THE OFFICIAL
Formula 1™
SEASON REVIEW 2011
FOREWORD BY BERNIE ECCLESTONE

Published in December 2011

A catalogue record for this book is available
from the British Library

ISBN 978 0 85733 108 3

Library of Congress control no. 2011932703

Managing Editor Steve Rendle

Design Richard Parsons, Lee Parsons, Dominic Stickland

Contributors Adam Cooper (race reports, driver interviews
and season overview), Tony Dodgins (round table, teams'
technical review and race report panels), Bruce Jones (race
results, team/car data panels and season statistics)

Photographs All by LAT (Steven Tee, Charles Coates,
Lorenzo Bellanca, Glenn Dunbar, Andrew Ferraro,
Steve Etherington, Andy Hone, Alastair Staley, Drew Gibson,
Jacob Ebrey), except lower image on p6-5 by Adam Cooper
Operations Manager LAT Tim Wright
Digital Technicians LAT Steve Carpenter, Tim Clarke,
Daniel Hutton, Chris Singleton, John Tingle

Illustrations Alan Eldridge

Publishing Director Mark Hughes

**Published by Haynes Publishing
in association with Haymarket Consumer Media**

Haynes Publishing, Sparkford, Yeovil,
Somerset BA22 7JJ, UK
Tel: +44 (0) 1963 442030
Fax: +44 (0) 1963 440001
E-mail: sales@haynes.co.uk
Website: www.haynes.co.uk

Haymarket Consumer Media, Teddington Studios,
Broom Road, Teddington, Middlesex TW11 9BE, UK
Tel: +44 (0) 208 267 5000
Fax: +44 (0) 208 267 5022
E-mail: F1Review@haymarket.com
Website: www.haymarket.com

Printed and bound in the UK by
Butler Tanner & Dennis Ltd, Caxton Road,
Frome, Somerset BA11 1NF

CONTENTS

FOREWORD

Obviously I would rather the championship was like it was before – the last corner of the last lap of the last race! But I think the racing has been good this year. People like to watch each race, and when they're watching the race they don't say, 'This is the championship position', and calculate the points. At the end of the race maybe they do, but during the race they just watch the race.

Sebastian is definitely the best guy there is at the moment. He reminds me a lot of Jochen Rindt – as everyone knows I was very close with Jochen. And he's a very relaxed guy and a good character. He has a good sense of humour, so he's easy to get on with.

I like Fernando too, he's a good friend of mine. He's suffered this year through no fault of his – the car isn't down to him.

Lewis went through a little bit of a bad period, which lots of people do in life, and I think he'll probably reflect on his performance. Meanwhile, Jenson has been on form, and why shouldn't he be as good as Lewis? He's done a good job this year. At the beginning of the year the McLaren wasn't as good as it is now, but they've fought on.

Massa and Webber, I don't understand both of them, to be honest! They're both very talented. A lot of these things depend on how good or bad the car is, and on top of that a bit of luck comes into life generally. And then it's a case of getting your act together, and I don't know what's happened to both of them. If you have a strong team-mate you should want to beat the guy.

Michael has improved a lot this year, and I'm very happy about that. You can't really judge the new guys, because again it depends on where they are with the car. Perez seems to be getting the job done, and di Resta is doing well.

The DRS has obviously been a big improvement, but as for KERS, it costs a lot of money, and all the public knows is that it doesn't work sometimes!

Pirelli have done what we asked them to do. It's just as difficult doing what they're doing as to make a tyre that lasts. If we said make a tyre that will go a whole race they could do it, obviously, but it isn't what we want.

India did a good job. When I went there two years before the race, it was just a big field. I was very happy with it.

As for next year, the people who have to get their act together are Ferrari. If they manage to do that, and I'm sure and I hope they will, we're going to have some good racing.

BERNIE ECCLESTONE

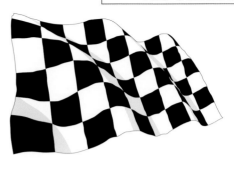

REFLECTING ON THE 2011 FORMULA ONE SEASON
VETTEL JOINS THE GREATS

THE SEASON

New Pirelli tyres, DRS and the reintroduction of KERS failed to upset the order, as Red Bull Racing maintained the upper hand, fending off challenges from McLaren and Ferrari

The 2010 FIA World Championship was one of the closest-fought in history, with four drivers still in contention at the final round in Abu Dhabi, and the destination of the title not confirmed until Sebastian Vettel crossed the line to win the race. It was the first time all year that the German had led the championship.

The 2011 season could not have been more different. Vettel won the opening race in Australia and logged such a strong run of early wins and podium finishes that by the middle of the year the opposition had pretty much conceded that it was all over. The mercurial German officially clinched his second crown in Japan, where so many titles have been won in the past, with four races still to run. In reality it was over long before that.

However, that's not to say that we had a boring season, and anyone who thought differently should perhaps reflect on some of the years of Michael Schumacher domination. McLaren, and to a lesser degree Ferrari, kept Vettel and Red Bull Racing on their toes, and ensured that we never went to a race weekend knowing that the dark blue cars were unbeatable, at least on Sundays.

The big story of 2011 was the return of Pirelli after an absence of 20 years. The Italian company was charged with the job of enlivening the racing by producing tyres that had a limited life, and few would deny that it succeeded in its task.

Tyres were a major talking point throughout the season, and certainly in the early races they played a critical role, as teams and drivers tried to get a handle on them. Lewis Hamilton's chase of Vettel in China – where the Lewis had an extra stop and the advantage of fresh rubber while Seb had pushed his tyres too far – was a highlight of the season.

Red Bull and others learned from that, and as the year went on tyres arguably played less of a role. Some drivers also complained that Pirelli had become too conservative, and a less-dramatic drop-off in performance reduced the chances of using strategy to gain ground.

The other big novelty was the DRS (see '2011 Rules' panel for details). The FIA trod a fine line as it experimented with the length and location of the DRS zones, and it didn't always get it right. In some races DRS seemed to have little value, and in others – notably Turkey – passing was clearly far too easy. The FIA's stated aim was to help drivers to get into a position where they could make a pass, rather than to do it for them.

However, the key technical story of the season was arguably the blown diffuser. Technical directors had predicted during the winter that exhaust development would be critical, and so it proved. Adrian Newey and Red Bull clearly proved masters of this complex technology, and the rest had to catch up.

There was a heated debate over the legality of such systems, and matters reached a head at Silverstone, when for one race only blowing was restricted. After that, the FIA allowed teams to

RIGHT Sebastian Vettel was the focus of attention all season

BELOW DRS – visible here in action on Michael Schumacher's Mercedes, with rear wing slot open – had a dramatic effect on overtaking

RULE CHANGES FOR 2012

Tyres aside, the most talked about change introduced to F1 in 2011 was the moveable rear wing – which the FIA rather belatedly christened DRS (Drag Reduction System).

It was a simple idea, designed to encourage overtaking. The driver was able to raise the upper-wing flap and create a 50mm slot, which reduced downforce by some 10%, cut drag, and gave a boost in straightline speed of around 5–10mph.

In races, drivers were initially able to use the DRS on one straight per lap, as nominated by the FIA. The timing system detected a car's proximity to the car ahead at a point some 200m before the preceding corner. If the driver was within a second, he received a signal to indicate that he could operate the wing in the DRS zone on the next straight.

In Montréal this was extended to cover two consecutive straights using a single detection point, and later the FIA felt confident enough in its technology to regularly use two totally independent DRS zones, with their own detection points.

DRS was not available in the first two laps after the start or after a safety-car restart, or when the track was wet. In practice and qualifying, drivers were free to use it anywhere in the search for lap time. However, under pressure from the GPDA (Grand Prix Drivers' Association), the FIA banned its use in some places, namely the Monaco tunnel and Eau Rouge at Spa.

In other aerodynamic changes, cars no longer had cockpit-adjustable front wings. As part of a package to reduce downforce, double diffusers were banned, as were F-Ducts or any other systems whereby the driver used his body to influence aerodynamics.

KERS (Kinetic Energy Recovery System) – for converting energy created under braking into a power boost – returned for the first time since 2009. Although KERS had remained within the rule book, the teams agreed not to use it in 2010. However, with energy recovery forming an important part of the upcoming turbo era, KERS was welcomed back.

The KERS rules were exactly as they were in 2009, with a button on the steering wheel providing a driver with an 80bhp boost for around 6.7s a lap. KERS was more valuable than it had been previously, however, as the car/driver weight limit had increased to 640kg. Thus, there was no longer an issue with heavier drivers being over the specified weight limit while running KERS – although lighter drivers had more ballast with which to play as they honed their cars.

New for 2011 was a paddock curfew, brought in to stop teams taking liberties by forcing their crews to work all night after shipping in newly developed parts at the last minute. With a typical European schedule, it meant that team members had to leave the paddock by midnight on Thursday and 1am on Friday, although four exceptions – in theory to be used for repairing crash damage – were allowed. Due to the existing parc fermé rules taking the cars away there was no need for a curfew on Saturday night.

ABOVE The highlight of Ferrari's season was Fernando Alonso's sole victory of 2011, in the British Grand Prix at Silverstone

OPPOSITE TOP Pirelli's tyres provided a new challenge for the teams and drivers, as they learned to cope with the characteristics of the new rubber

OPPOSITE BOTTOM KERS returned to F1 in 2011, requiring special precautions in the pitlane and garages to deal with the potentially dangerous high voltages involved

carry on, at least until the end of 2011. Some teams never fully mastered the technology, and it will be fascinating to see how the status quo is affected next season, when exhausts are not allowed to have any aerodynamic influence.

A second World Championship for Vettel moved the 24-year-old into the elite group of drivers who have won twice in a row, although no-one else has managed it at such a young age.

This year's title, on the face of it, came much more easily than the first. Last season early mechanical problems and mishaps, such as the controversial clash with Mark Webber in Turkey, badly compromised Vettel's title campaign.

In contrast, he started the 2011 season with an amazing run, establishing a lead that looked increasingly secure. He made virtually no mistakes, and demonstrated total mastery of the complex rules, making the most of DRS, KERS and tyre strategy to post win after win.

Even on days when not everything went to plan, he nearly always made the podium. He was also extremely adept at getting the car to work for him, as his string of pole positions demonstrated. Only in the

final two races did his luck run out, with a puncture that caused his retirement in Abu Dhabi and a gearbox problem that slowed him in Brazil.

"I think he's been phenomenal this year," said Red Bull Racing Team Principal Christian Horner. "I think the confidence he took out of winning the championship last year seemed to carry through the winter into Melbourne, and he's been absolutely peerless since then. He's raised the bar for sure.

"In reality, 2010 was a difficult year for him. It all came right in the end, but actually he had some difficult challenges and criticism and so on, which he shouldered brilliantly well behind the scenes last year. And I think he's just grown from that. He has emerged very clearly as an absolutely superb driver this year. He's marked himself down in history as a double World Champion, and as the youngest driver to do that.

"A lot of the races this year have been hard-fought for him. You've only got to think of Monaco, Barcelona, they were tough races. Operationally, as a team we've grown stronger, and he has as well. On days when we've had the best package we've utilised it, and on days when perhaps

we haven't had quite the best we've still maximised our opportunities."

Talent is one thing, but Vettel has also learned the value of hard work from his countryman and early mentor Michael Schumacher.

"Tactically he's very smart, he's very disciplined, he's very self-analytical," says Horner. "You'll see him in the paddock late on a Saturday evening. After qualifying he's usually one of the last to leave. He's hungry for information, he's hungry to improve. He's like a sponge, he soaks it all up."

One of Vettel's great strengths this year was his understanding of the Pirellis, and Mark Webber admitted that his team-mate got a much better handle on the supersoft. It wasn't a coincidence that in November 2010 Vettel returned to Abu Dhabi from his title victory tour in Europe to take part in the first Pirelli test. Other top drivers either chose not to do the test, or were allowed to take time off by their teams. Vettel was also the only F1 driver to visit Pirelli during the winter.

"I think he's understood the characteristics of what the tyre needs," says Horner. "Sometimes he's been able to make the stint length on that tyre remarkably

ABOVE Mark Webber finished the year on a high, winning in Brazil from team-mate Sebastian Vettel to give Red Bull Racing their third 1–2 finish of the season

ABOVE RIGHT Jenson Button drove a superb race in Canada, in difficult conditions, to win against all the odds after lying last at half-distance

OPPOSITE At times, Lewis Hamilton cut a solitary figure during a troubled season for the McLaren driver

long, and he's managed the tyres very well. Some of the laps he's done on a Saturday, under acute pressure, he's absolutely delivered."

Despite his devotion to duty, Vettel remains an extremely well-rounded individual. He's the same modest, witty and cheerful guy that he was when he first appeared, and he is immensely popular, not just with the public but, most significantly, his fellow drivers.

Vettel's performance was put into perspective by that of his team-mate. In 2010 Mark Webber was in the fight for the World Championship until the last race in Abu Dhabi. He won four races, took five pole positions, and was often able to give Vettel a hard time.

In 2011 things were very different. Webber had poles in Spain, Britain and Germany, reminding us of his one-lap pace. But in terms of race results, he was nowhere near his team-mate.

He received a welcome bonus in the finale in Brazil, inheriting the lead when Vettel had to slow with a gearbox problem. But aside from that, he only finished second twice, both times behind Vettel. In most races he was between third and fifth, beaten

not only by the other guy in the identical car, but often by various combinations of Lewis Hamilton, Jenson Button and Fernando Alonso.

Statistics don't always tell the full story, but there was nowhere for Webber to hide, and he knows better than anyone that next year he has to raise his game.

It's easy to forget that McLaren endured a nightmare build-up to the season. The team took a gamble on what became known as the 'Octopus exhaust', and the car proved both slow and unreliable through testing. Shortly before the first race, the team made the bold call to go back to a more standard arrangement. The car did not run on track in that form until Friday in Australia. Thankfully for the team, it worked, and the turnaround was another demonstration of the strength of the organisation.

Nevertheless, from the first race to the last, McLaren remained a step behind Red Bull on qualifying pace – only once, in Korea, did Hamilton manage to keep the RB7 off pole. And with the way racing unfolded in 2011, you had to start from the front. Despite DRS, KERS and the tyres mixing things up, there was no substitute for starting from pole,

opening up a lead, and then controlling the pit stops by reacting to what others did.

Vettel did that time and time again, and even on occasions when he didn't lead at the first corner, he made sure he was soon in front. He even managed it in Korea, as Hamilton's priceless pole was wasted within a few corners as Vettel slipped by.

Had the McLaren drivers been able to start from the top spot more often, or been able to pass Vettel on the first lap, the silver cars might have won more races. Nevertheless the final total of six wins – three apiece for Hamilton and Button – was a pretty healthy one.

Hamilton had an extraordinary season. There were moments of brilliance, such as his successful chase of Vettel in China, and a faultless lights-to-flag performance in Abu Dhabi. But there was also a string of controversial incidents that earned him a season ticket to the stewards' office, and resulted in various penalties. He had a series of unfortunate collisions with 2008 title rival Felipe Massa, and while Lewis wasn't always at fault, most of the time he was. There were other mistakes too, such as a clumsy collision with Kamui Kobayashi in Belgium.

The bottom line was that he found himself under unexpected pressure from Button, who, having found his feet at McLaren in 2010, really began to blossom. Lewis also had a few issues to deal with off-track, and at the end of the year he tellingly admitted that he envied the way Jenson had got his life together, with friends, family and management around him, creating what Hamilton called a 'bubble'.

Jenson would arguably win a most-improved driver award if there was such a thing, which might sound strange given that the guy won the World Championship in 2009. But this year he finally silenced the critics who suggested that he wasn't really from the top rank alongside Vettel, Hamilton and Alonso.

Button performed brilliantly all year, as his intelligent, methodical approach paid dividends in a year dominated by tyres and strategy. He scored superb rain-affected wins in Canada and Hungary, and then added his first dry success for McLaren with a great drive in Japan. Elsewhere, he put in a series of fine performances as he recorded a string of podiums, often bringing home a bagful of points on days when Hamilton had let himself and the team down. What

was still missing was the ultimate qualifying speed, although he did on occasion beat Hamilton.

There's no doubt that Ferrari had the third-fastest car in 2011, and that was proven beyond all doubt by Alonso, who qualified fifth with monotonous regularity. The red car simply wasn't quick enough, and the team admitted that the main weakness was aero. The team also struggled to get the most out of the tyres in qualifying, a trait that, conversely, often proved useful in races.

And regardless of where he qualified, Alonso was always in the thick of things on Sundays, often helped by great starts that propelled him up the order. The only win came at Silverstone – coincidentally or not, on the day when blown diffusers were restricted – but he also logged a string of podiums that ensured he was in the fight for second place in the championship all the way to the final round in Brazil. His biggest frustration was frequently losing places in the last stint, when the car invariably struggled on the prime tyres, and he was unable to defend himself.

"One thing became very clear this year for us," said Ferrari Team Principal Stefano Domenicali. "We had in any case a not very competitive car, but it was

very different depending on the condition of the tyres. We saw so many grands prix where the car was really competitive in the race, but when we were using the prime tyres it seemed like another car, and difficult to handle."

For Felipe Massa, in contrast, it was a disastrous season. Although he did occasionally out-qualify his team-mate, the Brazilian was rarely in the same league in races. To be fair, more than once his day was compromised by something going wrong, such as those clashes with Hamilton. That he failed to score a podium all year says everything.

Under British Technical Director Pat Fry, the team has undergone a reorganisation, and it plans to be more aggressive in the future.

Mercedes didn't make the expected step in 2011, and Michael Schumacher and Nico Rosberg had to be content with the fourth-best car, as their eventual championship positions attested. The younger man had the upper hand for most of the season, but there were signs of the old spark from Michael, who made an art form of gaining places on the first lap. He put in some charging drives, notably at Spa, where he went from the back to fifth. However, he also got

ABOVE Veteran multiple World Champion Michael Schumacher celebrated 20 years since his F1 debut at the Belgian Grand Prix by adopting this special helmet design for the weekend

OPPOSITE TOP Buddh International Circuit provided an impressive location for the first Indian Grand Prix – a track design universally praised by the drivers

OPPOSITE Felipe Massa and Lewis Hamilton tangle at Monaco – one of numerous controversial on-track clashes between the two drivers during the season

involved in a remarkable number of collisions with other drivers.

Rosberg, whose ultimate potential still remains hard to judge, was again a consistent points scorer. He even cheekily led a couple of races after making good getaways. The team has massively strengthened its technical staff for 2012, and expectations are high.

Lotus Renault's season was turned upside down even before it started, when Robert Kubica was injured in a rally accident, forcing the team to call on Nick Heidfeld. The team gambled on a front-exit exhaust system, and while it initially showed promise, it proved to be a blind alley.

Vitaly Petrov and Heidfeld both picked up a third place apiece in the first two races, but it was a false dawn, and later the Lotus Renaults struggled to make the top 10 as progress stalled. Heidfeld was eventually replaced by Bruno Senna, who showed flashes of talent, notably in qualifying.

Force India had a solid season, as rookie Paul di Resta forced Adrian Sutil to raise his game. Between them, they scored enough points to earn the team sixth in the championship, despite strong pressure from both Sauber and Toro Rosso. Sergio Perez proved a good find for the Swiss team, while Sébastien Buemi and Jaime Alguersuari were well-matched at Toro Rosso, both putting in some good races.

It was a terrible year for Williams, as rookie Pastor Maldonado and Rubens Barrichello found themselves battling to get out of Q1. The Venezuelan impressed at Monaco before Hamilton turfed him off the road, while Rubens spent the year fighting to continue his career into a 20th season in 2012. The team, meanwhile, has reorganised its technical department, and switches to Renault power in 2012.

It was another year of learning for the three sophomore teams. Lotus moved ahead of the others, but found itself in a no-man's land, unable to catch

RIGHT Red Bull's protégé, Australian Daniel Ricciardo, made the best of his opportunity with HRT

BELOW Williams had a difficult year, long-serving Technical Director Sam Michael leaving the team for McLaren, while Rubens Barrichello struggled to get the best from a flawed car

OPPOSITE Bruno Senna made a return as a grand prix driver, replacing Nick Heidfeld at Renault

those ahead. KERS would have closed the gap, but not by enough. Meanwhile, an ongoing legal fight with Group Lotus was finally concluded, and the team will be rebranded as Caterham for 2012. Heikki Kovalainen boosted his reputation, while the opposite happened to a lacklustre Jarno Trulli.

Virgin will also undergo a name change, in favour of Marussia. The team's second year was not much better than its first, much to the frustration of Timo Glock. Nick Wirth's CFD-only philosophy was discredited and the technical director was booted out, while former Renault man Pat Symonds worked quietly away in the background to build a new operation.

To many people's surprise, HRT was often able to compete with Virgin in qualifying and races, and Red Bull used the team as a training ground for Daniel Ricciardo, who may one day join Vettel at Red Bull. New investment from Spain led to the hiring of Pedro de la Rosa for next season.

At the front, however, it will be business as usual in 2012, with all the top drivers staying put. But will anyone be able to find the extra performance needed to beat Red Bull?

THE PANEL
CLOCKWISE FROM BOTTOM LEFT

MARTIN WHITMARSH
TEAM PRINCIPAL, McLAREN

MARTIN BRUNDLE
TV COMMENTATOR, *BBC*

CHRISTIAN HORNER
TEAM PRINCIPAL, RED BULL RACING

MARK HUGHES
JOURNALIST, *AUTOSPORT*

CHAIRED BY
TONY DODGINS
JOURNALIST, *AUTOSPORT*

ROUND TABLE

At the end of another classic season of racing, our panel of leading F1 paddock insiders get together to debate the topics that made the headlines during the year

With the introduction of new rules aimed at improving overtaking opportunities, and Pirelli's arrival as the new official F1 tyre supplier, the 2011 season provided plenty of topics for discussion by our expert panel.

DRS (Drag Reduction System), KERS (Kinetic Energy Recovery System) and tyre degradation brought new technical and strategy challenges for the teams, and required drivers to adjust their driving styles, benefiting some, while hampering others.

Red Bull Racing, under the technical guidance of Adrian Newey, was remarkably successful in adapting to the new regulations, with a dominant car/driver combination in the form of the consistently quick RB7 and reigning World Champion Sebastian Vettel.

McLaren's Jenson Button and Lewis Hamilton were Red Bull's closest challengers, but each had a very different season. Jenson reinforced his reputation with some controlled, intelligent drives, but for Lewis on-track controversies and off-track distractions got in the way.

Other themes included the role of driver stewards, the forthcoming changes for F1 TV coverage in the UK, and the likely direction of F1 as teams look ahead to safeguard the long-term future of the sport.

Q: Purists were concerned about the artificiality of DRS, KERS and degrading tyres. After the season we've had, what's the verdict?

Horner: The biggest effect has been the tyres. They have had the largest effect on the way the races have played out strategically. At some races DRS has been very successful, and at others perhaps it has been a little too easy to to pass, but that's the sort of thing that can be tuned out, hopefully, for next year. On the whole it has been very positive.

Brundle: I agree. I think it's the combination. KERS has had a new lease of life and become much more of a tool to defend rather than attack. Before, I think it was more one-dimensional. In conjunction with DRS and degrading tyres it has been good. It worries me that the tyres are getting better and better and we're losing that facility quickly, like we did in 2005 (when a single set of rubber had to last the whole race). Although it's a bit false in some ways, I've satisfied myself by saying that technology has created

the problem that racing cars can't follow each other because of aerodynamics. These engineers and designers can't forget what they know, so we're using technology in DRS to combat the problem that technology brought us. Overall, I'm a fan of it. As much because it will let back through faster cars that are out of position due to problems, safety cars, tyre stops, etc. You get a proper race.

Whitmarsh: I take the point that a lot of people don't understand, and don't want to understand, what DRS is, and I think that's a shame. But we did a survey, and there was an overwhelming view that people wanted more overtaking. Those of us involved in the show have a lot of data, and maybe a slightly better understanding, and we're intrigued by all the nuances and subtleties of strategy and tactics during the race. But we have to accept that there's a reasonable proportion of the fan base that either don't have the time to absorb that, or the data. I'm sure they're capable of it, but they don't have all that information. Therefore, good old-fashioned overtaking is what they

want to see. At a circuit like Abu Dhabi I think the tyres are getting better – we've had our day on tyres and perhaps we shouldn't rely on them. So, I think it's essential, and the nice thing about it is that the power of it can be tuned. It's a little bit nutty that you can DRS all through qualifying and then DRS only in certain places in the race. Maybe that adds an extra dimension, but it means your ratios are often a compromise. Maybe the real aficionado will enjoy and understand the subtlety of DRS, and others will say, 'Oh that's good, that car might get past here.' I'm not sure that it's ever too easy to overtake. Probably, for the fan, you can't have too many overtakes. We've heard that sometimes, and for a leading driver it's deeply frustrating when you know you have a faster car, but you're going to get 're-DRSed'.

Q: A case in point being Mark Webber pulling off that great pass of Alonso at Spa's Eau Rouge, just to have the Ferrari walk back past him with DRS next lap?

Fernando Alonso uses DRS to pass Mark Webber during the Belgian Grand Prix

Brundle: Exactly.

Whitmarsh: It may well be that you'll get lower-quality overtaking, because to overtake takes enormous skill and courage, and if you can wait for a straight and press a button, then arguably you have de-skilled the task.

Brundle: Yeah. The Schumacher fans were livid in Canada. As far as they were concerned he finished third and DRS finished fourth, because they just saw him as a sitting duck, even though he'd used those tools before to get up there.

Hughes: I understand the unease for the purist. Like Martin says, you can satisfy yourself that it's just technology solving a problem that technology has created.

Horner: I think we've had over 800 overtakes this year, which is quite a staggering statistic. Take India, the DRS wasn't that powerful, Monza it didn't really work and even in Korea, Mark versus Lewis, but then again at places like Montréal and Spa it was almost too powerful and you could just pick your side and go past.

Brundle: Istanbul was like that too.

Whitmarsh: As you go lower in drag you are going to have less DRS.

Hughes: It does seem that the more conservative Pirelli go with the tyres, the more like a Bridgestone race it becomes.

Whitmarsh: I think we've got to assume that's likely to happen. This year Pirelli was thrown in at the deep end and produced some tyres that initially gave a lot of headache and heartache to the drivers and engineers.

Horner: But some great races as well.

Whitmarsh: Some great races as well, exactly. It's a tough one for a tyre manufacturer, because having drivers and teams complain about the product is really not what they're in the sport for! On the one hand, quietly, we'll push on them and beat up on them – give us some high-degradation tyres – and if they deliver on that, the drivers can't help themselves, because they'll be in the lead, the tyres go away and in the heat of the moment afterwards they are going to say that it was these bloody tyres!

Brundle: But it has been the most powerful aspect of a very exciting season. Despite Christian's man dominating the year, it has been one of the most exciting I can remember, and just breathless at so many races, although that's fading now. Paul Hembery should be Prime Minister, I think. He brought along a product that was universally not quite ready for Formula 1, and somehow played that as 'that's what you asked for'.

Horner: Well it was designed to that specification, so…

Brundle: But now it's coming back into the normal range. I think Pirelli has done a brilliant job for Formula 1.

Hughes: Turned that negative into a positive.

Brundle: Yeah, brilliantly.

Hughes: He should be a car dealer, Martin.

Brundle: He should!

Q: Where does Sebastian Vettel stand in comparison with great champions of the past?

Hughes: I think you've got to start considering him right up there, because with the set of demands he has been presented with, he's just nailed it absolutely perfectly. You can say he's in the fastest car, but so is Mark Webber and Mark's no idiot.

Sebastian Vettel and Adrian Newey set new standards for excellence in 2011

Brundle: I remember thinking once he'd won the title in Abu Dhabi last year that he would just take off, but I had no idea by just how much. He's stopped the petulant mistakes he was making previously and has turned that into confidence. You can just see the boy thinking at all times. If the car was that dominant, every time he didn't win Mark Webber should have, and when he did win Mark should have finished second. But Mark finished second to him only twice (Istanbul and Spa). I think Vettel has been absolutely extraordinary and has set a whole new benchmark for how a Formula 1 driver should go about his trade.

Whitmarsh: I think he has been incredible. The comparative lack of mistakes, the smartness of the guy, you can just see. He has a very focused, humble approach to it all. He's a feet-on-the-ground guy who wakes up thinking about how he's going to win the following weekend. He's had a pretty good car, but as has been said, Mark is no slouch. I think the confidence he has had, and

Christian will know better, but in high-speed corners my sense is that you can just see, particularly in this era of exhaust blowing, the extreme confidence.

Horner: There aren't enough superlatives to describe how well he has performed this year, and he deserves all the credit that goes with it. He's a hugely popular member of the team. After winning in Abu Dhabi last year he raised his game and his confidence. Of all the races he has won, not many of them have been straightforward. You think back to Monaco and Barcelona, where the McLarens were giving us a very hard time. Last year was a tough year for him because he got some criticism. He won five races and was in a position to win another three had it not been for reliability issues. It was testimony to his commitment that having just won the World Championship and gone back to Europe after Abu Dhabi to do what was required of him in the media, he then got straight back on a plane to come back out to do the test in Abu Dhabi. That demonstrated his eagerness and commitment to understand at an early stage what these tyres were like and what was required. He went to Pirelli because he wanted to speak to the technicians and understand how the tyres were made. That's the kind of preparation he puts in. He's the benchmark at the moment, and also a tremendous ambassador for the sport. It's not often that nice guys come out on top in sport, but in this instance it's absolutely the case.

Q: When he equalled Nigel Mansell's record for laps led in a year, Christian, you made the point that both had been achieved in Adrian Newey cars. Adrian has a phenomenal record. What are his strengths?

Horner: He's a remarkable guy. What he's achieved in the sport is quite unique. I think that's 16 World Championships he's been involved in, drivers or constructors, across three teams. He's not a technical director in the sense that a modern technical director is a technical manager. He's still very involved in the architecture of the car, the shape and development of it, and manages to combine all the aspects in a modern F1 world that almost contradict each other. He can relate to the driver, he's obviously heavily focused on the aerodynamics, he's a very good race engineer and he has a very good mechanical understanding as well. So he encompasses all aspects, which, in the modern world, is quite unique.

Brundle: And he's a racer, isn't he? That's the thing that stands out most for me. When you see him crying on the pit wall after he has won a race. Whoa! That's just extraordinary.

Q: Are they very much your experiences of him as well, Martin?

Whitmarsh: He's a funny character. A lovely guy. He's a passionate, soft individual with a massive intellect, and so incredibly competitive. He's got all of those qualities, and has had an extraordinary career. Personally I think he should be relaxed at what he's done and retire! I've been telling him that for a number of years…

Q: He has been known to be ambitious and uncompromising with packaging. This year you had a smaller KERS installed in a hot place. With prescribed exhaust outlets costing downforce next year, can you risk that again?

Horner: I don't know. Innovation is something he inspires and encourages, and he's unrelenting in his pursuit of excellence. I think all testimony to the design and aero group. He dictates the tempo, but they have to go and turn that into reality. So far we've had a 100% reliability record, and we've put the KERS in probably the most environmentally unfriendly position that you could put some batteries on a race car! But they came up with solutions to accommodate that and make it work. It was quite a new technology for us; we didn't run the system in 2009, and therefore for Adrian to be relentless in saying where he wanted the KERS system… They kept coming back and saying 'I don't think this is possible.' He'd say, go away and think again, 'I'm not compromising either wheelbase or cooling!' In fairness, it was the whole group working in harmony and they found solutions.

Q: Jenson Button had a great season. Would you rate it even better than '09?

Whitmarsh: In '09, for a whole range of circumstances he had a flying start, but '09 Brazil was a turning point in my mind. I've been fortunate enough to be around a number of drivers who were trying to win their first World Championship. And the pressure on them is immense. It's theirs for the taking, but you also know it's theirs to throw away. Under those circumstances he drove that race with some really assertive overtaking and self-confidence and won it. He has always been a super-smooth driver. I didn't know him at all really, but by observation you wondered whether he had the hunger and passion, because he is such a laid-back, nice character. I thought, nothing ventured, nothing gained – probably we can't get him, but let's give it our best shot. A lot of people were telling him and his family they were nuts going to McLaren, to Lewis's team, but he's smart and brave. He knew exactly what he was doing, he knew he was putting himself up against a fearsome competitor who had dealt with every team-mate from karting all the way up to F1, and anyone who doubts his passion and drive just has to look at the determination. The determination with which he attacked his team-mate on a variety of occasions this year! And there have been two or three occasions where he's made the race, almost single-handed. Christian's guy has been in very strong positions and Jenson just hasn't given up. He's a super-nice guy, comfortable in his own skin. He doesn't have the need to prove or say who he is, but quietly has a level of determination that a lot of people underestimate.

The panel was impressed with Jenson Button's performance

Q: And Jenson has matured enormously since he arrived in F1?

Brundle: As a human being and an F1 driver, his stock, his credibility, is significantly higher than when he won the world title. He had half a season head-start then, a second-a-lap car advantage. He did a great job to save the title, and I said at the time and still stand by it being a very worthy title, but his credibility is even higher now.

Horner: He had a tremendous start in '09 after not knowing whether he was driving a couple of weeks before the start of the season. It looked like he was choking in the second half of the year but, after Sebastian, I'd say Jenson has been the next best driver of this year. He looks completely at ease with himself and his surroundings. He has driven some superb races, and I think these regulations and these tyres have played to the intelligent driver. It must be the hardest thing in the world to give away performance at the beginning of a stint in order to get it back, requiring enormous self-discipline. He seems to have managed that extremely well on many occasions this year.

Q: Lewis Hamilton by comparison has had a tough year. What have been the most influential factors there: frustration at Red Bull's competitiveness, pressure from within, personal issues?

Whitmarsh: It has been a host of things. He sets himself such high standards that he's not happy if he's not winning, and I think the world has high expectations of him and so he's had a lot of pressure. There's not one singular thing. It hasn't been one of his great seasons, but he's resilient and will fight back.

Hughes: I think you might also question if the Pirellis are naturally suited to his instinctive ways. He's good enough to adapt, I'm sure, but I think maybe he has had a tougher time than most. When overtaking was more difficult, he was one of the great overtakers and could do something that not many other people could. Now it's more about positioning yourself at the detection zones, which makes that facet of his driving stand out less.

Q: Yes, we all remember the move he pulled on Kimi at Monza in '07, so do you agree that DRS has taken away one of his advantages?

Brundle: I think it has. But for some reason all those audacious moves he got away with suddenly turned into front-wing crunching. It was as if that instinctive judgment had just gone missing. I'm absolutely convinced that hasn't lost any of his skill and speed, and the moment he fixes his head and his emotions, he'll be back. For me there are three world-class drivers out there just an ounce ahead: Vettel, Hamilton and Alonso. That's really hard on Jenson and others, but I still see Lewis right in there. I don't think there's anything missing at all, except that his head seems upside-down. He just wasn't applying himself. I think it was just crazy how he left his front wing in the action – again – in India, like at so many other races. It doesn't matter whose fault it is, if you put your car in a position where you have a 75% chance of somebody knocking your front wing off, it's pointless.

Q: Is it made that much more difficult to call by the likes of KERS and DRS?

Brundle: It's not affecting the other drivers, though. They're not tripping over each other. Michael's had a few, but he did before anyway!

Q: What about having ex-drivers on the stewarding panel. Has that helped?

Brundle: Very positive.

Whitmarsh: I think it has been. In terms of the governance of the sport it was a seemingly small thing but the confidence the drivers and teams now have of going to the stewards is much greater. Before it was a deeply frustrating thing for a driver to go to the stewards, with all due respect to them, and feel that they had to explain themselves. If there's a driver there, they can relate to what was going on. Not everyone will always agree with what they say, like players don't agree with referees, but I think it's healthy.

Horner: I absolutely agree. When you've got drivers of the calibre of Nigel Mansell in the stewards' room it inspires confidence.

Brundle: It's the job from hell though, isn't it?

Hughes: Another key thing is that it has taken away suspicion of motive. Whether or not you agree with the decision doesn't so much matter, you're confident now that there's no ulterior motive.

Q: Looking at the Sky/BBC TV deal for 2012, there was concern about falling viewer figures yet the Manchester derby attracted 2.28 million for a lunchtime kick-off – F1 start time – so how do we think the Sky/deferred BBC coverage numbers will compare?

Opinion was divided on the reasons for Lewis Hamilton's troubled season

The new Sky/BBC deal for TV coverage in the UK provided food for thought

Whitmarsh: Yes, and that was just a domestic football match. It meant virtually nothing in the scheme of things. [*Whitmarsh was jesting, in case you're wondering!*]

Brundle: Not a proper sport then, is that what you're saying?

Whitmarsh: Unless it's got Southampton playing – the slayers of Manchester United in 1976 of course!

Hughes: As everyone well remembers…

Brundle: Even Tony Fernandes wouldn't buy Southampton! No, they won't get the same numbers because terrestrial TV will always have an element of people watching because the TV is on.

Q: But if you take the Sky live numbers plus the BBC deferred numbers, what's the likelihood of the total actually being higher?

Whitmarsh: What you've actually got to do is accept that it has happened and consider it positively. This debate was going on in football a few years ago and everybody said it was a disaster.

You can't get football in the UK without Sky now, but look at the creativity and innovation they brought. There has been a lot of talk about Sky, but the reality is that the BBC were halfway out of the door at the time. So you can criticise Bernie, you can criticise Sky but, actually, it was the BBC that was doing a runner and someone had to step in and do something. We now have to accept that there is a whole range of opportunity, and we have to make it into something we can look back on in two or three years and say, actually, the show and the way it is done is better and more innovative and has created a sustained audience.

Horner: I think the Beeb has done such a wonderful job with Formula 1 over the past three years, have really raised the bar for F1 coverage, and I think Sky, to compete with that, are going to have to invest. By the sound of things they're going to be doing so pretty heavily. Faced with losing the BBC altogether, I think it was a masterstroke to be able to retain the Beeb and get the highlights programme for the races they won't be covering live at a prime time on a Sunday evening. And to bring in a new audience and the more in-depth and behind-the-scenes coverage that potentially Sky is going to bring. I think it was the best possible deal out of what was on the table. I think it is going to be really interesting.

Hughes: Also, every time we've changed the broadcaster it has been better than before: ITV was better than BBC, then when BBC took it back it was better again, so you want to come in, make a mark and show that you can do it better still. I'm sure that will happen again.

Brundle: I think there will be serious competition and, to an extent, they will aim at a slightly different audience. If you're not passionate about F1 you're not going to pay even 10p a month and sign a document, let alone what they will be charging. I think Sky is going to come up with fairly innovative concepts that will make it more accessible to the fans. I've been massively impressed and privileged to work with the BBC, and I'm disappointed – that's the word I'll use – that they chose to take this route, to fix their sports budget basically using Formula 1. That's what they've chosen to do. Sky will appeal to the people who tweet that we've only been on red button for an hour and a half, why are you going off air? That's the sort of people Sky is going to appeal to, the *Autosport* readers, the real core fans who can't get enough. Sky has got the platform, the resource and the budget to do that. And the BBC will still appeal to both the hard core and the more casual fans. Because, if you look at the BBC output now, it's got more of the *Top Gear* style and approach rather than a technical approach. What's interesting to me is that they haven't taken over cricket from Channel 4, they're going head-to-head with the BBC's best sports show. They're going to have to do something really special, and something I heard them say was that, while they won't match BBC numbers, one thing they can't do is to be seen to be not as good as the BBC. So F1 has got this situation where you have two mighty organisations going head-to-head, and personally I think that's good for the F1 fan.

Q: Third cars and customer cars have raised their heads again. With all the technical support deals being done, are we closer to full-blown customer cars, and would it be damaging?

Whitmarsh: I think conceptually, if the grid size starts to fall and we have to do it, we have to look at ways we can reduce cost, and there may be an element of that, but to go to full-blown customer cars at the moment would be the death of some of the teams. I think we have a duty of care to try to help the sport. If you could buy a Red Bull at the moment, why would you persevere as Caterham or Marussia or HRT? So I think customer or third cars now would be the wrong thing to do, but if there is some intelligent sharing that can be done, I don't think we should be afraid of that. If you took a picture of the Red Bull and Toro Rosso, you don't have to be a whizz aerodynamicist to see that they are different. Our car and the Force India are very different. But if you're being beaten by Force India, obviously there can be a degree of paranoia. The fact is that there are a number of wind tunnels, and we aren't fully using the wind tunnels we have (due to the Resource Restriction Agreement), so as soon as you've invited another team into your wind tunnel, there's a technical collaboration going on there. There's an inevitable transference of knowledge about how you test in a wind tunnel – because you say, 'come in to my wind tunnel, bolt your model on to my strut here, on to my data-gathering equipment, to my test routines' – and so it's not a black-and-white thing. There are people who get emotional about it, and I think we have to still get a lot smarter about how we efficiently operate. We are still spending too much money putting 24 cars on to a grid. But we've got to remain the technical pinnacle, the most advanced and technically differentiated.

Q: But isn't it a difficult thing to get across to the public what exactly is a technical collaboration, intellectual property, and what you can and can't do?

Horner: Do they care at the end of the day? What you've got to consider is that there are probably four teams that are solvent at the moment and the rest are struggling to be here. That's unsustainable in the long term. I think F1 needs to open its mind and consider, should there be further transfer of IP, should maybe chassis be interchangeable and perhaps you put your own aerodynamic package on to that mechanical platform? Because certainly, if it continues the way it's going, then it is unsustainable and you aren't going to have 12 teams that can all run with 500 people. The only thing that will get in the way of that kind of fundamental change will be ego. For an HRT to invest the kind of money and resource and personnel to diminish that seven-second gap is, over a period of time, hundreds of millions of euros. It's a pipe dream in many respects.

Whitmarsh: Do the cars look different and are they competing against each other? I think that's all that people care about.

Q: Many major sports generate a lot of coverage through money stories: we know Novak Djokovic has won $10m prize money, that Luke Donald looks like being the first player to top the US and European golf money lists in the same year. We've got possibly the most money-oriented sport there is. Are we not missing a trick by not publicising driver and team prize money?

Whitmarsh: I think we're different. There is equipment involved and the differentiators are the driver and the car that he's using. Then there's how good a job the team has done during the weekend – eliminating mistakes, optimisation, strategy, execution. So it would be very misleading. We are coy about money because we are businesses. It would be very misleading to say that Sebastian has had a superlative year and how much has he won in prize money? Zero. It's not the way we're structured. Then you're into how much Christian is paying him. We'd all like to know, but in fairness it's none of our business.

Horner: And it's why the constructors' championship has such pertinence to the teams. Because there are literally millions of dollars hanging on each position, and that's where a team has a choice whether they can go to facilitate cash flow and bring in a pay-driver, or take in two quality drivers to try to achieve a higher position in the championship.

Hughes: People understand that.

Q: But you have commentators talking about a sixth-placed constructors' championship battle worth millions, but we don't know exactly how much…

Brundle: But we've got this wonderful thing called a stopwatch, and that's how we rate ourselves. We don't need to rub people's noses in it with money. It's about who's fastest. That's all we want to know. We don't need to line people up and say how much money they're worth, particularly in these times.

Whitmarsh: I think one of the differences with tennis and golf is that the tournaments are

weighted in their importance and the players can dot around the world. They can do the Abu Dhabi Masters or whatever, but it won't be the same as the Open or the US Open. Here, the driver and team that does the best job wins the World Championship, and each grand prix is of equal status. The quality of the field in golf or tennis is generally decided by money. When you go to a championship where they're paying lots of money, all the top players are there. And a win there is weighted more heavily than in other places.

Hughes: As a fan I'd have zero interest in how much money the drivers made.

Horner: Yeah, I think it's irrelevant. I don't know how much Djokovic, Nadal or Federer earn, but I know they're the best three tennis players in the world.

Q: We have Concorde negotiations again next year and, presumably, difficult times. Bernie and CVC have proven what a lucrative business F1 is, so the obvious question is: why don't the teams get together and buy it?

Martin Whitmarsh suggested making more F1 data available to fans

Whitmarsh: We're not natural owners of the sport. There will be teams here who arguably could be equity participants, teams that clearly wouldn't want to be, and teams that would want to be and aren't able to be. I don't think it's an important aspect. I think what we need to do is work together to grow the sport. Bernie has done an extraordinary job to get it to where it is, and we have to work with the commercial-rights holder and the FIA to make the sport bigger. It can be made bigger if we work together with a clear strategy. And clearly we need a sustainable business model for all of the teams, which means controlling costs, talking about the distribution of money and all those type of things. There's challenge, but also a lot of opportunity, and personally I'm excited about the future of F1. Going into the digital-media era we are the most data-rich sport in the world, and it's amazing the appetite some of the younger fans have for information. And we're aflood with it. I think the basic proposition of brave,

young men in the most advanced vehicles in the world at the pinnacle of motorsport is fantastic. We talk about Concorde Agreement fights and so forth, but all these things are internal machinations, and actually the sport can be much bigger. We should be looking forward.

Q: But is it not a no-brainer to try and keep more money in the sport?

Brundle: That's oversimplifying. The teams' jobs are to compete against each other, and the skill sets of the people who run these businesses are different. I think that before you change the business model we have now, and a dictatorial type of business driver like Bernie, you have to come up with something you think is going to be better before you try to topple that regime. I would like to see more of the money that is generated by F1 filter down into the sport. It does upset me that it just gets hoovered up and goes straight out the top.

Q: Christian has pointed out that all but four teams are struggling. Is that not why?

Horner: But I think those teams will be taking home more money than a struggling Premiership football team at the moment. I think that, as Martin said, the teams aren't natural owners. You've only got to look at the NBA to see the trouble they have got themselves in, which has often been used as an example. I think the teams need to focus on being competitors. As Colin Chapman used to say, let the rules spell out what the championship is and I'll decide whether I enter or not. They've got that choice, and year after year they come back. It's not our job to run the sport, it's our job to put on the best possible show. I think it will be an interesting 12 months ahead.

Hughes: I think that a significant part of the money generated by the FIA/teams/rights holder arrangement is not so much reinvested as simply taken, and I think that's wrong.

THE DRIVERS

All 28 drivers who competed in F1 during 2011 tell us about their campaigns, in World Championship order, led by back-to-back World Champion Sebastian Vettel

1 **SEBASTIAN VETTEL**
RED BULL RACING

"IT REALLY HAS BEEN A YEAR WHERE I'VE JUST GROWN. I'VE LEARNED A LOT THIS YEAR WHICH I CAN TAKE INTO NEXT YEAR"

"This season has been a year of growth. I was talking to a friend just recently who is very, very wise. I said that it has been a very difficult year, but he said it hasn't been a difficult year, it's been a year of growth – which was one of the most positive things I've learned this year.

It really has been a year where I've just grown. I've learned a lot this year which I can take into next year. So I feel positive about it, and I think in the future I'll look back on this season and smile and say, 'I needed that.'

I like to think of the good things that I've done. I've had three grand prix wins this year, which isn't as many as I would hope for, but I'm still grateful for them. Obviously they were positive races where I was able to excel to where I should be.

I think if I looked at the season and I didn't win one grand prix, it could be a lot worse, couldn't it? It's not too bad, but it can always be better. As I said, if I look back on this year, whilst it's not been a year where I've won the most grands prix or won the championship, it's been the year where I've learned quite a bit.

I think I will come out a stronger person. I can't say that I'm there yet, but I think when I get to the winter, when I reflect on the whole season, I think I will be. I'm about to turn 27, and I think I'm definitely a lot wiser than I was when I started this season, and that's always a positive, because you move forward.

It's about striking a balance. You can be too intense, and you can be not serious enough. It's really trying to strike a balance. I've been racing since I was eight years old, and I still don't have the right formula for it. Obviously the car has a big impact on that. Every year is a journey towards finding that solution, finding the right ingredients.

Last winter I spent five or six hours a day, six days a week, training. It was so much work and so much dedication, it was a bit too serious, I think. I'm still very fit now, even though I've had a year where I've not been training anywhere near as much. I think it's about keeping the training up – maybe I can do less training, but more effective – and the most important bit is the time in between that you spend with family and friends, making sure I enjoy that more. That's the most important thing, that's what gets your mind more ready and in better shape for the next season.

I think there are a lot of lessons we've learned. Every year we try to arrive with a car that's the best. Obviously we've struggled for the last couple of years. Since 2009 we have started better in 2010 and we kind of started better in 2011. I think we'll take those experiences, and with next year's car, we'll start on the right track. And if we're able to start on the right track, I think we have the strength to stay ahead and compete with anyone.

5 LEWIS HAMILTON
McLAREN

I have been with the team since I was 13 years old. I think I have quite a unique relationship with the team, and regardless of how tough a year it has been, or how many problems we have had, I stay very close to their hearts, and I think they're the same with me. They continue to support me, and it's great to see that when they're having tough times, us as drivers, Jenson and me, are able to lift them and vice versa.

You cannot really predict what's going to happen with Red Bull, but they have been very competitive the last two and a half years so we have to assume they're going to be competitive next year, but we all start from scratch and have another chance to win again. I think one thing is for sure: we're all determined to win the championship, so whatever the case, it won't be easy for any of us."

NATIONALITY British
DATE OF BIRTH 7/1/85
PLACE OF BIRTH Stevenage, England
GRANDS PRIX 90
WINS 17
POLES 19
FASTEST LAPS 11
POINTS 723
HONOURS F1 World Champion 2008; GP2 Champion 2006; European F3 Champion 2005; British Formula Renault Champion 2003; World Kart Champion 2000

"I WILL NEVER GIVE UP. I WAS ALWAYS PUSHING HARD TO GET BACK TO THE RIGHT DIRECTION FOR FIGHTING FOR VICTORIES IN THE CHAMPIONSHIP"

look at Barcelona, Fernando was fighting with Sebastian at the front, then he took new tyres and he lost one lap. It's not just related to me, it's related to both drivers. I think this was part of our car this season.

There were some good races. I think Malaysia was a very good race, China as well. I had so many problems in the pit stops in Turkey, but it was a good race. Monte Carlo was OK, but anyway I had a problem with Lewis! When you don't have what you want, there's always a little bit of frustration. Monaco was one of those races.

Silverstone wasn't a great result, but it was acceptable. I tried to pass Lewis on the last lap, but this was really a normal situation, nothing compared with Monaco. Germany was a good race, but I had a problem with the pit stop on the last lap. In Hungary I went off the track in the wet, it was the beginning of the race. The pace was very good, but I lost too many places there.

So there were also some problems that didn't help my results at the end, and it could have been a little bit better than it was, for all these problems I had. I cannot say I am 100% happy, even counting these problems. But anyway, I will never give up. I was always pushing hard to get back to the right direction for fighting for victories and the championship.

So it was definitely not a positive championship, but anyway I think it's important to be fresh in mind, and work to be at a completely different level, and I'm sure I can be next year.

I think definitely I have to be more consistent, race-by-race. As I said, many things happened in so many races this season, so I have to be more consistent, and being more consistent and having a good car, I'm sure this is the direction to go.

The target is always to fight for the podium, to try to see if we have the possibility to even get to fight for the victory. That's always the target. It's not easy, but that's always the direction we take. We're working very hard for next year, already developing the car, trying to put all the ideas for the new car, trying to see everything that we weren't so happy about this year, to try to make the car stronger next year.

At the top of the list are always the downforce and the efficiency, that's what makes the car very, very quick. But then you have all the other areas which are important as well – the engine side, the way you do the chassis, the suspension, the mechanical parts. We need to be perfect in everything. For sure, when you win a championship you need to be perfect in all the areas.

When you don't have a good season, the next year is always a fresh start. The motivation is very high to work very hard for the start of next year and a better season. Everybody wants it inside the team, and I want it even more."

6 FELIPE MASSA
FERRARI

NATIONALITY Brazilian
DATE OF BIRTH 25/4/81
PLACE OF BIRTH
São Paulo, Brazil
GRANDS PRIX 153
WINS 11
POLES 14
FASTEST LAPS 15
POINTS 582
HONOURS
Euro F3000 Champion 2001;
European Formula Renault
Champion 2000

"There have been many important lessons this season, and not just for me. For me it was a difficult season, but also for the whole team, so there were many lessons that we need to put on paper, for the developing of next year's car and for the work for next season.

There were many disappointments. Definitely we didn't have the car we expected, and then in many races many things happened to me. We didn't have a great pace in qualifying, especially in the first part of the season.

For sure Fernando did a better job in qualifying, and clearly it was something I was struggling with a little bit. I improved a lot in the last races in terms of performance in qualifying.

I've had tyre problems before, but I think this year it's something that we saw in both cars. For example if you

7 NICO ROSBERG
MERCEDES GP

"In 2011 we took a step back, unfortunately, which wasn't ideal for all of us. On the other hand, it has been good because it made it clear that we didn't have what it took to win as a team, so we had to strengthen it up.

And that's what's happening – the message from Mercedes is clear, we have to do whatever it takes to win the championship, so they're pushing big time. The final news was Aldo Costa and Geoff Willis coming, which was fantastic. It's clear that they are going for it, because those two are absolutely top guys in F1.

There were some bright spots – I could have won in China, but I ran out of fuel, which was very frustrating. Monza could have been really good if I hadn't been taken out at the start. I'm pleased with my own performances, I feel like I've had a good year, and I'm generally quite happy. But next year is going to be good, we're going to have a much better car and it's going to be a lot more enjoyable.

Now I can fully concentrate flat-out to help push the team forward. It was very clear in the summer, with all the new people coming on board, that this team was 150% committed to becoming the best in F1. It's fantastic to be part of that project to help lead the team towards better things, and I just look forward to it.

For me it will be such an amazingly special thing to be standing on the top step of a podium having won a race with a Silver Arrow. It will be spectacular. And that's what my dream is, and I want to achieve that now. This team means business, and they're doing what it takes to become the best.

With Ross leading again, he's been there and done it before, and he knows what it takes. He's been strongly implementing all his changes in the summer, and even more now, going forward step by step. Of course I know that I need to be a little bit more patient, for a little longer, but that's OK, I can accept that.

It's going to be difficult – the gap to the front is quite large at the moment. Next year the goal will be consistently going for podiums. That will be a good step for us, and then we'll take it from there."

NATIONALITY German
DATE OF BIRTH 27/6/85
PLACE OF BIRTH Wiesbaden, Germany
GRANDS PRIX 108
WINS 0
POLES 0
FASTEST LAPS 2
POINTS 306.5
HONOURS GP2 Champion 2005; German Formula BMW Champion 2002

8 MICHAEL SCHUMACHER
MERCEDES GP

"I've said before that the first part of my career finished with Ferrari, and this is like a new chapter. I'm excited about the Mercedes chapter, because it somehow all started at Mercedes, when I joined F1, and now I'm rejoining the team and working together with friends that I know from the past.

And this is a big challenge. It became bigger than we anticipated for the reasons that are known, but it's a good challenge, and it's an interesting one. It's a challenge that I feel has a lot of potential to have a successful ending, which I'm excited about and look forward to.

It isn't about age, it's about the racing. I still have the hunger to compete and race, after moments that I didn't, at least at the high professional level in F1. I always kept racing motorcycles and go-karts. It just somehow came back to F1. I did not expect it to, but it did, and it's just fun.

There's clearly been progress in terms of how we work together, how we maximise the potential of the car. Yes, at the beginning you're a bit rusty and you need time to maximise your own skills, but thereafter it's how you work and proceed to get the best out of the car, how you understand this, who you work with, and what you've got to achieve this. That is something we have definitely improved a lot this year.

I'm quite happy with the way we're heading, how we operate, how we work the car through a weekend. I'm reasonably happy with what we were managing out of our available resources. You can, at the end of the day, be happy or not happy, because you know exactly whether or not you did a good job.

It took some while to maximise that potential. Talking about our general performance, you have to assess where you are, what needs to be done, and then to transform it. You'd rather do this early than late, and we have to understand that we're later than we hoped to be.

There's no point in talking about particular races I'm happy or not happy with. The point is that I think it was after Budapest, towards Belgium, where clearly we were able to achieve more with the car."

NATIONALITY Germany
DATE OF BIRTH 3/1/69
PLACE OF BIRTH Kerpen, Germany
GRANDS PRIX 288
WINS 91
POLES 68
FASTEST LAPS 75
POINTS 1517
HONOURS F1 World Champion 1994, 1995, 2000, 2001, 2002, 2003, 2004; German F3 Champion 1990; German Formula Konig Champion 1988

9 ADRIAN SUTIL
FORCE INDIA

"It was a bit difficult at the beginning of the season, I wasn't really there, and I had my difficulties with the new tyres a little bit, especially in qualifying. But then, after a few updates on the car, and after I turned into my better shape again, the pace was there.

We can see every year that we're improving. It shows what I did in the last few years, and it gives me a good feeling, and it shows what the whole team is capable of doing.

It wasn't the easiest season for me at the beginning, but I pulled myself up again, and that is sometimes even more important. The last 10 or 12 races it was quite obvious, I think. I think I've shown everyone what I'm able to do – more I can't do.

You have to perform every time, every race, you have to perform as if it's your last race. I'm OK with this, that's how it works here in F1. In some races you're doing badly, and you're suddenly nowhere. Then you do a few good races and you're up at the top again. It's just a very fast business here, and I know how it is.

I would say from Monaco on we were quite competitive. Canada was a good qualifying, but we just didn't make it in the race with the tricky conditions, and a few mistakes from myself. Valencia was quite good, and from there on every second race I was in the points, and good points.

Sixth in Germany was a great result. I think in Singapore we were very strong and competitive in the race, also at Suzuka. It could have been a little bit better, but the safety car caught me out, and that's the main reason why I lost the points.

It was the other way around from last season, when we were much stronger at the beginning, and we had difficulties at the end of the season. Still I believe from ultimate performance the 2010 car was a little bit better. At the beginning of that season I was able to be really far at the front, like P5 in Malaysia.

That wasn't possible this year. This year we had three categories in F1, and we were in the front of the middle pack, and everyone else in front of us was too far away. But I would still say it turned out to be a good season."

NATIONALITY German
DATE OF BIRTH 11/1/83
PLACE OF BIRTH Graefeling, Germany
GRANDS PRIX 90
WINS 0
POLES 0
FASTEST LAPS 1
POINTS 95
HONOURS Swiss Formula Ford Champion 2002

10 VITALY PETROV
RENAULT

"Definitely physically and mentally, and with the performance I did, I can feel I made a good step forward, I improved myself. But I'm not so happy with the performance that we did with me and the team this year. Yes, we started at a really, really high level, and the first few races we were good enough. With 80% of my driving I'd get easily into Q3, and I could fight in the top eight.

Australia was an amazing day for me really, because it was my first podium, and I couldn't believe it happened. All the weekend was fantastic, we made no mistakes and we did a fantastic strategy, and the car was brilliant to drive. Then we had some bad weekends, and also the tactics that we chose.

The problem was our front exhaust, because we couldn't develop it. I think we didn't expect that the Pirelli tyres would have so much degradation. If we still had Bridgestone tyres, maybe our technology would be a good step.

With a rear-exhaust car, other teams could still develop this area. Toro Rosso made an improvement – they brought a new exhaust and they found one second. This is a good, good step. We couldn't do anything. We brought a lot of different parts for the track, but it wasn't working. It was maybe half a tenth or a tenth, which was nothing.

We struggled at the slow tracks where you need traction and a good exit from the corners. At high-speed tracks like Suzuka, we were good. We weren't the quickest, but we were eighth or ninth. This is why this season wasn't as expected.

I think the changes will be better for the team. It's like football – when a new coach joins a team, what he does first of all is look at the team and watches where the players are playing. Then he puts the people in the right places, where they should be playing. Then the team becomes more competitive and plays stronger. This is actually what we try to do inside the team. The team principal tries to change some people, to move them around and try to profit from this."

NATIONALITY Russian
DATE OF BIRTH 8/9/84
PLACE OF BIRTH Vyborg, Russia
GRANDS PRIX 38
WINS 0
POLES 0
FASTEST LAPS 1
POINTS 64
HONOURS Formula 1600 Russia Champion 2005; Lada Revolution Champion 2005; Lada Cup Champion 2002

11 NICK HEIDFELD
RENAULT

"I have to say, especially in the beginning, the team was very open and very helpful with everything, and I did settle in very quickly. If you look back at the interviews I gave then, I had a very good feeling within the team.

You always hoped, especially with the exhaust being the only one in the field, that it might be the thing that promoted us to the front. Especially before the first race, you don't know.

Qualifying at the first race wasn't nice, I think I was out in Q1 with the traffic, and then I had a damaged car in the race. But at least Vitaly showed with a podium how good the pace was. Then, at the second race in Malaysia, I had a podium.

I think the whole team did a good job. At some points this year the team was criticised for not doing the right thing in qualifying. It's easy to say from the outside, but I think this is what partly helped us in the beginning of the year, and also in Malaysia. I didn't do many laps in qualifying, but this gave me the possibility to have fresher tyres. Of course,

it can be a gamble if you just do one shot in qualifying, but then you have a benefit later.

So, early in the season we were going quite strongly. It was obvious that we fell back a little. I had some better races, some worse races, sometimes bad luck. That's the way it went. I think Barcelona was very nice, if you look at the race. The car burned in practice so I couldn't do qualifying, but I still finished P8 from last position or something, just behind the two Mercedes. It's another if, but one lap more, and I would have had those two as well.

I think I had a good season, although it was not the best season of my career. Vitaly outqualified me – there were sometimes reasons for it, but nobody wants to hear them. And Vitaly also did a good job. He's a lot more self-confident, and I think that has helped him a lot as a driver. But I think what matters most in the end are the points.

I think it's obvious how I felt when it ended, but that is behind me now. Now I'm trying to do the best for the future."

NATIONALITY German
DATE OF BIRTH 10/5/77
PLACE OF BIRTH Mönchengladbach, Germany
GRANDS PRIX 185
WINS 0
POLES 1
FASTEST LAPS 2
POINTS 259
HONOURS Formula 3000 Champion 1999; German F3 Champion 1997

12 KAMUI KOBAYASHI
SAUBER

"The first part of the season was great, we had good pace to score points always, and we were very consistent. Then in Valencia we struggled, but in the British GP we came back to our pace, but we had a gearbox failure, and we couldn't score any points. After that, the FIA changed the exhaust rules, and we struggled a lot, while the other teams were improving a lot. We had a misunderstanding and finally we went the wrong way.

The team itself was stronger than last year, and at the beginning of the season we did a great job. But when they changed the rules, it wasn't really nice for us. The team has improved in every area, I don't want to say just one thing. We have more people, and they've got more experience.

Monaco was a very nice race, I was very happy with the result, fifth place. In Canada we had brilliant pace in the wet, although finally I finished seventh. But it was a great show for us, and I was very happy.

Japan was so disappointing! It was a good qualifying time from myself, and we started

seventh, which was great. But unfortunately it was not a good day on Sunday! Our pace was not good, and our tyre selection was a little bit different from the others as well, as we were playing a little bit of a different game, which was quite difficult for us.

I was quite happy with the DRS in the beginning – it had a big effect in the races on overtaking, but later it wasn't so effective. It looked less powerful. I think spectators were getting bored again! We have to be more aggressive with the tyres, the DRS, everything.

It was quite strange in my second year being the experienced driver in the team. It's more work – let's say as a rookie it's much easier! Sergio is a nice guy, and he's fast as well. Our driving styles are a little bit different – we're just different people.

This year we had a good start, but at the end we struggled because of development. We have to find a way to be competitive from the beginning of the season to the end. I think that's our target. I'm confident that we can begin the next season well."

NATIONALITY Japanese
DATE OF BIRTH 13/9/86
PLACE OF BIRTH Hyogo, Japan
GRANDS PRIX 40
WINS 0
POLES 0
FASTEST LAPS 1
POINTS 65
HONOURS European & Italian Formula Renault Champion 2005; Japanese Kart Champion 2001; Suzuka Kart Champion 2000; Japanese Cadet Kart Champion 1997

13 PAUL DI RESTA
FORCE INDIA

NATIONALITY British
DATE OF BIRTH 16/4/86
PLACE OF BIRTH Uphall, Scotland
GRANDS PRIX 19
WINS 0
POLES 0
FASTEST LAPS 0
POINTS 27
HONOURS DTM Champion 2010; Formula 3 Euroseries Champion 2006; British Super 1 Kart Champion 2001

"I think, looking back at the year, you can say it was reasonably positive. There have been highs and lows and, given how long the season is, it's going to be like that. There were times when we didn't maximise it, and when I've made mistakes or the team has made mistakes.

We came in with ambitions of being sixth in the constructors' championship. We started very slowly, but with a change of philosophy that we started during the winter, we turned it around, and we were in a strong position.

Going to Australia, we'd accepted that the performance was probably not going to be quite where it needed to be to score points. But we put ourselves in a good position in qualifying, and we had good race pace. The main thing was that our reliability was key, and in the end that paid off. By China we already had an upgrade, and the performance level was massively boosted by that.

Qualifying at Silverstone was a highlight. It was obviously a wet Friday, and we seemed to be fairly happy. We had limited track time and straight into qualifying, and all I can say is that the pre-race work we'd done paid off, and we qualified sixth.

The first part of the race I was seventh and still going very strongly, until we had a problem in the pit stop. There was a bit of confusion, but at the end of the day the team wasn't trying to compromise me, it was just a genuine mistake.

Up and down the paddock people still expected us to be quick at Monza and Spa. But Monza was probably one of the hardest races that we had, we weren't that competitive in a straight line. You might say we were lucky, but we extracted what we could out of it, and managed to get an eighth place.

You'd expect Hungary to be one of our weaker tracks, and it was one of the strongest results. We went forward quite a bit. We started 11th, and went forward to seventh, and it was quite an action-packed race with some rain.

And it just continued on, although we were up against it, because Toro Rosso had huge upgrades. You'd have to say Singapore was a highlight, given that it was genuine performance that got us where we were."

14 JAIME ALGUERSUARI
TORO ROSSO

NATIONALITY Spanish
DATE OF BIRTH 23/3/90
PLACE OF BIRTH Barcelona, Spain
GRANDS PRIX 46
WINS 0
POLES 0
FASTEST LAPS 0
POINTS 31
HONOURS British F3 Champion 2008; Italian Formula Renault Winter Series Champion 2006

"In the races I think we've achieved our maximum. We know our good points, we know where the potential is on the tyres, we know how to deal with that – the team and myself. In qualifying we lacked performance, and therefore to be behind Force India was not really our position, although we should be really happy to be in front of Williams.

The car was missing downforce, but we knew how to maintain a good pace in the race, and I would say our car used the tyres less than the others. We could go faster in the races than in qualifying.

With the new tyres it was difficult for me to adapt myself and adapt the car, the set-up and so on, but we got it during the season.

It's just a matter of understanding the tyres from the mechanical balance point of view and from the driver's point of view. In that sense the team has done a fantastic job on Sundays, better than the other teams.

I think Canada was a very good race, because it was a very difficult race. Silverstone was good as well, and Nürburgring. Our best results came at Monza and in Korea.

In Hungary there was potential to finish seventh, but we finished 10th in the end. We changed tyres just when it started raining, and with cold tyres it was very difficult. I made a mistake and three cars passed me. It was a good race, and we had really good pace too.

I think Giorgio Ascanelli is one of those people you have to meet in life – he helped me to understand F1 and to understand this motorsport world. The team can be very happy with the progress, and they will do more next year, because it's building up, the team has more experience, and they know what to do. I think next year we should target to be sixth in the constructors' championship.

I think the team has done a fantastic job, and my team-mate and myself have done a really good job. Hopefully I can show my performance next year with a better car with Toro Rosso, if I'm still here. I hope to bring even better results. I know what I can do, and I will try my best to one day battle for the drivers' championship, because I think I can."

15 SEBASTIEN BUEMI
TORO ROSSO

"I think it's pretty clear that we have done better than last year. Obviously, in the championship we were in front of Williams. At the beginning of the year the main objective was to finish in the top eight, and we had a good fight with Sauber and Force India. On the other hand you always want to be better, and you're never happy!

I think I used most of the opportunities I had to score points. I lost quite a few points at Monza, we lost a bit of time in the pit stop, otherwise I could have finished eighth instead of 10th. So there were a few points here and there that we lost. Still, I think we improved quite a lot compared with last year.

I think we had a good car to start with. The middle of the season was a bit hard, but we still kept our position, especially in the races. Then we improved a bit, but it was still hard. In Hungary I was eighth – I started 23rd and it was a very good race, maybe the best race I did in my F1 career.

Then we were on an upward trend – at Spa we could have scored a lot of points if we didn't have those incidents, and at Monza we were both in the points.

In general I think we improved the car very well from mid-season to the end. I think we were improving the car race after race and this is why we could actually catch up the other guys. We were maybe a little bit too slow developing the car in the middle of the year. It's only the second year that the team is building the car, so it takes a bit of time to get into the rhythm, but I think we definitely got a lot of lap time through the blown diffuser.

It's the second year we've built our own car. The first year we had nothing ready, and the team did a fantastic job just to put the car together, because it was so hard. You're on your own, and it's very difficult. But now we start to have experience, we have a wind tunnel, we have CFD, everything starts to go in the right direction. You could not expect a small team to have results like this in two months, so now we see that it's going better."

NATIONALITY Swiss
DATE OF BIRTH 13/10/88
PLACE OF BIRTH Aigle, Switzerland
GRANDS PRIX 55
WINS 0
POLES 0
FASTEST LAPS 0
POINTS 29
HONOURS Italian Kart Champion 2003; European & Swiss Junior Kart Champion 2002; Swiss Super Mini Kart Champion 2000

16 SERGIO PEREZ
SAUBER

"I think it's been quite a good season. Probably when you look at the points it doesn't look so great, but if you consider my season, they took my points away in Australia, and then I missed two very important races where my team-mate scored very good points, in Monaco and Montréal.

I had a very bad accident in Monaco, and it took me three races to be 100% again. In Canada it was impossible to drive, Valencia was very difficult, and Silverstone was very tough. Nürburgring was better, and Budapest was fine.

For me, if I look back, I did a mega-effort in Valencia to do the race. After the accident I didn't expect that it was going to take so long. So it was a big effort, and I finished 11th there. Nürburgring as well was very, very tough for me, but I did a good race.

Silverstone was super hard, because it was the second race after my accident, and my head still wasn't feeling right. But it was another good result, seventh like in Australia. That was quite a good race in difficult conditions, especially as I wasn't 100%.

In a few races I was very unlucky. Malaysia wasn't such a good race, I was unlucky because something from a Toro Rosso hit my car and I couldn't finish. In Monza I was easily P7 when I had a mechanical failure, and we could have scored good points there.

I think its been a good season. The speed is there, so I'm happy. Of course it always helps to come into F1 and straight away show yourself. For me it worked quite well from the first race in Australia, straight away.

You realise that F1 is completely another world compared to what you're used to from GP2 or other categories, in terms of media, in terms of how busy you are during the season. There's a lot more of everything. But it's fun, it's what I always dreamed about, and I'm very happy to have finally achieved it.

I think Sauber is a great team to start your career with, because it's a team that can teach you very well. You learn a lot, and they push you a lot. I'm very happy, and I think I have shown a lot of promise in my season of F1."

NATIONALITY Mexican
DATE OF BIRTH 26/1/90
PLACE OF BIRTH Guadalajara, Mexico
GRANDS PRIX 18
WINS 0
POLES 0
FASTEST LAPS 0
POINTS 14
HONOURS British F3 Champion 2007

17 RUBENS BARRICHELLO
WILLIAMS

NATIONALITY Brazilian DATE OF BIRTH 23/5/72 PLACE OF BIRTH São Paulo, Brazil GRANDS PRIX 325 WINS 11 POLES 14 FASTEST LAPS 17 POINTS 658 HONOURS British F3 Champion 1991; European Formula Opel Champion 1990

"At the beginning of the testing we didn't have a very well balanced car, but we were able to do things with it. We ran a lot lower ride height than last year, and we were able to get the benefits from it. And all of a sudden we kept on breaking the floor, and they kept saying, 'We can fix it, we can fix it.'

By the time we got to the first race, it wasn't fixed, so we had to raise the car a great amount, and then we lost so much. By the time the car was fixed, the other teams had made huge developments on other stuff. So we were never able to conquer that. You can see the likes of Toro Rosso, they got a much better car towards the end of the season, which we did last year.

The car has some good things, but the bad ones actually outweighed the good ones. The driveability wasn't good, it was killing the rear tyres, and then, with the KERS situation, we were killing the rear tyres too, so it was a bit of a difficult one.

All the races you kind of have fun, even though you're racing for 12th or 13th. In Korea, for example, I was flat-out to the end, I had a better tyre choice than Bruno and Perez, and I was able just to catch and overtake them. My lap in most of the qualifying sessions was like a pole-position lap, but I put the car in 12th or 13th. It's been down from the point of view of TV viewers not seeing that, but on my side, I've been going home really happy."

18 BRUNO SENNA
RENAULT

NATIONALITY Brazilian DATE OF BIRTH 15/10/83 PLACE OF BIRTH São Paulo, Brazil GRANDS PRIX 26 WINS 0 POLES 0 FASTEST LAPS 0 POINTS 2 HONOURS None

"It was a very difficult situation in the beginning of the year, with not knowing what was happening, then Nick getting the drive, and then jumping into the car in the middle of the season. All these things were very difficult.

At the time of Robert's accident I was coming into the team, and I'd been there a week when everything happened. So it was a crazy mess. I was super-happy already with the fact that I had a job, because I didn't have one at the start of the year. When I got the news that I was going to test the car I was very nervous, as everything happened so fast.

When Nick got the drive, it was a bit disappointing because I wanted to drive, but not because I felt replaced. It was simply because I wanted to drive. At the

end of the day it happened the way it happened, and I got the drive eventually. It was just one of those things.

It has been pretty decent. Monza was a very good race, and Spa was a very good race, apart from the first corner! Even with the drive-through the safety car kind of put me back into contention. The only poor race I felt I had was Korea.

I think it took the edge off last year's bad image. The poor performance, even though it doesn't come from you, it rubs off on you. In 2010 I'm sure I could have had the best race of my life, and still no-one would have noticed it! There's still some of that, but that bitter taste is kind of going away. I think I'm on the map much better than I've ever been."

19 PASTOR MALDONADO
WILLIAMS

NATIONALITY Venezuelan DATE OF BIRTH 9/3/85 PLACE OF BIRTH Maracay, Venezuela GRANDS PRIX 19 WINS 0 POLES 0 FASTEST LAPS 0 POINTS 1 HONOURS GP2 Champion 2010; Italian Formula Renault Champion 2004

"I think it was really difficult for me, especially at the beginning of the season, because when I started I had just 800km of testing before the race. In the first races I only did a few laps, so it was so difficult for me to adapt myself to keep the pace, especially during the race.

I've been very quick and clean over one lap, like always, but it was really difficult to understand the car in the long runs, especially with the Pirelli tyres, when there was a big difference between the compounds. After we started to finish the races I was understanding the car a bit more, and improving myself race after race.

It was a difficult situation in the team, because when everything is wrong, everyone is down. But I enjoyed my time with Williams, because I learned a

lot, especially with Rubens. We were working so hard to try to improve the car as soon as we could. Even if the problems were there, we were pushing so hard to solve them.

Monaco was the race of the year for me. In qualifying I was P8, and I was running P6 near the end, until the problem with Hamilton. I had the opportunity because I knew the track very well, and I knew the car isn't the most important thing at Monaco. And when I knew the opportunity was there I was pushing all through the weekend, with confidence. I was so disappointed about the end of the race, but anyway, I did a great job. At Spa I got the first point of my career, starting from 21st, so it was a great race."

20 PEDRO DE LA ROSA
SAUBER

NATIONALITY Spanish DATE OF BIRTH 24/2/71 PLACE OF BIRTH Barcelona, Spain GRANDS PRIX 85 WINS 0 POLES 0 FASTEST LAPS 1 POINTS 35 HONOURS Formula Nippon Champion 1997; Japanese GT Champion 1997; Japanese F3 Champion 1995; British & European Formula Renault Champion 1992; Spanish Formula Ford Champion 1990

"It's an amazing year for me. If at the beginning of the year someone would have told me what was going to happen, I would never have believed it!

The bottom line is that I had a huge opportunity to develop the tyres with Pirelli, but not only the slicks, we had a lot of laps developing the intermediates and the full wets, in very different climates, which was fantastic. I started in October 2010, and we went to Valencia, Paul Ricard, Barcelona, Bahrain and Abu Dhabi – day and night and dry and wet!

And then I had the opportunity to come back to McLaren, which always makes you learn. That's the good thing about being there – even if your role is very limited at the track, you never stop learning in the simulator. You're active and you're learning, and you're working with the most clever engineers out there.

And then I had the chance to race in Canada with Sauber, which was completely unexpected, until Friday P2. It was incredible, very stressful, because I didn't know the car. The biggest issue was I didn't know the systems, the KERS or the DRS. It was very different – I even raced with mechanics' overalls! I finished 12th, but I should have been higher up. I will never forget, at the restart for the second part of the race, I had Alonso in front of me, and Jenson behind. And 48 hours before, I was just having lunch while they were running around! I felt I was an extremely lucky reserve driver to have this opportunity."

21 JARNO TRULLI
LOTUS RACING

NATIONALITY Italian DATE OF BIRTH 13/7/74 PLACE OF BIRTH Pescara, Italy GRANDS PRIX 256 WINS 1 POLES 4 FASTEST LAPS 1 POINTS 246.5 HONOURS German F3 Champion 1996; World Kart Champion 1995; European Kart Champion 1994

"I think we were a bit too optimistic at the beginning of the season when we said that we wanted to be in the midfield. Obviously the reality was that we found out pretty soon that we didn't make the step that we were expecting to.

On top of that, I think my season has been pretty hard because of the fact that I struggled with the power steering until Hungary, and even after that I couldn't use it at every race because the new version wasn't able to cope with the forces at certain circuits.

The season was much better than last year, because last year was horrible. But this year I had more struggles with the car, and with the feeling. I expected to be much further up on the grid, but we have to take it as an experience and say that if we want to make a step, we really need to work harder and invest more in the team.

I don't know if it was a mistake to have no KERS, because if you take a look at where we were, we were almost a second and a half off, so for this year it wasn't worth having, considering the cost. In fact, all three new teams didn't go for it. Next year we'll have three or four tenths in the pocket compared to this year.

I think we have to make quite a big step in terms of performance, and especially aerodynamics, if we really want to chase the midfield. It's pretty clear that we have half a car that is a World Champion car, and the rest that we design and look after is not up to the performance that we expect."

22 HEIKKI KOVALAINEN
LOTUS RACING

NATIONALITY Finnish DATE OF BIRTH 19/10/81 PLACE OF BIRTH Suomussalmi, Finland GRANDS PRIX 90 WINS 1 POLES 1 FASTEST LAPS 2 POINTS 105 HONOURS World Series by Nissan Champion 2004

"I feel my performances this year have been good, I feel that I am in the right frame of mind, self-confidence is on the right level, and I'm on top of things much better than previously in my career. I'm comfortable with the situation, and I feel I need a quick car to do the business again.

I feel that the race performances have been strong. It's hard to back it up with the results, because all I can show is my consistency, and my lap times through the race.

In an ideal world, everything would happen here at Team Lotus. I've been here since the beginning, and obviously next year it's crucial that we make the step forward, and we build on that.

We're growing, so I think we have a pretty good base for next year. The gap to the cars behind shows that we've made a good step forward. That's the thing that we should take from this year.

KERS would give us on average three-tenths every lap for free, obviously helping at the start and in race situations. It's still not enough, and I think the main improvement will come from the aerodynamic side. We need a more efficient aero package, more time in the wind tunnel. Now we've started to use the Williams wind tunnel as well, it will help us.

I think realistically you can't do it in two years. It took Red Bull six or seven years to make it, so it will take a lot of time for us as well. I think the progress so far is as good as we could have hoped for."

23 VITANTONIO LIUZZI
HISPANIA RACING TEAM

NATIONALITY Italian DATE OF BIRTH 6/8/81 PLACE OF BIRTH Locorotondo, Italy GRANDS PRIX 81 WINS 0 POLES 0 FASTEST LAPS 0 POINTS 26 HONOURS Formula 3000 Champion 2004; World Kart Champion 2001; Italian Kart Champion 1996

"I have to say it has been a challenging season! At least until the middle of the year we were fighting closer with our direct competitors. We had some interesting races where we were fighting for position with Virgin, and also sometimes with Lotus. In most wet races we could fight with faster cars, like Silverstone and Montréal.

Most of the early races we could fight with Virgin, the gap was really close, sometimes we were ahead and sometimes behind in qualifying. Later we suffered, because they clearly had better pace, and when there were dry conditions, it wasn't easy to fight with them.

I have to say the first part of the championship was more or less what I expected, because we were in a proper fight, then the second part of the season has been a bit slower. We didn't grow the way we were expecting, we didn't grow the way that we wanted. But on the other hand, there were a few changes in the team which might change the long-term plan. It seems that the new owners are pushing very hard, but these changes slowed down the development.

Of course, compared to what I had at Force India, there was a huge difference in terms of downforce and so on. The whole package was quite far behind. But in a way, where we are now was where Force India started, and they started with a team that already existed, so it was easier. We started from zero. It's normal, we know that we are a small team with a small budget, and this was the pace we were expecting to have this year."

24 JEROME D'AMBROSIO
VIRGIN RACING

NATIONALITY Belgian DATE OF BIRTH 27/12/85 PLACE OF BIRTH Etterbeek, Belgium GRANDS PRIX 19 WINS 0 POLES 0 FASTEST LAPS 0 POINTS 0 HONOURS Formula Master Champion 2007; Belgian Formula Renault 1600 Champion 2003

"For sure, the car wasn't where we wanted it to be, and it hasn't been easy to drive. On the other hand, I've learned a lot with this car. I think that in terms of difficulty, I expected it to be difficult to drive the car.

But what I didn't expect was the amount of stuff that you have to put together to be on top of your game during a Saturday and Sunday, all the parameters you have to go through, and you have to highlight and understand 100%. You realise that in F1, experience really does count.

I know I'm not fighting for the win, I'm not fighting for points. I'm fighting to grow and to improve all the time. We have our own little race in a race, with our references, and I always try to be on top of my game. It's important not to lose that rhythm, and to push all the time.

When everything goes well, it's all right, but then you have a weekend when maybe it's raining. When things don't go exactly together, then experience counts, like at Silverstone where we had only one dry practice to set up the car. You can't go in the wrong direction and then back off. This is where Timo sometimes still had an advantage over me.

We've all been through tough times, but we've stayed united, kept on pushing, and kept on going forwards. I still have a lot to learn, and a lot to do. I still love driving the car. Maybe it's not a Red Bull, but it's still an F1 car, and I am lucky to be one of these 24 drivers."

25 TIMO GLOCK
VIRGIN RACING

NATIONALITY German DATE OF BIRTH 13/3/82 PLACE OF BIRTH Lindenfels, Germany GRANDS PRIX 73 WINS 0 POLES 0 FASTEST LAPS 1 POINTS 51 HONOURS GP2 Champion 2007; German Formula BMW Champion 2001; German Formula BMW Junior Champion 2000

"We had another quite difficult start to the year, and we had to realise that we weren't on the pace and couldn't reach the targets that we had before the season. So the team had to make decisions, and during the season, which is always quite difficult. In the end, the team came up and said 'we have to change this and this.'

Quite clearly what we want in the future is to be somewhere in the top 10, and at some point fight at the top. The decision was right to work with McLaren – if you get a chance like this you have to grab it, and the team did. It's very positive for the future, and it shows we want to grow together in the next couple of years.

The big topic in F1 is aerodynamics, and that's where we were clearly behind everyone. Mechanically we were OK, but in every direction we can improve if we are quite far behind. But I think we made a massive step in terms of how everyone was working together.

There were quite a lot of races where I got a lot out of the car. For me it was always difficult to compare with anything, because Lotus was quite far ahead. Monza was pretty good for us in terms of qualifying speed – with a DRS that wasn't working properly we were only four-tenths away from those guys.

Valencia was good in terms of the race pace, and I would say nearly all of the races I'm quite happy with – at least in the part where we were really racing, and not being penalised by the blue flags! I think I got everything out of the car."

NATIONALITY Indian DATE OF BIRTH 14/1/77
PLACE OF BIRTH Madras, India GRANDS PRIX
28 WINS 0 POLES 0 FASTEST LAPS 0 POINTS 0
HONOURS Formula Asia Champion 1996; British
Formula Ford Winter Champion 1994

26 NARAIN KARTHIKEYAN
HISPANIA RACING TEAM

"Inside me, I'm very, very happy about my season, because I believe in myself, but at the end of the day, you are directly compared to your team-mates.

The Indian GP was one of the catalysts for me to come back to F1. At the beginning of the season obviously, coming from NASCAR, it took a bit of getting used to.

However, I feel I adapted quite well to it, to be honest. But at the back of the grid you can't really interest anyone. At least with the Jordan in the wet and so on I was very fast. But with HRT it was very hard!

I did only one and a half days of testing. We didn't qualify in Australia – we did three laps – so Malaysia was where the season started. I was 0.9s off Liuzzi, and then in China I was 0.2s slower, so I was getting faster.

Then, for Silverstone, the team did a deal with Red Bull for Ricciardo, so I was out. They run on a shoestring, so a little bit more money from someone else, you get dumped! But that's life at that back of the grid.

Later I did some FP1 sessions – Singapore was damp, Suzuka was a good session, and then Korea was completely wet. But still I was very happy in India. I was only a couple of hundredths slower than Daniel in qualifying, and he's rated very highly, so I think I proved a point, that I can still get up there.

I'm 34 years old, so I probably have only two years left. But there's a lot of interest in India, people want to buy into teams, so why not?"

NATIONALITY Australian DATE OF BIRTH 1/7/89
PLACE OF BIRTH Perth, Australia GRANDS PRIX 11
WINS 0 POLES 0 FASTEST LAPS 0 POINTS 0
HONOURS British F3 Champion 2009; Formula
Renault 2.0 WEC Champion 2008

27 DANIEL RICCIARDO
HISPANIA RACING TEAM

"It has definitely been a busy year, doing three different roles at different points throughout the year! I think, looking back on it all, it has been pretty good.

The Renault World Series was OK, but I would definitely have loved to have won more races. The Friday mornings were going quite well with Toro Rosso, and that probably helped to open up the opportunity at HRT. Since I've been with HRT there's definitely been progress, especially in the last few races, so I'm pretty happy.

Silverstone was hectic, that's probably a summary of the weekend! From Wednesday I was making a seat, meeting my engineer, and obviously there was a bit of media attention as well, as it was my first Grand Prix.

The result was not so spectacular, I'm well aware of that. But I finished the race – there's probably not really much more that could have come out of it, never having done any long runs on the tyre, and not sitting in the car for very long. It wasn't the easiest one to start with, and coming in at mid-season probably isn't easy, full stop!

But from then on, we definitely made progress pretty quickly. Budapest went quite well, at least the consistency and the way I was able to make the tyre last. And the conditions were also quite tricky.

Monza qualifying was a pretty good result. We missed parts of FP2 and FP3, so I was going in quite fresh. Korea was one of the strongest races, again not doing many dry laps before the race, but having a good race pace and mixing it up with the Virgins was good."

NATIONALITY Indian DATE OF BIRTH 19/1/84
PLACE OF BIRTH Chennai, India GRANDS PRIX
11 WINS 0 POLES 0 FASTEST LAPS 0 POINTS 0
HONOURS FV6 Asia Champion 2006; Formula 2000
Asia Champion 2001; Formula Maruti Champion 2000

28 KARUN CHANDHOK
LOTUS RACING

"Unfortunately, there wasn't a full-time race seat going, and then Tony Fernandes came up with this idea for me to be involved with the team and do a number of Fridays, gain a bit more experience, and get involved with the simulator programme.

Then Tony called me and said, 'I'd like to put you in the car in Germany'. I didn't really care how or why they arrived at that decision. You have to take any opportunity that comes.

The worst part was that the first time I did a lap in the dry was in Germany! I went off in Australia, it rained in Turkey, it rained at Silverstone, and in Valencia the gearbox broke at the end of the pitlane.

Everything was quite different to last year with HRT.

Lotus used different brakes, which was the big problem, because I flat-spotted every set of tyres on Friday! We changed things for Saturday to bring it more in line with what I wanted.

Tony said he'd be happy if I qualified within a second of Heikki, and I was within 0.8s of him, and given the limited mileage that was OK. The race wasn't great. I made a good start and I think I was about P16 coming out of Turn 4, and then Perez shoved me wide, so I went over the grass and ended up last. From there it was a struggle. I made a mistake in the quick chicane and went off, but I finished. Overall I was quite pleased with how I did.

Obviously I would love to have done India or races later in the year once I had a bit more mileage.

THE TEAMS

Red Bull Racing set the pace, with McLaren and Ferrari chasing hard, while the midfield battle was intense as teams adapted to new Pirelli tyres, DRS and the return of KERS

RED BULL

FERRARI

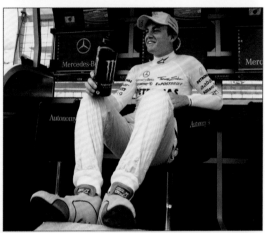

RENAULT

SAUBER

WILLIAMS

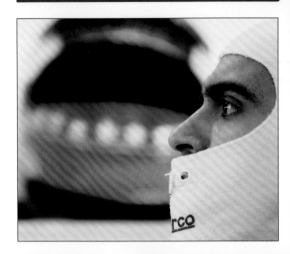

RED BULL

THE TEAM

PERSONNEL

CHAIRMAN Dietrich Mateschitz
TEAM PRINCIPAL Christian Horner
CHIEF TECHNICAL OFFICER Adrian Newey (above)
HEAD OF AERODYNAMICS Peter Prodromou
CHIEF DESIGNER Rob Marshall
HEAD OF CAR ENGINEERING Paul Monaghan
HEAD OF RACE ENGINEERING Ian Morgan
CHIEF ENGINEER, VEHICLE DYNAMICS Mark Ellis
TECHNICAL DIRECTOR, RENAULT ENGINES
Rob White
TEAM MANAGER Jonathan Wheatley
CHIEF ENGINEER, RENAULT ENGINES Fabrice Lom
DRIVERS Sebastian Vettel, Mark Webber
RACE ENGINEER (Vettel) Guillaume Rocquelin
RACE ENGINEER (Webber) Ciaron Pilbeam
SUPPORT TEAM MANAGER Tony Burrows
TEST/THIRD DRIVER Daniel Ricciardo
CHIEF MECHANIC Kenny Handkammer
TOTAL NUMBER OF EMPLOYEES 525
NUMBER IN RACE TEAM 85
TEAM BASE Milton Keynes, England
TELEPHONE +44 (0)1908 279700
WEBSITE www.redbullracing.com

TEAM STATS

IN F1 SINCE 1997 as Stewart Grand Prix then Jaguar Racing
FIRST GRAND PRIX Australia 1997 **STARTS** 263
WINS 27 **POLE POSITIONS** 38 **FASTEST LAPS** 22
PODIUMS 60 **POINTS** 1,492.5 **CONSTRUCTORS' TITLES** 2
DRIVERS' TITLES 2

SPONSORS

Red Bull, Infiniti, Total, Renault, Rauch, Pepe Jeans, FXDD, Casio, Geox, Singha Beer, Alpinestars, Red Bull Mobile, Hangar-7, Platform Computing, Siemens, Pirelli,

 1 SEBASTIAN VETTEL   **2 MARK WEBBER**

LEADING THE WAY WITH EXHAUST BLOWING

By Adrian Newey
Chief Technical Officer

"The big thing for 2011 was the banning of double diffusers. Given the level of development we'd achieved, it was a huge reduction in downforce, so it was trying to recover as much as we could.

Last year we found the exhausts to have a powerful effect, and that's what we concentrated on. We went to the position we did very early on, somewhere around August/September 2010.

We got to that position in the tunnel and developed it a fair bit from there. It's a tricky area to make work, but we had a lot of time to create a really big benefit. The car seemed pretty reasonable from the first test.

We then got on to understanding the Pirellis, which was a very rapid learning curve. With weight distribution fixed, it was the usual things; camber angles, pressures, and so on.

The amount of rubber flying off caused us early problems, going down brake ducts and radiator ducts. They don't rubber-in the track as much either, so track evolution is very different.

We learned from 2010, when we wasted a lot of points early on, but the main reason for getting RB7 out early was the tyres. We wanted to learn with the new car.

KERS PACKAGING PROVED A CHALLENGE

The smaller KERS decision concerned a better overall package. We were conscious that in 2009, with ostensibly the same regulations, if you compromised packaging too much accommodating KERS, you ended up slower. All I can say is, we're comfortable with the decision we made.

The reliability issue we struggled with on the car was KERS, particularly early season. We didn't get it running for the first couple of tests and that certainly hurt us. Part of the problem was undoubtedly the packaging route we chose – putting it at the back of the car in an area that's pretty hot and has lots of vibration.

The other thing was that KERS isn't our bread and butter. We're really a bunch of mechanical engineers and aerodynamicists, not electrical installation and control engineers.

One problem was the long lead times with some components, so when problems were identified they took a long time to fix.

TYRE DEGRADATION DICTATED PACE

There was an element of not being able to use all of the car's performance in the race, for sure. The degradation of the tyres could self-level things a bit.

Initially, we were trying to go as slowly as we could to win the race. Also, while we had a working KERS in qualifying, generally speaking a couple of laps into the race, the thing had broken. Sebastian in particular very much drove to the slowest pace he could to conserve the tyres, because we just didn't know how they were going to last.

There was a bigger gap between the two drivers this year. Seb's a very smart young man and is learning all the time. His experience continues to grow. In 2010 he made some driving mistakes that cost points. This time he made no mistakes to speak of.

Mark also found the Pirellis much more difficult to get on with than the Bridgestones. The Pirellis are very intolerant of high amounts of slip.

RADIO AND TYRE WARM-UP ISSUES

Of the races that got away, China was very frustrating. Of all the stupid things, the car's radio aerial snapped off, and so when we wanted Seb to come in, he didn't get the message. We hadn't realised the radio wasn't working. We didn't intend to do one less stop, but the radio failure threw our strategy to pot. The car had very good inherent pace and it was a silly reason to lose a race.

In Canada, Seb had good pace all through the wet phase and was able to draw away at will. Then, on that final stint after the red flag, we struggled with tyre warm-up in cold conditions and Jenson didn't. That was a story that came back to haunt us a bit at Silverstone, Nürburgring and Hungary. I'd agree that McLaren got pretty much instant temperature, Ferrari struggled and we were in between.

It's difficult to understand whether that's something fundamental to the car, or whether it's something we can tune. We tried to remove it a bit, but the pattern remained.

THE EXHAUST-BLOWING CONTROVERSY

In Barcelona, McLaren pushed us after we'd had a big qualifying margin, and I think that was more the traditional, early-season KERS

ENGINE
MAKE/MODEL Ferrari 056
CONFIGURATION 2398cc V8
(90 degree)
SPARK PLUGS NGK
ECU FIA standard issue
FUEL Shell V-Power
OIL Shell Helix Ultra
BATTERY Not disclosed

TRANSMISSION
GEARBOX Ferrari
FORWARD GEARS Seven
CLUTCH Not disclosed

CHASSIS
CHASSIS MODEL Ferrari 150 Italia
FRONT SUSPENSION LAYOUT
Independent pushrod-activated
torsion springs
REAR SUSPENSION LAYOUT
Independent pushrod-activated
torsion springs
DAMPERS Not disclosed
TYRES Pirelli
WHEELS BBS
BRAKE DISCS Brembo
BRAKE PADS Not disclosed
BRAKE CALIPERS Not disclosed
FUEL TANK Not disclosed
INSTRUMENTS
Ferrari/Magneti Marelli

DIMENSIONS
LENGTH Not disclosed
WIDTH Not disclosed
HEIGHT Not disclosed
WHEELBASE Not disclosed
TRACK, FRONT Not disclosed
TRACK, REAR Not disclosed
WEIGHT 640kg (including
driver and camera)

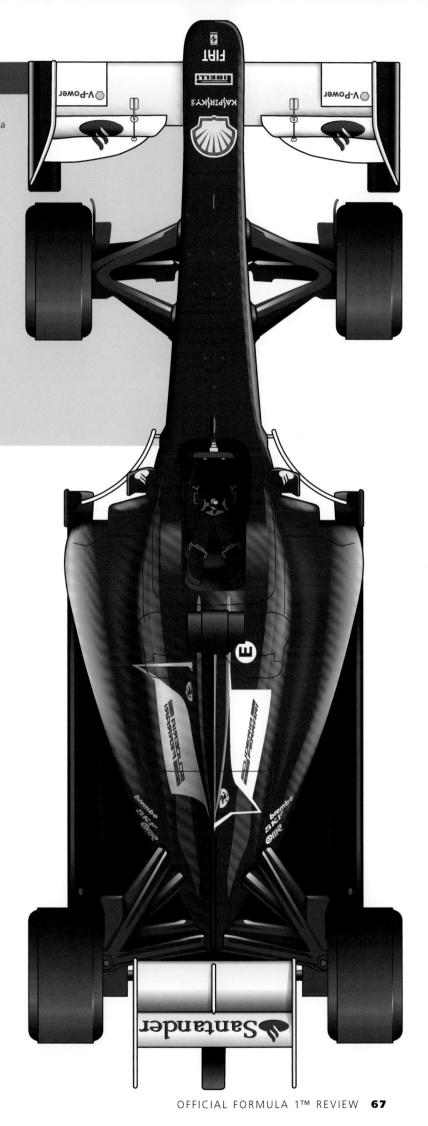

and it took all of the 2007–08 winter to get to the point of running the way they do now. Whether it was worth it then I don't know, but now that would have paid off.

We must have run in the order of 10 different exhaust/diffuser combinations. There were different lengths, angles and diameters of pipe.

We tried running more rake, and it was simply a trade-off of where the downforce was. You're trading centre-of-gravity height and losing out a bit. It's down to the way the exhaust interacts with the floor and the tyre, and you're trying to stop the air coming in underneath the tyre, so if you lift up the rake, you change the area you're blowing.

How you optimise your front wing when it's close to the ground is one reason you do it. The other – our main driving force at Silverstone – was that's where the downforce was. So it wasn't a challenge running it there, you had to run it and make sure it was working as you'd expect.

You use the exhaust gas to seal the floor. The high-pressure area in front of the tyre is trying to come around into the low-pressure area under the diffuser and you blow to stop it.

So it's like a curtain/skirt, and you blow at various points depending where you want to send the gas down.

The fact that we had our most competitive race with the Silverstone interpretation of off-throttle blowing did suggest we weren't getting as much out of the technology as some.

The very high exhaust-blowing rates have been one of the areas where we've struggled with correlation. The corner entry side of it, when your throttle's still open at 90% but you're not putting any fuel through, or only a little, we predict very well. But we haven't predicted that well at higher blowing levels, and that effectively means our floor is optimised at a lower level than the others.

SILVERSTONE VICTORY THE HIGHLIGHT OF THE YEAR
Silverstone made people run at the level we were already running at. They didn't have time to re-optimise their cars. If you'd given them a couple of weeks they would have done. The teams that took a real bad step there were McLaren, Renault and to some degree Mercedes. Red Bull had a similar gap to us. It looked like they didn't use KERS in qualifying there, which is why we looked that bit closer."

MERCEDES

HONING THE TEAM FOR THE NEXT STEP

By Ross Brawn
Team Principal

"We probably wouldn't have created the car concept we did if we'd understood and anticipated the exhaust technologies. The short wheelbase and other things we did were not as advantageous as we thought.

We rather shot ourselves in the foot with the cooling system, which was quite different to the norm in terms of the two-tiered radiators. When we solved the teething problems they actually worked very well, but those problems hurt us in the development stakes early on.

The two-tiered radiators were to keep the car short, because obviously a single radiator is much longer. The reason we wanted a short car was that with the diffuser-height changes from 2010 we thought that would be the way to go, but it wasn't the case.

We thought we would want a nice short, flat area of the floor, because we'd struggle to keep the diffuser working the way we wanted, but of course the exhaust technologies solved that problem straight away. There was then no need for a short floor, which has compromises in terms of weight distribution, fuel height and all sorts of other factors.

EXPERIENCE WILL FEED INNOVATION

It became clear at the end of last year that there was perhaps more going on in the exhaust area than we'd understood. We then started to look at when you wanted the exhaust to work and the so-called hot-blowing and other strategies become very relevant.

We have a good, bright group of people, but perhaps they were stretched and we didn't have enough depth to anticipate these areas.

Adding to that depth with Geoff Willis and Aldo Costa will be a real asset for the people we already have. They will have the extra mentoring and experience.

All the teams come up with different ideas, and they have a different magnitude of effect. Last year it was the F-duct, the year before the double diffuser – a peak for us that was born out of the team we had in Japan, which was huge. There's no doubt that a good big team will always beat a good little team.

REAR-TYRE DEGRADATION

Pirelli did a very good job. The respect for them among the teams has gone up, because I know when we decided to go to Pirelli some teams were a little bit nervous. But I think they've done a great job. It's been perfect for F1. When I say great job, I don't know about the absolute performance of the tyres – but it's not a tyre war and that was not their objective.

Their brief was to produce a decent tyre and make sure everyone had the same tyres and that they were consistent, and that's exactly what they did. We also told them we wanted tyres with more degradation, and again that's exactly what they've done. You can't criticise them at all.

We had some fairly high rear degradation initially, and the higher centre of gravity with the shorter car and some other factors came into it. At tracks like Monaco and Singapore that was an area we weren't too strong in.

When we were at tracks that are front-tyre limited, and China was one of them, the car seemed to perform very well. We got better in that respect – Singapore wasn't another Monaco for us – but rear-tyre degradation is something we have to address for next year.

Pirelli had some development tyres for the teams to try in Abu Dhabi aimed at improving that aspect. But we can't complain because other teams did a better job of looking after them.

DRS PROVED TO BE A STRONG POINT

Developing the new DRS went well. We had a little problem in the beginning at certain yaw angles, or in certain cross winds when it was a bit reluctant to re-attach once the flap came back down.

For some curious reason it seemed to affect Michael more than Nico. We had theories about helmet shape and various other things, but never really concluded why. Their helmets are slightly different shapes and the flow on to the rear wing was a little different. You could swap the wing over and the problem would stay with Michael.

It was something very marginal, and so we just came back a little bit on the design of the wing and from that point on it was solid and performed well. The DRS was one of the strongest aspects of the car.

THE TEAM

PERSONNEL
TEAM PRINCIPAL Ross Brawn (above)
CHIEF EXECUTIVE OFFICER Nick Fry
CHIEF OPERATING OFFICER Rob Thomas
VICE-PRESIDENT, MERCEDES-BENZ MOTORSPORT Norbert Haug
MANAGING DIRECTOR, MERCEDES-BENZ HIGH-PERFORMANCE ENGINES Thomas Fuhr
CHIEF OPERATING OFFICER Rob Thomas
TECHNICAL DIRECTOR Bob Bell
CHIEF DESIGNER John Owen
HEAD OF AERODYNAMICS Loic Bigois
HEAD OF VEHICLE ENGINEERING & DYNAMICS Craig Wilson
CHIEF ENGINEER Russell Cooley
DRIVERS Nico Rosberg, Michael Schumacher
SPORTING DIRECTOR Ron Meadows
CHIEF RACE ENGINEER Simon Cole
SENIOR RACE ENGINEER (Rosberg) Jock Clear, then Tony Ross
SENIOR RACE ENGINEER (Schumacher) Mark Slade, then Peter Bonnington
CHIEF MECHANIC Matthew Deane
TEST/RESERVE DRIVERS Sam Bird, Anthony Davidson
TOTAL NUMBER OF EMPLOYEES 450
NUMBER IN RACE TEAM 47
TEAM BASE Brackley, England
TELEPHONE +44 (0)1280 844000
WEBSITE www.mercedes-gp.com

TEAM STATS
IN F1 SINCE 1999, as BAR, then Honda Racing, then Brawn GP
FIRST GRAND PRIX Australia 1999
STARTS 226 **WINS** 9 **POLE POSITIONS** 8
FASTEST LAPS 4 **PODIUMS** 33 **POINTS** 875
CONSTRUCTORS' TITLES 1 **DRIVERS' TITLES** 1

SPONSORS
Petronas, Aabar, Autonomy, Deutsche Post, MIG Bank, Allianz, Graham London, Henri Lloyd, Monster Energy, Pirelli, Standox, Alpinestars, Endless, Lincoln Electric, Sandvik, Star Trac, STL

7 MICHAEL SCHUMACHER　　**8 NICO ROSBERG**

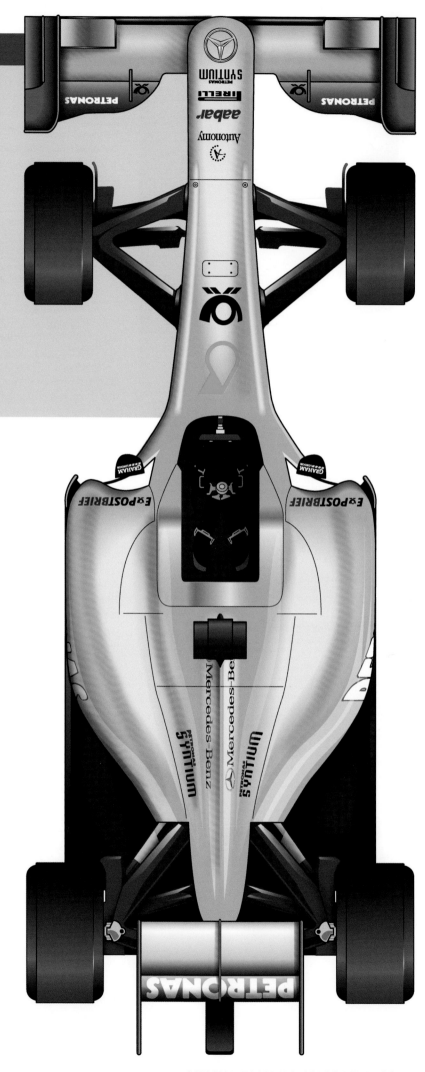

ENGINE
MAKE/MODEL Mercedes-Benz FO108Y
CONFIGURATION 2400c V8 (90 degree)
SPARK PLUGS NGK
ECU FIA standard issue
FUEL Petronas
OIL Petronas
BATTERY Not disclosed

TRANSMISSION
GEARBOX Mercedes GP
FORWARD GEARS Seven
CLUTCH Not disclosed

CHASSIS
CHASSIS MODEL Mercedes MGP W02
FRONT SUSPENSION LAYOUT
Wishbones and pushrod-activated
torsion springs and rockers
REAR SUSPENSION LAYOUT
Wishbones and pushrod-activated
torsion springs and rockers
DAMPERS Penske

TYRES Pirelli
WHEELS BBS
BRAKE DISCS
Not disclosed
BRAKE PADS
Not disclosed
BRAKE CALIPERS
Brembo
FUEL TANK Not disclosed
INSTRUMENTS
Not disclosed

DIMENSIONS
LENGTH 4800mm
WIDTH 1800mm
HEIGHT 950mm
WHEELBASE Not disclosed
TRACK, FRONT
Not disclosed
TRACK, REAR
Not disclosed
WEIGHT 640kg (including
driver and camera)

MERCEDES GP
PETRONAS
FORMULA ONE™ TEAM

DRIVERS WORK HARD TO AID DEVELOPMENT

Michael put some good races together, but Nico still tended to be quicker in qualifying and we had no strong theory as to why. There was a period when perhaps Michael was focusing a bit more on race performance, but like all these situations, Nico responded.

They both bounce off each other a bit, which is healthy if it's constructive. Michael seemed to find more confidence, and Monza was a great help in terms of his self-esteem. It all counts. They both worked incredibly hard at getting the best out of the car. Both are very professional and put a big effort in with their engineers, at the track and away from it.

What they require from the car is pretty similar. One may be doing a bit of the development programme, knowing that he can jump on to the other's set-up if it's a blind alley, and that's a good position to be in.

I think Nico is very, very good. I'm delighted with his performance, but where he sits in terms of the overall ladder, I don't know. A race win would make a huge difference to his confidence, and I'm very excited about what would develop if we can give it to him. I do think he's right up there, but until you get these guys in the same cars, you never know.

STRENGTHENING THE TEAM FOR 2012

Perhaps we'd hoped that we could compete at the level we needed in 2011, but we couldn't. We've strengthened the team now and Aldo and Geoff are just two head counts, so not a major impact on the Resource Restriction Agreement (RRA). They may want to strengthen the team in some areas, but we have some head-room and are now working up to the limits of the RRA.

The coming year should really be the one when Red Bull, Ferrari and McLaren come down to the RRA limits. They will have had the advantage of the high numbers in 2011, but this winter, if people are respecting the RRA, we should see changes to teams to bring them all to the same level – a level that we are moving up to."

RENAULT

THE TEAM

PERSONNEL

CHAIRMAN Gerard Lopez
TEAM PRINCIPAL & MANAGING DIRECTOR
Eric Boullier
CHIEF OPERATING OFFICER Patrick Louis
TECHNICAL DIRECTOR James Allison (above)
DEPUTY TECHNICAL DIRECTOR Naoki Tokunaga
HEAD OF AERODYMANICS Dirk de Beer
SPORTING DIRECTOR John Wickham
CHIEF DESIGNER Martin Tolliday
CHIEF RACE ENGINEER Alan Permane
ENGINE SUPPORT LEADER Riccardo Penteado
CHIEF MECHANIC Gavin Hudson
DRIVERS Nick Heidfeld, Vitaly Petrov, Bruno Senna
RACE ENGINEER (Heidfeld and Senna) Simon Rennie
RACE ENGINEER (Petrov) Ayao Komatsu
TEST/THIRD DRIVERS Jan Charouz, Fairuz Fauzy, Romain Grosjean, Ho-Pin Tung
TOTAL NUMBER OF EMPLOYEES 518
NUMBER IN RACE TEAM 90
TEAM BASE Enstone, England
TELEPHONE +44 (0)1608 678000
WEBSITE www.lotusrenaultgp.com

TEAM STATS

IN F1 SINCE 1977–85 then from 2002 **FIRST GRAND PRIX** Britain 1977, then Australia 2002 **STARTS** 301 **WINS** 35 **POLE POSITIONS** 50 **FASTEST LAPS** 31 **PODIUMS** 98 **POINTS** 1382 **CONSTRUCTORS' TITLES** 2 **DRIVERS' TITLES** 2

SPONSORS

Group Lotus, Genii, Boeing Research & Technology, Trina Solar, Total, TW Steel

9 NICK HEIDFELD   **9 BRUNO SENNA**   **10 VITALY PETROV**

NEW TYRES NEGATED EXHAUST DEVELOPMENT

By James Allison
Technical Director

"When we ran a blown exhaust in 2010, it gave us downforce, and plenty of it, but with a rather unpleasant handling effect on our car with the Bridgestone tyres. Every time you put your foot down and got the downforce it was all at the rear and you had a whole heap of understeer.

We pursued rearwards-blowing until quite deep into the development of the R31, then changed course in mid-August.

There are only a few places an exhaust can come out and impinge on a downforce-generating surface. One of the hypothetical benefits of a forward exhaust is that you get most of the lift from the middle of the car and don't get that nasty understeer effect.

It took us a while in CFD to actually find a front-blowing layout that worked. We knew that if we blew exhaust on a curved bit of the car it would generate downforce, but getting one that was competitive with a rearward blower took a while.

Eventually, we got one that was somewhat better than our best rear blower, which was very similar to a Red Bull concept, though I wouldn't pretend we were getting as much out if it as they have.

TYRE CHARACTERISTICS UNEXPECTED

Wind on to the start of the year, and you find out that the Pirellis actually have a very different characteristic to the Bridgestones. They suffer more under combined load and so, as you come out of the corner, when you want traction, the rear becomes unhappy quite quickly. What you really want is a load more rear downforce!

We basically had a car that was fairly snappy and difficult all year in those combined conditions. And a car that was ugly as hell at all the circuits where those conditions predominate – Monaco, Hungary, Singapore. In those places very few of the redeeming features were to be seen, and the nastiness was on display at every corner. That's the block we found ourselves in.

Our early-season gap to Red Bull was much the same as it had been at the end of the previous year, but then we were overhauled by a whole heap of people who had initially not been as imaginative as Red Bull. We were also in the vanguard of the off-throttle blowing, where other people cottoned on later and caught up.

FORWARD EXHAUST PROVED A HANDICAP

Our exhaust configuration was very, very fussy. When the geometry was as beautiful as we could make it, it wasn't bad. But it didn't take much by way of stone damage, or some parts that didn't fit absolutely perfectly, for a lot of the downforce to go.

To give an example, the exhaust played very directly on quite an aggressively curved part of the flow, the leading edge of the sidepod. And that piece gets very hot. It can't be made of carbon, it has to be made of metallic material.

You can't make the whole thing out of metal – it would be too heavy. So there's a join between the carbon and metal. You have a join quite close to a place that's generating an awful lot of downforce, and if that joint's not beautiful you do toss away a lot of your downforce.

At the point we carried out our rear-blowing experiment in Germany, we hadn't started talking about changing the rules for 2012, so it was abundantly clear we were getting well beaten by Red Bull, McLaren and Ferrari, and a whole bunch of mid-grid teams were nudging in front, having started well behind. It was pretty clear that we needed to re-evaluate.

We could already tell that the tyres really didn't suit the balance characteristic of the car. So, we made up a configuration closely related to our best one at the point we'd frozen rear-blowing development in September 2010, did a bit more work on it, copied a couple of the trends we'd seen on other cars – cut-outs around the tyre, etc – and ran it at Duxford.

There was plenty of rear downforce available in corner-exit conditions, but because we basically had to graft on to our existing diffuser package, we were unable to control the performance of the floor at lower rear ride heights. In the higher-speed corners, the diffuser was unstable and stalled.

Then it became clear that this configuration wasn't going to be available for 2012 in any case, so we couldn't justify re-inventing the wheel. We just had to take it on the chin. There's also a weight penalty

of around 5kg for a forward exhaust, as it's much
harder to cool.

Elsewhere, we switched from a 50% to a 60% model,
capable of running ride heights, yaw values and steer
values that the other model couldn't get to. With the
broader envelope we were able quite quickly to improve
the wings, floors and flicks.

DRIVERS MADE THE BEST OF CHALLENGING CAR
I can't really gauge the loss of Robert Kubica. Robert is
super-quick and was settling into the car pretty well. I'm
sure he would have made our bright start to the season
even brighter. But I'd be kidding myself if I thought that
just having Robert would have steered us out of the mire
we subsequently found ourselves in. It was too far away
for God himself to have put the thing on pole!

Vitaly Petrov surpassed expectations, and did a
creditable job for us, as did Bruno Senna stepping in
mid season – a tough thing to do. And Nick Heidfeld
put in some good performances as well.

DEVELOPMENTS LESS EFFECTIVE THAN HOPED
We had as many updates as in 2010, but they were
less effective. Our new wing for Suzuka didn't appear,
because both prototype versions broke in the factory.
That approach will be at the heart of next year's car.

Our KERS was massively lighter than the '09 system,
which was a troublesome arrangement with bits all over
the place and awkward connections between them. Our
KERS guys did a fabulous job and the new package was
properly competitive in total weight and usability.

Our ambitions are higher than running around
trying to cling on to fifth place. It's too simplistic to say
that one thing, a forward exhaust, defined our season.
But the Technical Director has to make decisions of this
type, and if I could have had a time machine, I wouldn't
have made that one. But, everyone knew it was my
decision, and from the bottom of the company to the top,
no-one gave me a hard time – that, I have to say, is one of
the nice things about our team. They all knew we were
doing something exciting and new, and we enjoyed it
while it was good."

FORCE INDIA

THE TEAM

PERSONNEL
TEAM PRINCIPAL & MANAGING DIRECTOR Vijay Mallya
CHAIRMAN Saharasri Subrata Roy Sahara
CO-OWNER Sahara India Pariwar
DEPUTY TEAM PRINCIPAL Robert Fernley
CHIEF OPERATING OFFICER Otmar Szafnauer
TECHNICAL DIRECTOR Andrew Green
PRODUCTION DIRECTOR Bob Halliwell
CHIEF DESIGNER 2011 Ian Hall
HEAD OF R&D Simon Gardner
HEAD OF AERODYNAMICS Simon Phillips
SPORTING DIRECTOR Andy Stevenson
DRIVERS Paul di Resta, Adrian Sutil
CHIEF ENGINEER Dominic Harlow (above)
RACE ENGINEER (Sutil) Bradley Joyce
RACE ENGINEER (di Resta) Gianpiero Lambiase
TEST/THIRD DRIVER Nico Hulkenberg
HEAD OF CAR BUILD Nick Burrows
RACE TEAM OPERATIONS MANAGER Mark Gray
NO 1 MECHANICS Chris King & Chris Borrill
TOTAL NUMBER OF EMPLOYEES c300
NUMBER IN RACE TEAM 45
TEAM BASE Silverstone, England
TELEPHONE +44 (0)1327 850800
WEBSITE www.forceindiaf1.com

TEAM STATS
IN F1 SINCE 1991, as Jordan, then Midland, then Spyker until 2007 **FIRST GRAND PRIX** USA 1991 **STARTS** 407
WINS 4 **POLE POSITIONS** 3 **FASTEST LAPS** 3
PODIUMS 21 **POINTS** 389 **CONSTRUCTORS' TITLES** 0
DRIVERS' TITLES 0

SPONSORS
Kingfisher Lager Beer, Kingfisher Airways, Alpinestars, STL, Schroth Racing, Medion, Vladivar, Whyte & Mackay, Royal Challenge, Doublemint, EADS, Airbus, UB Group, Reebok, AVG, UPS Direct, Samsung, BGN Events

14 ADRIAN SUTIL   **15** PAUL DI RESTA

VICE-FREE CAR ENABLED CONSISTENT RESULTS

By Dominic Harlow
Chief Engineer

"Losing double diffusers obviously made you think and develop the exhaust-blown diffuser technology. That, coupled with the tyres and KERS, were the major things. And a big change was the pullrod rather than pushrod rear suspension. But it all went together pretty well and didn't impose any real boundaries on design.

Our KERS packaging was a much better solution than the sidepod-mounted units of 2009. It was practical, serviceable and safe, but certainly a massive engineering project. The package was mounted beneath the fuel cell, but was completely contained within the survival cell, with just the electric motor outside, on the engine.

Rather than having two modules in the sidepods, you get to shrink everything down. You've got to recover that volume still on the survival cell, but the compromise is probably better.

The gains from the exhaust-blown diffuser were a lot better with the evolved concept we introduced during the year. We started fairly conservatively, perhaps even more conservatively than in 2010, and then introduced a more aggressive concept along the lines of what the top teams were doing – using the exhaust around the tyre foot – and certainly it was a good area to exploit.

CAR AN IMPROVEMENT ON 2010
We'd lost James Key and then Mark Smith. Technically, I don't think we lost out, but meeting the tight deadlines with the track testing is incredibly difficult with that month of February, which is just pure hell for everybody. It's flat-out, a million problems at once, and when you break continuity it's just a little bit harder still.

The VJM04's biggest strength was that it was a go-anywhere type of car and straightforward for the engineers and drivers to set up. It was quite adaptable, and we didn't seem to have an Achilles heel in the wet, or low downforce versus high downforce.

We didn't experience enormous rivalry between ourselves and Mercedes, or anyone else for that matter, but if we're improving on the previous year, that's probably the biggest motivator. It's nice sometimes when you know you've beaten Michael Schumacher or something like that, it's fantastic, but in the long run we're about bettering ourselves.

To make another step you can always invest more in your facilities and, nowadays, R&D and wind-tunnel testing. For engineers, that's a satisfying thing to get your teeth into and it's the way this sport and bigger industry is moving.

UPGRADES DELIVERED RESULTS
We had a big upgrade package for Barcelona, then took it off, but we came on song around Silverstone time. It was a case of two steps forward, one step back – and just catching up with development to make that a fully competitive package. It was something we needed to get to the track as quickly as possible and then start learning with.

As well as learning about the car from an engineering point of view, it was moving forward in the tunnel as well, and those two things came together and started to deliver. We had the performance in Canada, but that race was determined by other things, then at Silverstone we didn't deliver on a well-performing car. Then we started to go forward.

In terms of componentry on the car, the big upgrade was obviously centred on getting performance from the exhaust. There was floor, pods, pretty much everything bodywork-related. Just the front and rear wings carried over, and they've had their own development path.

We were quite neutral on the one-off Silverstone regulations, able to cope with both scenarios, and I think it's a credit to our aero department that their understanding of that area had moved on massively since 2010. We were able to react and debate that issue, and do what we needed to do and minimise the impact. We'd much rather not have had that discontinuity and, looking back, it was something that was fortunately overcome by the teams in a good way.

The DRS development partly centres around where you think you're going to race. We were in that midfield pack and you can make yourself a bit less vulnerable by having some speed there.

TEAM COPED WELL WITH NEW TYRES
Relative to the tyres, I think we had a learning process like everyone else and were in a reasonably good place for most of the races.

TECHNICAL SPECIFICATIONS

ENGINE
MAKE/MODEL Mercedes-Benz
FO 108Y
CONFIGURATION 2400cc V8
(90 degree)
SPARK PLUGS NGK
ECU FIA standard issue
FUEL Mobil
OIL Mobil 1
BATTERY Not disclosed

TRANSMISSION
GEARBOX McLaren
FORWARD GEARS Seven
CLUTCH AP Racing

CHASSIS
CHASSIS MODEL Force India VJM04
FRONT SUSPENSION LAYOUT
Aluminium uprights with
carbon-fibre composite wishbones,
trackrod and pushrod. Inboard
chassis-mounted torsion springs,
dampers and anti-roll bar

REAR SUSPENSION LAYOUT
Aluminium uprights with carbon-fibre
composite wishbones, trackrod and
pullrod. Inboard gearbox-mounted
torsion springs, dampers and anti-roll bar
DAMPERS Penske
TYRES Pirelli
WHEELS BBS
BRAKE DISCS Carbone Industrie
BRAKE PADS Carbone Industrie
BRAKE CALIPERS
AP Racing
FUEL TANK ATL
INSTRUMENTS McLaren
Electronic Systems

DIMENSIONS
LENGTH 5100mm
WIDTH 1800mm
HEIGHT 950mm
WHEELBASE 3500mm
TRACK, FRONT 1480mm
TRACK, REAR 1440mm
WEIGHT 640kg (including
driver and camera)

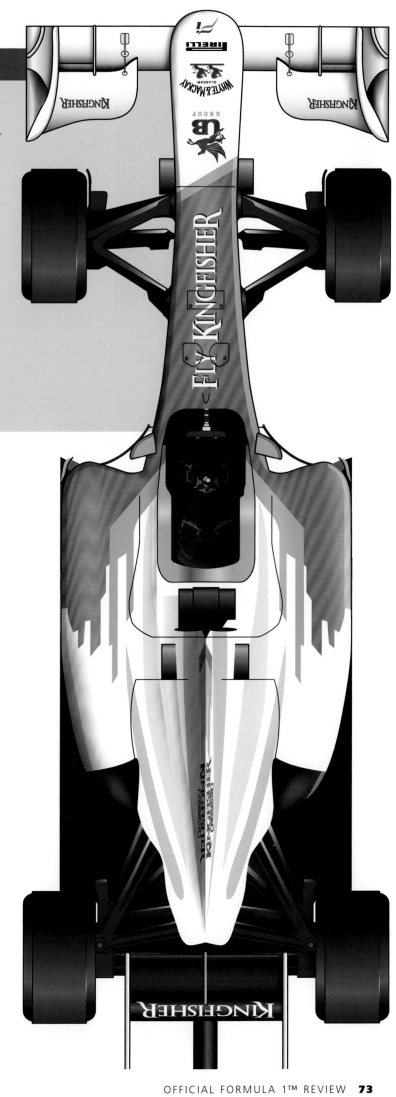

Certainly it's a big difference in terms of managing the degradation compared to where we were with the Bridgestones.

The overriding factor was the level of downforce with the harder compounds. That's what I see, that with the quicker cars the prime-to-option delta is that little bit smaller. It's probably more significant for the top three teams, and then down from there it becomes more similar. Beyond that, we're comfortable that the tyres all did what they said on the tin.

RULES STABILITY MEANS REFINING CAR FOR 2012
Next year, I think, is going to be refining what you've got, with the next couple of seasons likely to have a more consistent technical platform than recently, with all the tyre changes and so forth. Then preparing ourselves for what in the future will be a big change in power/drivetrain. But at the same time there's always that big innovation that may come, and the fascination of what it's going to be.

The loss of exhaust-blown diffusers means a lot of downforce will need to be recovered. It's too early to guess the difference in numbers, but we'll be back to where we were, I suspect.

RUNNING THREE DRIVERS BROUGHT BENEFITS
Paul had a good season. We were happy working with him in 2010, and it was obvious straight away that he was very good all round. He just carried on from there in the races this year. I would like to have seen him have a bit better luck at a few of them; Hungary was a great drive and at Spa the safety car was one of those things.

I think the drivers are constantly motivated by their desire to beat their team-mates, and the way it may also have benefited Adrian was in the extra feedback that Paul gave the team. That helps raise everyone, and coupled with Adrian's experience and knowledge of the circuits, we had a good line-up.

Nico Hulkenberg proved another very good asset, and fitted in very well. He's bright, with good feedback and good speed. We used him a lot in the simulator, on Fridays, and he brought a lot of resource.

Incorporating someone on Friday who's not going to race was a decision we make on a 'bigger picture' basis. At Monaco, for instance, you ran the race drivers on the Thursday because it's better to get those guys on the track, but overall we thought it brought us more than it lost us."

SAUBER

THE TEAM

PERSONNEL

TEAM PRINCIPAL & OWNER Peter Sauber
CHIEF EXECUTIVE OFFICER Monisha Kaltenborn
TECHNICAL DIRECTOR James Key (above)
OPERATIONS DIRECTOR Axel Kruse
CHIEF DESIGNER Matt Morris
HEAD OF AERODYNAMICS Seamus Mullarkey
TEAM MANAGER Beat Zehnder
HEAD OF TRACK ENGINEERING Giampaolo Dall'Ara
DRIVERS Pedro de la Rosa, Kamui Kobayashi, Sergio Perez
RACE ENGINEER (de la Rosa/Perez) Marco Schüpbach
RACE ENGINEER (Kobayashi) Francesco Nenci
CHIEF ENGINE ENGINEER Ernest Knoors
TEST/THIRD DRIVER Esteban Gutierrez
CHIEF MECHANIC Urs Kuratle
TOTAL NUMBER OF EMPLOYEES 280
NUMBER IN RACE TEAM 59
TEAM BASE Hinwil, Switzerland
TELEPHONE +41 44 937 9000
WEBSITE www.sauberf1team.com

TEAM STATS

IN F1 SINCE 1993, as Sauber until 2005 **FIRST GRAND PRIX** South Africa 1993 **STARTS** 325 **WINS** 1 **POLE POSITIONS** 1 **FASTEST LAPS** 2 **PODIUMS** 22 **POINTS** 585 **CONSTRUCTORS' TITLES** 0 **DRIVERS' TITLES** 0

SPONSORS

Claro, TELMEX, Disensa, NEC, CuerTequila, Mexico, Interproteccion, Certina, Emil Frey, Mad Croc

16 KAMUI KOBAYASHI **17 SERGIO PEREZ** **17 PEDRO DE LA ROSA**

LACK OF BLOWN DIFFUSER PEGGED CAR'S PACE

By James Key
Technical Director

"Every team faced the problem of designing a car around no tyre information, deciding what to do with suspension and aero-map targets. We saw the initial Pirelli data, and although things changed, it showed a weak rear tyre compared to what we were used to.

We figured the need to design a car that could cope with that, and left it open for lots of set-up tools, lots of different ways to change low- and high-speed balance.

The Melbourne disqualifications for rear-wing infringement were absolutely gutting, because it was exactly the start to the season we wanted. We had a large update package for Melbourne and the wing was part of that.

Basically, the top-surface profile of the flap's concave radius was less than 100mm. Concentrating so hard on performance, that somehow slipped through. We checked all the other wings and they were fine. We had three different types and it was just this one wing, this one design.

NEW TYRES PROVIDED A CHALLENGE

The car was balanced and easy on the tyres, but that was a disadvantage at times. It could be balanced over a big window, but the downside was that you couldn't get tyre temperatures in cold conditions. The drivers were good at conserving the tyres too, particularly Sergio.

In the middle of year we wondered whether we needed to concentrate more on qualifying. But then the race advantage disappears. The worst case was Nürburgring; damp and cold with very little loading on tyres, and a low-grip surface. That really hurt us.

But it was about the whole package. You can't have tunnel vision about the way the tyre works, and then find the aero doesn't match the way you want to set up the car. It has to fit. It sort of did, but not fully.

The car was substantially different from the 2010 car. It was a lot more complicated with all the mechanical work we did. The wheelbase was a bit longer and the cooling layout quite substantially different.

We got really good support from Ferrari, who we talked to when they were at the conceptual stage with the gearbox.

EXHAUST DEVELOPMENT DIFFICULTIES

The Red Bull-type exhaust layout was our nemesis. We missed a lot of lap time not having that on the car. We looked at a lot of outboard-blown stuff over the winter and couldn't really get it to work in the tunnel. But in February it kicked in and we saw how powerful it was.

In Shanghai, we introduced the first parts as a test item. Up to that point, CFD, the wind tunnel and even the 1:1 model had all shown the same, so we were quite confident. But on the track it didn't correlate.

From that point forward we were just plodding along with it, re-iterating. We got to test it in Turkey and Barcelona, and in Barcelona we began to see the effects we expected. The biggest problem was that by installing it on the floor where it was, we actually lost a lot more downforce than we should have.

So the redevelopment of the diffuser, the bodywork, the brake ducts was all falling apart. It became a complicated and expensive project. And at that time the FIA said 'hang on, we're not sure about these engine maps' and all that kicked off.

It looked fairly clear that the engine-mapping side, a very powerful part of it all of course, was going to get re-clarified. We absolutely agreed with the FIA from the outset on that, because we think you're not supposed to use the engine for aero.

Considering what we thought was going to happen from Silverstone, coupled with the high expense and the issues of developing the car around it, meant that we binned the project. We decided to go back to what we were doing and guarantee some updates later. Then, of course, the Silverstone interpretation didn't stay and that disadvantaged us.

We dipped back into it briefly when we were developing the package we took to Suzuka. The best we could have done would have been to introduce it probably in Singapore, and then you've got five races to sort it out, something that didn't work first time around. It was a tricky call and just didn't fall right for us.

MAPPING AND AERO UPGRADES

As a customer team you're always slightly disadvantaged because you haven't got control, but Ferrari were pretty good. We ran their latest software, and although we'd got

ENGINE
MAKE/MODEL Ferrari 056
CONFIGURATION 2398cc V8 (90 degree)
SPARK PLUGS Not disclosed
ECU FIA standard issue
FUEL Shell V-Power
OIL Shell Helix Ultra
BATTERY Not disclosed

TRANSMISSION
GEARBOX Ferrari
FORWARD GEARS Seven
CLUTCH Not disclosed

CHASSIS
CHASSIS MODEL Sauber C30
FRONT SUSPENSION LAYOUT Upper and lower wishbones, inboard springs and dampers actuated by pushrods

REAR SUSPENSION LAYOUT
Upper and lower wishbones, inboard springs and dampers actuated by pushrods
DAMPERS Sachs
TYRES Pirelli
WHEELS OZ Racing
BRAKE DISCS Brembo
BRAKE PADS Brembo
BRAKE CALIPERS Brembo
FUEL TANK ATL
INSTRUMENTS Ferrari/Magneti Marelli

DIMENSIONS
LENGTH 4935mm
WIDTH 1800mm
HEIGHT 1000mm
WHEELBASE Not disclosed
TRACK, FRONT 1495mm
TRACK, REAR 1410mm
WEIGHT 640kg (including driver and camera)

Sauber F1 Team

an in-blown diffuser and not an out-blown one like theirs, there was still a pretty powerful effect.

We got our first hot-blown maps for winter testing and had off-throttle hot blowing by Nürburgring, then significant updates at Monza. We got some understeer from that. We didn't know what to expect given our diffuser, but it was quite powerful. We also resolved some of the issues we had with braking stability.

The Suzuka upgrade was a standard aero update. We targeted low-speed performance, because we still felt that was a bit of a disadvantage. We also targeted better efficiency, because we saw that at the start of the year our straightline speeds were very good, but as the season went on, others developed. We had a new wing at Silverstone, which was OK, but not quite there. So we completely changed the philosophy.

The big question was the trade-off between the activated DRS phase and normal. We did two wings so that we had options; a slightly lower-downforce one with more drag reduction for race conditions, and a higher-downforce wing with a bigger activation delta for qualifying, and chose on a race-by-race basis which to go for.

DRIVERS DIFFERING STRENGTHS A POSITIVE
Sergio Perez was really good. He came in at a very complicated time, with DRS, KERS, the tyres, no testing and a very good team-mate – and adapted well. He's very confident, and his race pace was always impressive. He's a rookie driver, which you saw sometimes, but he made very few mistakes.

The drivers have different styles. Sergio likes a more neutral car, and Kamui likes a bit more stability, some understeer. He's more a high-speed corner type of driver, whereas Sergio was good at Monaco, Hungary and Singapore – street circuits and windy stuff.

Sergio had a big accident at Monaco and was right not to race in Canada. He was fit enough at Valencia, but maybe still suffering a bit mentally.

Having an experienced guy like Pedro de la Rosa back in the car gave us another opinion. In Canada we thought we had a bit of a kerb issue, but Pedro said, 'No, it's nothing to do with the kerbs, it's to do with front-tyre temperature. Get that up and the issue goes away.' That was the first time we'd heard that. That sort of thing can be useful."

TORO ROSSO

THE TEAM

PERSONNEL

TEAM OWNER Dietrich Mateschitz
TEAM PRINCIPAL Franz Tost
TECHNICAL DIRECTOR Giorgio Ascanelli (above)
TEAM MANAGER Gianfranco Fantuzzi
CHIEF DESIGNER Ben Butler
CHIEF ENGINEER Laurent Mekies
DRIVERS Jaime Alguersuari, Sébastien Buemi
TECHNICAL CO-ORDINATOR Sandro Parrini
LOGISTICS MANAGER Domenico Sangiorgi
RACE ENGINEER (Buemi) Riccardo Adami
RACE ENGINEER (Alguersuari) Andrea Landi
TEST/THIRD DRIVERS Daniel Ricciardo, Jean-Eric Vergne
CHIEF MECHANIC Gérard Lecoq
ASSISTANT CHIEF MECHANIC Domiziano Facchinetti
NO 1 MECHANIC (Buemi) Gabriele Vergnana
NO 1 MECHANIC (Alguersuari) Alberto Gavarini
RELIABILITY MANAGER Gianvito Amico
TEAM LEADER ENGINE ENGINEER Ernest Knoors
RACE ENGINES MANAGER Mattia Binotto
TOTAL NUMBER OF EMPLOYEES c250
NUMBER IN RACE TEAM 50
TEAM BASE Faenza, Italy
TELEPHONE +39 (0)546 696111
WEBSITE www.scuderiatororosso.com

TEAM STATS

IN F1 SINCE 1985, as Minardi until 2005 **FIRST GRAND PRIX** Brazil 1985 **STARTS** 449 **WINS** 1 **POLE POSITIONS** 1 **FASTEST LAPS** 0 **PODIUMS** 1 **POINTS** 148 **CONSTRUCTORS' TITLES** 0 **DRIVERS' TITLES** 0

SPONSORS & PARTNERS

Red Bull, Red Bull Mobile, Hangar-7, Falcon Private Bank, CEPSA, USAG, Nova Chemicals, VW, Siemens, OMP, Pirelli, Advanti Racing

18 SEBASTIEN BUEMI   **19** JAIME ALGUERSUARI

MAKING THE MOST OF LIMITED RESOURCES

By Giorgio Ascanelli
Technical Director

"People likened the STR6 to the twin-floor 1992 Ferrari, but that wasn't in the equation, because the expansion of the diffuser in those days was about seven times as much as it is now!

The elimination of the many appendices that characterised past F1 cars and the disappearance of the double-deck diffuser meant that we had to think about where to go to pick up air to generate energy.

With our concept, the exhaust was more difficult to install; you have to make a kink in it. How could we get to a higher velocity of exhaust without destroying the engine?

There was a nice magazine article about a company memo where the technical director of Mercedes was asked how much you actually lose with these convoluted exhausts. Very little, he said. Well, we weren't able to lose very little! But I think the solution that we put on the car in Japan was good.

USING RESOURCES TO BEST EFFECT

I'd like to think this year has been about what we've done right rather than what someone else has done wrong. It's a fact that we're still very much away from the FOTA limits on aerodynamics. With a traditional car I think we would have been a solid eighth, not fighting with Sauber and Force India for sixth and seventh.

We believe, and I'm confident in what I'm saying, that every bit of work we did brought us an advantage, and I'd say that there are more renowned teams where that wasn't the case.

Part of it is probably my conservative attitude, because I have to spend our money well. We just can't produce novelty at the same rate as those with more resources. Clint Eastwood used to say that when a man with a rifle meets a man with a pistol, the man with a pistol is a dead man. And it's fact.

DEVELOPING AND LEARNING

Take the rear of the car and what people called our Barcelona update. I wouldn't call it development, we simply couldn't make the gearbox in time to start the season.

Then we had a few goes at DRS, which only started working properly at Spa. We were working on F-duct last year when we should have been thinking about DRS.

It meant that at the first test we had a fixed rear wing, and then at the second test we had a fixed wing with an adjustable flap, which is not a DRS. The criterion to design a wing with DRS is completely different – you have to minimise drag when the DRS is activated and maximise downforce, roughly speaking. We were caught off guard because we were busy with other things.

There's been continuous work with the front wing and it was difficult to follow the tyres. Singapore was quite a good example. The temperature changed and you had to change the front wing flap like you put an umbrella up and down in the rain! It was that sensitive.

Then there was the second update at Valencia, which was well played because it got us out of synch from the updates of the biggest guys, which meant we scored a point at Valencia, and then at Silverstone we scored points because of a fantastic race from Alguersuari and some misfortunes around the field.

A blown exhaust is not something we had in the tunnel. From March we had it, and we had to learn how to make it work. Ferrari gave us the possibility of hot blowing from Spa onwards, but it's not just hot blowing, it's what to do with it. The point is again, I don't start spending energy on something I may have. I must have it and then I can start spending energy.

Our numbers have come up a bit. Last year we were below par in aero and increased that, hiring people by February. Then we discovered that the drawing office was the bottleneck, because we generated more parts than the drawing office could do. My designers are doing an excellent job, but we're not Williams – we haven't a legacy of nine championships. We've got young kids. They're bright, they're good and keen, but they need experience.

PACE: QUALIFYING VERSUS RACE

The drivers' attentive, conservative attitude brought us many points.

At Monza there was carnage at the first corner and our two guys stayed out of trouble. It's hard to make a jump if you're conservative, but there's value too. I believe they're treasuring the opportunity.

TECHNICAL SPECIFICATIONS

ENGINE
MAKE/MODEL Ferrari 056
CONFIGURATION 2398cc V8
(90 degree)
SPARK PLUGS Not disclosed
ECU FIA standard issue
FUEL Not disclosed
OIL Not disclosed
BATTERY Not disclosed

TRANSMISSION
GEARBOX Not disclosed
FORWARD GEARS Seven
CLUTCH Sachs

CHASSIS
CHASSIS MODEL Toro Rosso STR6
FRONT SUSPENSION LAYOUT
Upper and lower carbon wishbones,
torsion-bar springs and anti-roll bars

REAR SUSPENSION LAYOUT
Upper and lower carbon wishbones,
torsion-bar springs and anti-roll bars
DAMPERS Sachs
TYRES Pirelli
WHEELS Advanti Racing
BRAKE DISCS Brembo
BRAKE PADS Brembo
BRAKE CALIPERS Brembo
FUEL TANK ATL
INSTRUMENTS
Scuderia Toro Rosso

DIMENSIONS
LENGTH Not disclosed
WIDTH Not disclosed
HEIGHT Not disclosed
WHEELBASE Not disclosed
TRACK, FRONT Not disclosed
TRACK, REAR Not disclosed
WEIGHT 640kg (including
driver and camera)

SCUDERIA Toro Rosso

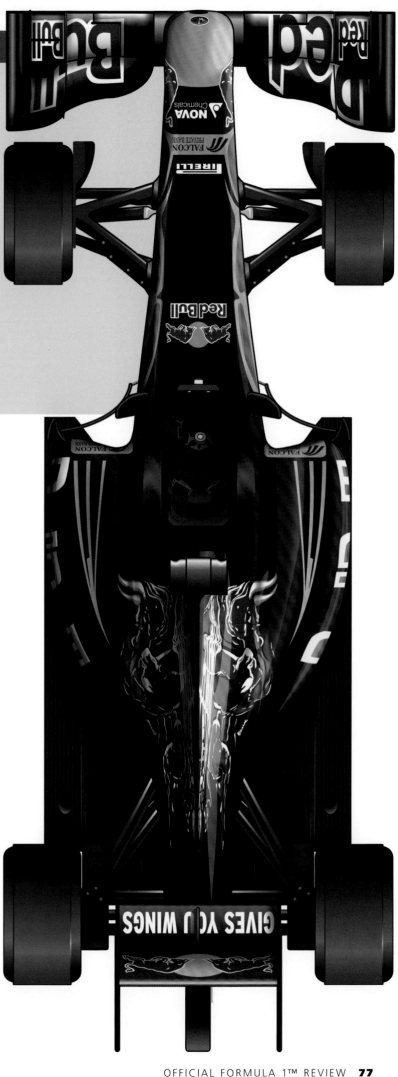

Sébastien tried hard enough to put it in the wall in practice at Monza and I wasn't disappointed with him. Gilles Villeneuve said that if you want to go to the limit, you need to know where it is.

The biggest riddle was that we weren't faster in qualifying. They seemed to have the need to start 24th to finish 10th! I have to thank the people who brought in *parc fermé* – because if we could change the car between qualifying and race we'd be bloody confused!

I think a component of the engine settings explained part of that – the fact that the engine setting was allowed to be changed between Saturday and Sunday and then that was denied. The situation didn't change substantially for us. We couldn't deliver sudden performance and that was probably our biggest limitation.

A STEADY JOB FROM DANIEL RICCIARDO
Sébastien seemed to be generally quicker in qualifying and Jaime better in the race. Ricciardo is a good kid, but I didn't think he was daring enough.

Every Friday morning he was within a tenth of his team-mate, but every weekend he did he was lucky because we had a second set of tyres for development and he could get in the groove.

But if you're within one tenth of your team-mate and don't put a foot wrong, that's good. He never put a wheel off the circuit, so he had margin, which was a good sign.

Maybe he was targeting doing what he needed without taking risks. I don't think he did a bad job and I rate his feedback, I enjoyed his smiling face around the paddock but, on the other side, frankly, I think he could have done more and missed the chance to do more.

I think he had the bullets in his belt and simply didn't shoot them. He was content with what he achieved, which is wise, but… It was Thomas Edison who said genius was one per cent inspiration and 99 per cent setting high targets. But I think he's bright.

None of the three guys is a bad driver. I cannot say I'm unhappy with any of them, but whether they have that extra bit? I haven't seen it yet. Having said that, I didn't see it in Vettel the first time he drove for us. It took about seven races."

WILLIAMS

THE TEAM

PERSONNEL
TEAM PRINCIPAL Sir Frank Williams
DIRECTOR OF ENGINEERING Patrick Head
CHAIRMAN Adam Parr
CHIEF EXECUTIVE OFFICER Alex Burns
TECHNICAL DIRECTOR Sam Michael (above), then Mike Coughlan
HEAD OF AERODYNAMICS Jason Somerville
CHIEF OPERATIONS ENGINEER Mark Gillan
CHIEF DESIGNER Ed Wood
TEAM MANAGER Dickie Stanford
DRIVERS Rubens Barrichello, Pastor Maldonado
RACE ENGINEER (Barrichello) Tom McCullough
RACE ENGINEER (Maldonado) Xevi Pujolar
TEST/THIRD DRIVER Valtteri Bottas
CHIEF MECHANIC Carl Gaden
TOTAL NUMBER OF EMPLOYEES 500
NUMBER IN RACE TEAM 47
TEAM BASE Grove, England
TELEPHONE +44 (0)1235 777700
WEBSITE www.attwilliams.com

TEAM STATS
IN F1 SINCE 1973 **FIRST GRAND PRIX** Argentina 1973
STARTS 623 **WINS** 113 **POLE POSITIONS** 126
FASTEST LAPS 130 **PODIUMS** 296 **POINTS** 2680
CONSTRUCTORS' TITLES 9 **DRIVERS' TITLES** 7

SPONSORS
AT&T, Randstad, PDVSA, Venezuela Tourism, Hatch McGregor, Oris, Pirelli, Ridge Solutions, Thomson Reuters, GAC, Interbrand, MAN, PPG, Rays, Sparco

11 RUBENS BARRICHELLO **12** PASTOR MALDONADO

NEW REAR-END DESIGN BRINGS CHALLENGES

By Sam Michael
Technical Director

"As soon as double diffusers were banned we looked and said, 'Right, the fastest single-diffuser car in 2009 was the Red Bull, and Adrian Newey designed it with a very low gearbox and driveshafts.' It was still a pretty competitive package against the double-diffuser Brawn.

We'd taken a lot of photos of that car and decided that we were going to go a whole step lower. We embarked on that pretty early, around March 2010, because we had to do a lot of work to make the driveshafts survive.

A NEW LOW-LINE GEARBOX CONCEPT
Making the gearbox small was quite straightforward, because it's basically a box section. People were saying, 'Oh, you're going to lose all the stiffness', but it was no less stiff than a normal gearbox.

The reason is quite simple: you have your gear cluster and you have your box around that cluster. The traditional gearbox grows up to the corners of the engine, and what you do behind that in a typical pushrod car is dig all the back of the gearbox out and bury your dampers in there. But, as soon as you do that, you open the top skin of the 'box, so it loses strength.

With our gearbox, we've still got the casing around the cluster, which gives about 98% of the strength. The stuff on top doesn't do anything from a bending point of view, so we didn't lose any torsional stiffness compared to the previous 'box – it's exactly the same. When we first embarked on it we didn't actually realise that – it was only when we did the stress analysis.

For the driveshafts, we went to the Cologne (Toyota) electric dyno that you can put the whole rear suspension on, took an old 'box, put the upright in the new position and did a 3,500km sign-off.

In the early tests we had some big failures, but worked them out. After that, no problems. The only time we had a failure was with Rubens in Australia when stones in a driveshaft boot dried out the joint. That was nothing to do with the angle. We had no problems with either the drive or gearbox, and power loss was less than 0.5bhp.

AERODYNAMIC DEVELOPMENTS
By dropping the gearbox height, the airflow to the rear lower wing is better. When we got rid of the double diffuser and looked at the rear lower wing for this year, it had increased downforce three-fold. It became very clear you had to make the rear lower wing work. The car's whole concept was about that.

Unfortunately, the engine/engine cover restricted us in taking full advantage of the low wing. The engine is homologated and you cannot change it. That's why the cover was shrink-wrapped around it. It looked pretty ugly, but you can't change that – that's as small as we could make it. The Renault is different in that the back of their trumpet tray funnels very heavily. It's not like that on the Cosworth.

We changed the front wing because of what Red Bull was doing. They had changed the concept and were running their nose much closer to the ground, especially the front-wing endplates.

You increase the efficiency of the wing significantly, because you're running it more in ground effect. Secondly, it helps unload the centre of the wing and gets more airflow to the diffuser. You end up with a better car everywhere.

It's got to still be legal of course. We run a fairly standard rake. Red Bull definitely run more than us. I think that's to do with the way their diffuser works. We just made sure the wing deflected as much as the regulations allow.

If you run more rake you have a centre of gravity height increase straight away. So you have to have a diffuser designed to work around a high rear ride height. Our diffuser wouldn't do that. Red Bull obviously started with that type of philosophy.

LAGGING BEHIND WITH BLOWN DIFFUSER
On reflection, we probably spent too much energy for the company's resources making the gearbox work. Going from a high-pushrod gearbox to a pullrod consumed a lot of the design office. It created quite a bit of conflict in the middle of 2010. It was something we had to push very hard on the aero side.

That took a lot of energy away from areas like the exhaust. We didn't do a top job on

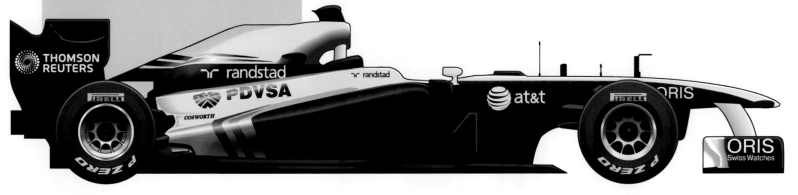

ENGINE
MAKE/MODEL Cosworth CA2011
CONFIGURATION 2400cc V8
SPARK PLUGS Not disclosed
ECU FIA standard issue
FUEL Not disclosed
OIL Not disclosed
BATTERY Not disclosed

TRANSMISSION
GEARBOX WilliamsF1
FORWARD GEARS Seven
CLUTCH Not disclosed

CHASSIS
CHASSIS MODEL Williams FW33
FRONT SUSPENSION LAYOUT
Carbon-fibre double wishbones with composite toelink and pushrod-activated springs and anti-roll bar

REAR SUSPENSION LAYOUT
Carbon-fibre double wishbones and pullrod-activated springs and anti-roll bar
DAMPERS WilliamsF1
TYRES Pirelli
WHEELS RAYS
BRAKE DISCS Not disclosed
BRAKE PADS Not disclosed
BRAKE CALIPERS Not disclosed
FUEL TANK Not disclosed
INSTRUMENTS WilliamsF1

DIMENSIONS
LENGTH 5000mm
WIDTH 1800mm
HEIGHT 950mm
WHEELBASE 3300mm
TRACK, FRONT Not disclosed
TRACK, REAR Not disclosed
WEIGHT 640kg (including driver and camera)

the blown exhausts, even though our 2010 blown diffuser worked pretty well. We took our eye off the ball with that.

In terms of running the exhausts down where Red Bull were, we didn't think of that, so we spent most of the year catching up on blown diffusers.

We started with just the traditional coke-bottle-exit exhaust. The first time we ran the Red Bull-type was Shanghai, but it didn't work, we had problems with burning. It took us about six races to get it sorted. After Shanghai, we didn't run it for two races, tried it in Monaco practice, but didn't race it. It took us quite a while to get the plume to work.

We also didn't have blowing in the tunnel until later in the season, and so we were doing it all on CFD. From a mapping point of view we didn't do any hot blowing, we could only do cold blowing.

At Silverstone, we looked better because everyone else's hot blowing was restricted and it was also the first time we ran the new diffuser. The Red Bull-type exhaust layout was also about 5kg heavier than the traditional one, and so sometimes Rubens couldn't use ballast. It was only Spa/Monza time that the floor was working properly.

Saying all that, we still expended significant development effort. By Singapore we were on our 11th front wing, ninth diffuser, eighth rear wing and fourth floor. We'd also done quite a bit of work on a different suspension system.

Most of the time we found that the car was rear-limited, with corner-entry oversteer. It was fairly typical to get to that limit. It's where you should end up, even the fastest car. If not, the car's not set up properly or the driver isn't at the limit.

Our KERS was quite heavy – over 30kg. The harvesting and brake balance still needed to be better, and the componentry was all done on a budget with a control system developed with Cosworth.

ROOKIE DRIVER MADE GOOD PROGRESS
We got a bit of flak signing Pastor, but I was pleased with him, I think he's really good. He ran Rubens pretty close all year, and I rate Rubens. I think he'll be better again in his second year after learning all the tracks. He definitely deserves his place in F1. His first four or five races were pretty rough, but that's what you get with a rookie."

LOTUS

THE TEAM

PERSONNEL
TEAM PRINCIPAL Tony Fernandes
DEPUTY TEAM PRINCIPALS Kamarudin
Meranun & S.M. Nasarudin
CHIEF EXECUTIVE OFFICER Riad Asmat
CHIEF TECHNICAL OFFICER Mike Gascoyne (above)
TECHNICAL DIRECTOR Mark Smith
SPORTING DIRECTOR Dieter Gass
CHIEF OPERATING OFFICER (UK) Keith Saunt
HEAD OF OPERATIONS (ASIA) Mia Sharizman
HEAD OF VEHICLE TECHNOLOGY DESIGN
Elliot Dason-Barber
CHIEF ENGINEER Jody Egginton
HEAD OF LOGISTICS Graham Smith
TEAM MANAGER Graham Watson
DRIVERS Heikki Kovalainen, Jarno Trulli
RACE ENGINEER (Trulli) Gianluca Pisanello
RACE ENGINEER (Kovalainen) Juan Pablo Ramirez
RESERVE DRIVER Karun Chandhok
THIRD DRIVER Luiz Razia
TEST DRIVERS Ricardo Teixeira, Davide Valsecchi
CHIEF MECHANIC Nick Smith
TOTAL NUMBER OF EMPLOYEES 240
NUMBER IN RACE TEAM 70
TEAM BASE Hingham, England & Kuala Lumpur, Malaysia
TELEPHONE +49 (0)1953 851411
WEBSITE www.teamlotus.co.uk

TEAM STATS
IN F1 SINCE 2010 **FIRST GRAND PRIX** Bahrain 2010
STARTS 38 **WINS** 0 **POLE POSITIONS** 0
FASTEST LAPS 0 **PODIUMS** 0 **POINTS** 0
CONSTRUCTORS' TITLES 0 **DRIVERS' TITLES** 0

SPONSORS
GE, Dell, Caterham Cars, AirAsia, Tune Group.com,
NAZA, CNN, EQ8

20 HEIKKI KOVALAINEN   **21** JARNO TRULLI   **21** KARUN CHANDHOK

A STEP IN THE RIGHT DIRECTION

By Mike Gascoyne
Chief Technical Officer

"In 2010 we did a car in Cologne with a group of contractors, so 2011, in some ways, wasn't our first season. But it was with a completely new, young design team and a new engine/gearbox package.

The big change was the switch to a Renault engine and Red Bull gearbox and hydraulics. The other positive was that the aero programme had been in existence much longer and we were able to put things like blown diffusers on the car. It was a lot more up-to-date than the previous year's car, but it was still a considerable effort. Our head of composites, for example, didn't arrive until November.

We wanted to be racing at the Toro Rosso/Williams/Sauber/Force India level and didn't manage it. We are still new to it, still smaller than them and still putting it together. Which is why we operated in that little bubble.

But we became a proper F1 team, with our own design office, aero programme, factory and race team. That was reflected in our level of performance compared to the other new teams. We moved two seconds away from them, and in Singapore we beat Renault.

The other thing is that we didn't put KERS in. It was always going to be a step too far.

FACTORY MOVE A STEP FORWARD
Although we have a good aero programme, Aerolab and our own CFD facility, we're still only operating at around 60% of the level of the other teams and the Resource Restriction Agreement. Moving forward, we have the Williams wind-tunnel programme, we've got Mark Smith and a stable design team doing its second car.

Tony Fernandes has been realistic, hence the factory move. Being stuck out in Norfolk can make it hard to recruit and then retain people – I was born and bred here and I can see it's a problem. If, in a year's time, we're at Leafield and the Williams tunnel is operating 24/7, there is real reason to say that we will go and race the other independents.

BLOWN DIFFUSER KEY TO 2011 PACE
Technically, our biggest problem was that we were still 12 months behind, and the key thing has been the blown diffuser. We implemented one like those used at the end of 2010, but other teams then took a massive step forward.

This has been a problematic area. Simulating a blown diffuser is difficult, and getting it to work full-size is equally difficult. When we went to our outboard exhaust, it didn't do anything to start with. You didn't see on the track what you saw in the tunnel. Take that and KERS and there's our deficit. We got caught out and then it was a resource issue – all the aero testing, mapping and throttle settings.

We had an update for the start of the season, a big update for Turkey, and then the next big package was Singapore. If you look at the stats, we kept pace with the leading teams and caught some of the midfield teams, like Williams.

The car was pretty circuit-dependent. We struggled most at places like Suzuka and the low-speed tracks were better, probably as the downforce wasn't bad, but the efficiency wasn't great. We just didn't have the necessary performance from the blown diffuser.

EXPERIENCED DRIVERS AN ADVANTAGE
Having two experienced drivers has been an advantage since day one. In Jarno we had the guy who, if he gets it right on a qualifying lap, can be the quickest guy out there. Heikki is very consistent, a quick and strong racer in all conditions. As soon as we have wet qualifying Heikki gets into Q2 – every single time.

Heikki's confidence has grown. He suffered being Lewis's team-mate – he was very unsettled. In the car he was fine, but out of it things got to him. This year he became stronger. On those occasions when Jarno was quicker, Heikki didn't panic. In qualifying at Suzuka Jarno looked really quick on the first run on the hard tyre. A year ago Heikki would have overdriven it and gone backwards, but this time he responded and beat Jarno by a tenth. People say that Jarno was usually out-performed by Heikki in qualifying and he was, but it was different after we changed the power steering – then he wasn't.

I've always said that Jarno's strength is also his biggest weakness. He's the most sensory driver I've ever worked with. That's what ultimately gives him that extra couple of tenths

TECHNICAL SPECIFICATIONS

ENGINE
MAKE/MODEL Renault RS27-2011
CONFIGURATION 2400cc V8
SPARK PLUGS NGK
ECU FIA standard issue
FUEL Total
OIL Total
BATTERY GS Yuasa

TRANSMISSION
GEARBOX Red Bull Technologies
FORWARD GEARS Seven
CLUTCH AP Racing

CHASSIS
CHASSIS MODEL Lotus T128
FRONT SUSPENSION LAYOUT
Double wishbone pushrod
REAR SUSPENSION LAYOUT
Double wishbone pullrod
DAMPERS Penske, Multimatic
TYRES Pirelli
WHEELS BBS
BRAKE DISCS Carbone
Industrie, Hitco
BRAKE PADS Carbone
Industrie, Hitco
BRAKE CALIPERS AP Racing
FUEL TANK ATL
INSTRUMENTS McLaren
Electronic Systems

DIMENSIONS
LENGTH Approx 5000mm
WIDTH Not disclosed
HEIGHT 950mm
WHEELBASE More than 3000mm
TRACK, FRONT Not disclosed
TRACK, REAR Not disclosed
WEIGHT 640kg (including driver
and camera)

that he's always had over his team-mates. He has fantastic feel when a car is good, but take that away and he can't drive it. Someone like Fernando Alonso, however, just deals with that.

POWER-STEERING PROBLEMS
With the power steering, the drivers were asking for more assistance, and so we produced a system that had more. But inherently the more friction they have, the bigger the 'dead' band and the less responsive they are.

As soon as Jarno tried the new power steering he said, 'Yes, it's lighter, but I can't feel the car'. It was basically a new system, not a simple redesign, because all the piston sizes were different. We tried some things that didn't work and had to redo it – immediately a three-month process.

The redesigned steering has less friction but is actually a lot heavier to use, so we couldn't use it everywhere. Going through somewhere like 130R at Suzuka or Eau Rouge at Spa, it wouldn't have given enough assistance, which is why we didn't use it at those two races.

Heikki and Karun could feel the new steering, but it made no difference to them. Jarno said it totally transformed the car and immediately started telling us what he needed at the front and back. Go back to the old one and he couldn't tell you what the car was doing. It was absolutely black and white, no bullshit.

Jarno put the new steering on in Hungary; he'd been half a second off Heikki all year, and here he outqualified him. Then change back for Spa and he can't drive the car. He's super-sensitive and that's what gives him his speed. Next year we'll take what we've got and tweak it so that we've got a bit more assistance. We were led down a path by the drivers and just got it wrong.

Overall it has been disappointing, but securing two consecutive 10th-place constructors' championship finishes to become a 'column one' team [*a reference to F1's revenue distribution*] was the target. The financial rewards are massive, you can invest to move up, and the shareholders' investment is repaid.

Our backers been supportive and taken a long-term view. Tony has made comments about heads on the block in 2012, but actually he means his as well as everyone else's. We have to step up."

HRT

THE TEAM

PERSONNEL

TEAM OWNER Thesan Capital
CHIEF EXECUTIVE OFFICER Saul Ruiz de Marcos
TEAM PRINCIPAL & MANAGING DIRECTOR
Colin Kolles
TECHNICAL DIRECTOR Geoff Willis (up to September)
CHIEF DESIGNER Paul White (up to September)
CHIEF RACE & TEST ENGINEER Antonio Cuquerella
SPORTING DIRECTOR & TECHNICAL CO-ORDINATOR
Jacky Eeckelaert (above)
TEAM MANAGER Boris Bermes
DRIVERS Narain Karthikeyan, Vitantonio Liuzzi,
Daniel Ricciardo
RACE ENGINEER (Karthikeyan & Ricciardo) Angel Baena
RACE ENGINEER (Liuzzi) Richard Connell
TEST/THIRD DRIVER Narain Karthikeyan
CHIEF MECHANIC Soren Morgenstern
TOTAL NUMBER OF EMPLOYEES Not disclosed
NUMBER IN RACE TEAM Not disclosed
TEAM BASE Madrid, Spain & Greding, Germany
TELEPHONE +34 (0) 91 220 0100
WEBSITE www.hrtf1team.com

TEAM STATS

IN F1 SINCE 2010 **FIRST GRAND PRIX** Bahrain 2010
STARTS 38 **WINS** 0 **POLE POSITIONS** 0
FASTEST LAPS 0 **PODIUMS** 0 **POINTS** 0
CONSTRUCTORS' TITLES 0 **DRIVERS' TITLES** 0

SPONSORS

TATA, TATA Motors, OMP, Base Batteries, Panda Security,
IMAR, Construzioni

22 NARAIN KARTHIKEYAN   **22** DANIEL RICCIARDO   **23** VITANTONIO LIUZZI

RELIABILITY THE KEY TO IMPROVING RESULTS

By Jacky Eeckelaert
Sporting Director & Technical Co-ordinator

"I've been with Hispania Racing Team (HRT) since the start. I left Honda in February 2009 after finishing the Brawn car, then had a year's gardening leave before I could start in F1 again, on 1 March 2010.

That was a long time for me to do nothing! Honda said I could work in motor racing, but not F1, so I worked with Colin Kolles in LMP1. That team was the basis of HRT. In January 2010 Bernie called Colin and said he'd found someone to pay the Dallara bills that Campos couldn't pay and he wanted the team on the grid.

The Carabantes had money, but no team; Colin had a team, with trucks he'd bought from Super Aguri. So it was a case of taking two Audi sportscars out of the truck and putting two F1 cars in!

I flew down to Italy with Geoff Willis and discovered two naked monocoques and a few cartons of wishbones and uprights!

DEVELOPMENT LIMITED BY BUDGET

We made it through to the end of last year, and from then to now the main development has been adapting the cars to the Williams gearbox, with the new rear axle, and to the single-diffuser rules.

We then had to make an aero package that recovered the downforce lost by the double diffuser. All this was done in CFD and by simulation. The budget was extremely limited. But no complaints – everybody was paid, and so were the bills, but the excess needed to build a new car and do proper development wasn't there.

It was the Dallara car, the same chassis as 2010, with different bodywork, a new 'box and a different rear axle. We didn't lose downforce, but normally you'd be able to do continuous wind-tunnel development. That didn't happen.

The Pirellis made the car a bit easier to balance, and we had some modifications to the front wing with CFD that improved things, but it was still a slow car due to lack of downforce.

DRIVERS GOT THE BEST FROM THE CAR

I was happy we had Liuzzi in the car, because he's a known quantity. We know the guy is quick. He's a good reference, and if you

compare the other two drivers we have had in the car, then you can see that Narain is not a slow driver. Not at all.

Ricciardo, same thing. He takes his time to come up to speed, but in the end is the same speed or similar – sometimes faster, sometimes slower. He got there very quickly for a rookie, and without any mistakes; no spins, not even a flat spot, nothing. That's impressive. There were lots of others, even those with more experience like Bruno Senna, flying off left and right.

In India, Daniel was doing a very impressive first stint and then at the pit stop the wheel nut was not fixed properly and he had to come back in. Therefore he finished behind Narain, but he had been pulling away. He gets more out of the car than is really in it, especially in race conditions. I think he has big potential.

STRATEGY DETERMINED BY CAR'S PACE

As with 2010, we based our strategy around being lapped. We know we will be lapped twice in a race, and you plan your stops around when it's going to happen – it's better to come in than have 11 or 12 blue-flag periods costing you three seconds per car. So it's like a free stop if you like! This year was a bit easier than last, because with the Bridgestones it was mostly one or two stops and with Pirelli it's two, three or four. So, by the time they're lapping us they're basically coming in themselves, so we could stay out a bit longer.

A NEW TEAM STRUCTURE FOR 2012

Thesan Capital took over as owners in July, and now there's a budget for a completely new car next year. Then there was a stop in August for three weeks, so we started in September, which is already late.

The plan is now to have two HRTs – a technical office based in Munich and the racing team in Valencia. Germany isn't like the UK, but there's a lot of high-precision mechanical industry, composites, etc. If your design group is there, all the people supplying parts are in the neighbourhood. It's easier than Spain for contacts and meetings.

For the moment HRT doesn't own a wind tunnel, and so we rent the Mercedes one. They have two, and we use one because with the

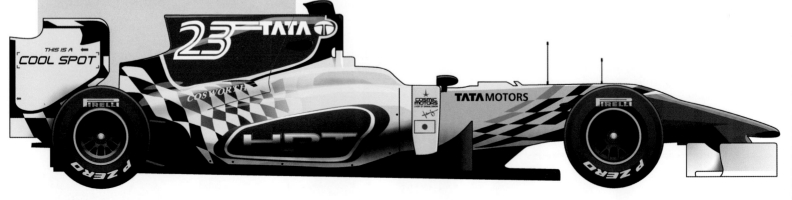

TECHNICAL SPECIFICATIONS

ENGINE
MAKE/MODEL Cosworth CA2011
CONFIGURATION 2400cc V8
SPARK PLUGS Champion
ECU FIA standard issue
FUEL BP
OIL BP
BATTERY GS Base

TRANSMISSION
GEARBOX Williams
FORWARD GEARS Seven
CLUTCH AP

CHASSIS
CHASSIS MODEL HRT F111
FRONT SUSPENSION LAYOUT
Carbon-fibre double wishbone with
pushrod operating torsion springs
and anti-roll bar via rocker

REAR SUSPENSION LAYOUT
Carbon-fibre double wishbone with
pushrod operating torsion springs
and anti-roll bar via rocker
DAMPERS Penske
TYRES Pirelli
WHEELS BBS
BRAKE DISCS Brembo
BRAKE PADS Brembo
BRAKE CALIPERS Brembo
FUEL TANK ATL
INSTRUMENTS McLaren
Electronic Systems

DIMENSIONS
LENGTH Not disclosed
WIDTH Not disclosed
HEIGHT Not disclosed
WHEELBASE Not disclosed
TRACK, FRONT Not disclosed
TRACK, REAR Not disclosed
WEIGHT 640kg (including
driver and camera)

Resource Restriction Agreement they can only use one.

Next year's HRT will therefore be the first that's been near a wind tunnel. From the little bit we have done already, it seems to be a good step forward, but the level of the existing teams is extremely high.

You have to be realistic. We aren't a team of 500 people. The design group in Munich at the latest count was 64 people, and I think the rest of the team – mechanics and people working at the track – will be another 60.

All we could do was try and make the car reliable which, actually, in 2010 we managed to do and finished 11th and not 12th. I think the total development then was a new ATL fuel cell, some sensors and a wiring loom! And this year again, we have beaten Virgin on reliability. People don't realise how tough it is.

PREPARING FOR FUTURE REGULATION CHANGES
When you look at other teams building a new car, they're starting from a good base. The rule changes on the exhaust exits, and hopefully on engine mapping, are going in the right direction and are well-defined. They might be an advantage for us, because if you've got freedom of where the exhausts are blowing, it's massive.

We have also extended our technical collaboration with Williams. For the moment it's limited to the gearbox and, for next year, the KERS system, but at least we can now go in that direction, because in two years' time we go to new engine rules and KERS will be a much more important thing. It will be 120bhp and the amount of time you can use it will be much more, nearly the whole lap.

Where that will leave us is a question for the future. We will have to see what's on the market for an engine. And it's not only engine, but gearbox, because the engine will be revving lower and we will have the same power, which means higher torque. That means that the gearbox we have now, which is made for a maximum 300Nm torque, will not last anymore.

So the whole powertrain has to be new, and it will be much more complex in terms of internal aerodynamics, because you have to cool the turbo, two motor generator units – one linked to the turbo and one linked to the engine – and more powerful batteries. So it will be a completely different story and we need to start early."

VIRGIN

THE TEAM

PERSONNEL
CHIEF EXECUTIVE OFFICER Andy Webb
TEAM PRINCIPAL John Booth (above)
CHIEF DESIGNER John McQuilliam
ENGINEERING DIRECTOR Nickolay Fomenko
SPORTING DIRECTOR & PRESIDENT Graeme Lowdon
CHIEF ENGINEER Dave Greenwood
TEAM MANAGER Dave O'Neill
DRIVERS Timo Glock, Jerome d'Ambrosio
RACE ENGINEER (Glock) Michael Harre
RACE ENGINEER (d'Ambrosio) Mark Hutcheson
TEST/THIRD DRIVERS Robert Wickens, Sakon Yamamoto
CHIEF MECHANIC Richard Wrenn
NO 1 MECHANIC (Glock) Kieron Marchant
NO 1 MECHANIC (d'Ambrosio) Lee Adams
TOTAL NUMBER OF EMPLOYEES 165
NUMBER IN RACE TEAM 47
TEAM BASE Banbury, England
TELEPHONE +49 (0)1295 517270
WEBSITE www.marussiavirginracing.com

TEAM STATS
IN F1 SINCE 2010 **FIRST GRAND PRIX** Bahrain 2010
STARTS 38 **WINS** 0 **POLE POSITIONS** 0
FASTEST LAPS 0 **PODIUMS** 0 **POINTS** 0
CONSTRUCTORS' TITLES 0 **DRIVERS' TITLES** 0

SPONSORS
Armin Racing Watches, CNBC, CSC, Kappa, LDC, Monroe, MusicMagpie, QNet, Quantel, Quick, Ring Automotive, SMA University, Soleco, UST Global, Nexa, Autocolour, Pirelli, Perkin Elmer, RTR, Servotest

24 TIMO GLOCK   **25** JEROME D'AMBROSIO

BUILDING SOLID FOUNDATIONS FOR THE FUTURE

By John Booth
Team Principal

"Our first objective was to improve operating procedures and reliability and go up a step in performance, but we weren't foolish enough to think we were going to leap on to the back of Force India in a year.

By the end of the first test it became obvious that we'd achieved two objectives, but the third was sadly lacking.

Aerodynamically it wasn't working. Nick Wirth pretty much took it on the chin and beavered away to rectify the problem.

We did the first test in Valencia with the old car on Pirellis and I think every day we were P6/7/8 and thinking, 'Bloody hell, we get the new car, which Nick says is two seconds a lap quicker, and we'll be away…'

It didn't happen and there's evidence that we were actually a bit worse off than last year. But with the new tyres and the blown-exhaust technology, which we didn't have, it's hard to know what was causing the gap.

If you watched the car on-circuit or the onboard footage, it didn't look horrible. It was corner entry speed that we lacked, which is downforce and exhaust technology. But the performance wasn't anywhere near where it should have been.

A CHANGE OF DIRECTION AFTER TURKEY
We had an upgrade for Turkey; a floor, new front wing, high nose and some attempt at a blown exhaust, although we didn't have the technology to map it. It was comprehensive, but brought no gain.

It was at that point our investors said we had to go in a different direction. Perhaps we were trying to do something that isn't possible with CFD. Until we could control our own destiny, it was difficult to see a way forward. We knew it would be a long, hard path.

We had a void of probably six weeks post-Turkey, while the McLaren negotiations were taking place, which was difficult for all concerned. Pat Symonds had started putting together a design team, which consists mainly of people who were already at Banbury – there's some really bright, renowned people and some good young talent.

Pat started forming that into the structure he wanted, and we had a couple of spin-offs, including a nice little upgrade for Monza. But both our rivals had upgrades at the same time and we negated each other, but moved slightly closer to the tail of the field. The interesting thing was that the promised figures correlated pretty much with what we saw from the car, which was encouraging.

We're learning all the time. We've been in the dark a lot of the time about where the aero map is for the car. We did a bit of mapping in Spain after Monza, and constantly applied that to the car, so I think we got a bit more out of it. But we weren't in a wind tunnel.

We started using the McLaren tunnel at the end of October, and the relationship has been growing stronger since day one. They actually started things rolling before the contract was signed, so there's an eagerness on their side to make it work as well.

PREPARING FOR THE 2012 SEASON
It's a late start in terms of the 2012 car and I think it will have more impact throughout next year than at the start. But I'm sure the new car will be a lot better than the one that started this year. We're a bit on the edge, but it will be there for the first test. What we're short of is development time.

The building work for the new factory is well underway and the plan was to move in when we got back from the Brazilian GP. It's not big enough to put freight and logistics in – we've got another building for that – but all the car crew and race team offices are in the same building now.

When we started, I didn't think it was going to be that important but, on reflection, I now spend most of my time at Banbury and can nip into the design office, into finance, go and see acquisitions, and rather than write an email, which can cause a whole chain of trouble, it's much better. You go and sit down with someone for 10 minutes and the job's ticked off.

We started the year with our 79 people, and Nick had about 60 on the F1 project. By the time our vacancies are filled – the

TECHNICAL SPECIFICATIONS

ENGINE
MAKE/MODEL Cosworth CA2011
CONFIGURATION 2400cc V8
(90 degree)
SPARK PLUGS Champion
ECU FIA standard issue
FUEL BP Castrol
OIL BP Castrol
BATTERY Not disclosed

TRANSMISSION
GEARBOX Marussia Virgin Racing/Xtrac
FORWARD GEARS Seven
CLUTCH AP Racing

CHASSIS
CHASSIS MODEL Virgin MVR-02
FRONT SUSPENSION LAYOUT
Double wishbone with pushrod
REAR SUSPENSION LAYOUT
Double wishbone with pushrod

DAMPERS Penske
TYRES Pirelli
WHEELS BBS
BRAKE DISCS Hitco
BRAKE PADS Hitco
BRAKE CALIPERS AP Racing
FUEL TANK ATL
INSTRUMENTS McLaren
Electronic Systems

DIMENSIONS
LENGTH 5200mm (approx)
WIDTH 1800mm (approx)
HEIGHT 950mm (approx)
WHEELBASE 3300mm (approx)
TRACK, FRONT 1800mm
TRACK, REAR 1800mm
WEIGHT 640kg (including
driver and camera)

MARUSSIA VIRGIN RACING

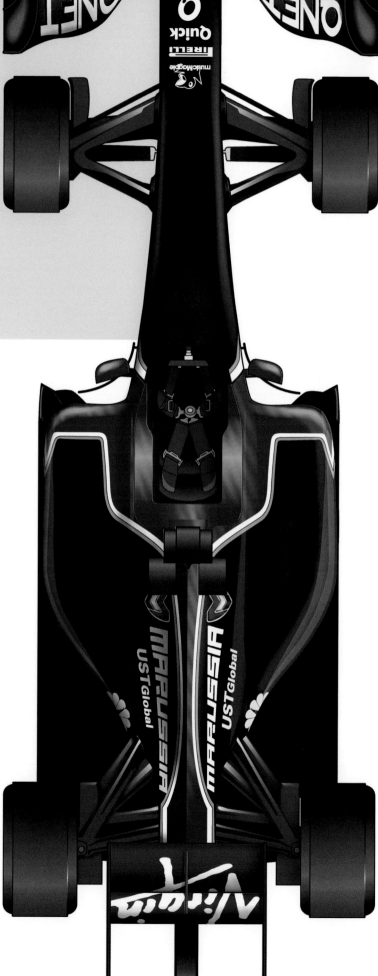

problem is that everyone is on notice periods in F1 and a lot of those we're employing now won't be able to start until March – we'll be up to 205.

That's still small compared to most, but this is the structure Pat wants. Ours is a much broader technical partnership with McLaren, and I think the Force India one is more specific. You do see influences on the Force India car when you look closely.

MAXIMUM EFFORT FROM THE DRIVERS
It was great to get Timo Glock signed again. One, he's a bloody great driver, and two, it would be nice for him to see it through after taking the pain. It gave the garage a boost to see that Timo has faith in the way we're going. There's no question in my mind that he's a top eight driver. Drop him into a Red Bull and he'd be right up there.

What's incredible about Timo, and I watch it quite carefully, is that he always gives 100%, particularly in races. He never wavers from that.

Jerome d'Ambrosio did a fantastic job to beat Timo in qualifying at Suzuka. He was absolutely nowhere on Friday and asked us just to set his car like Timo's. Through Saturday morning he got better and better.

Jerome was normally a few tenths shy, but in Japan Timo said he'd given it everything in qualifying and only made a tiny mistake that cost him maybe a couple of hundredths. So Jerome did a great job. Timo was the first one to go and shake his hand. He was bloody great about it. Boiling inside, I'm sure, but he didn't let any of it show!

FINANCING THE FUTURE
We've got a financial plan in place for the next four years, and hopefully some interesting announcements coming along soon.

Again, though, we won't have KERS. Don't get me going on that! The cost is £5–8 million… we could get a wind tunnel running for that, which would be worth a lot more than four tenths from where we are.

If you're looking for that last four tenths, fine, but that £8 million would be a massive boost to our development budget. It's the biggest waste of money there has been in F1 since active suspension."

THE RACES

In one of the longest F1 seasons in history, the action started in Melbourne in March and ran through to São Paulo in late November, taking in India for the first time

AUSTRALIA

2011 FORMULA 1 QANTAS AUSTRALIAN GRAND PRIX
MELBOURNE

DOMINANT DEFENDER

Sebastian Vettel had the best possible start to the defence of his World Championship by dominating what became the season opener after the cancellation of the Bahrain GP

New tyres, movable wings and the return of KERS may have been the big talking points in Australia, but the changes did nothing to upset the momentum of the Sebastian Vettel/Adrian Newey combination.

Vettel and Red Bull Racing started the 2011 season in Melbourne as they finished in 2010, with a dominant victory. The result was not entirely unexpected, given the form that the RB7 had shown in testing.

However, the relative ease with which the German won didn't necessarily mean that his team would have things all its own way as the season progressed. Indeed, Vettel's team-mate Mark Webber could finish only fifth after struggling to get on the pace, while worries over reliability meant that the team didn't run its KERS system after Friday. Perhaps the others would have a chance, after all.

KERS and DRS provided plenty of talking points, but the first weekend of the season was really all about the new Pirellis. Following the two recent Barcelona tests there was doom and gloom among the drivers, and suggestions that four or five pit stops might become the norm. And that would

ABOVE At the first corner Sebastian Vettel already has a healthy lead that he would extend to 2.4s by the end of the first lap

BELOW Michael Schumacher retired on the first lap after hitting Jaime Alguersuari's Toro Rosso

OPPOSITE Jenson Button battles with Felipe Massa before passing the Ferrari off-track, landing the Englishman a drive-through penalty

perhaps push the sport over the borderline between being interesting, or becoming a farce.

In the end, that didn't happen. From the very beginning of practice on Friday, it became clear that the tyres were lasting a lot longer than expected, and thus teams had to rethink some of the strategies that they had pre-planned for Australia.

In qualifying, Vettel set a time that was nearly 0.8s quicker than that of nearest rival Lewis Hamilton. Things didn't quite go the way of local hero Webber, and the Aussie found himself pushed down to third.

"I think the key is always to finish the race, to see the chequered flag," said Vettel. "Last year, half way through, we had to retire. But I am quite confident. We had a very, very good preparation in the winter. We hardly suffered any reliability issues. The car was reliable from the first minute and obviously not too slow, so things are looking good. But it is a hard race with the new tyres.

"It's a bit like racing into the unknown. We can kind of guess how the tyres will behave, but in the end we will have to see how it is. Also, racing all the others, having probably more than one stop, it will be quite entertaining for us. There are a lot of things that we need to keep an eye on and focus on, but today was the base and couldn't have been any better."

Having launched the MP4-26 car late – to make better use of the winter for R&D – McLaren had struggled through testing with lack of reliability and, more worryingly, lack of performance. A gamble on an advanced exhaust and floor concept, reflecting one of the key areas where bold designers could still make gains, failed to pay off.

Less than a fortnight before the first race, the team decided to throw away the new stuff and go with something a little more conventional. It was a huge job, but the revised parts made it to Australia on time and they transformed the car, even though they hadn't been run on track before practice. Against the odds, McLaren was Red Bull's strongest challenger in Australia, and Hamilton duly qualified second. He was backed up by Jenson Button in fourth, the latter having a scrappy Q3 session.

Ferrari had been expected to push RBR hardest, but Fernando Alonso had to settle for fifth after struggling for grip. Felipe Massa, who had a spin in Q3, was down in eighth. Vitaly Petrov did a brilliant job to put the Renault sixth, leading to speculation on what Robert Kubica might have done in the same car.

INSIDE LINE
VITALY PETROV
LOTUS RENAULT DRIVER

"My first podium in my 20th grand prix feels great, alongside Sebastian and Lewis – both World Champions!

It was a difficult winter for the team. Testing seemed quite long and then of course Robert (Kubica) had his accident. We had the new exhaust and we didn't know how it would work. We spent quite a long time trying to understand the aerodynamics and a lot of things, and really when we came to Melbourne we didn't know where we were, we didn't know how quick our car was, but it looks like we are quite strong. Not like Red Bull and McLaren, but still strong.

Some people wondered if I could lead the team, but I don't think I need to answer anything now… yes!

The whole weekend was pretty good for us. After the last test we came here with some new parts, and right from free practice our car looked very good. Qualifying sixth – behind only the Red Bulls, McLarens and Alonso – was not too bad, and I think the whole team can be proud of the job we did.

My start was OK. I tried to attack Fernando, but then I saw Jenson was in front so I had to brake early, then, as they went out wide, I just released the brake and passed them both.

Nobody knew what the situation with the tyres was going to be and what the strategy would be. Sebastian stopped twice and he was comfortable, but I was not so far behind Lewis, who also stopped twice. I was watching Mark Webber in front of me, pushing as hard as I could, then, when he pitted, I pushed to the maximum I could without destroying the tyres.

I tried to pull away from Fernando, and during the middle of the race I didn't understand where I was or what I should do because of the different strategies, with Mark and Fernando stopping one more time.

My radio wasn't working very well, so I just tried to save the tyres and push as hard as I could – and everything worked out well.

Fernando was getting close towards the end, but I was still confident. It's not so easy to pass, and even if he attacked, my tyres were still in quite good shape and I had good traction out of the last corner. I also got some good breaks with the lapped cars. I think we deserved the podium."

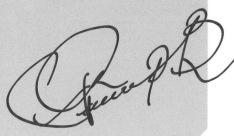

BRAVE NEW WORLD?

After Bahrain's cancellation, the waiting was finally over. There were several 'expectations' born of winter testing: a multi-stop race, as the new Pirelli control rubber wore rapidly; overtaking that was possibly too easy thanks to the new DRS (Drag Reduction System) rear wings and the reintroduction of Kinetic Energy Recovery Systems (KERS); a McLaren team with its back to the wall, facing another start to the year like '09; and Red Bull still the team to beat.

Christian Horner's troops performed to the script, at least in the shape of Sebastian Vettel, who was peerless and promptly won the race from pole position, remaining in control throughout. The reigning World Champion's team-mate, Mark Webber, though, once again had a disappointing afternoon at home, fifth place being the maximum he could manage, equalling his result with Minardi in 2002. Despite similar telemetry traces to Vettel (steering inputs, brake pressure, etc) Mark found he was wearing the Pirellis at a higher rate and needed an extra stop, dropping him behind Petrov and Alonso, even though the Ferrari pitted three times too. The phenomenon left him scratching his head.

Elsewhere, there were surprises. Talk of four and five stops as the tyres fell apart proved well wide of the mark. In fact, rookie Sergio Perez started on the hard tyre, made just one pit visit, and finished seventh! Unfortunately for the Mexican, both Saubers were then excluded for rear wing infringements…

McLaren made a mockery of testing 'form' when it dropped the complicated 'octopus' exhaust system that had been compromising balance and strangling power. The team was competitive all weekend, with Lewis Hamilton the closest challenger to Vettel.

What of KERS/DRS? Well, Melbourne was perhaps not the best barometer of its likely influence on the action over the year. There was talk of a double DRS zone, with drivers allowed to make use of the device on the run to Turn 3 as well, but in the end the FIA went with just the single zone, on the main straight, which proved a tad too short. So, in fact, we saw only three DRS-assisted overtakes all afternoon: Alonso on Rosberg, Button on Massa and Massa on Buemi.

KERS was the same as '09 and so, we knew, was worth about three-tenths over the lap. But what was this? Red Bull wasn't using its KERS. Christian Horner said that after reliability concerns on Friday, they switched it off. But the hot story was that Adrian Newey, expecting the RB7s to be starting at the front and not needing to overtake, had ordered a 'mini-KERS' that would protect the RB7s off the line without compromising packaging, and hence efficiency, for the rest of the race.

"Journalistic fantasy," Horner smiled, "but now I'm worried that Adrian will think it's a good idea…"

The big concern for Red Bull was that without KERS the dark blue cars would lose out to those behind on the run from the start. However, that didn't prove to be the case, as Vettel and third qualifier Mark Webber both managed to defend their positions. In fact, from the dirty side of the grid, Hamilton and Button made very average starts from second and fourth places.

On the first lap Vettel pulled out a massive 2.4s lead over Hamilton, and in a race uninterrupted by safety cars, he never came under any threat, although Hamilton was close enough to ensure that there was no margin for error.

In the end, we had the sort of convoluted spectacle that Pirelli had been charged with creating, with teams trying three-, two- and one-stop strategies. And even within those basic choices there were various permutations in terms of when the primes and options were used, and the lengths of the stints.

The guy with the maximum flexibility was Vettel. KERS or no KERS, he had such a margin that he could have run a whole variety of strategies, and still won the race. In the end he went for a simple two-

stop, running option/option/prime. The first driver to stop, on lap 11, after making clear on the radio that the rears were going away, was Webber. Vettel, too, was heard on the radio saying his rears were going, and came in on lap 14.

Could we draw conclusions about the Red Bull working its tyres hard? That certainly tallied with the RB7's qualifying pace, but then subsequently Vettel was able to safely complete a two-stopper. Webber in contrast needed three stops, getting just 15 laps out of the primes that he took on at his first change.

"It was a bit of a voyage into the unknown, because nobody fully knew how the tyres were going to react," said Team Principal Christian Horner. "But I think we got our strategy just right, and it was great to win Pirelli's first race back in F1.

"There was one crucial stage where, after the first stop, Sebastian emerged behind Jenson, who got a drive-through penalty anyway. Tactically, if they could have held Sebastian up it would have put him behind Lewis after the stop.

"But he made a fast and fair move on Jenson, and that was decisive for the rest of the race, and then it was a matter of controlling his pace. We were unsure

OPPOSITE TOP Lewis Hamilton was Vettel's closest pursuer all weekend, qualifying and finishing in second place

OPPOSITE BOTTOM F1 rookies Sergio Perez (Sauber) and Pastor Maldonado (Williams) made a promising debut, Perez finishing an impressive seventh before both Saubers were disqualified for a rear-wing infringement

ABOVE Force India's new signing, Paul di Resta, outqualified his experienced team-mate, Adrian Sutil, and ran strongly to finish ninth

Vitaly Petrov qualified sixth and drove a spirited race for Renault, withstanding race-long pressure to take the third step on the podium

BELOW Sebastian Vettel and Red Bull Racing celebrate after starting the 2011 season as they finished in 2010, with a dominant performance to win from pole position

harmed the aero performance, but he still kept up a good pace and finished a comfortable second.

Button could have been on the podium, but received a drive-through penalty for passing Massa by running off-track. The Englishman would have been OK had he let the Brazilian back through, but the penalty demoted him to sixth.

"We saw that Mark's tyres went off very quickly, we saw Sebastian's go off," said McLaren's Martin Whitmarsh. "At that point Lewis was in reasonable shape. But we didn't really know at the first stop. I think we were slightly lighter on tyre wear, but by the time we got to the second stop we already had the floor damage, and therefore it really didn't matter too much.

"I don't think we could have one-stopped, but who knows? I think here if you can stop before the cars around you, and still make it to the end of the race with the nominated number of stops that you planned, then you're going to be quicker after the stop quite clearly. But if you stop too early, you've really got to stretch – if you're two-stopping – the second and third stints."

There was an unexpected face on the podium, as Vitaly Petrov put in a perfect race to reward the Renault team with third place. In the closing laps he was being caught by Fernando Alonso, but the Russian stayed 1.2s clear. Having gone wide at Turn One and lost ground, Alonso was happy enough with fourth, knowing that he'd beaten at least two potential title rivals in the shape of Webber and Button.

Like the RBR guys, Alonso and Massa had also made very early stops on laps 12 and 13. Both then ran three-stoppers, with the Brazilian having to run a final stint of just 10 laps, which was hardly ideal. With fresher tyres than everyone else, he subsequently set the fastest lap of the race just three laps from home, while fellow late stoppers Alonso and Webber were next fastest. That gave us a hint of a scenario that many expected to see in 2011, with those on new tyres reeling in those who had stuck it out and paid the price when their old rubber dropped over the edge.

The big surprise was Sauber rookie Sergio Perez, who finished seventh on the road after an amazing single-stop run that saw him do 34 laps on the supposedly more fragile option tyre. He finished ahead of team-mate Kamui Kobayashi, but after the race both men were disqualified for a rear-wing infringements, much to the team's embarrassment.

That promoted Massa to seventh, after an undistinguished run for the Brazilian driver. STR's Sébastien Buemi moved up to eighth, while the Force Indias of Adrian Sutil and new recruit Paul di Resta inherited ninth and 10th.

It was a bad day for Mercedes, as both Michael Schumacher and Nico Rosberg retired due to accident damage from mid-field collisions. Schumacher tangled with Jaime Alguersuari on the first lap, while Rosberg was hit by an over-optimistic Rubens Barrichello. Clearly the team had a lot of work to do.

if we were going to do an additional stop or not, but as it was, the tyres worked out very well, and we got away with a two-stop.

"We went into the race planning to do both to the same strategy, but Mark quite quickly got into more issues with his own tyres..."

Webber was simply off the pace in the first two stints, and had to settle for fifth place.

McLaren, meanwhile, didn't seem to have any tyre issues, with Hamilton and Button running 16 and 17 laps respectively on their opening sets of primes. The former's challenge to Vettel ended when he suffered damage to his floor and this

SNAPSHOT FROM
AUSTRALIA

CLOCKWISE FROM RIGHT
The Melbourne skyline provides the backdrop to the Albert Park circuit; messages for the injured Robert Kubica from his Renault team; a marshal keeps his eyes on things; fanatical Ferrari fans; Michael Schumacher meets Australian three-times World Champion Sir Jack Brabham; smiley, happy, pretty person; the Sauber team send their tribute to the victims of the Japanese earthquake; leading GP2 racer and Ferrari test driver Jules Bianchi ponders his future; Lewis Hamilton crouches to compare his second-placed McLaren MP4-26 with the opposition in *parc fermé* after the race; Pirelli's tyres proved far more durable than expected

RACE RESULTS
AUSTRALIA MELBOURNE

RACE DATE March 27th
CIRCUIT LENGTH 3.295 miles
NO. OF LAPS 58
RACE DISTANCE 191.110 miles
WEATHER Sunny & dry, 18°C
TRACK TEMP 23°C
ATTENDANCE 298,000
LAP RECORD Michael Schumacher, 1m24.125s, 141.016mph, 2004

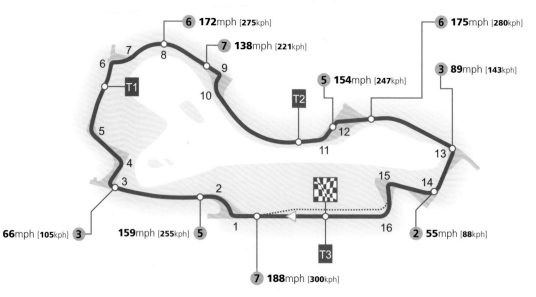

PRACTICE 1				PRACTICE 2				PRACTICE 3				QUALIFYING 1			QUALIFYING 2	
	Driver	Time	Laps		Driver	Time	Laps		Driver	Time	Laps		Driver	Time		Driver	Time
1	M Webber	1m26.831s	20	1	J Button	1m25.854s	32	1	S Vettel	1m24.507s	15	1	S Vettel	1m25.296s	1	S Vettel	1m24.090s
2	S Vettel	1m27.158s	19	2	L Hamilton	1m25.986s	31	2	M Webber	1m25.364s	14	2	L Hamilton	1m25.384s	2	L Hamilton	1m24.595s
3	F Alonso	1m27.749s	20	3	F Alonso	1m26.001s	28	3	L Hamilton	1m25.553s	15	3	V Petrov	1m25.543s	3	M Webber	1m24.658s
4	N Rosberg	1m28.152s	16	4	S Vettel	1m26.014s	35	4	J Button	1m25.567s	16	4	F Alonso	1m25.707s	4	J Button	1m24.957s
5	R Barrichello	1m28.430s	24	5	M Webber	1m26.283s	33	5	V Petrov	1m25.906s	18	5	K Kobayashi	1m25.717s	5	F Alonso	1m25.242s
6	J Button	1m28.440s	29	6	M Schumacher	1m26.590s	31	6	F Alonso	1m26.121s	16	6	S Perez	1m25.812s	6	K Kobayashi	1m25.405s
7	L Hamilton	1m28.483s	26	7	F Massa	1m26.789s	34	7	K Kobayashi	1m26.417s	17	7	N Rosberg	1m25.856s	7	V Petrov	1m25.582s
8	M Schumacher	1m28.690s	14	8	S Perez	1m27.101s	39	8	N Rosberg	1m26.520s	17	8	J Button	1m25.886s	8	N Rosberg	1m25.606s
9	K Kobayashi	1m28.725s	13	9	R Barrichello	1m27.280s	34	9	N Heidfeld	1m26.746s	17	9	M Webber	1m25.900s	9	F Massa	1m25.611s
10	V Petrov	1m28.765s	15	10	N Rosberg	1m27.448s	23	10	M Schumacher	1m26.856s	15	10	M Schumacher	1m25.962s	10	S Buemi	1m25.882s
11	F Massa	1m28.842s	20	11	J Alguersuari	1m27.525s	31	11	S Buemi	1m27.008s	17	11	F Massa	1m26.031s	11	M Schumacher	1m25.971s
12	N Heidfeld	1m28.928s	14	12	V Petrov	1m27.528s	29	12	F Massa	1m27.011s	15	12	S Buemi	1m26.232s	12	J Alguersuari	1m26.103s
13	A Sutil	1m29.314s	19	13	N Heidfeld	1m27.536s	22	13	J Alguersuari	1m27.066s	14	13	A Sutil	1m26.245s	13	S Perez	1m26.108s
14	S Buemi	1m29.328s	21	14	S Buemi	1m27.697s	30	14	P di Resta	1m27.087s	15	14	R Barrichello	1m26.270s	14	P di Resta	1m26.739s
15	P Maldonado	1m29.403s	24	15	K Kobayashi	1m28.095s	35	15	A Sutil	1m27.180s	15	15	P Maldonado	1m26.298s	15	P Maldonado	1m26.768s
16	D Ricciardo	1m29.468s	23	16	P di Resta	1m28.376s	33	16	R Barrichello	1m28.068s	7	16	J Alguersuari	1m26.620s	16	A Sutil	1m31.407s
17	S Perez	1m29.643s	18	17	A Sutil	1m28.583s	31	17	S Perez	1m28.077s	9	17	P di Resta	1m27.222s	17	R Barrichello	No time
18	N Hulkenberg	1m31.002s	20	18	P Maldonado	1m29.386s	29	18	H Kovalainen	1m29.772s	17	18	N Heidfeld	1m27.239s			
19	H Kovalainen	1m32.428s	13	19	H Kovalainen	1m30.829s	22	19	J Trulli	1m30.003s	18	19	H Kovalainen	1m29.254s			
20	J d'Ambrosio	1m35.282s	17	20	J Trulli	1m30.912s	23	20	T Glock	1m30.261s	15	20	J Trulli	1m29.342s			
21	T Glock	1m35.289s	15	21	J d'Ambrosio	1m32.106s	36	21	P Maldonado	1m30.496s	5	21	T Glock	1m29.858s			
22	K Chandhok	No time	1	22	T Glock	1m32.135s	30	22	J d'Ambrosio	1m30.704s	18	22	J d'Ambrosio	1m30.822s			
23	N Karthikeyan	No time	0	23	V Liuzzi	No time	1	23	N Karthikeyan	1m41.554s	1	23	V Liuzzi	1m32.978s			
24	V Liuzzi	No time	0	24	N Karthikeyan	No time	0	24	V Liuzzi	No time	1	24	N Karthikeyan	1m34.293s			

Best sectors – Practice			Speed trap – Practice			Best sectors – Qualifying			Speed trap – Qualifying		
Sec 1	S Vettel	28.414s	1	L Hamilton	196.042mph	Sec 1	S Vettel	28.088s	1	K Kobayashi	195.234mph
Sec 2	S Vettel	22.520s	2	K Kobayashi	195.421mph	Sec 2	S Vettel	22.320s	2	S Perez	194.799mph
Sec 3	S Vettel	33.552s	3	S Buemi	195.172mph	Sec 3	S Vettel	33.045s	3	N Rosberg	194.737mph

Sebastian Vettel
"I had a good getaway, but didn't know if it was enough. Then I saw Lewis and Mark battling, so I got a cushion on lap 1 and tried to hold the gap for the first stint."

Jenson Button
"I was surprised to see Vitaly up the inside. Then I got stuck behind Felipe, as I got a poor exit, and that was my worst move, as he was so slow and hard to pass."

Fernando Alonso
"I got away well at the start, but Button headed for me and I had to go wide to avoid a clash. Luckily, the strategy was right and helped me make up places."

Michael Schumacher
"I had quite a good start, but was then hit in Turn 3, which punctured my right rear and damaged the floor. We then decided to stop the car for safety reasons."

Nick Heidfeld
"I got hit on lap 1, and it's a shame, as I'd gone from 18th to 12th by the first corner. The damage was quite severe, mostly to the right-hand bodywork."

Rubens Barrichello
"I was pushed out at the start, then was doing a lot of passing until the incident with Rosberg. I wasn't planning on passing him, I was defending from Kobayashi."

Mark Webber
"I wasn't quick, like in qualifying, so we need to understand the reason why. I lost the last position to Fernando during the pit stops and that was it for me really."

Lewis Hamilton
"Second is a great result. To be able to pressure Sebastian so soon this year was encouraging. If it hadn't been for the poor start, I could have been in the fight."

Felipe Massa
"In the second part of the race, I had degradation on the rear tyres. When Button overtook me, cutting the chicane, I expected him to be penalised."

Nico Rosberg
"It was a tough race until I saw Rubens in my mirror. He was quite far back, so I was surprised he hit me. I immediately thought that was it and I had to pull over."

Vitaly Petrov
"I made a great start to get ahead of Alonso and Button, and was able to run in clean air and look after my tyres. Our two-stop strategy was the right decision."

Pastor Maldonado
"We don't know what happened with the car, so we will have to look into the problem. There was absolutely no warning, we just stopped and that was it for us."

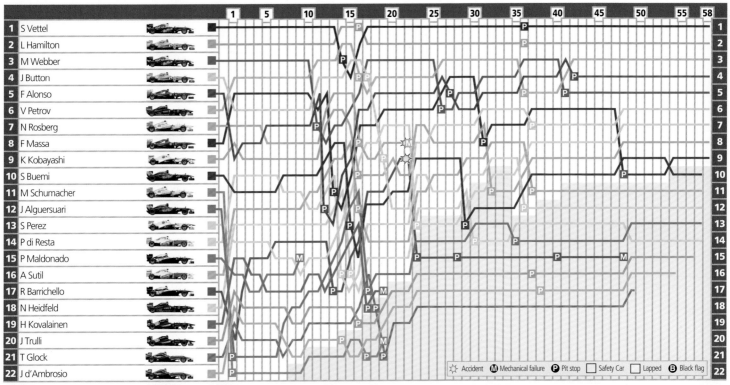

		1	5	10	15	20	25	30	35	40	45	50	55	58	
1	S Vettel														1
2	L Hamilton														2
3	M Webber														3
4	J Button														4
5	F Alonso														5
6	V Petrov														6
7	N Rosberg														7
8	F Massa														8
9	K Kobayashi														9
10	S Buemi														10
11	M Schumacher														11
12	J Alguersuari														12
13	S Perez														13
14	P di Resta														14
15	P Maldonado														15
16	A Sutil														16
17	R Barrichello														17
18	N Heidfeld														18
19	H Kovalainen														19
20	J Trulli														20
21	T Glock														21
22	J d'Ambrosio														22

☼ Accident Ⓜ Mechanical failure Ⓟ Pit stop ☐ Safety Car ☐ Lapped Ⓑ Black flag

QUALIFYING 3

	Driver	Time
1	S Vettel	1m23.529s
2	L Hamilton	1m24.307s
3	M Webber	1m24.395s
4	J Button	1m24.779s
5	F Alonso	1m24.974s
6	V Petrov	1m25.247s
7	N Rosberg	1m25.421s
8	F Massa	1m25.599s
9	K Kobayashi	1m25.626s
10	S Buemi	1m27.066s

GRID

	Driver	Time
1	S Vettel	1m23.529s
2	L Hamilton	1m24.307s
3	M Webber	1m24.395
4	J Button	1m24.779s
5	F Alonso	1m24.974s
6	V Petrov	1m25.247s
7	N Rosberg	1m25.421s
8	F Massa	1m25.599s
9	K Kobayashi	1m25.626s
10	S Buemi	1m27.066s
11	M Schumacher	1m25.971s
12	J Alguersuari	1m26.103s
13	S Perez	1m26.108s
14	P di Resta	1m26.739s
15	P Maldonado	1m26.768s
16	A Sutil	1m31.407s
17	R Barrichello	No time
18	N Heidfeld	1m27.239s
19	H Kovalainen	1m29.254s
20	J Trulli	1m29.342s
21	T Glock	1m29.858s
22	J d'Ambrosio	1m30.822s

RACE

	Driver	Car	Laps	Time	Avg. mph	Fastest	Stops
1	S Vettel	Red Bull-Renault RB7	58	1h29m30.259s	128.117	1m29.844s	2
2	L Hamilton	McLaren-Mercedes MP4-26	58	1h29m52.556s	127.583	1m30.314s	2
3	V Petrov	Renault R31	58	1h30m00.819s	127.387	1m30.064s	2
4	F Alonso	Ferrari F150 Italia	58	1h30m02.031s	127.359	1m29.487s	3
5	M Webber	Red Bull-Renault RB7	58	1h30m08.430s	127.208	1m29.600s	3
6	J Button	McLaren-Mercedes MP4-26	58	1h30m24.563s	126.830	1m29.883s	2
D	S Perez	Sauber-Ferrari C30	58	1h30m36.104s	126.560	1m29.962s	1
D	K Kobayashi	Sauber-Ferrari C30	58	1h30m47.131s	126.304	1m30.384s	2
7	F Massa	Ferrari F150 Italia	58	1h30m55.445s	126.112	1m28.947s	3
8	S Buemi	Toro Rosso-Ferrari STR6	57	1h29m38.705s	125.706	1m30.836s	2
9	A Sutil	Force India-Mercedes VJM04	57	1h29m54.974s	125.327	1m31.526s	2
10	P di Resta	Force India-Mercedes VJM04	57	1h30m23.766s	124.661	1m31.941s	2
11	J Alguersuari	Toro Rosso-Ferrari STR6	57	1h30m28.923s	124.543	1m30.467s	3
12	N Heidfeld	Renault R31	57	1h30m43.901s	124.200	1m32.377s	2
13	J Trulli	Lotus-Renault T128	56	1h30m53.536s	121.806	1m32.550s	2
14	J d'Ambrosio	Virgin-Cosworth MVR-02	54	1h29m34.518s	119.182	1m34.523s	2
NC	T Glock	Virgin-Cosworth MVR-02	49	1h31m02.637s	106.402	1m35.789s	2
R	R Barrichello	Williams-Cosworth FW33	48	Transmission	-	1m31.404s	3
R	N Rosberg	Mercedes MGP W02	22	Accident damage	-	1m33.503s	1
R	H Kovalainen	Lotus-Renault T128	19	Water leak	-	1m34.918s	1
R	M Schumacher	Mercedes MGP W02	19	Accident damage	-	1m35.319s	1
R	P Maldonado	Williams-Cosworth FW33	9	Transmission	-	1m34.102s	0

CHAMPIONSHIP

	Driver	Pts
1	S Vettel	25
2	L Hamilton	18
3	V Petrov	15
4	F Alonso	12
5	M Webber	10
6	J Button	8
7	F Massa	6
8	S Buemi	4
9	A Sutil	2
10	P di Resta	1

	Constructor	Pts
1	Red Bull-Renault	35
2	McLaren-Mercedes	26
3	Ferrari	18
4	Renault	15
5	Toro Rosso-Ferrari	4
6	Force India-Mercedes	3

Fastest lap
F Massa 1m28.947s
(133.568mph) on lap 55

Fastest speed trap
J Button   194.737mph
Slowest speed trap
H Kovalainen   181.875mph

Fastest pit stop
1 M Webber   22.520s
2 S Vettel   22.603s
3 J Button   22.681s

Adrian Sutil

"It wasn't a bad race. Coming from 16th wasn't easy; my start was good and there were a lot of cars at the first corner, but I made up places by the end of lap 1."

Kamui Kobayashi

"I got by Alonso at the start, who passed me later. I struggled to warm the first set of softs. I had a big moment when Rubens and Nico crashed in front of me."

Sebastien Buemi

"I came 10th, but maybe eighth or ninth was possible. It's a shame that Jaime and I clashed at the first corner and it's not the first time that it has happened."

Jarno Trulli

"It was really good to finish the race and to show there's some pace in the car, despite some of the problems we have had to work through this weekend."

Narain Karthikeyan

Failed to qualify due to 107% rule.

Timo Glock

"I was behind Jarno, then caught him and got past in the pit stop. Unluckily, the front-left wheel was loose at the stop and I had to drive round for a lap very slowly."

Paul di Resta

"I had a fight with Kobayashi, but that let one of the Toro Rossos by and I lost momentum. Our pace was just a little bit behind. Then, later, I had to conserve fuel."

Sergio Perez

"I'll never forget this race. After we changed to the soft tyre, I thought I had to push, but then realised I could manage the tyres and we decided to go to the end."

Jaime Alguersuari

"Into Turn 2, Michael cut the corner as he was having a go around the outside,. He touched my front wing but he couldn't have avoided it."

Heikki Kovalainen

"Until the retirement, I was pleased with my race. I had a good start and was staying with Alguersuari and Perez until a water leak finished my race."

Vitantonio Liuzzi

Failed to qualify due to 107% rule.

Jerome d'Ambrosio

"I'm happy to have finished my first grand prix. I started well and felt comfortable, even though I think I could have gone a bit faster at the end of the race."

2011 FORMULA 1 PETRONAS
MALAYSIA GRAND PRIX
KUALA LUMPUR

SEB DOES IT AGAIN

The Malaysian GP proved to be very different from the Australia race, with non-stop action thanks to high tyre wear, 59 pit stops and DRS-assisted overtaking – but Vettel still won again

After the finish of the Malaysian GP the paddock was buzzing. The identity of the winner might not have been much of a surprise, but we had just witnessed one of the most extraordinary dry-weather and safety-car-free races that we have seen in many years.

Melbourne was never going to be a true litmus test for F1, 2011-style, but in Sepang we got the full load. Multiple tyre stops, passing precipitated by use of the DRS, and KERS also playing a role, not just in the action on the track, but due to the fact that it didn't always work.

It was a truly fascinating race, but you needed a slide rule and a degree in astrophysics to follow it in detail. Even seasoned team bosses had a look of 'what just happened?' when you talked to them post-race.

Sebastian Vettel made it look easy, but of course it was anything but. He did part of the job by taking pole, and laid another foundation stone for his win by getting to the first corner safely in the lead. It was already very clear that, even with easier passing, the best way to guarantee yourself a win in this new era was to get in front, run at your own pace, control

INSIDE LINE
JENSON BUTTON
McLAREN DRIVER

"I have to be satisfied with that: second place, 18 points and second place in the championship, although two races in, that's hardly significant!

People are pointing out that the margin Red Bull has in the race is less than in qualifying, and a lot of it is everyone still trying to understand the tyres and strategy. It was a really confusing race, trying to understand the pit stops and whether it was worth looking after tyres or not throughout the stints.

It's very difficult to understand what to do. If you try and preserve the tyres, sometimes you make the situation worse, as you're not carrying as much speed through a high-speed corner, you get less downforce and you damage the tyres more. It's quite a tricky situation to be in, but as we went through the race I think we understood the tyres a lot more, and we didn't get down to the canvas, so a big 'thank you' to the team. They did a magnificent job today with the pit stops and the strategy.

With these tyres, as soon as they go, they go. It's what they are supposed to do and it's exactly what they do. I had the wrong balance on the first stint and I thought that the rears would be OK, but they went off a lot earlier than I expected. I didn't expect the Ferraris and the Renault to be as consistent as they were, and our degradation was bigger, so we made a few set-up changes in the stops and improved from there – so a big thanks to the guys.

Sebastian and I stopped three times, which worked, while Mark, Fernando and Lewis stopped four times. In the last stint, when we put the prime tyre on, the car came alive and I had so much more grip. I had a feeling that the prime wasn't going to go the same way as the option tyre and my pace was much better in the last stint.

It was a fun race and I had a couple of really good battles. I had the team telling me to back it off and look after the tyres, but in a racer's mind you want to push as hard as you can and catch the leader. Even though it wasn't really on, you've still got to give it a go. I think I kept Sebastian honest!"

your tyres as best you could, and react to the stops of those immediately behind.

In Australia, Red Bull was so confident in its one-lap pace that it was even able to abandon KERS. McLaren was closer in Sepang, but still RBR felt able to make compromises to the set-up for qualifying that would pay off on Sunday, when tyre usage was all-important. It was a risk, and it worked for Vettel, although Mark Webber found himself stranded in third place on the grid, behind Lewis Hamilton.

This time, Vettel had a huge bonus at the start in the form of Nick Heidfeld, who got in front of Hamilton and rode shotgun. We'll never know what might have happened if Lewis had been able to stick behind Vettel in those opening laps – we might have seen a very different race. But while he had some unexpected help, Seb did the rest himself.

"He had a great start, led into the first corner and then his pace was excellent," said Christian Horner. "He was able to build a lead, which gave us options. We then responded to the cars behind us, and we then had the option of going a three- or a four-stop. In the end, we didn't need to do a four-stop, and he brought the car home with a very, very mature and level-headed drive.

"I think you have to be flexible. We didn't know whether it was going to be a three-, four- or five-stop in that race to be honest with you, but I think you have to go into a race and have the flexibility to change."

The pursuit was led at various times by Heidfeld, Hamilton, Alonso and Button, but Vettel always had things under control. The only thing that gave some cause for concern was KERS. A little over halfway through the race, he was told not to use it.

"We elected to turn it off," said Adrian Newey. "More than anything, just not to cause any reliability problems. If we'd been pushed then we could

LEFT A busy start saw the two Renaults make lightning getaways around the outside from sixth and eighth on the grid, Nick Heidfeld moving into second place, ahead of Lewis Hamilton, and Vitaly Petrov fifth behind Jenson Button

BELOW HRT's new 2011 livery failed to improve the car's pace, F1 returnee Narain Karthikeyan qualifying last and retiring after 14 laps due to overheating

have managed [to use] it – we might have taken a different decision – but by that stage of the race we had a bit of a gap, so we took the safe route."

KERS continued to be RBR's Achilles heel, and the fact that Webber's system packed up right at the start was a major worry. Vettel may have been able to keep up a good race pace without it for the second half the race, but had he been without it at the start this time, it's highly unlikely that he would have made it to Turn One in front.

"The reality is that it's a system in its infancy," said Newey. "We're not a manufacturer team, so we're having to develop KERS ourselves, which hasn't been our area of expertise in the past, and on a limited resource, limited budget and limited experience, so we're on a rapid learning curve. How long it will take us to get to the top of that curve remains to be seen."

Malaysia was a good weekend for McLaren, and specifically Jenson Button. The silver cars were quick all weekend, and close enough to the Red Bull to really pile on the pressure in qualifying.

In the race, Button did a perfect job, and while he was fourth and behind his team-mate early on,

what mattered was that he'd edged his way into second by the end, and was close enough to Vettel to keep the German on his toes. Intriguingly, he was happiest on the hard tyres in the closing laps. Over the winter there had been a lot of talk about Button's smooth style potentially saving his tyres.

"Jenson did a great, patient job," said Martin Whitmarsh. "He thought the car was at its best at the end. We could see how long the stint was, so we were urging him to take it easy. Ten laps to go he was urging us – he wanted to push, he was saying let's see what Red Bull's got.

"We were saying 'no don't do that, look after the tyres!' He felt he was right in the sweet spot. At some point he was catching or maintaining the gap to Sebastian. I think by then Sebastian was controlling that to a little degree as well, and we felt 'why take the risk and let the tyres go off?' We had another driver who was having a torrid time with the tyres at that time…"

We didn't get to see what might have happened had Hamilton been able to stick with Vettel at the start – but even if he had got ahead at some stage, Lewis would still have got into the tyre problems that he faced in his fourth stint.

"The launch was fine, it was a reasonable start," said Whitmarsh. "The Renaults attacked down the outside, and I think it was a good clean attack. Lewis was a bit bottled up on the inside. Thereafter he was behind Nick, who had good end-of-straight speed, better than ours. And therefore it was difficult to deal with it, and therefore he lost time.

"When we stopped, I guess he was 7–8secs behind Sebastian. At the end of that run it was probably only 4secs, and he'd passed Nick, so that was a reasonable position to be in. For the next stop he didn't quite get away cleanly on the paddles, so he came out behind Petrov. That cost him a little bit,

TALKING POINT
THE THINGS PEOPLE DO

Ten days between Oz and Malaysia – a chance for drivers to relax in the sun, do some light training and prepare for the humidity of Sepang? Jenson Button was more ambitious. He flew to Hawaii with trainer Mike Collier to compete in the Lavaman Triathlon – a 1,500m swim, 40km cycle ride and 10km run.

The winner was 25-year-old German

Erich Wegscheider, a professional triathlete making his debut in the elite ranks, who completed the event in 1h53m31s, with a 3min winning margin despite only taking the lead midway through the run from John Flanagan, who only just came up short at the US Olympic open water swimming trials. Wegscheider averaged 5m34s per mile for the 6.25-mile run, his benchmark 10km time being 34m25s.

Button finished 191st (2h39m18s) of the 1,039 competitors, which might not sound remarkable, but wait… What you need to know is that Jenson suffered a puncture on the cycling leg and sat by the roadside awaiting a replacement wheel for half an hour.

Wegscheider took 20m23s for his open water near-mile swim; Button's time was 23m03s – which ranked Jenson 51st at that discipline.

Remarkably, though, Jenson's 10km time of 37m34s, which translates to a pace of 6m04s per mile, was beaten by only eight athletes – highly impressive in such company.

The fastest cycling leg was Wegscheider again, in 57m18s, with Jenson's puncture resulting in an unrepresentative 1h36m16s. If you average out 51st and ninth from the other two disciplines and give Jenson a top 30 bike time instead, you arrive at an event time of 2h05m42s, which would have placed him 18th overall!

Button is keen to tackle the full Iron Man extreme distance, but McLaren is less enthusiastic – it can take two months to properly recover!

"When you're doing a triathlon, you're aiming to be at the top end of your aerobic capacity just before you dip into your maximal," explained

Collier. "What we do, very much for the start of the year, is work on base endurance – the reason being that it's the stuff that really brings drivers' weights down. You want them to be as lean as they possibly can be and Jenson, at the moment, has about 8% body fat.

"Once you know their racing weight you can play around a bit. We are aiming to compete in the London Triathlon in August, and so between now and then we will work a little bit more on the aerobic stuff and towards anaerobic higher-end training. That's why we were really pleased to see that 10km time now."

So much for relaxation… Button's inspiration, apparently, came from meeting a trio of Iron Man triathletes training in Lanzarote, and taking some tips.

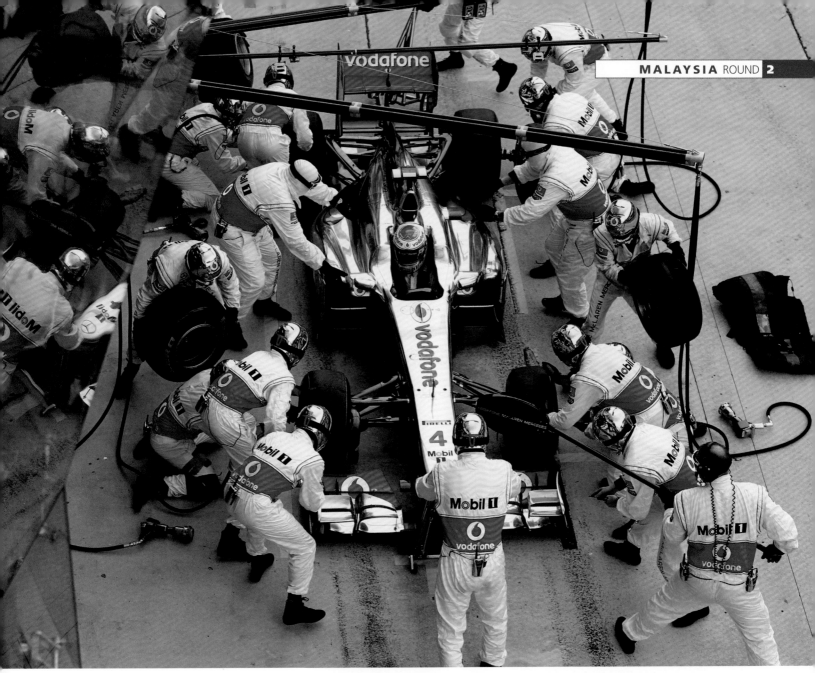

but he got past. For the next stint he was on a new prime, and it was fine, he was more or less matching Vettel [on options].

"Then, for what we hoped would be his last stop, we had a used prime. He stopped a bit short, so the gunman had to re-adjust, so he lost a second or two there, that put him behind Jenson, and he was also having to defend from Webber at that point. And he just couldn't get those tyres going..."

A three-stopper requires four sets, and for most drivers who made Q3 that meant taking the start on the options they set their times on, followed by two stints on options they used earlier in qualifying, and then a run to the finish on new primes.

Hamilton wasn't able to do that for the simple reason that due to a brake-locking moment one of his option sets couldn't be used. That meant his third stint had to be on the new primes, and they actually worked quite well. The problem was the fourth stint – and for that he had to use primes that had already been run in qualifying.

The team had no reason to suspect that they would be troublesome – used options worked fine for everybody – but that particular set proved

ABOVE Lewis Hamilton and Fernando Alonso battled hard on lap 45, resulting in eventual contact that forced the Ferrari driver to pit for a new nose. Both drivers were hit with 20s penalties after the race

BELOW Sebastian Vettel shares the victory champagne with Red Bull Racing's Chief Technical Officer, Adrian Newey

disastrous for Lewis, who couldn't get up to speed. And it was while using them that he got into a spectacular fight with Fernando Alonso, who was himself handicapped by an inoperative DRS. In the end, Lewis got so fed up with that set that he insisted on coming in with just four laps to go. It cost him a spot to Alonso, so the team wasn't entirely happy.

"He was immediately in defensive mode, and it was a question of getting the tyres overheated, or struggling with them," said Whitmarsh. "We obviously wanted to go to the end on those tyres, but in the end the driver's got to make the call. He felt he had to stop.

"He was twice behind Renaults, which was unhelpful, a couple of little stops which weren't quite right, but having to run a used prime was probably the real race-influencing factor."

When Lewis came in for the rubber equivalent of a 'splash and dash', the team literally had only his sixth-best set available, also primes that had done some mileage on Saturday. They were good enough to cover those last four laps, but it was hardly ideal.

After dropping back in the middle of the race, Heidfeld took advantage of trouble for others to climb back up to a superb third. He finished ahead of Webber, who dropped down to ninth at the start. He then used a four-stop strategy to move up the order, despite his lack of KERS. He ran mini-stints of 10–12–10–11–13 laps, always ensuring that he was on reasonably fresh rubber, while also using those stops to find clean air.

Felipe Massa was fifth, after losing valuable time with a stuck wheel at his first pit stop. He headed home Alonso, who, as already mentioned, was hampered when his DRS failed early on. Later in the race, the Spaniard was challenging Hamilton for third when he damaged his front wing, and had to make an extra pit stop.

Hamilton's aforementioned struggles dropped him to seventh. After the race, Alonso received a 20s penalty for causing a collision with the Brit. It would have dropped him behind Hamilton, but ironically Lewis received a similar penalty for changing his line more than once while defending his position. Alonso thus retained sixth, while Lewis dropped back to eighth.

Seventh went instead to Kamui Kobayashi, who battled with Michael Schumacher for much of the race, eventually finishing ahead of the German's Mercedes, while Paul di Resta took an impressive tenth place for Force India.

SNAPSHOT FROM
MALAYSIA

CLOCKWISE FROM RIGHT
Kamui Kobayashi speeds past
Sepang's distinctive grandstands
during Friday practice; a marshal
operates the circuitside signalling
lights from the FIA control box;
Pirelli's engineers attempt to create
a 'human' F1 car; a warm welcome
always awaits visitors to Malaysia;
Sebastian Vettel visualises his lap
before heading out for qualifying;
Bernie Ecclestone has an animated
conversation on his mobile; Red Bull
Racing's Adrian Newey weighs up
the opposition in *parc fermé* after
the race; Nick Heidfeld celebrates
his well-earned third place with the
Renault team; a pensive Michael
Schumacher seen in the viewfinder
of one of the TV cameras

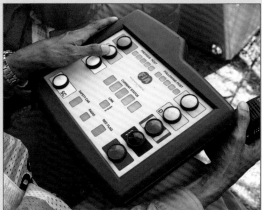

RACE RESULTS
MALAYSIA
SEPANG

Official Results © [2011]
Formula One Administration Limited,
6 Princes Gate, London, SW7 1QJ.
No reproduction without permission.
All copyright and database rights reserved.

RACE DATE April 10th
CIRCUIT LENGTH 3.444 miles
NO. OF LAPS 56
RACE DISTANCE 192.864 miles
WEATHER Bright and humid, 30°C
TRACK TEMP 37°C
ATTENDANCE 105,018
LAP RECORD Juan Pablo Montoya, 1m34.223s, 131.991mph, 2004

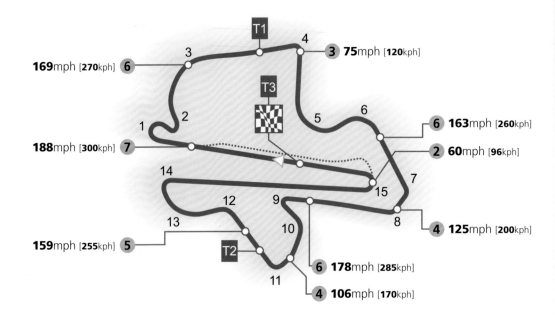

PRACTICE 1

	Driver	Time	Laps
1	M Webber	1m37.651s	22
2	L Hamilton	1m39.316s	16
3	M Schumacher	1m39.791s	29
4	N Hulkenberg	1m40.377s	23
5	P Maldonado	1m40.443s	31
6	F Massa	1m40.453s	22
7	N Heidfeld	1m40.525s	6
8	R Barrichello	1m40.581s	21
9	F Alonso	1m40.601s	23
10	N Rosberg	1m40.646s	29
11	A Sutil	1m40.734s	21
12	D Ricciardo	1m40.748s	23
13	J Alguersuari	1m40.770s	24
14	K Kobayashi	1m40.872s	27
15	J Button	1m40.927s	16
16	J Trulli	1m41.620s	21
17	S Vettel	1m41.627s	18
18	S Perez	1m41.642s	24
19	T Glock	1m42.154s	18
20	J d'Ambrosio	1m42.540s	20
21	D Valsecchi	1m44.054s	18
22	V Liuzzi	1m45.228s	20
23	N Karthikeyan	1m46.267s	10
24	V Petrov	1m47.932s	4

PRACTICE 2

	Driver	Time	Laps
1	M Webber	1m36.876s	24
2	J Button	1m36.881s	30
3	L Hamilton	1m37.010s	23
4	S Vettel	1m37.090s	30
5	M Schumacher	1m38.088s	26
6	F Massa	1m38.089s	31
7	N Rosberg	1m38.565s	25
8	N Heidfeld	1m38.570s	16
9	F Alonso	1m38.583s	27
10	J Alguersuari	1m38.846s	31
11	P Maldonado	1m38.968s	25
12	R Barrichello	1m39.187s	30
13	V Petrov	1m39.267s	17
14	K Kobayashi	1m39.398s	29
15	S Perez	1m39.603s	34
16	P di Resta	1m39.625s	31
17	A Sutil	1m39.809s	28
18	S Buemi	1m40.115s	31
19	T Glock	1m40.866s	24
20	J Trulli	1m41.890s	19
21	N Karthikeyan	1m43.197s	15
22	V Liuzzi	1m43.991s	14
23	H Kovalainen	1m44.886s	4
24	J d'Ambrosio	No time	0

PRACTICE 3

	Driver	Time	Laps
1	L Hamilton	1m36.340s	11
2	M Webber	1m36.630s	16
3	J Button	1m36.762s	14
4	N Heidfeld	1m37.115s	14
5	S Vettel	1m37.175s	14
6	F Alonso	1m37.284s	11
7	V Petrov	1m37.297s	17
8	F Massa	1m37.762s	12
9	K Kobayashi	1m38.059s	18
10	M Schumacher	1m38.300s	20
11	N Rosberg	1m38.307s	20
12	S Perez	1m38.448s	17
13	A Sutil	1m38.464s	16
14	P Maldonado	1m38.597s	15
15	S Buemi	1m38.665s	14
16	R Barrichello	1m38.681s	16
17	J Alguersuari	1m38.716s	14
18	P di Resta	1m38.864s	13
19	H Kovalainen	1m39.260s	19
20	J Trulli	1m39.699s	15
21	J d'Ambrosio	1m41.215s	17
22	T Glock	1m41.414s	18
23	V Liuzzi	1m43.147s	6
24	N Karthikeyan	1m43.383s	11

QUALIFYING 1

	Driver	Time
1	F Massa	1m36.744s
2	L Hamilton	1m36.861s
3	F Alonso	1m36.897s
4	M Schumacher	1m36.904s
5	K Kobayashi	1m36.994s
6	J Button	1m37.033s
7	V Petrov	1m37.210s
8	N Heidfeld	1m37.224s
9	N Rosberg	1m37.316s
10	S Vettel	1m37.468s
11	J Alguersuari	1m37.677s
12	A Sutil	1m37.693s
13	S Buemi	1m37.693s
14	S Perez	1m37.759s
15	M Webber	1m37.924s
16	P di Resta	1m38.045s
17	R Barrichello	1m38.163s
18	P Maldonado	1m38.276s
19	H Kovalainen	1m38.645s
20	J Trulli	1m38.791s
21	T Glock	1m40.648s
22	J d'Ambrosio	1m41.001s
23	V Liuzzi	1m41.549s
24	N Karthikeyan	1m42.574s

QUALIFYING 2

	Driver	Time
1	J Button	1m35.569s
2	L Hamilton	1m35.852s
3	S Vettel	1m35.934s
4	M Webber	1m36.080s
5	F Alonso	1m36.320s
6	N Rosberg	1m36.388s
7	F Massa	1m36.557s
8	V Petrov	1m36.642s
9	K Kobayashi	1m36.691s
10	N Heidfeld	1m36.811s
11	M Schumacher	1m37.035s
12	S Buemi	1m37.160s
13	J Alguersuari	1m37.347s
14	P di Resta	1m37.370s
15	R Barrichello	1m37.496s
16	S Perez	1m37.528s
17	A Sutil	1m37.593s

Best sectors – Practice

Sec 1	V Petrov	24.891s
Sec 2	L Hamilton	32.173s
Sec 3	L Hamilton	39.185s

Speed trap – Practice

1	P di Resta	192.500mph
2	N Rosberg	192.438mph
3	A Sutil	192.190mph

Best sectors – Qualifying

Sec 1	S Vettel	24.665s
Sec 2	S Vettel	31.569s
Sec 3	L Hamilton	38.617s

Speed trap – Qualifying

1	A Sutil	193.495mph
2	M Schumacher	193.246mph
3	N Rosberg	192.998mph

Sebastian Vettel

"I made a good start, then I saw Lewis behind me so I was surprised going into Turn 1, as I saw something black in my mirrors. It was a good thing."

Jenson Button

"I took a lot of wing out, which was a mistake as I had understeer which also hurt the rears. I dialled in more front wing at each stop and my pace kept getting better."

Fernando Alonso

"If the movable rear wing had worked all the time, I could have passed Hamilton. He defended well and, unfortunately, we touched: that broke my wing."

Michael Schumacher

"My race was exciting near the end, but full of ups and downs before. It was mainly about managing the tyres. However, we have to work on our race pace."

Nick Heidfeld

"I moved up to P2 at the start, but Sebastian was much quicker. Later, I got lucky with Alonso having a problem, but it was great getting ahead of Lewis."

Rubens Barrichello

"A hydraulic problem forced me out. I was running at the back when we had to retire due to an early stop to change a punctured tyre picked up after a collision."

Mark Webber

"We had KERS failure and, for the first four laps, I was trying to pass cars, but they were coming back at me on the straights. I fought back with a good strategy."

Lewis Hamilton

"There were a lot of factors that made it hard: the delay at the stop, being chased by two cars when I was trying to look after my tyres, being hit by Fernando."

Felipe Massa

"It was a shame to have lost time at my first stop: but for that problem I could have fought my way to the podium, as my pace was very good with the soft tyres."

Nico Rosberg

"I had a poor start which made it very hard to score. Our pace wasn't good enough, and it was difficult to push, so we couldn't perform at the level we wanted."

Vitaly Petrov

"It was a strong run in an unusual race. I made a mistake which shouldn't have had the effect it had. I went wide and the car took off on the kerb, landing hard."

Pastor Maldonado

"I had a misfire from lap 3. I tried to stay out, but we had to bring the car in. I'm now looking ahead to China where I'll be pushing to complete a race distance."

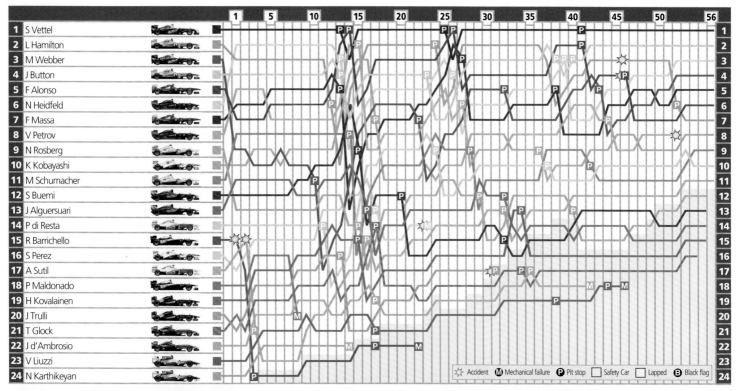

1	S Vettel	
2	L Hamilton	
3	M Webber	
4	J Button	
5	F Alonso	
6	N Heidfeld	
7	F Massa	
8	V Petrov	
9	N Rosberg	
10	K Kobayashi	
11	M Schumacher	
12	S Buemi	
13	J Alguersuari	
14	P di Resta	
15	R Barrichello	
16	S Perez	
17	A Sutil	
18	P Maldonado	
19	H Kovalainen	
20	J Trulli	
21	T Glock	
22	J d'Ambrosio	
23	V Liuzzi	
24	N Karthikeyan	

☆ Accident Ⓜ Mechanical failure Ⓟ Pit stop ☐ Safety Car ☐ Lapped Ⓑ Black flag

QUALIFYING 3

	Driver	Time
1	S Vettel	1m34.870s
2	L Hamilton	1m34.974s
3	M Webber	1m35.179s
4	J Button	1m35.200s
5	F Alonso	1m35.802s
6	N Heidfeld	1m36.124s
7	F Massa	1m36.251s
8	V Petrov	1m36.324s
9	N Rosberg	1m36.809s
10	K Kobayashi	1m36.820s

GRID

	Driver	Time
1	S Vettel	1m34.870s
2	L Hamilton	1m34.974s
3	M Webber	1m35.179s
4	J Button	1m35.200s
5	F Alonso	1m35.802s
6	N Heidfeld	1m36.124s
7	F Massa	1m36.251s
8	V Petrov	1m36.324s
9	N Rosberg	1m36.809s
10	K Kobayashi	1m36.820s
11	M Schumacher	1m37.035s
12	S Buemi	1m37.160s
13	J Alguersuari	1m37.347s
14	P di Resta	1m37.370s
15	R Barrichello	1m37.496s
16	S Perez	1m37.528s
17	A Sutil	1m37.593s
18	P Maldonado	1m38.276s
19	H Kovalainen	1m38.645s
20	J Trulli	1m38.791s
21	T Glock	1m40.648s
22	J d'Ambrosio	1m41.001s
23	V Liuzzi	1m41.549s
24	N Karthikeyan	1m42.574s

RACE

	Driver	Car	Laps	Time	Avg. mph	Fastest	Stops
1	S Vettel	Red Bull-Renault RB7	56	1h37m39.832s	118.495	1m41.539s	3
2	J Button	McLaren-Mercedes MP4-26	56	1h37m43.093s	118.435	1m41.264s	3
3	N Heidfeld	Renault R31	56	1h38m04.907s	117.996	1m41.547s	3
4	M Webber	Red Bull-Renault RB7	56	1h38m06.216s	117.970	1m40.571s	4
5	F Massa	Ferrari 150 Italia	56	1h38m16.790s	117.758	1m41.999s	3
6	F Alonso	Ferrari 150 Italia	56	1h38m37.080s*	117.355	1m40.717s	4
7	K Kobayashi	Sauber-Ferrari C30	56	1h38m46.271s	117.173	1m42.095s	2
8	L Hamilton	McLaren-Mercedes MP4-26	56	1h38m49.789s**	117.103	1m41.512s	4
9	M Schumacher	Mercedes MGP W02	56	1h39m04.728s	116.809	1m42.491s	3
10	P di Resta	Force India-Mercedes VJM04	56	1h39m11.395s	116.678	1m42.883s	3
11	A Sutil	Force India-Mercedes VJM04	56	1h39m21.211s	116.486	1m42.973s	3
12	N Rosberg	Mercedes MGP W02	55	1h37m45.770s	116.267	1m41.778s	3
13	S Buemi	Toro Rosso-Ferrari STR6	55	1h38m13.721s	115.716	1m42.659s	3
14	J Alguersuari	Toro Rosso-Ferrari STR6	55	1h38m23.108s	115.532	1m43.744s	2
15	H Kovalainen	Lotus-Renault T128	55	1h38m23.523s	115.524	1m43.677s	2
16	T Glock	Virgin-Cosworth MVR-02	54	1h37m52.361s	114.026	1m43.357s	2
17	V Petrov	Renault R31	52	Steering	-	1m41.054s	3
R	V Liuzzi	HRT-Cosworth F111	46	Handling	-	1m46.521s	3
R	J d'Ambrosio	Virgin-Cosworth MVR-02	42	Electrical	-	1m45.346s	2
R	J Trulli	Lotus-Renault T128	31	Clutch	-	1m45.280s	1
R	S Perez	Sauber-Ferrari C30	23	Electrical	-	1m43.298s	1
R	R Barrichello	Williams-Cosworth FW33	22	Hydraulics	-	1m45.516s	2
R	N Karthikeyan	HRT-Cosworth F111	14	Overheating	-	1m49.385s	0
R	P Maldonado	Williams-Cosworth FW33	8	Misfire	-	1m45.689s	0

* 20s penalty for causing a collision with Hamilton   ** 20s penalty for making more than one change of direction in defending against Alonso

CHAMPIONSHIP

	Driver	Pts
1	S Vettel	50
2	J Button	26
3	L Hamilton	22
4	M Webber	22
5	F Alonso	20
6	F Massa	16
7	N Heidfeld	15
8	V Petrov	15
9	K Kobayashi	6
10	S Buemi	4
11	A Sutil	2
12	M Schumacher	2
13	P di Resta	2

	Constructor	Pts
1	Red Bull-Renault	72
2	McLaren-Mercedes	48
3	Ferrari	36
4	Renault	30
5	Sauber-Ferrari	6
6	Toro Rosso-Ferrari	4
7	Force India-Mercedes	4
8	Mercedes	2

Fastest lap
M Webber 1m40.571s
(123.295mph) on lap 46

Fastest speed trap
N Heidfeld 186.162mph
Slowest speed trap
N Karthikeyan 174.978mph

Fastest pit stop
1 S Vettel 21.893s
2 M Webber 21.991s
3 M Webber 22.069s

Adrian Sutil
"The first few laps weren't brilliant, as I lost my front wing touching Barrichello's rear tyre. Then I pitted for the softs, then another set of hards, then softs."

Kamui Kobayashi
"I had a good car, the team did a great job, and I'm happy we scored our first points. The strategy with only two stops was a bit risky, but it worked out well."

Sebastien Buemi
"I made a good start, but at my first stop I thought the limiter hadn't been engaged. I pressed it, which deactivated it, so I sped in the pitlane and got a stop-go."

Jarno Trulli
"The anti-stall kicked in, but I recovered. After the first stop I locked a front wheel and had to make up ground again. I got by Timo, but then the clutch failed."

Narain Karthikeyan
"I'd have liked to have finished, but didn't. There were some problems with the water temperatures so we had to retire in order to not damage the engine."

Timo Glock
"I got ahead of Trulli into Turn 1, but was only able to defend the position for so long. I was able to look after the tyres, so we could stick to a two-stop strategy."

Paul di Resta
"I'm quite happy, but I couldn't hold off Michael, as he had fresh tyres and we had to stop earlier for my third stop than predicted. I didn't want to risk the point."

Sergio Perez
"Something came off Buemi's car which hit my car. The extinguisher went off and the electrics cut out. It was a shame I couldn't finish the race, as the car felt good."

Jaime Alguersuari
"I need to analyse this race with the engineers, as I don't understand what happened: we were slow and the tyre degradation was much higher than on Friday."

Heikki Kovalainen
"That was a good race. The balance was good on both sets of tyres and the strategy worked well. We pitted at the right times and I didn't have any problems."

Vitantonio Liuzzi
"It's a shame I didn't finish, but I had an issue with the rear wing and had to stop. It's a shame as I had a really good start where I was able to pass a few cars."

Jerome d'Ambrosio
"I'm happy, but I won't want to recall that I stopped with less than 15 laps to go, although my goal was to improve on Saturday and Sunday in Melbourne."

2011 FORMULA 1 UBS CHINESE GRAND PRIX
SHANGHAI

LEWIS AT HIS BEST

Lewis Hamilton brought an end to Sebastian Vettel's winning streak with a superb drive at Shanghai, a three-stop strategy enabling him to use fresh tyres to pass Vettel with four laps to go

After the Chinese GP it was hard to find anyone who hadn't enjoyed the race, although the folk at Ferrari were looking a little downbeat. As in Malaysia, people were bubbling about the spectacle they had just witnessed. Grand prix racing 2011-style was starting to look pretty good.

Three races into the season, Lewis Hamilton and McLaren had found a way to unseat the seemingly unstoppable Sebastian Vettel. And while in the end it was pretty close – and Seb still went home with 18 points – Shanghai suggested that there would be plenty of opportunities in 2011 for Red Bull to get things not quite right on Sunday, despite having the fastest car on Saturday.

In Q3 Vettel was a massive 0.7s ahead of Jenson Button, who in turn just edged out McLaren team-mate Hamilton by a mere 0.042s. Nico Rosberg showed that Mercedes had made progress and jumped Ferrari by taking fourth, ahead of Fernando Alonso, who started fifth for the third time in three races.

Missing from Q3 (and indeed Q2) was Mark Webber. The Aussie lost most of the morning practice session to an electronic problem and went into qualifying knowing he wouldn't have KERS. Like the other top drivers, he

made it to Q3 with two sets of soft tyres to spare, Hamilton was able to save a set simply by waiting in the garage when Vettel and Button did their first runs. By keeping a brand-new set, Lewis gave himself maximum flexibility for Sunday.

If Hamilton was feeling confident thanks to that ace up his sleeve, he was to get a fright before the start when the car failed to fire in the garage. It took a huge effort from the crew to get him to the end of the pitlane just seconds before the red light that would have relegated him to a pitlane start. The repair job was finished on the grid, after Lewis drove around with the rear part of his engine cover missing.

At the start, things were to get better, and very quickly, for both Lewis and McLaren. Having failed to take advantage of the Red Bull's KERS-less RB7s in Australia, this time both McLaren drivers charged past Vettel before the first corner to secure a 1–2.

Basically it was tyre performance that dictated the subsequent McLaren strategy, and pointed the team towards three stops rather than the anticipated two.

A bizarre thing happened at the first stops. Somehow, Jenson failed to get the message to stop, and instead of coming in, went sailing past the pits at the end of lap 13. And by complete coincidence, radio problems meant that Vettel – himself due in on lap 13 – also failed to show up in the pitlane. When Button did come in, he tried to stop at RBR's box, distracted, he later said, because he was looking at his steering wheel to make an adjustment.

It had a knock-on effect for Hamilton. He was supposed to come in on lap 14, but because Jenson had to take his slot, he had to wait for one more lap.

It proved to be a double whammy for McLaren. Driving through the RBR pits cost Jenson precious time, and allowed Vettel to jump him. But pushing Hamilton's stop back a lap was just as damaging, because it was a lap too far for the set of tyres that Lewis had worked so hard in qualifying.

ABOVE Polesitter Sebastian Vettel bogged down at the start and the two McLarens swept past, Jenson Button taking the lead

BELOW Button mistakenly enters the Red Bull Racing pit box, delaying Vettel – who waits behind him

OPPOSITE After leading mid-race, Nico Rosberg later battled hard with Felipe Massa, the two finishing fifth and sixth respectively

set a time on the hard tyres early in the session, but as slower cars put on softs, he tumbled down the order.

RBR felt confident that Webber could get through with a second set of hards, thus saving softs for later in the session. However, the car left the garage too late, and instead of getting two laps, the first to warm up the tyres, Webber only got one. It was slower than his earlier lap and he found himself bumped down to 18th. The only consolation was that he had three brand new sets of soft tyres for the race...

Although ultimately it wouldn't play a particularly important role in the race, Hamilton showed some forward thinking. Alone among the top drivers who

INSIDE LINE
LEWIS HAMILTON

McLAREN DRIVER

"We cut it fine in the garage! The car just wouldn't start. It was very, very curious. We have had it not start initially several times in the past, so I thought it was nothing, but as they kept trying it was clearly becoming a concern. I didn't want to be asking questions all the time, so I just said 'how long have we got until the pitlane closes?' It was six minutes, I didn't think it was going to be too big a problem, but in the end I think we made it with 30 seconds to spare. I was nervous that just as I got to the pitlane exit light, it would go red, but fortunately it didn't.

From three-quarters of a second down in qualifying, third on the grid, to the win and 25 points – fantastic! I managed to save a set of tyres in qualifying compared to my rivals, but I don't think that was the only thing. All my tyres were in good condition and without that I wouldn't have overtaken Jenson.

I'm absolutely overwhelmed. It feels like a long, long time since I won. We went out to the last Barcelona test with an upgrade package and it really wasn't working. The reliability was a disaster, we couldn't even get past 20 laps. The team pushed very hard in the space of a week-and-a-half, two weeks, and it was just incredible what they were able to bring to Australia.

Australia was our first race distance, and the car has been great. It really has been great. Red Bull are doing a fantastic job. They are very, very fast. They have got a wonderful car and they are doing the job, and we are pushing with absolutely everything to try and close the gap. I think today we were similar pace in the race, perhaps they were a tiny bit quicker, but I think it was just due to us being a little bit smarter on the strategy and making it work, and fortunately it did today.

I think my emotion at the end just comes from the desire to win, the desire to be better and the desire to compete against the toughest drivers in the world. When you haven't won for a while it feels like an eternity. I was confident going into the race, but for a while I thought I wasn't even going to be in it!"

TALKING POINT
TIME TO THINK?

The Chinese Grand Prix was superb entertainment, but the strategists noted interesting things.

Mark Webber, despite being eliminated in Q1 and starting 18th, was able to finish just 7.5s behind Lewis Hamilton's winning McLaren. He was much further back at the end of the opening lap...

Think about that. He was able to drive a quicker race through traffic than the race winner, who was neither on the wrong strategy nor cruising at the end. Hamilton was as flat-out as the Pirellis allowed him to be as he chased down Rosberg, team-mate Button and the two-stopping Vettel and Massa.

In the past, with a first stint spent in among the tail-enders, such a thing would have been unthinkable. But now that DRS and KERS (although not in Webber's case) have facilitated overtaking, and limited opening-stint time loss, interesting strategy permutations have opened up.

Webber would have been even quicker with an operational KERS, and it would have been interesting to see whether he would have made a net gain on Vettel's sister Red Bull, had Sebastian not been switched to a two-stopper when he lost out to both McLarens on the run to Turn 1. That was clearly a slower overall strategy as things worked out.

"We did that with Sebastian because we thought that it would give him a chance to beat both McLarens, having fallen behind them," Red Bull Team Principal Christian Horner explained.

Webber went into the race with four brand new sets of tyres. His fastest race lap was 1m38.99s. Nobody else even lapped in the 1m39s bracket and his race best was 1.42s quicker than winner Hamilton's.

The question was: would any of the leading teams take Webber's race on board and gamble on trying the same thing, deliberately forsaking Q3?

For sure, you wouldn't want to have to drive a race like Webber's in Shanghai every time out. Chances are that if your races were routinely that 'busy' you would lose a front wing and probably lose out on consistency over time to the more conventional 'run-from-the-front' strategy.

Given what we'd seen of the Ferrari's race speed relative to its single-lap pace, the strategy could have been worth a try for them. Anything that put Ferrari slightly out of sync with everyone else could have worked to its advantage. Against that is the fact that the car was struggling to heat its tyres on one lap, and so taking the prime in Q1 might see it marooned there.

Ferrari may have felt that its tyre-heating issue compromised its ability to make best use of the strategy, but certainly Mercedes and Renault also had enough pace to make it worth a look. It would be interesting to see if there would be any strategy gamblers in future races.

The tyre performance fell over the edge, and Hamilton was passed by Felipe Massa. After the stops he was also behind Rosberg and Vettel, as well as the yet-to-stop Alonso and Vitaly Petrov. Like Lewis, Jenson also lost a little lap time by taking his tyres further than they were intended to go.

"It cost Jenson position and it cost him time," said Martin Whitmarsh of the pit mishap. "Within the stop itself it cost over 2 seconds and it cost a position; the fact that he stopped a lap later than he should have done cost Lewis time and track position as well, as that last lap was when Massa got by and he should have stopped by then.

"It was pretty calamitous, simple way of looking at it. We were first and second, and we were, whatever, fifth and seventh after the first stops, so at that point we knew we had to do something different. That partly prompted the view that we had to change strategy. In the end, that would be the right way to go."

That decision was not confirmed until after the first stops played out. In fact Lewis had taken on his 'magic' new set for the simple reason that the team anticipated a long second stint and two stops. New tyres last for longer, it was as simple as that. The decision to go for three stops, however, meant that Lewis didn't get full use out of his special set, because he didn't need to make use of their longevity after all.

Button came in for the second time on lap 24, and Hamilton on lap 25, both men having run just 10 laps on their second sets of tyres. Meanwhile, RBR responded to the stops for Jenson and Lewis by leaving Vettel out on a two-stopper, on the basis that the team felt firstly that doing something different was the way to beat McLaren, and secondly the RB7's tyre wear was much improved since Australia, and Seb could deal with long stints on his second and third sets.

When Vettel didn't pit McLaren knew straight away that he was on a two-stop strategy, and the true picture of the race emerged. Button and Hamilton now had to make full use of their shorter stints, go as hard as possible, and pass anyone they came up against as soon as they could.

And it was during that third stint that the McLaren boys had their own little fight, Lewis passing Jenson on lap 34 – without any DRS help – in a decisive move at Turn One. Lewis, however, relied on his team-mate leaving him space.

"I don't enjoy those moments, personally,"

OPPOSITE Jaime Alguersuari qualified a career-best seventh, but was forced to retire after losing his right-rear wheel, which had not been tightened correctly at his first pit stop

ABOVE With 12 laps to go, Lewis Hamilton was 4.6s behind leader Sebastian Vettel, but on fresher tyres he chased down the Red Bull to take the lead with six laps to run

They were now on the hard tyres for the run to the flag. Jenson had to run 18 laps, and Lewis 17. Having pitted on lap 31, Vettel had to make his tyres last for 25 laps, and that was where the race was won and lost.

On his first flying lap after that final stop, Lewis was 5.8s behind Vettel. But Rosberg and Massa were between them, so it was far from clear-cut that the McLaren would be able to catch and attack Vettel. But this was the sort of racing that Lewis was born to do. He was soon past Rosberg, hampered by having to run in fuel-conservation mode, and by lap 44 he had taken Massa.

With 12 laps to go, he was 4.6secs behind Vettel. It certainly looked like he could do it, but the chase proved even easier than anyone expected. As Vettel's tyres approached the end of their useful life, he was powerless to stop the McLaren, and DRS played no role in the pass. For the last five laps, Lewis was at the head of the field. It was a truly impressive performance.

"It was a guy who had to keep calm when his car was in bits, pulling out of the garage with seconds to go," said Whitmarsh. "A guy who then had to make a great start, a guy who then had to recover from leading the race to being fifth or sixth after the first stop. He had to be aggressive, but still make his tyres last, and when you're attacking other cars and looking after delicate tyres, that's a real challenge."

"It was always going to be marginal on the two-stop," said Christian Horner of Vettel's race. "But just about achievable, and it very, very nearly worked. We were within four laps of winning the grand prix, having been third at the start.

"Once you commit to it, you've got to go for it, and there's no crystal ball to say it's going to work. It very nearly did for Seb today, and it's still massively valuable points. To be slightly disappointed with second shows how far the team has come..."

Struggling more than Lewis with his rear tyres in the closing laps, Button got by Massa and Rosberg, but then himself fell prey to the flying Webber, and had to settle for fourth.

From 18th on the grid, Webber started on the hard tyre and then ran three stints on the new softs that he hadn't used after his qualifying disaster. Consistently the quickest man on the track, he charged up the order in the closing laps, taking Button for third on the penultimate lap.

"With Mark we ran quite a creative strategy, a three-stop starting on the prime, and he drove a fantastic race," said Horner. "He needed to make it work. He knew before the race that it was going to rely on him making that work, and passing a lot of cars today, and he did exactly that. It was fantastic for him to finish just seven seconds behind the race winner."

Rosberg held on for fifth after his challenge faded over the second half of the race, while Massa's two-stop strategy failed in the same manner as Vettel's, and he tumbled down to sixth after looking like a podium contender early on.

He did at least beat team-mate Alonso, having overtaken the Spaniard at the start. Alonso subsequently lost a lot of time – and spoiled a set of tyres – while trying to fight his way past Michael Schumacher. The latter finished eighth, while the final points went to Petrov and Kamui Kobayashi.

ABOVE Heikki Kovalainen qualified and raced ahead of his team-mate, Jarno Trulli, and finished 16th, ahead of both Sergio Perez's Sauber and Pastor Maldonado's Williams

BELOW After a disastrous qualifying session, Mark Webber drove a stunning race from 18th place on the grid to finish third, making the most of three sets of brand-new soft tyres to carve through the field

Whitmarsh admitted. "But it's very clear that's how we run our team. Jenson was pretty robust as well. He certainly wasn't trying to let him by. I'm always relieved when the two cars separate in one piece after such manoeuvres, but it was good, I'm sure it was great for TV, and if anyone needed to be convinced that our drivers are racing each other, then they got that."

Getting past Button was a crucial move, much like Vettel's pass on Jenson in Australia. Although Lewis was now in front, Jenson still made his final stop first, because now the advantage was to stop later rather than earlier. They came in on laps 37 and 38 respectively, both having done 13 laps on their second sets of soft tyres.

SNAPSHOT FROM
CHINA

CLOCKWISE FROM RIGHT

The circuit's trademark grandstands provide a backdrop to the action; Shanghai's illuminated waterfront skyline; a masked McLaren engineer watches over Lewis Hamilton during a pit stop; the colourful flags of the competing drivers' nations; a squad of mysterious rollerbladers got all fired up before the start, apparently pursued by umbrella-wielding girls in hot pants; a mechanical octopus of cooling fans in the pitlane; two of Sebastian Vettel's fans make their feelings known; the crowd take their positions ready for an action-packed afternoon; the friendly face of Chinese policing; Virgin Racing's Jerome d'Ambrosio prepares to outqualify his team-mate on Saturday

RACE RESULTS
CHINA
SHANGHAI

Official Results © [2011]
Formula One Administration Limited,
6 Princes Gate, London, SW7 1QJ.
No reproduction without permission.
All copyright and database rights reserved.

RACE DATE April 17th
CIRCUIT LENGTH 3.390 miles
NO. OF LAPS 56
RACE DISTANCE 189.680 miles
WEATHER Overcast and dry, 22°C
TRACK TEMP 31°C
ATTENDANCE 163,700
LAP RECORD Michael Schumacher,
1m32.238s, 132.202mph, 2004

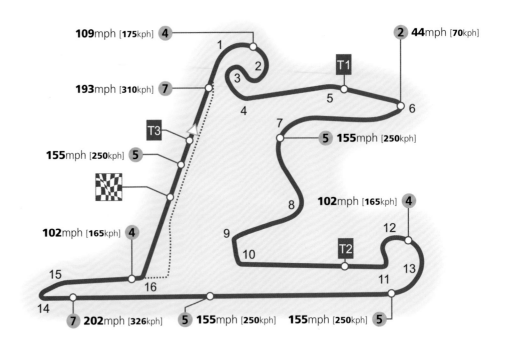

109mph [175kph] 4
2 44mph [70kph]
193mph [310kph] 7
T1
155mph [250kph] 5
155mph [250kph] 5
102mph [165kph] 4
102mph [165kph] 4
T2
202mph [326kph] 7   155mph [250kph] 5   155mph [250kph] 5

PRACTICE 1

	Driver	Time	Laps
1	S Vettel	1m38.739s	23
2	M Webber	1m39.354s	27
3	L Hamilton	1m40.845s	21
4	J Button	1m40.940s	22
5	N Heidfeld	1m40.987s	5
6	F Massa	1m41.046s	25
7	S Perez	1m41.189s	20
8	P Maldonado	1m41.222s	20
9	V Petrov	1m41.231s	16
10	S Buemi	1m41.328s	21
11	N Rosberg	1m41.361s	23
12	F Alonso	1m41.434s	15
13	N Hulkenberg	1m41.494s	20
14	H Kovalainen	1m41.579s	13
15	P di Resta	1m41.610s	18
16	D Ricciardo	1m41.752s	20
17	R Barrichello	1m41.939s	25
18	M Schumacher	1m42.301s	23
19	K Kobayashi	1m43.792s	20
20	J d'Ambrosio	1m44.089s	20
21	V Liuzzi	1m44.359s	18
22	T Glock	1m44.438s	11
23	L Razia	1m44.542s	9
24	N Karthikeyan	1m45.019s	23

PRACTICE 2

	Driver	Time	Laps
1	S Vettel	1m37.688s	34
2	L Hamilton	1m37.854s	22
3	J Button	1m37.935s	31
4	N Rosberg	1m37.943s	34
5	M Schumacher	1m38.105s	29
6	F Massa	1m38.507s	
7	A Sutil	1m38.735s	35
8	N Heidfeld	1m38.805s	26
9	V Petrov	1m38.859s	31
10	M Webber	1m39.327s	33
11	K Kobayashi	1m39.538s	33
12	P Maldonado	1m39.667s	37
13	S Buemi	1m39.771s	18
14	F Alonso	1m39.779s	17
15	J Alguersuari	1m39.828s	25
16	R Barrichello	1m39.925s	32
17	S Perez	1m39.953s	30
18	H Kovalainen	1m40.476s	30
19	J Trulli	1m41.482s	32
20	N Karthikeyan	1m42.902s	25
21	V Liuzzi	1m43.850s	3
22	J d'Ambrosio	1m44.008s	35
23	T Glock	1m44.747s	12
24	P di Resta	No time	0

PRACTICE 3

	Driver	Time	Laps
1	S Vettel	1m34.968s	13
2	J Button	1m35.176s	15
3	L Hamilton	1m35.373s	14
4	N Rosberg	1m35.677s	18
5	F Alonso	1m35.818s	17
6	F Massa	1m35.971s	15
7	V Petrov	1m36.098s	18
8	A Sutil	1m36.125s	15
9	M Schumacher	1m36.141s	14
10	P di Resta	1m36.370s	18
11	N Heidfeld	1m36.404s	16
12	K Kobayashi	1m36.582s	18
13	S Perez	1m36.596s	17
14	S Buemi	1m36.717s	16
15	M Webber	1m36.896s	5
16	J Alguersuari	1m36.953s	14
17	R Barrichello	1m37.007s	20
18	P Maldonado	1m37.304s	18
19	H Kovalainen	1m38.176s	12
20	J Trulli	1m38.739s	12
21	T Glock	1m39.938s	17
22	J d'Ambrosio	1m39.998s	16
23	V Liuzzi	1m40.593s	17
24	N Karthikeyan	1m40.881s	18

QUALIFYING 1

	Driver	Time
1	N Rosberg	1m35.272s
2	V Petrov	1m35.370s
3	F Alonso	1m35.389s
4	F Massa	1m35.478s
5	M Schumacher	1m35.508s
6	S Vettel	1m35.674s
7	P di Resta	1m35.702s
8	N Heidfeld	1m35.910s
9	R Barrichello	1m35.911s
10	J Button	1m35.924s
11	S Perez	1m36.046s
12	L Hamilton	1m36.091s
13	A Sutil	1m36.092s
14	S Buemi	1m36.110s
15	P Maldonado	1m36.121s
16	J Alguersuari	1m36.133s
17	K Kobayashi	1m36.147s
18	M Webber	1m36.468s
19	H Kovalainen	1m37.894s
20	J Trulli	1m38.318s
21	J d'Ambrosio	1m39.119s
22	T Glock	1m39.708s
23	V Liuzzi	1m40.212s
24	N Karthikeyan	1m40.445s

QUALIFYING 2

	Driver	Time
1	L Hamilton	1m34.486s
2	J Button	1m34.662s
3	S Vettel	1m34.776s
4	V Petrov	1m35.149s
5	F Alonso	1m35.165s
6	F Massa	1m35.437s
7	S Buemi	1m35.500s
8	J Alguersuari	1m35.563s
9	N Rosberg	1m35.850s
10	P di Resta	1m35.858s
11	A Sutil	1m35.874s
12	S Perez	1m36.053s
13	K Kobayashi	1m36.236s
14	M Schumacher	1m36.457s
15	R Barrichello	1m36.465s
16	N Heidfeld	1m36.611s
17	P Maldonado	1m36.956s

Best sectors – Practice

Sec 1	S Vettel	25.094s
Sec 2	S Vettel	28.334s
Sec 3	L Hamilton	41.487s

Speed trap – Practice

1	S Buemi	201.883mph
2	V Petrov	200.454mph
3	N Heidfeld	200.205mph

Best sectors – Qualifying

Sec 1	S Vettel	24.839s
Sec 2	S Vettel	27.936s
Sec 3	S Vettel	40.931s

Speed trap – Qualifying

1	N Heidfeld	200.454mph
2	V Petrov	200.392mph
3	P Maldonado	200.081mph

Sebastian Vettel
"I lost places to Jenson and Lewis at the start. I came out in the lead and tried to stay on two stops, but I was out on the hard tyre and could see Lewis closing in."

Jenson Button
"I lost out to Sebastian at the first stop. I was looking at the steering wheel to adjust a switch: when I looked up, I thought I was in my box, but it was Red Bull's."

Fernando Alonso
"I made a bad start, Felipe got by me and a Force India nearly did the same. After the first stop, I lost too much time behind Michael, losing touch with the leaders."

Michael Schumacher
"That was a lot of racing. I had a lot of fun and I'm pleased to see the hard work of our guys paid off this weekend. We have made a big step forward with our car."

Nick Heidfeld
"My start was poor, but I was aggressive into Turn 1 and made up a few places. Then I began having KERS problems and couldn't always use full power."

Rubens Barrichello
"We ran a two-stop strategy, while others did three, but I don't think that it made much of a difference, as the car just isn't performing as well as it should."

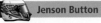

Mark Webber
"I made a mistake at Turn 2 on my in-lap and my race went from there. I was 17th after 15 laps, but I had a few sets of tyres left from qualifying, so that really helped."

Lewis Hamilton
"This race is in my top three of wins, with Silverstone and Monaco in 2008. I exist, I live and I breathe to win: I love winning and I couldn't be happier."

Felipe Massa
"It's a shame not finishing higher. It seems, from qualifying to race, that we discover another car: yesterday, we weren't on the pace, today we fought with the leaders."

Nico Rosberg
"We have made a big step and will have better races in future. Leading the race for such a long time was great, but we had some issues with fuel consumption."

Vitaly Petrov
"To finish ninth is good, since we didn't qualify well. As the strategy was OK, we're annoyed that we didn't challenge higher up the order and gain more points."

Pastor Maldonado
"I'm pleased that we finished, as we have more data to analyse how the FW33 is working over a race distance. My car felt OK, but we need to find more speed."

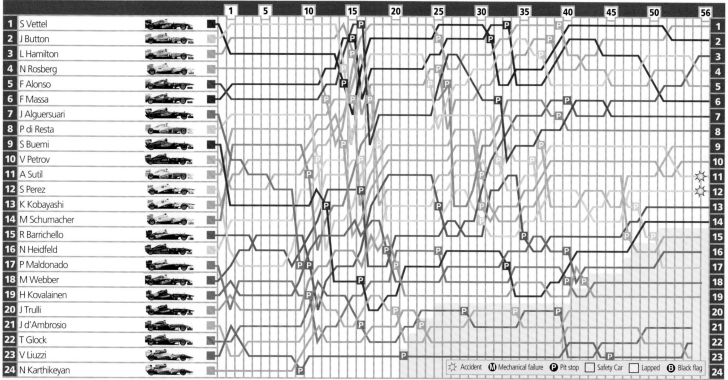

1	S Vettel		
2	J Button		
3	L Hamilton		
4	N Rosberg		
5	F Alonso		
6	F Massa		
7	J Alguersuari		
8	P di Resta		
9	S Buemi		
10	V Petrov		
11	A Sutil		
12	S Perez		
13	K Kobayashi		
14	M Schumacher		
15	R Barrichello		
16	N Heidfeld		
17	P Maldonado		
18	M Webber		
19	H Kovalainen		
20	J Trulli		
21	J d'Ambrosio		
22	T Glock		
23	V Liuzzi		
24	N Karthikeyan		

Accident · M Mechanical failure · P Pit stop · Safety Car · Lapped · B Black flag

QUALIFYING 3

	Driver	Time
1	S Vettel	1m33.706s
2	J Button	1m34.421s
3	L Hamilton	1m34.463s
4	N Rosberg	1m34.670s
5	F Alonso	1m35.119s
6	F Massa	1m35.145s
7	J Alguersuari	1m36.158s
8	P di Resta	1m36.190s
9	S Buemi	1m36.203s
10	V Petrov	No time

GRID

	Driver	Time
1	S Vettel	1m33.706s
2	J Button	1m34.421s
3	L Hamilton	1m34.463s
4	N Rosberg	1m34.670s
5	F Alonso	1m35.119s
6	F Massa	1m35.145s
7	J Alguersuari	1m36.158s
8	P di Resta	1m36.190s
9	S Buemi	1m36.203s
10	V Petrov	No time
11	A Sutil	1m35.874s
12	S Perez	1m36.053s
13	K Kobayashi	1m36.236s
14	M Schumacher	1m36.457s
15	R Barrichello	1m36.465s
16	N Heidfeld	1m36.611s
17	P Maldonado	1m36.956s
18	M Webber	1m36.468s
19	H Kovalainen	1m37.894s
20	J Trulli	1m38.318s
21	J d'Ambrosio	1m39.119s
22	T Glock	1m39.708s
23	V Liuzzi	1m40.212s
24	N Karthikeyan	1m40.445s

RACE

	Driver	Car	Laps	Time	Avg. mph	Fastest	Stops
1	L Hamilton	McLaren-Mercedes MP4-26	56	1h36m58.226s	117.294	1m40.415s	3
2	S Vettel	Red Bull-Renault RB7	56	1h37m03.424s	117.190	1m41.321s	2
3	M Webber	Red Bull-Renault RB7	56	1h37m05.781s	117.142	1m38.993s	3
4	J Button	McLaren-Mercedes MP4-26	56	1h37m08.226s	117.093	1m40.623s	3
5	N Rosberg	Mercedes MGP W02	56	1h37m11.674s	117.024	1m41.166s	3
6	F Massa	Ferrari 150 Italia	56	1h37m14.066s	116.976	1m41.678s	2
7	F Alonso	Ferrari 150 Italia	56	1h37m28.848s	116.680	1m42.070s	2
8	M Schumacher	Mercedes MGP W02	56	1h37m29.252s	116.672	1m41.215s	3
9	V Petrov	Renault R31	56	1h37m55.630s	116.148	1m41.261s	2
10	K Kobayashi	Sauber-Ferrari C30	56	1h38m01.499s	116.032	1m42.577s	2
11	P di Resta	Force India-Mercedes VJM04	56	1h38m06.983s	115.924	1m42.614s	2
12	N Heidfeld	Renault R31	56	1h38m10.965s	115.846	1m42.406s	2
13	R Barrichello	Williams-Cosworth FW33	56	1h38m28.415s	115.504	1m42.031s	2
14	S Buemi	Toro Rosso-Ferrari STR6	56	1h38m28.897s	115.494	1m41.696s	3
15	A Sutil	Force India-Mercedes VJM04	55	1h36m58.956s	115.185	1m41.157s	3
16	H Kovalainen	Lotus-Renault T128	55	1h37m12.024s	114.927	1m42.672s	2
17	S Perez	Sauber-Ferrari C30	55	1h37m15.434s	114.860	1m41.643s	3
18	P Maldonado	Williams-Cosworth FW33	55	1h37m20.363s	114.763	1m41.702s	3
19	J Trulli	Lotus-Renault T128	55	1h37m34.174s	114.492	1m42.052s	2
20	J d'Ambrosio	Virgin-Cosworth MVR-02	54	1h37m24.115s	112.604	1m44.806s	2
21	T Glock	Virgin-Cosworth MVR-02	54	1h37m54.356s	112.025	1m44.381s	2
22	V Liuzzi	HRT-Cosworth F111	54	1h38m12.137s	111.687	1m43.384s	2
23	N Karthikeyan	HRT-Cosworth F111	54	1h38m13.309s	111.664	1m46.081s	1
R	J Alguersuari	Toro Rosso-Ferrari STR6	9	Lost wheel	-	1m45.700s	1

CHAMPIONSHIP

	Driver	Pts
1	S Vettel	68
2	L Hamilton	47
3	J Button	38
4	M Webber	37
5	F Alonso	26
6	F Massa	24
7	V Petrov	17
8	N Heidfeld	15
9	N Rosberg	10
10	K Kobayashi	7
11	M Schumacher	6
12	S Buemi	4
13	A Sutil	2
14	di Resta	2

	Constructor	Pts
1	Red Bull-Renault	105
2	McLaren-Mercedes	85
3	Ferrari	50
4	Renault	32
5	Mercedes	16
6	Sauber-Ferrari	7
7	Toro Rosso-Ferrari	4
8	Force India-Mercedes	4

Fastest lap
M Webber 1m38.993s
(123.181mph) on lap 42

Fastest speed trap
V Petrov 200.827mph
Slowest speed trap
N Karthikeyan 190.885mph

Fastest pit stop
1 M Schumacher 20.522s
2 L Hamilton 20.533s
3 L Hamilton 20.567s

Adrian Sutil
"I was unlucky with the incident with Perez, but I also had tyre problems, as they didn't last as long as we thought and I was just struggling the whole time."

Kamui Kobayashi
"When I got close to Adrian we came across another driver who didn't see me. We touched and I got a hole in my nose. Later, I did the last 26 laps on the hard tyres."

Sebastien Buemi
"I'm frustrated that I failed to score. I had a poor start, got passed by Heidfeld, then began to feel understeer, so we changed the wing, meaning an extra stop."

Jarno Trulli
"I had a good start and then Heikki and I pulled away from the cars behind. My first stop wasn't great and I'm still having issues with the tyre degradation."

Narain Karthikeyan
"We met our main objective which was to finish. I don't think the Virgins are that far ahead of us, which is good for future races. We now have to improve the car."

Timo Glock
"I had a good start, managed to stay in front of the HRT and passed Jerome when he had a moment. But a wheel didn't go on in the last stop, delaying me."

Paul di Resta
"I came very close to scoring, but just missed out at the end when the tyres had gone. Having gone into the race without heavy fuel runs may have compromised us."

Sergio Perez
"I lost places at the first corner. I wanted to get the most out of my tyres, as I was pressed by Vitaly, but lost the rear when I was on the inside of Adrian and hit him."

Vitaly Petrov
"I struggled for grip from the rear tyres, so we decided to pit early. Then, straight after leaving the pits, the car felt unstable and then a wheel came off."

Heikki Kovalainen
"That is our best performance. It's not the highest place, but we beat two midfield cars in a straight fight, so I'm happy, with my performance and the team's."

Vitantonio Liuzzi
"We performed better than in Malaysia and closed the gap on Virgin. But I had a drive-through penalty due to a problem at the start where I moved too soon."

Jerome d'Ambrosio
"I'm very pleased with my race. I made progress throughout the meeting and my pace was much better than in the previous two races, which is also good."

2011 FORMULA 1 DHL TURKISH GRAND PRIX
ISTANBUL

THREE OUT OF FOUR

Sebastian Vettel recovered from a heavy crash in practice to dominate qualifying and the race, shadowed by Mark Webber, to take Red Bull Racing's first 1–2 finish of the 2011 season

The Turkish GP proved to be a major test for the 2011 rules. The apparent ease with which people could pass in the DRS zone created a lot of comment, while all the top runners made four stops, and thus used five sets of tyres to run the 58 laps. And that wasn't expected before the start, and certainly not by Pirelli.

The pressure of performing multiple pit stops was really beginning to tell on the top teams, as the inevitable mistakes crept in. Indeed it was a challenging afternoon for all concerned, and the man who got it just right was Sebastian Vettel, who made up for the previous year's disastrous collision with his third victory of the season.

There were no surprises when Vettel and team-mate Mark Webber locked out the front row. However, the way the team did it was what caught the eye. Having done no dry running on Friday after a big crash in the morning rain, Vettel was fastest from the start of Saturday morning practice in his repaired car.

In Q3 he set a time so far ahead of everyone else that he didn't bother to go out at the end to defend it. By staying in the pits, he saved a set of new, soft tyres.

Like Vettel, Webber also settled for his first-run time and preferred to save a set of tyres, but his second place – he was 0.4s off his team-mate – looked far more vulnerable

ABOVE Sebastian Vettel leads into Turn 1, with Nico Rosberg moving up to second ahead of Mark Webber, Lewis Hamilton and the chasing pack

OPPOSITE TOP Michael Schumacher had a poor weekend, finishing the race a lapped 12th

OPPOSITE BOTTOM The two Renaults battled fiercely, Nick Heidfeld prevailing to finish seventh while Vitaly Petrov was eighth

to attack. However, none of the drivers who went out for a final run and used up their last set of soft tyres were able to beat him.

Both McLaren drivers had disappointing last efforts, and third place went instead to Nico Rosberg. Lewis Hamilton had to settle for fourth, two places ahead of Jenson Button, who didn't improve on his last lap. The McLarens were split by Fernando Alonso, the Ferrari driver starting fifth, as he had done in all three previous races.

As in Australia, from the very first corner Vettel was safely ahead of his most dangerous rivals. In Melbourne he had Vitaly Petrov riding shotgun, and this time it was Rosberg. He was well clear of any threat when DRS

became active on the third lap, and thereafter he was able to work his tyres only as hard as he needed to, driving smoothly and precisely while his pursuers were attacking, defending and generally sliding around.

Vettel pitted in response to those behind, always with plenty of margin to allow for any mistakes. And he didn't make one over the course of what was a perfect afternoon for the German.

Vettel's 'precautionary' fourth stop was an interesting strategy twist. Although he was caught out in Shanghai when Hamilton reeled him in on fresher rubber, his lead was so big this time that in normal circumstances there was never going to be a repeat.

INSIDE LINE
SEBASTIAN VETTEL
RED BULL RACING DRIVER

"Three wins from four races – I have to be happy!

I was pretty much in control from start to finish. It was a bit of a comfortable situation having Nico behind me at the beginning for at least the first five laps, because I was able to open a gap maybe quicker

than if Mark had been behind. Throughout the race I had this cushion and we were able to react to other people.

Actually, this one is for the guys. I wrecked the car on Friday in the wet, but they got it back together and everyone played a role – not only my mechanics, but Mark's also. You always feel bad when you go back into the garage after you've done something like that. But when I walked in on Saturday morning the mechanics gave me the impression that nothing happened, nothing is wrong and it's business as usual. That helps a lot. People I see in the paddock, I see them from time to time, but people I see in the garage, I'm working with them all year long and it means a lot if they make you comfortable.

In the first two stints you had to really see where you were – the tyres are tricky to handle, and again today we saw different strategies with different people. The tyres go away from you at some stage and you have to deal with it. There was nobody out there today with no tyre wear! We expected this circuit to be extremely challenging, and especially around Turn 8 it was difficult to handle.

I could have afforded to stay out on my first set of primes at the end, but you have to be prepared for what might come. I could have made it easily to the chequered flag, which would have saved us the pit-stop time, 15–20 seconds, but then again, if something happens and there's an accident and a safety car comes out, you can be in trouble.

You are on a used tyre obviously, and those that have stopped for fresh rubber suddenly get the gap back and are in much better shape, so you have to guard against that. So I think it was the right thing to come in another time, even though it was just a very short fourth stint after the third stop. I'm happy with how we communicated during the race and how we reacted and I think since China we have definitely made a step forward."

The reason for stopping a fourth time was the risk of a late-race safety car. If the field had closed up and he'd lost all that advantage, then at the restart he would have been an easy target for Webber, Alonso and maybe others on newer tyres. Fortunately for RBR, Seb didn't have to constantly explore the limits of his KERS system. Clearly things were getting better with the team's Achilles heel, but Christian Horner hinted that there could still be a weakness when the RB7 was involved in a real fight.

"We made a good step forward this weekend," he explained. "We had a trouble-free run with Seb today, and we had some small issue with Mark because he was pushing the system very hard when he was racing Fernando. Definitely the modification we've made as we've learned more about the technology has paid dividends this weekend."

In China Webber moved from 18th on the grid to third at the finish. He had to work just as hard in Turkey to convert second on the grid into second at the flag. He had the misfortune to start on the dirty side, and that gave Rosberg a helping hand. In the past we'd seen Webber convert a bad initial start into a total disaster later round the first lap, but this time he held his ground when Hamilton attacked.

TALKING POINT
ACTION OVERLOAD?

When the Drag Reduction System (DRS) was announced, it offended the purists. Overtaking is a part of racing, went the argument, but it's only an element. It should be meaningful overtaking. DRS, they thought, in combination with the new tyre regulations, meant there was potential for lots of meaningless passing. The analogy was made between football and basketball; far better to watch a tight game and wait for the breakthrough goal, than to be watching baskets every few seconds.

In Melbourne, however, those fears weren't realised. In fact, we saw just three DRS overtakes all afternoon. That, though, was due to the DRS zone being relatively short. Turkey was a different story. At Istanbul Park, you almost couldn't help but pass. It led to the kind of frustration that saw Michael Schumacher simply turn into Vitaly Petrov at the chicane, almost like a rookie Formula Ford driver.

On top of that, no fewer than 13 of the 24 cars made four pit stops during the race. For the director in Bernie Ecclestone's TV nerve centre, it must have been a nightmare. Action everywhere, but how much of it significant?

And, as Sebastian Vettel pointed out, what about the people in the grandstands?

"Obviously every race is different," he said, "and it's difficult to produce a tyre that is a two-stopper everywhere, but I think the real hard time is for the spectators at the circuit. Sure, if they have a video wall in front of them it's possible for them to follow, but after the first stint, especially when you have pit stops every ten to 15 laps, I think it makes it really difficult for the people coming here to follow.

"You maybe understand the first five or the first ten, but then not everyone is following the leader or the guy in P2 or P3. It's obviously very early to judge because we've only had four races and in one of them it was possible to one-stop, but maybe we need to think about it."

It's a tough balancing act for Pirelli. They were tasked with providing tyres that make the racing exciting, and that is what they have attempted to do. Vettel's point about the circuits all being different is a valid one. We will see one/two stop races at some tracks, and three/four stop races at others.

As Fernando Alonso put it: "It's what people asked for last year. We saw two stops in Canada and people enjoyed that race. Fans, journalists, everyone, were asking for more of a show, more pit stops, more fun. Now we have all of that, if people are still not happy, we need to see what they want…"

Webber used up his tyres fighting with Rosberg, and that encouraged him to come in early on lap 10, although he was by no means the first.

All the teams had learned from China, where McLaren and Red Bull were busy eyeing each other and were caught out, failing to respond when Rosberg pitted. When they emerged from their stops, the Mercedes was in front, and it was a case of 'where did he come from?'

In Turkey, Vitaly Petrov pitted on lap eight, and the cars that had been immediately in front of him – Hamilton and Massa – came in a lap later. The lap after that, Webber was followed down the pitlane by Alonso and Rosberg, and then it was Vettel's turn. While some of those who stopped were already experiencing tyre issues, others could have stayed out longer, but were compelled to respond. These first stops were so early that the cars concerned went into the four-stop zone.

"It's like a chess match," said Horner. "That first move can dictate what happens later on."

And later on is what counted. China proved that in 2011 races were all about what happens in the final stint, and Turkey gave us a new twist on that. In effect Webber paced himself brilliantly, not panicking when passed by a flying Alonso at half distance. He knew he had an ace up his sleeve for that final stint. While attention had been focussed on the efforts of the top teams to save new soft tyres for the race, it was equally handy to quietly set aside a set of new hard tyres for that crucial final stint – and that's what Mark had done.

"We had the benefit of an extra set of primes for the end of the race, because we didn't use them yesterday, versus Alonso," said Horner. "Alonso was quick on the option, and managed to get past us on the option. The team stayed calm; they knew they had that last set of tyres to have a crack at him with, and he made it stick.

"What was fascinating about today is that 12 months ago losing a place, as Mark did to the Ferrari, would have been 'game over' for him, and he would have

consolidated the third. With the way that the strategy now works, with the tools that the drivers now have, with the DRS and the KERS and the strategic element that you apply to races these days, it gave him a crack at getting that position back, which he made work for him."

At first glance, Alonso's run to third place came out of the blue, but the signs had been there all season. While the latest updates helped to ensure that he was closer to pole in terms of lap time, the red cars had shown good race pace since the first race in Australia.

In all of the first three races he had had a bad first lap, having been pushed wide in Australia and getting away badly in both Malaysia and China. And each time he ended up behind his team-mate. By the time he found some clear air and got going, the podium was out of reach, and a wing-breaking clash with Hamilton in Malaysia didn't help.

In Turkey, not only did Alonso not lose a place on the first lap, but he gained one when Hamilton ran wide. He was then able to keep up with Webber, perhaps even to the surprise of his own team. Fourth became third when Rosberg slipped back, and then, on lap 29, Fernando passed Webber in a straight fight, so well was the car performing on the soft tyres.

OPPOSITE Jenson Button and Lewis Hamilton had an intense battle in the early laps, passing and re-passing each other several times, ruining their first sets of tyres in the process

TOP Michael Schumacher and Felipe Massa battled for 11th place towards the end of the race, the Ferrari driver coming out on top. Here they have just passed Jaime Alguersuari's Toro Rosso, with an already twice-lapped Narain Karthikeyan's HRT ahead

ABOVE Massa overtook Hamilton into the hairpin for sixth place on the in-lap for both drivers' first pit stops, but the Ferrari's stop was a poor one and Hamilton re-passed the Brazilian driver on the way out of the pitlane

ABOVE Sébastien Buemi laps Heikki Kovalainen's Lotus on his way to a strong ninth place, with Michael Schumacher, Rubens Barrichello and Adrian Sutil following. The Toro Roso driver was running seventh with two laps to go, but was unable to hold off the two Renaults on fresh rubber

BELOW Sebastian Vettel receives a hug from his father, Norbert, after another dominant performance to take his third win from four races

"First of all we need to remember that during all the races the pace was not too bad, everywhere," said Stefano Domenicali. "Unfortunately, when you start so far behind, the real problem is you cannot show your race pace because you have to do a good start, try to get out of the traffic, destroying the tyres...

"That's the real issue. I would say generally that we have confirmed that the race pace has improved, because today, honestly, we were lapping on the same lap time or faster on the soft than Webber, and very close or the same lap time with Vettel."

Webber bided his time and took full advantage of his new hard tyres to reclaim the position, Fernando having

to run his final stint on tyres he'd used in qualifying. The car didn't have the performance on the primes that it had enjoyed on the options, and the extra edge Webber had from his new set made the Australian's pass for second inevitable.

McLaren lost out to Mercedes in qualifying and Ferrari in the race, and that was clearly not a situation that anyone in the camp was happy with, given the momentum it appeared to have after the superb win in China. The team went into the Turkey weekend with a built-in handicap when scheduled upgrades had to be postponed after a new part failed on the factory rig, so the car wasn't in the intended optimum spec. Nevertheless, from his fourth grid spot Hamilton could have had a much better race than he did. No one criticised Lewis for having a go at Webber on the first lap. It's easy to say that in the DRS era you don't have to take risks at the start like you used to, but he's an instinctive racer, and he saw an opportunity. The problem was that not only did his move fail to come off, it cost him places to Alonso and Button, and left him with a lot to do.

An interminable 14sec delay in the pits at his third stop didn't help but was out of Lewis's control, and in the end he was relieved to cross the line in the same position that he started from.

Rosberg fell back in the middle part of the race when running on the hard tyre, but he moved ahead of Button in the final stint to claim fifth. Jenson had opted for a three-stop strategy, but ultimately his final stint on hard tyres proved to be too long, and he could not maintain sufficient pace. Behind him, Renault showed good speed again, as Nick Heidfeld took seventh and Petrov eighth. Sébastien Buemi moved up the order nicely to claim ninth for STR, while Kamui Kobayashi took the final point, after starting last.

While his team-mate was on the podium, Felipe Massa had a frustrating run to 11th, and Michael Schumacher finished 12th after another eventful race that included a stop for a new nose after an early clash with Petrov.

SNAPSHOT FROM
TURKEY

CLOCKWISE FROM RIGHT

Kamui Koyayashi in action with the Turkish countryside as a backdrop; a warm welcome from the local marshals; this particular grid girl attracted plenty of attention from the photographers; Sebastian Vettel wrecked his car after a heavy crash during damp Friday morning practice; Vettel faces the press after his Friday crash; Lewis Hamilton wonders at the speed of the Red Bull Racing RB7; the first European race provides the first opportunity for the teams to show off their latest paddock hospitality centres, in this case that of Mercedes GP; radio headsets are essential for communication between team members; Karun Chandhok drove for Lotus in Friday morning practice

RACE RESULTS
TURKEY ISTANBUL

RACE DATE May 8th
CIRCUIT LENGTH 3.317 miles
NO. OF LAPS 58
RACE DISTANCE 192.386 miles
WEATHER Sunny and dry, 24°C
TRACK TEMP 34°C
ATTENDANCE 115,000
LAP RECORD Juan Pablo Montoya, 1m24.770s, 138.056mph, 2005

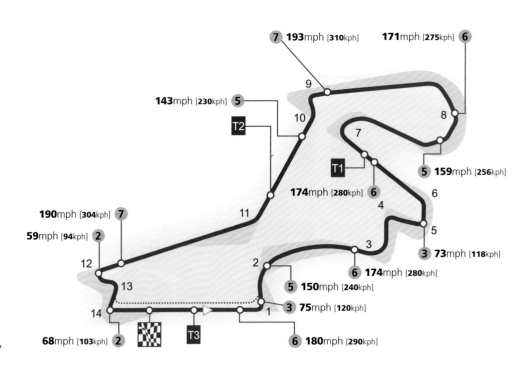

PRACTICE 1

	Driver	Time	Laps
1	F Alonso	1m38.670s	13
2	N Rosberg	1m40.072s	14
3	M Schumacher	1m40.132s	18
4	N Heidfeld	1m40.338s	9
5	V Petrov	1m40.401s	10
6	K Kobayashi	1m40.421s	16
7	F Massa	1m40.697s	14
8	D Ricciardo	1m41.094s	18
9	S Buemi	1m41.178s	22
10	N Hulkenberg	1m41.347s	16
11	M Webber	1m42.564s	5
12	P Maldonado	1m42.597s	7
13	P di Resta	1m43.525s	11
14	R Barrichello	1m43.913s	5
15	K Chandhok	1m43.986s	6
16	V Liuzzi	1m44.787s	20
17	S Vettel	1m44.954s	4
18	T Glock	1m45.183s	15
19	J d'Ambrosio	1m45.237s	11
20	N Karthikeyan	1m48.461s	8
21	J Trulli	1m51.676s	6
22	S Perez	1m55.791s	13
23	J Button	2m00.666s	4
24	L Hamilton	No time	1

PRACTICE 2

	Driver	Time	Laps
1	J Button	1m26.456s	26
2	N Rosberg	1m26.521s	29
3	L Hamilton	1m27.033s	31
4	M Schumacher	1m27.063s	21
5	M Webber	1m27.149s	31
6	F Massa	1m27.340s	37
7	V Petrov	1m27.517s	37
8	P di Resta	1m27.725s	37
9	S Perez	1m27.844s	32
10	A Sutil	1m28.052s	37
11	F Alonso	1m28.069s	27
12	S Buemi	1m28.153s	36
13	N Heidfeld	1m28.475s	35
14	J Alguersuari	1m28.765s	32
15	P Maldonado	1m28.828s	19
16	R Barrichello	1m28.946s	20
17	J Trulli	1m29.409s	39
18	K Kobayashi	1m29.637s	27
19	H Kovalainen	1m30.281s	37
20	J d'Ambrosio	1m31.035s	28
21	T Glock	1m31.221s	22
22	N Karthikeyan	1m31.230s	29
23	V Liuzzi	1m31.989s	30
24	S Vettel	No time	0

PRACTICE 3

	Driver	Time	Laps
1	S Vettel	1m26.037s	17
2	M Schumacher	1m26.038s	17
3	M Webber	1m26.404s	16
4	N Rosberg	1m26.420s	19
5	J Button	1m26.578s	17
6	L Hamilton	1m26.726s	14
7	V Petrov	1m26.755s	20
8	F Alonso	1m26.819s	12
9	F Massa	1m26.883s	12
10	S Buemi	1m27.080s	16
11	S Perez	1m27.121s	20
12	P Maldonado	1m27.255s	18
13	A Sutil	1m27.318s	19
14	N Heidfeld	1m27.379s	17
15	R Barrichello	1m27.528s	19
16	P di Resta	1m27.644s	18
17	J Alguersuari	1m27.724s	15
18	K Kobayashi	1m27.976s	19
19	H Kovalainen	1m28.911s	15
20	J Trulli	1m29.697s	17
21	J d'Ambrosio	1m31.097s	25
22	T Glock	1m31.175s	19
23	V Liuzzi	1m31.375s	19
24	N Karthikeyan	1m32.009s	15

QUALIFYING 1

	Driver	Time
1	F Massa	1m27.013s
2	S Vettel	1m27.039s
3	M Webber	1m27.090s
4	L Hamilton	1m27.091s
5	F Alonso	1m27.349s
6	J Button	1m27.374s
7	A Sutil	1m27.392s
8	P Maldonado	1m27.396s
9	V Petrov	1m27.475s
10	N Rosberg	1m27.514s
11	S Buemi	1m27.620s
12	P di Resta	1m27.625s
13	M Schumacher	1m27.697s
14	S Perez	1m27.778s
15	N Heidfeld	1m27.901s
16	J Alguersuari	1m28.055s
17	R Barrichello	1m28.246s
18	H Kovalainen	1m28.780s
19	J Trulli	1m29.673s
20	J d'Ambrosio	1m30.445s
21	V Liuzzi	1m30.692s
22	T Glock	1m30.813s
23	N Karthikeyan	1m31.564s
24	K Kobayashi	No time

QUALIFYING 2

	Driver	Time
1	S Vettel	1m25.610s
2	N Rosberg	1m25.810s
3	L Hamilton	1m26.066s
4	M Webber	1m26.075s
5	M Schumacher	1m26.121s
6	F Alonso	1m26.152s
7	F Massa	1m26.395s
8	J Button	1m26.485s
9	V Petrov	1m26.654s
10	N Heidfeld	1m26.740s
11	R Barrichello	1m26.764s
12	A Sutil	1m27.027s
13	P di Resta	1m27.145s
14	P Maldonado	1m27.236s
15	S Perez	1m27.244s
16	S Buemi	1m27.255s
17	J Alguersuari	1m27.572s

Best sectors – Practice
Sec 1	N Rosberg	31.841s
Sec 2	S Vettel	30.253s
Sec 3	M Schumacher	23.575s

Speed trap – Practice
1	K Kobayashi	200.268mph
2	S Perez	200.143mph
3	L Hamilton	198.714mph

Best sectors – Qualifying
Sec 1	S Vettel	31.493s
Sec 2	S Vettel	30.040s
Sec 3	J Button	23.503s

Speed trap – Qualifying
1	S Perez	200.454mph
2	L Hamilton	198.466mph
3	J Button	198.466mph

Sebastian Vettel
"It was a great result, especially after I gave the team so much work on Friday. I got a gap in the first stint. Then I did two short stints, which was the right thing."

Jenson Button
"It's a pity to finish so far back after everything in the first stint seemed to go so well. My battle with Lewis was fun, but we went the wrong way on strategy."

Fernando Alonso
"I was stuck behind Rosberg for too long: maybe I could have forced him to push more. In the end, Webber passed me as he had the benefit of new tyres."

Michael Schumacher
"I'm not very happy, but I'm responsible for the result. The incident with Petrov dictated my race: we were very close and I was surprised that we touched."

Nick Heidfeld
"It's always good to score, but I could have finished even higher. I was stuck in traffic, so overtaking was difficult and Vitaly made contact with me."

Rubens Barrichello
"We struggled with straightline speed and at various stages I couldn't use KERS, which made it difficult to defend and I struggled with it, locking up under braking."

Mark Webber
"The team pitted me earlier than expected, as they were worried about undercuts approaching. Ferrari saw the same thing and it became a race with Fernando."

Lewis Hamilton
"I made a mistake on lap 1 out of Turn 3 when I was trying to go around Webber. If I hadn't dropped behind Fernando and Jenson, I could have got to third."

Felipe Massa
"I did the first stop at the right time, but lost the place I'd taken off Hamilton. Then I had problems at the third and fourth stops, so we all have to work on this."

Nico Rosberg
"My start was fantastic to pass Mark and be second, but then I struggled with my tyres. Our strategy worked out well to bring me back into a decent position."

Vitaly Petrov
"Michael hit my car, then I was stuck behind slower drivers after my first stop. If this hadn't happened, my race could have been much stronger."

Pastor Maldonado
"It was very hard to maintain a consistent pace as I had oversteer. I had better pace towards the end on primes but made a mistake by speeding in the pits."

Lap markers: 1, 5, 10, 15, 20, 25, 30, 35, 40, 45, 50, 55, 58

1	S Vettel
2	M Webber
3	N Rosberg
4	L Hamilton
5	F Alonso
6	J Button
7	V Petrov
8	M Schumacher
9	N Heidfeld
10	F Massa
11	R Barrichello
12	A Sutil
13	P di Resta
14	P Maldonado
15	S Perez
16	S Buemi
17	J Alguersuari
18	H Kovalainen
19	J Trulli
20	V Liuzzi
21	T Glock
22	N Karthikeyan
23	J d'Ambrosio
24	K Kobayashi

Legend: ☆ Accident Ⓜ Mechanical failure Ⓟ Pit stop ☐ Safety Car ☐ Lapped Ⓑ Black flag

QUALIFYING 3

	Driver	Time
1	S Vettel	1m25.049s
2	M Webber	1m25.454s
3	N Rosberg	1m25.574s
4	L Hamilton	1m25.595s
5	F Alonso	1m25.851s
6	J Button	1m25.982s
7	V Petrov	1m26.296s
8	M Schumacher	1m26.646s
9	N Heidfeld	1m26.659s
10	F Massa	No time

GRID

	Driver	Time
1	S Vettel	1m25.049s
2	M Webber	1m25.454s
3	N Rosberg	1m25.574s
4	L Hamilton	1m25.595s
5	F Alonso	1m25.851s
6	J Button	1m25.982s
7	V Petrov	1m26.296s
8	M Schumacher	1m26.646s
9	N Heidfeld	1m26.659s
10	F Massa	No time
11	R Barrichello	1m26.764s
12	A Sutil	1m27.027s
13	P di Resta	1m27.145s
14	P Maldonado	1m27.236s
15	S Perez	1m27.244s
16	S Buemi	1m27.255s
17	J Alguersuari	1m27.572s
18	H Kovalainen	1m28.780s
19	J Trulli	1m29.673s
20	V Liuzzi	1m30.692s
21	T Glock	1m30.813s
22	N Karthikeyan	1m31.564s
23*	J d'Ambrosio	1m30.445s
24	K Kobayashi	No time

*5-place grid penalty for ignoring yellow flags

RACE

	Driver	Car	Laps	Time	Avg. mph	Fastest	Stops
1	S Vettel	Red Bull-Renault RB7	58	1h30m17.558s	127.751	1m29.937s	4
2	M Webber	Red Bull-Renault RB7	58	1h30m26.365s	127.549	1m29.703s	4
3	F Alonso	Ferrari 150 Italia	58	1h30m27.633s	127.519	1m30.279s	4
4	L Hamilton	McLaren-Mercedes MP4-26	58	1h30m57.790s	126.814	1m30.108s	4
5	N Rosberg	Mercedes MGP W02	58	1h31m05.097s	126.645	1m30.573s	4
6	J Button	McLaren-Mercedes MP4-26	58	1h31m16.989s	126.370	1m31.167s	3
7	N Heidfeld	Renault R31	58	1h31m18.415s	126.337	1m30.158s	4
8	V Petrov	Renault R31	58	1h31m25.726s	126.168	1m30.618s	4
9	S Buemi	Toro Rosso-Ferrari STR6	58	1h31m26.952s	126.140	1m31.360s	3
10	K Kobayashi	Sauber-Ferrari C30	58	1h31m35.579s	125.942	1m31.038s	3
11	F Massa	Ferrari 150 Italia	58	1h31m37.381s	125.901	1m31.118s	4
12	M Schumacher	Mercedes MGP W02	58	1h31m43.002s	125.772	1m31.153s	4
13	A Sutil	Force India-Mercedes VJM04	57	1h30m20.932s	125.475	1m32.070s	3
14	S Perez	Sauber-Ferrari C30	57	1h30m20.963s	125.474	1m30.797s	4
15	R Barrichello	Williams-Cosworth FW33	57	1h30m31.456s	125.232	1m32.079s	3
16	J Alguersuari	Toro Rosso-Ferrari STR6	57	1h30m31.610s	125.228	1m29.894s	4
17	P Maldonado	Williams-Cosworth FW33	57	1h30m52.155s	124.756	1m32.044s	3
18	J Trulli	Lotus-Cosworth T128	57	1h31m23.869s	124.035	1m32.862s	3
19	H Kovalainen	Lotus-Cosworth T128	56	1h30m21.373s	123.264	1m32.695s	3
20	J d'Ambrosio	Virgin-Cosworth MVR-02	56	1h31m07.701s	122.219	1m34.971s	2
21	N Karthikeyan	HRT-Cosworth F111	55	1h30m26.738s	120.943	1m33.948s	3
22	V Liuzzi	HRT-Cosworth F111	53	1h30m24.932s	116.584	1m34.699s	4
23	P di Resta	Force India-Mercedes VJM04	44	Loose wheel	-	1m32.519s	4
NS	T Glock	Virgin-Cosworth MVR-02	0	Gearbox	-	-	0

CHAMPIONSHIP

	Driver	Pts
1	S Vettel	93
2	L Hamilton	59
3	M Webber	55
4	J Button	46
5	F Alonso	41
6	F Massa	24
7	N Heidfeld	21
8	V Petrov	21
9	N Rosberg	20
10	K Kobayashi	8
11	M Schumacher	6
12	S Buemi	6
13	A Sutil	2
14	P di Resta	2

	Constructor	Pts
1	Red Bull-Renault	148
2	McLaren-Mercedes	105
3	Ferrari	65
4	Renault	42
5	Mercedes	26
6	Sauber-Ferrari	8
7	Toro Rosso-Ferrari	6
8	Force India-Mercedes	4

Fastest lap
M Webber 1m29.703s
(133.416mph) on lap 48

Fastest speed trap
S Perez 198.652mph
Slowest speed trap
N Karthikeyan 187.032mph

Fastest pit stop
1 S Vettel 20.112s
2 N Rosberg 20.308s
3 M Schumacher 20.379s

Adrian Sutil

"The three-stop was the right choice and the softs felt the better race tyre, so I stayed on them as long as I could. In the final laps I had fun fighting with Perez."

Kamui Kobayashi

"I had promised Peter (Sauber) to score points. It's just one point, as I lost time with a puncture from touching Buemi. Otherwise, I could have finished seventh."

Sébastien Buemi

"If I hadn't lost two places in the final laps, I could have finished seventh. But I couldn't even hold the steering wheel as there was so much vibration from the tyres."

Jarno Trulli

"I had another really good start, but was blocked in the first turn. Early on, I started fighting with the tyres, so we changed to a three-stop strategy that worked."

Narain Karthikeyan

"I should be happy with the fact that I got another finish under my belt. I've now finished two races out of three, so I need to get more comfortable in the car."

Timo Glock

"It was frustrating to experience a problem with fifth gear going to the grid. The team did a great job to try to get me back on track, but it just wasn't possible."

Paul di Resta

"The pace didn't seem quite there and that's why we decided to make a fourth stop. However, the team told me to stop as there was an electronics problem."

Sergio Perez

"I had good pace and so it's a real shame what happened on lap 1. Pastor was braking quite hard in front of me, I couldn't avoid him and broke my front wing."

Jaime Alguersuari

"I did my best, pushing hard from the start, but I suffered from degradation on the rears in what was meant to be the final stint, requiring a fourth pit stop."

Heikki Kovalainen

"That was tough. I had two issues, with a hydraulic leak which affected the DRS and the diff, and I think the strategy didn't work out how we'd have liked."

Vitantonio Liuzzi

"This was a positive weekend until qualifying. In the race, we had a problem with both front tyres and need to work on this to make sure there's no repeat."

Jérôme d'Ambrosio

"I was on my own, as I was faster than the HRTs, but couldn't keep up with the Lotuses, but it was good for me to manage the tyres and change to a two-stop."

FORMULA 1 GRAN PREMIO
DE ESPAÑA SANTANDER 2011
CATALUNYA

RED BULL FIGHTER

Local hero Fernando Alonso was an early leader, but in a race that was all about tyres Sebastian Vettel once again prevailed, repelling a strong challenge from a charging Lewis Hamilton

E very race thus far in 2011 had given us another lesson in how a grand prix might unfold under the new rules. In Spain, a track notorious for dull Sunday afternoons instead produced a gripping contest, with the three top teams – and three of the most celebrated drivers of the era – involved in the lead battle.

It was a fascinating event, and one that produced some surprises. With all the talk about the importance of qualifying, who would have imagined that a driver could jump straight from fourth – on the dirty side of the grid – into the lead? Or that after leading until lap 19, the same driver would be lapped by the finish?

For the first time in 2011, Sebastian Vettel didn't take pole, the German losing out to team-mate Mark Webber by a margin that was less than the loss the World Champion faced by not having KERS when it mattered. Lewis Hamilton took third place, despite locking up on his quick lap. Jenson Button was fourth for most of Q3 as, like the Red Bull drivers, the McLaren men decided to stick to a single qualifying lap and save a set of tyres. Right at the end, Fernando Alonso managed to sneak between the McLarens to take fourth place, thus moving out of fifth spot for the first time in 2011.

Vettel wasn't too concerned about losing pole to his team-mate, and on Sunday all his efforts were focused on getting past Webber into Turn One. He managed it, but he didn't expect that they would both lose out to Alonso.

Having already pulled out an awesome qualifying lap to get himself into fourth place on the grid, Fernando made a superb start, taking advantage of the fact that the RBR guys were so focused on fighting each other. It helped, too, that there was a relatively long run down to Turn One, and the Ferrari was able to get a tow. But mainly it was down to the Spaniard's opportunism and bravery as he went for a gap that was fast diminishing.

Button, meanwhile, had a bad first lap, dropping from fifth to 10th. Thereafter he switched to a three-stop strategy, while all the quick guys went for four stops, as in Turkey.

Alonso had respectable pace while on soft tyres, but he clearly wasn't going as fast as Vettel would have been able to in clear air, so RBR's game plan was out of the window.

In an attempt to resolve the situation, Vettel was the first runner to stop for new tyres, coming in on lap 9 as his softs began to edge towards their sell-by date. The

timing committed him to a four-stopper, and thus did the same for those who responded to him.

What we saw then was quite unexpected. Sebastian came out mired in traffic – made up of some very competitive cars. But with a quick car and, crucially, fresher tyres, it was not a drama. In the space of a lap he passed Button, Massa and – with some DRS help – Rosberg. He'd taken on used options in the stop, so they were effectively just nine laps younger than those on the other cars, and yet the difference in performance was extraordinary.

Ferrari reacted immediately by bringing Fernando in, while Webber followed him into the pits. Having run fourth, Hamilton pitted on the next lap and – thanks to a great in-lap – managed to get ahead of Webber, defeating the undercut.

Vettel's busy out-lap meant that Alonso stayed in front, so RBR chose to try the undercut again, and at the first possible opportunity. Seb pitted again on lap 18 after just nine laps on that second set of option tyres. It was a very late call, and Alonso was already committed to carrying on for another lap.

A lap later, Alonso and Webber pitted together once more. This time, Vettel did get ahead of the Ferrari, helped by the fact that he now had his single set of brand-new options, which gave him a boost on his out-lap. Down the straight he also had a handy DRS tow from backmarker Timo Glock.

The problem for Seb was that he was already on his third and final set of softs after just 18 laps. They were at least the new ones, so that gave him a bit of extra mileage to play with, but clearly he was going to have to go a long way on the hards.

"At that stage of the race we'd obviously taken an aggressive undercut at the second stop," said Christian Horner. "And those tyres were going to have to go a long, long way. It was a matter of then managing the race to make sure the tyres

LEFT The partisan crowd erupted when Fernando Alonso made a perfect start from fourth on the grid to scythe past Lewis Hamilton and the duelling Red Bulls before Turn 1.

OPPOSITE BOTTOM Pastor Maldonado hustled his Williams through to Q3 for the first time to qualify ninth, but slipped to 13th on the first lap, and was further hampered by a four-stop strategy to finish an eventual 15th

INSIDE LINE
STEFANO DOMENICALI
FERRARI TEAM PRINCIPAL

"A fantastic qualifying lap from Fernando saw us, for the first time this year, get a place on the two front rows of the grid. At the start of the race Fernando made an incredible getaway, which took him into the lead. That was a position clearly superior to the worth of our package.

On the soft tyres we could keep the best cars behind us, as Fernando showed, but then on the hard tyres we did not stand a chance. We could only think of defending our position as much as possible.

There is no denying that being lapped hurt. It was even more painful after seeing a driver of Fernando's calibre putting on such a breathtaking display at the start and then fighting like a lion to keep drivers with clearly faster cars behind him for almost 20 laps.

We need to give Fernando and Felipe a car with which they can fight all the way to the end of a race and not just in the first part. On a track that favours cars with a lot of aerodynamic downforce, ours was lacking in that area, something that

was glaringly obvious, especially on the new hard tyres brought here by Pirelli.

We never managed to get the hard tyre to work, and our pace was at least two seconds off that of the first four. We will continue to work on improving the car and finding the aerodynamic downforce that we are lacking. We now go into a run of three races that will see the use of the soft and supersoft tyres. We hope that will produce a different situation.

Red Bull and McLaren were clearly quicker than us, and it was only down to Fernando's talent that we managed to hold them off in the first part of the race. We knew we had an aerodynamic downforce deficit, but

we did not expect to be that far off in terms of race pace.

From a strategy point of view I think we made the right choices, trying to cover our main rivals throughout the whole race. Sure, it put the pit-stop guys under a lot of pressure, pushing things to the limit with a rival car in the pitlane at the same time. They did a good job. We just need to improve the car and we will work flat-out, as always."

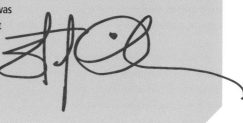

near-identical strategies, and thus we might have expected Vettel to at least hold on to that gap, if not increase it. And yet, some 30 laps down the road, they were nose to tail, just 0.7s apart, with 12 laps in which to decide who would get the biggest trophy...

In other words, this was an awesome and unexpectedly strong performance by Hamilton and McLaren, and one that showed that Red Bull's huge lap-time advantage in qualifying meant relatively little come Sunday.

"We did some good stops, consistent stops, all day today," said Martin Whitmarsh. "The worst stop was probably Lewis's last one, which wasn't a bad stop, but had that been the very quickest, I think he would have exited alongside Sebastian, and that would have been very entertaining for sure."

At lap 50, the gap between them was 1.9s, with 16 laps to go, and Lewis was on tyres that were just one lap younger than Sebastian's, but that still gave him a slight lap-time bonus on every lap to the flag.

Once again Hamilton began closing the gap, getting down to just 0.7s by lap 54, with 12 to go in which to find a way past. In the end, he didn't quite make it. Nevertheless, it was a fascinating game of cat and mouse, and Seb didn't really need the 'Try to shake him off' message from engineer Rocky...

Lewis consistently had the benefit of DRS, but couldn't make it pay, perhaps because he couldn't quite squeeze enough momentum out of his seventh gear ratio. Seb, meanwhile, was allowed by the team to activate KERS again, and used it defensively as best he could.

On some laps – including a couple of crucial ones near the end when his tyres were potentially a concern – Vettel earned himself a DRS activation off backmarkers, which gave him welcome respite. In the end, he did just enough to stay ahead.

"It's very difficult, because you're almost racing yourself, because you know if you abuse the tyre, you

TOP Sebastian Vettel passes Jenson Button, with Felipe Massa as his next target, as he carves through the field on fresh, soft tyres following his early first pit stop on lap 9

ABOVE Vitantonio Liuzzi retired with gearshift problems at HRT's home race, while team-mate Narain Karthikeyan was the last classified finisher, five laps down in 21st place

OPPOSITE TOP Michael Schumacher and Nico Rosberg battled for much of the race to finish sixth and seventh, Schumacher having the upper hand with Rosberg suffering from radio and DRS failures

OPPOSITE BOTTOM Fernando Alonso has just emerged sideways from his pit to run side-by-side with Mark Webber down the pitlane after the third of four pit stops for both drivers

didn't degrade too much, and then you end in a world of pain."

If it was a challenge for Vettel, it was even worse for Alonso. He and Ferrari were well aware that they would struggle more than the others once they switched to hards. But by chasing RBR's strategy Fernando had used two sets of softs by lap 19. And, unlike Seb's, his third set was old, so they weren't going to last as long as those on the Red Bull.

Hamilton, meanwhile, had sat dutifully in fourth during the first stint, and then jumped Webber, despite making his first stop a lap later than the Australian. In terms of the bigger picture, after the first stints, Lewis also had, in effect, two laps' worth of tyre use in hand over Vettel, the man he was ultimately racing.

At the second stops, Lewis ran five laps longer than Seb, and four more than Alonso. The Ferrari had new tyres, but Lewis now had clean air, and some great laps ensured that he emerged from his second stop, on lap 23, still in front of Fernando, and behind new leader Vettel.

So, as of lap 24, the battle for the lead became a straight fight between Vettel and Hamilton, the two separated by 4.9s. They would subsequently run

TALKING POINT
FERRARI'S TYRE TROUBLE

Barcelona exposed the problems that gave Ferrari such a difficult start to the year. A lone podium for Fernando Alonso in Turkey was the team's best result after five races, and Alonso left his home grand prix already 67 points adrift of Sebastian Vettel in the world championship.

Alonso's performance was electrifying. The Ferrari pace on the hard prime Pirelli tyre was not strong enough to allow the team to use it to escape Q1. Instead, Alonso and Massa had to waste a set of options.

In Q2, the Ferrari was eight-tenths away from the McLaren pace, but after a searing lap in Q3, Alonso put the Ferrari fourth on the grid, splitting Hamilton and Button.

"If I had another 20 goes at it I don't think I could do that lap again!" Alonso said.

On Sunday afternoon he was just as spectacular off the line, charging inside the Red Bulls into Turn 1 to lead the race. On the option tyre the Ferrari was not the quickest car, but it was strong enough to lead the first two stints of the race.

The crowd loved it but, unbelievably, between the point at which Ferrari bolted on a set of primes and the end of the race, Alonso was lapped. Team principal Stefano Domenicali was not slow to praise his driver and have the team shoulder responsibility.

Between Spain and Monaco, Ferrari announced a major restructure of its technical department, with Aldo Costa leaving his role as Technical Director and Pat Fry, who joined the team from McLaren, taking on responsibility for the chassis side as de facto Technical Director.

The problem seemed to be lack of downforce, a factor largely responsible for the car's inability to generate heat in the harder-compound Pirellis, which largely explained Alonso's problems later in the race.

With Monaco and Montréal next on the calendar, the harder-compound Pirelli would not be called upon, and so the team's problems would be disguised. And, already, while Costa was still at the helm, a development programme had been put in place to address the issues.

While Domenicali admitted that the Costa decision had been a tough one, he felt it had to be made. Alonso, who had just committed to Ferrari until the end of 2016, worked with Fry during his year at McLaren in 2007, where the pair had a strong relationship.

Fifth place in the 2011 championship, after losing it so narrowly at the last race of 2010, was not what Alonso had in mind. For the moment, Ferrari felt that the upcoming venues would work in its favour, and that the first true test of progress would be Silverstone, where temperatures were likely to be low and the hard Pirelli would be used once again.

ABOVE After missing qualifying due to a major exhaust fire, Nick Heidfeld – seen here having passed Pastor Maldonado's Williams – had to start at the back of the grid but fought his way up the field to finish eighth

BELOW Three green bottles... Winner and defending World Champion Sebastian Vettel shared the podium with former title holders Lewis Hamilton and Jenson Button

might run out towards the end of the race," said Horner. "You've got to have tremendous mental poise to deal with that, especially when you're running in the lead of a grand prix. He coped with that tremendously well."

Meanwhile, Button made his three-stop strategy work brilliantly. It meant that he was able to run a much bigger chunk of the race on soft tyres – stretching his three sets out to 48 laps, compared with the 29 of some of his rivals – and that got him ahead of Webber/Alonso, into a comfortable third place, which is where he probably would have finished without his bad start.

He ran stints of 14, 16 (his new set) and 18 laps on his soft tyres, and paid little or no heed to what any other frontrunners were doing, with no jumping into the pits to cover the guy ahead or behind. He left himself with a tidy little 18-lap run to the flag on new, hard tyres.

It took RBR a while to get Webber ahead of Alonso, the Aussie managing it after the Ferrari pitted in response to a 'phantom' stop, only for Mark to carry on past the pits. On the harder tyre, Fernando went backwards from there at an astonishing rate.

Webber was 12 seconds behind Button at the end. As for Alonso, from the lap he lost the lead, to the point when Vettel lapped him shortly before the flag he lost ground at over 2s a lap relative to the Red Bull driver. He was so slow on the hard tyres that his best overall lap time was set on softs, on lap 22, with 44 laps of fuel still in the red car...

Michael Schumacher silenced his critics with a solid run to sixth, finishing just ahead of team-mate Nico Rosberg. Starting at the back, Nick Heidfeld did a brilliant job to climb up to eighth, helped by having plenty of new tyres, and a strategy that saw him start on the unloved hard, enabling him to run softs from his first stop to the end of the race.

Sergio Perez became the first Mexican to score points in 30 years when he took ninth, ahead of Sauber team-mate Kamui Kobayashi, who recovered from a first-lap puncture. The only top driver to retire was Felipe Massa, who was at the bottom of the top 10 when he stopped with gearbox failure.

In China, the top six were covered by 15s, and 14 cars finished on the lead lap. In Spain, the top four alone were spread over 47s, and everyone up to and including fifth-placed Alonso was lapped. The same guy may have been winning most of the races, but behind him 2011 was proving to be anything but predictable.

SNAPSHOT FROM
SPAIN

CLOCKWISE FROM RIGHT
Fernando Alonso leads his home race in front of a partisan crowd; a Renault mechanic sprays identification markings on a Pirelli tyre; Mark Webber controls his enthusiasm as Fernando Alonso congratulates him on taking pole position; Michael Schumacher and Nico Rosberg pose with MotoGP star Jorge Lorenzo; the Williams chefs prepare lunch; former Manchester United goalkeeper Peter Schmeichel was a guest in the paddock; Lewis Hamilton discusses details of his McLaren MP4-26 with an engineer; sunny smiles from sunny Spain; Virgin Racing's Timo Glock and Jerome d'Ambrosio play table football with Spanish footballers Jordi Amat, Alvaro Vazquez and Javi Lopez

RACE RESULTS
SPAIN
BARCELONA

RACE DATE May 22nd
CIRCUIT LENGTH 2.892 miles
NO. OF LAPS 66
RACE DISTANCE 190.872 miles
WEATHER Sunny & dry, 25°C
TRACK TEMP 34°C
ATTENDANCE 185,130
LAP RECORD Kimi Räikkönen,
1m21.670s, 127.500mph, 2008

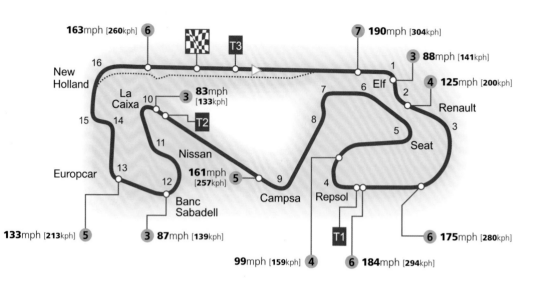

PRACTICE 1

	Driver	Time	Laps
1	M Webber	1m25.142s	27
2	S Vettel	1m26.149s	20
3	N Rosberg	1m26.379s	29
4	F Alonso	1m26.480s	27
5	S Perez	1m26.738s	26
6	L Hamilton	1m26.988s	19
7	M Schumacher	1m27.016s	32
8	N Heidfeld	1m27.132s	21
9	J Button	1m27.138s	22
10	R Barrichello	1m27.212s	20
11	V Petrov	1m27.241s	22
12	D Ricciardo	1m27.471s	23
13	P Maldonado	1m28.005s	11
14	N Hulkenberg	1m28.027s	26
15	A Sutil	1m28.163s	22
16	F Massa	1m28.654s	28
17	K Kobayashi	1m28.819s	23
18	J Alguersuari	1m28.995s	9
19	H Kovalainen	1m29.231s	21
20	J d'Ambrosio	1m30.896s	18
21	T Glock	1m31.235s	24
22	V Liuzzi	1m31.268s	23
23	J Trulli	1m31.418s	12
24	N Karthikeyan	1m32.106s	25

PRACTICE 2

	Driver	Time	Laps
1	M Webber	1m22.470s	35
2	L Hamilton	1m22.509s	27
3	S Vettel	1m22.826s	37
4	J Button	1m23.188s	32
5	F Alonso	1m23.568s	34
6	N Rosberg	1m23.586s	35
7	M Schumacher	1m23.981s	30
8	F Massa	1m24.278s	30
9	K Kobayashi	1m24.290s	33
10	N Heidfeld	1m24.366s	31
11	S Perez	1m24.483s	38
12	V Petrov	1m24.786s	43
13	S Buemi	1m25.296s	33
14	R Barrichello	1m25.303s	38
15	J Alguersuari	1m25.457s	34
16	P Maldonado	1m25.603s	43
17	P di Resta	1m26.073s	32
18	H Kovalainen	1m26.417s	37
19	A Sutil	1m27.123s	20
20	J Trulli	1m27.189s	34
21	J d'Ambrosio	1m28.036s	36
22	T Glock	1m28.062s	28
23	N Karthikeyan	1m29.469s	28
24	V Liuzzi	1m29.476s	31

PRACTICE 3

	Driver	Time	Laps
1	S Vettel	1m21.707s	6
2	M Webber	1m21.791s	17
3	M Schumacher	1m23.057s	16
4	L Hamilton	1m23.068s	13
5	J Button	1m23.214s	14
6	N Rosberg	1m23.397s	18
7	K Kobayashi	1m23.669s	17
8	V Petrov	1m24.043s	18
9	F Alonso	1m24.270s	11
10	R Barrichello	1m24.318s	18
11	F Massa	1m24.322s	17
12	S Perez	1m24.329s	19
13	P Maldonado	1m24.399s	17
14	S Buemi	1m24.535s	16
15	A Sutil	1m24.695s	18
16	J Alguersuari	1m24.722s	14
17	P di Resta	1m25.223s	19
18	H Kovalainen	1m26.236s	11
19	J Trulli	1m27.000s	20
20	T Glock	1m27.706s	20
21	V Liuzzi	1m28.330s	17
22	J d'Ambrosio	1m29.057s	18
23	N Heidfeld	1m29.200s	6
24	N Karthikeyan	1m29.562s	16

QUALIFYING 1

	Driver	Time
1	M Schumacher	1m22.960s
2	V Petrov	1m23.069s
3	P Maldonado	1m23.406s
4	F Alonso	1m23.485s
5	F Massa	1m23.506s
6	N Rosberg	1m23.507s
7	M Webber	1m23.619s
8	K Kobayashi	1m23.656s
9	S Buemi	1m23.962s
10	J Alguersuari	1m24.049s
11	S Vettel	1m24.142s
12	S Perez	1m24.209s
13	P di Resta	1m24.332s
14	L Hamilton	1m24.370s
15	J Button	1m24.428s
16	A Sutil	1m24.648s
17	H Kovalainen	1m25.874s
18	J Trulli	1m26.521s
19	R Barrichello	1m26.910s
20	T Glock	1m27.315s
21	V Liuzzi	1m27.809s
22	N Karthikeyan	1m27.908s
23	J d'Ambrosio	1m28.556s
24	N Heidfeld	No time

QUALIFYING 2

	Driver	Time
1	S Vettel	1m21.540s
2	M Webber	1m21.773s
3	J Button	1m22.050s
4	L Hamilton	1m22.148s
5	N Rosberg	1m22.569s
6	M Schumacher	1m22.671s
7	F Alonso	1m22.813s
8	P Maldonado	1m22.854s
9	V Petrov	1m22.948s
10	F Massa	1m23.026s
11	S Buemi	1m23.231s
12	S Perez	1m23.367s
13	J Alguersuari	1m23.694s
14	K Kobayashi	1m23.702s
15	H Kovalainen	1m25.403s
16	P di Resta	1m26.126s
17	A Sutil	1m26.571s

Best sectors – Practice
Sec 1	M Webber	22.685s
Sec 2	S Vettel	30.633s
Sec 3	M Webber	28.270s

Speed trap – Practice
1	K Kobayashi	202.691mph
2	P di Resta	202.132mph
3	F Massa	201.883mph

Best sectors – Qualifying
Sec 1	S Vettel	22.605s
Sec 2	M Webber	30.425s
Sec 3	M Webber	27.881s

Speed trap – Qualifying
1	A Sutil	202.070mph
2	P di Resta	200.827mph
3	M Schumacher	200.019mph

Sebastian Vettel
"At the start I didn't understand where Fernando came from! He went inside Mark, I went outside. I couldn't get close enough to use DRS, but got him with the stop."

Jenson Button
"I was on the outside into Turns 1 and 3, leaving me 10th, so I didn't think third was on, but as the others pitted so early, and as my tyres still felt good, I advanced."

Fernando Alonso
"The best bit of the race was the start. I tried to do the maximum, keeping the quickest ones behind me for around 20 laps, but then there was nothing I could do."

Michael Schumacher
"We managed to make the most of our chances. I had a good start; going through the middle was tight, but it worked out. Then it was about holding position."

Nick Heidfeld
"I'm satisfied with eighth after starting last. Just like in Turkey, with one or two laps more I could have gained one or two more places from the two Mercedes."

Rubens Barrichello
"Starting on primes meant the base wasn't good, but we had the option, so it should have been better, but we had problems in the pit stop, then with KERS."

Mark Webber
"Fernando got a phenomenal start. From then on, it was a chess game. People were covering each other's pit stops and I really didn't do much racing on track."

Lewis Hamilton
"We were quicker than the Red Bulls, except through the high-speed stuff. I pushed as hard as I could and with a few more laps it might have been different."

Felipe Massa
"Towards the end, I couldn't select gears and I had to stop at the side of the track: it was a fitting end to a terrible weekend. Luckily, we start again at Monaco."

Nico Rosberg
"I lost radio communication early on and my DRS wasn't working properly. I had fun battling with Michael for sixth place, although I wasn't able to attack."

Vitaly Petrov
"I'm disappointed not to make better use of my grid position. It seems my qualifying position had little effect, so we need to analyse why that happened."

Pastor Maldonado
"It was a difficult race. I didn't have a great start, which is something we need to work on. I then struggled to keep on the pace and our strategy didn't help us."

	Driver		1	5	10	15	20	25	30	35	40	45	50	55	60	66	
1	M Webber																1
2	S Vettel																2
3	L Hamilton																3
4	F Alonso																4
5	J Button																5
6	V Petrov																6
7	N Rosberg																7
8	F Massa																8
9	P Maldonado																9
10	M Schumacher																10
11	S Buemi																11
12	S Perez																12
13	J Alguersuari																13
14	K Kobayashi																14
15	H Kovalainen																15
16	P di Resta																16
17	A Sutil																17
18	J Trulli																18
19	R Barrichello																19
20	T Glock																20
21	V Liuzzi																21
22	N Karthikeyan																22
23	J d'Ambrosio																23
24	N Heidfeld																24

☆ Accident Ⓜ Mechanical failure Ⓟ Pit stop ☐ Safety Car ☐ Lapped Ⓑ Black flag

QUALIFYING 3

	Driver	Time
1	M Webber	1m20.981s
2	S Vettel	1m21.181s
3	L Hamilton	1m21.961s
4	F Alonso	1m21.964s
5	J Button	1m21.996s
6	V Petrov	1m22.471s
7	N Rosberg	1m22.599s
8	F Massa	1m22.888s
9	P Maldonado	1m22.952s
10	M Schumacher	No time

GRID

	Driver	Time
1	M Webber	1m20.981s
2	S Vettel	1m21.181s
3	L Hamilton	1m21.961s
4	F Alonso	1m21.964s
5	J Button	1m21.996s
6	V Petrov	1m22.471s
7	N Rosberg	1m22.599s
8	F Massa	1m22.888s
9	P Maldonado	1m22.952s
10	M Schumacher	No time
11	S Buemi	1m23.231s
12	S Perez	1m23.367s
13	J Alguersuari	1m23.694s
14	K Kobayashi	1m23.702s
15	H Kovalainen	1m25.403s
16	P di Resta	1m26.126s
17	A Sutil	1m26.571s
18	J Trulli	1m26.521s
19	R Barrichello	1m26.910s
20	T Glock	1m27.315s
21	V Liuzzi	1m27.809s
22	N Karthikeyan	1m27.908s
23	J d'Ambrosio	1m28.556s
24	N Heidfeld	No time

RACE

	Driver	Car	Laps	Time	Avg. mph	Fastest	Stops
1	S Vettel	Red Bull-Renault RB7	66	1h39m03.301s	115.616	1m27.162s	4
2	L Hamilton	McLaren-Mercedes MP4-26	66	1h39m03.931s	115.603	1m26.727s	4
3	J Button	McLaren-Mercedes MP4-26	66	1h39m38.998s	114.925	1m27.518s	3
4	M Webber	Red Bull-Renault RB7	66	1h39m51.267s	114.690	1m27.187s	4
5	F Alonso	Ferrari 150 Italia	65	1h39m13.856s	113.662	1m28.737s	4
6	M Schumacher	Mercedes MGP W02	65	1h39m31.695s	113.323	1m29.463s	3
7	N Rosberg	Mercedes MGP W02	65	1h39m32.570s	113.306	1m29.155s	3
8	N Heidfeld	Renault R31	65	1h39m33.015s	113.298	1m26.958s	3
9	S Perez	Sauber-Ferrari C30	65	1h39m53.605s	112.908	1m27.247s	3
10	K Kobayashi	Sauber-Ferrari C30	65	1h39m58.323s	112.820	1m27.615s	3
11	V Petrov	Renault R31	65	1h40m11.150s	112.579	1m29.592s	3
12	P di Resta	Force India-Mercedes VJM04	65	1h40m17.511s	112.460	1m29.469s	3
13	A Sutil	Force India-Mercedes VJM04	65	1h40m23.337s	112.351	1m28.791s	3
14	S Buemi	Toro Rosso-Ferrari STR6	65	1h40m29.839s	112.230	1m30.049s	3
15	P Maldonado	Williams-Cosworth FW33	65	1h40m30.081s	112.225	1m29.391s	4
16	J Alguersuari	Toro Rosso-Ferrari STR6	64	1h39m13.809s	111.914	1m29.132s	4
17	R Barrichello	Williams-Cosworth FW33	64	1h39m15.964s	111.874	1m26.891s	4
18	J Trulli	Lotus-Renault T128	64	1h40m11.203s	110.846	1m30.783s	3
19	T Glock	Virgin-Cosworth MVR-02	63	1h40m27.140s	108.825	1m31.635s	3
20	J d'Ambrosio	Virgin-Cosworth MVR-02	62	1h39m18.879s	108.325	1m32.549s	3
21	N Karthikeyan	HRT-Cosworth F111	61	1h39m10.631s	106.725	1m32.848s	3
R	F Massa	Ferrari 150 Italia	58	Gearbox	-	1m29.081s	3
R	H Kovalainen	Lotus-Renault T128	48	Accident	-	1m30.618s	3
R	V Liuzzi	HRT-Cosworth F111	28	Gearbox	-	1m33.884s	1

CHAMPIONSHIP

	Driver	Pts
1	S Vettel	118
2	L Hamilton	77
3	M Webber	67
4	J Button	61
5	F Alonso	51
6	N Rosberg	26
7	N Heidfeld	25
8	F Massa	24
9	V Petrov	21
10	M Schumacher	14
11	K Kobayashi	9
12	S Buemi	6
13	A Sutil	2
14	S Perez	2
15	P di Resta	2

	Constructor	Pts
1	Red Bull-Renault	185
2	McLaren-Mercedes	138
3	Ferrari	75
4	Renault	46
5	Mercedes	40
6	Sauber-Ferrari	11
7	Toro Rosso-Ferrari	6
8	Force India-Mercedes	4

Fastest lap
L Hamilton 1m26.727s
(120.071mph) on lap 52

Fastest speed trap
S Perez 205.114mph
Slowest speed trap
V Liuzzi 187.032mph

Fastest pit stop
1 N Rosberg 19.534s
2 L Hamilton 19.761s
3 S Vettel 19.887s

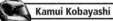

Adrian Sutil
"I did the opposite strategy to Paul by starting on primes, which were slow to start with. Then, as I ran the options, the race came to me and I moved forward."

Kamui Kobayashi
"I lost time on lap 1, as I was pushed into the gravel and then another car hit me, which resulted in a left-rear puncture. I had to pit and was relegated to last."

Sébastien Buemi
"I made a good start, passing Massa, Button and Maldonado, but Button and Massa got by again. I was then unlucky to lose a lot of time when I got lapped."

Jarno Trulli
"I gained places at the start. With softs our car was better than with hards and that gave us a good first couple of stints. Annoyingly, I then had an exhaust problem."

Narain Karthikeyan
"The tyres were degrading, especially the rears. The early laps were OK, but the rear started giving problems. I also had trouble with my seat and burnt my back."

Timo Glock
"It was a struggle going into Turn 1. Liuzzi got past me, as he had a better line, but I got past him after the first stop, which meant that I could then go at my own pace."

Paul di Resta
"We compromised our qualifying by saving tyres, which was definitely the right approach, but we were just missing a bit more pace to do any more than we did."

Sergio Perez
"It was a hard fight for points. My first points in F1 are special for me. The team had a good strategy and did a perfect job at the stops. Today is a turning point."

Jaime Alguersuari
"I did my maximum, pushing lap after lap, while trying to look after my tyres. After 12 laps, my tyres were gone, which is why I ended up doing a four-stop race."

Heikki Kovalainen
"It's a shame that my afternoon came to an end like that. I made a mistake on the entry to Turn 4 and went off, but up until that point the race was pretty good."

Vitantonio Liuzzi
"I passed a few cars into Turn 1, then pulled away from both Virgins. After the first stop, I lost grip in the rear. I also started feeling issues with the upshift."

Jerome d'Ambrosio
"It was a good race, better than qualifying. I had a good first stint, but when we hit traffic it turns into a completely different race. Here you lose a lot of time."

FORMULA 1 GRAND PRIX DE MONACO 2011
MONTE CARLO

ONE-STOP TRIUMPH

Sebastian Vettel gambled on making a set of prime tyres last for an astonishing 62 laps, winning a classic late-race showdown between three cars on three different strategies

A t Monaco, we were treated to a superb and utterly compelling contest that saw Sebastian Vettel, Fernando Alonso and Jenson Button running nose to tail as the laps ticked away. Having run one-, two- and three-stop strategies respectively, they had ended up in the same place at the same time, but with tyres of widely varying age and thus potential performance. And then, the red flag robbed of us a proper conclusion to the race, and gave Vettel a get-out-of-jail-free card.

A stoppage had also turned qualifying on its head, generating a grid made up of times set on the Q3 first runs, and leaving Lewis Hamilton stranded down in ninth place.

The red flag in qualifying was caused by Sergio Perez, who had driven superbly to make it to Q3, only to lose control under braking for the chicane. He hit the wall on the right and then slid into the barrier. He was knocked unconscious, but fortunately there were no ill-effects.

That red flag came with 2m26s of the session to go. The drivers had completed only one run and, in the end, they were not able to go faster after the restart. No one suffered more than Hamilton. Having been fastest in Q1 and Q2, he had chosen to make only one run in Q3 as he tried to save a set of new tyres for the race.

The red flag came before he had set his time. After the

"Pole position is the first thing you have to achieve in Monaco, and in Q3 the lap I had was just spot-on. McLaren, especially Lewis, looked very competitive. He was a bit unlucky, obviously trying a different strategy that in the end caught him out with the red flag.

There was a bit of a shadow over qualifying when you see a colleague (Sergio Perez) crash and not jump out immediately. You sit there asking for updates and it's difficult to keep the focus.

The race was unbelievable. I had a good first stint and pulled a gap to Jenson. I targeted going longer on the options, but Jenson came in, we reacted, but had a problem at the stop, so lost track position.

I went on to the hard tyre, Jenson went on the soft and he was pulling away like crazy. At one stage I was P2, 15 seconds behind with him still pulling away and the victory seemed far away. I knew that once he was 19–20s ahead it would be quite difficult – that's the time you need in hand for a pit stop.

Then he came in for another set of softs which, to be honest, at that stage was a surprise. The safety car came out and we were back in the lead but it was quite difficult to stay ahead.

Jenson was much quicker on the soft tyres, but it's very difficult to pass here. Fernando was on a similar strategy. Probably they were a bit cleverer with the safety car to bring him in and put on a new set of hard tyres. The lap Jenson pitted we initially wanted to react and pit as well, but I said 'let's try to one-stop'.

There were 33 laps to go. I had quite a good feeling on the tyres I had. I saw that the only chance to win the race was to try to stay out. It was really close. I think it was 20 laps under pressure with Fernando and Jenson behind. I knew it's difficult to pass, obviously, but it was getting closer and closer and I think it would have been a difficult last six laps.

But then we caught the big group. They crashed in front of us, so there was another safety car and a suspended race, allowing us to change tyres. The roulette wheel favoured me today!"

session was restarted, he had just one lap, and struggled with handling on cold tyres. He could only manage seventh – and then had that time deleted for jumping the chicane, sending him back to ninth.

Vettel took pole, while Button gave McLaren something to cheer by taking second, ahead of Mark Webber, who was nearly half a second off his team-mate. Alonso wasn't able to follow up on his good practice form, but was still a threat in fourth.

Pole is normally a secure place to start at Monaco, and Vettel probably felt a little more comfortable about having Button right behind rather than Hamilton or Alonso. In fact, his biggest concern was the presence of Webber in third. For once, the guy in second place on the grid held on to his position at the start, and Alonso pushed Webber down to fourth, so Vettel didn't have to worry about having Mark on his tail.

Even better for Vettel, Button slipped back in the early laps, and with no immediate pressure in his mirrors, Seb was able to find a good rhythm, putting in quick times while protecting his supersofts as best he could.

On lap 16, Button dived into the pits to take on new supersofts, the deficit to Vettel having been cut to less than 3s in traffic. Vettel came in next lap, and neither Seb nor his crew should have been under any undue pressure for what should have been a very routine covering operation.

But the request to fit supersoft tyres, to shadow what Jenson was doing, didn't get through to the mechanics. After a delay, Vettel left on primes. And Jenson had gone past, having also banged in a superb out-lap on his fresh ex-qualifying supersofts.

By the time Vettel completed lap 17, his first out of the pits on the less favourable softs, he was 4.1s behind – a remarkable turnaround and a massive headache for RBR. The only positive was that having used both tyre compounds, Seb could, in theory, now get to the finish without another stop.

Initially it looked like an impossible ask, given that the tyres would have to last 62 laps, significantly more than anyone in the paddock had anticipated. The only real hope was that some safety-car interludes would calm things down, allowing him to conserve his tyres.

"We then said 'OK this isn't a disaster, we need to change our strategy here and work our way out of it'," said Horner. "So then there were a whole load of different permutations that we were looking at, whether to stop again, whether to go on the supersoft at the end, whether to go on another set of softs…"

Vettel couldn't allow Button to get far enough ahead that the McLaren could make a second stop and come out still in front. If he did that, and put on the softs, it would be 'game over'. They would then be on the same tyres, both in a position to get to the end, but Jenson's would be that much fresher.

For a while, it looked like Jenson might do it, but Vettel hung in there, keeping the margin at 13–14s. Jenson had lost momentum. McLaren had to do something, choosing to bring him in on lap 33.

They knew he would come out still behind Vettel, but it was a question of either, a) putting him on to softs and creating a potential race to the flag with Jenson on

OPPOSITE TOP Sebastian Vettel sprints into the lead at the start, ahead of the fast-starting Jenson Button and Fernando Alonso, as Michael Schumacher rams the rear of Lewis Hamilton's McLaren

OPPOSITE BOTTOM Mark Webber dropped down the field after a slow pit stop, but recovered well and made some impressive passes to finish fourth

TOP Lewis Hamilton was handed a drive-through penalty after this clumsy move on Felipe Massa at the Loews hairpin

ABOVE Pastor Maldonado was running an excellent fifth until he fell victim to another over-optimistic move by Lewis Hamilton five laps from the flag, relegating him to an eventual 18th, and last, place

tyres that were 17 laps younger than Seb's, or, b) taking another set of supersofts and giving Jenson some pace and overtaking potential, but the necessity to make a third stop for softs. In the end, Jenson went for the latter choice. No sooner had he made the stop than the safety car came out after Felipe Massa crashed in the tunnel shortly after contact with Hamilton.

It was crunch time for Vettel – he could pit under the safety car, and drop back behind Jenson, or stay out and try to get his already well-used tyres to the end. There were still some 44 laps to run, and it looked like a daunting task, but he chose to go for it.

Jenson was behind him in the safety-car queue, albeit with the lapped Heidfeld, Buemi and Barrichello in the way, preventing him from being in a position to immediately attack Seb at the restart.

By lap 41, just three laps after the green, Button was right on Seb's tail. Jenson could go for it because he could use up those tyres. Indeed he had to go for it, because he had to find a way to squeeze in a third stop for softs, and that meant getting past Vettel. Seb, meanwhile, just had to focus on the long game and somehow stay ahead while preserving his tyres. However, Jenson couldn't find a way by, and McLaren's attention was diverted towards Alonso.

Ferrari had made a great call under the Massa safety car. Having watched Button take the supersofts on lap 34, the team put Alonso on to softs on the basis that a 44-lap run to the finish was feasible. With Jenson stuck behind Vettel, Fernando was closing in. Button had to stop again at some stage, and McLaren brought him in for softs on lap 48, after he'd run 15–18–15 laps on his three sets of supersofts. At the end of lap 49, Jenson's out-lap on the new tyres, Vettel was 5.9s clear of Alonso, and Button was third, a further 14s behind the Ferrari.

Now it was a question of the maths, with everyone's tyres losing performance by the lap. Vettel's were 33 laps old, Alonso's had done 15, and Button's just the one.

Seb knew that his pursuers would catch him, and he really had to use his head. Alonso was in striking distance by lap 57, and Jenson joined the party on lap 62. With 16 laps to go, it was now all about survival for Vettel.

"We were trying it as we went along!" said Adrian Newey. "It was unexplored territory, put it that way. We knew that the tyres would last a lot longer than the options, but we didn't know exactly how much longer."

Under the most intense pressure, Vettel gave his more experienced pursuers a master class in defensive driving. Alonso was saving himself for a late attack, while Button was being patient, and had a feeling that his rivals would both end up in the wall.

OPPOSITE TOP Jenson Button chases Fernando Alonso and Sebastian Vettel in the closing laps

OPPOSITE BOTTOM Vitaly Petrov suffered an injured ankle after several cars tangled on lap 67, his extraction resulting in a red flag

ABOVE Button's tyres are changed on the grid before the restart – a scene repeated for Alonso and Vettel – leading to a processional finish

TALKING POINT
WE WERE ROBBED!

Heading to the Monaco Grand Prix there was much discussion about how long Pirelli's supersoft tyre was going to last. People were talking about 'qualifying' tyres returning to F1 and predicting that the front-runners could be pitting for new rubber as early as lap five.

It could not have been further from the truth. After the first day's running Pirelli was confident of getting more than half a race distance out of both the prime (soft) tyre and the option (supersoft)!

Suddenly, people were talking about one-stop races, although the maths showed that two stints on options and one on primes would probably be the quickest way.

Early on, Vettel converted his pole and pulled away from Button, but when Jenson stopped first and Red Bull reacted, the World Champion had a slow stop. He returned to the fray on the hard tyre in second place, with Button on the soft, and now it was Jenson's turn to romp away.

The timing of tyre stops and safety cars distilled the race down to the fact that if Vettel was to take his first Monaco win, he needed to make a set of Pirelli primes last 62 laps! Behind him, Alonso was on fresher supersofts and caught him with around 20 laps to go.

Behind the Ferrari, Button was on newer primes and reeled in the pair of them. The race could not have been more beautifully poised if you had scripted it yourself.

Alonso got very close into Ste Devote on one lap, jinking right to have a look and also looking threatening under braking for the harbour chicane.

There is no doubt that Fernando was going to pull a move, as he admitted. "I was waiting to see how his tyres coped in the last laps but if they hadn't gone away I was still going to go for it," Alonso said. "I had nothing to lose."

Button was potentially quickest of the three, but could see a drama unfolding right in front of him and wasn't about to do anything rash. He was right there, ready to pick up any pieces, and if there weren't any to be had, would have a go himself.

So what happened? A red flag for a multiple crash that momentarily trapped Vitaly Petrov in his Renault. And what does the rule book say in such circumstances? Before any restart, cars can be worked upon and tyres changed. The drama had been pricked like an over-inflated balloon.

They all bolted on fresh tyres and ran, in Monaco fashion, untroubled to the end. Pirelli's Paul Hembery spoke for everyone when he said it was a rule that needed to be looked at…

Sadly, we were robbed of potentially the most exciting finish in years when the red flag came out, the three leaders having somehow slipped through the carnage, as Hamilton, Jaime Alguersuari and Vitaly Petrov tangled in front of them at the Swimming Pool.

Believing he was hurt, Petrov stayed in the car and shouted 'hospital, hospital' into his radio. Told extraction might take 20 minutes, Race Director Charlie Whiting decided to suspend the race rather than let it run to the flag under a safety car.

So we still had a race, but with a catch. Under a race suspension, teams are allowed to work on their cars during the interval, and they are also allowed to change tyres.

So, for the final six-lap sprint, Vettel and Alonso were able to fit used supersofts, while Button faced a double whammy. Not only did he lose the tyre advantage he had before the stoppage, but he had no supersofts left, so had to take softs, albeit a new set. After the restart, the last few laps were a formality for Vettel.

"He drove an absolutely immaculate race," said Horner. "And he made it work, even without the restart he would have held on. It was a straightforward race to the finish, and on the options we were relatively comfortable. The only danger was that he would go for the fastest lap on the last lap, so I'm grateful that he didn't!"

Alonso put in a great performance, and the man himself was pretty confident that he could have found a way past Vettel and held off Button. Jenson, arguably, was the best placed of the three before the stoppage.

"We were going for the win," said Martin Whitmarsh of Jenson's prospects. "I think we had a good strategy and I think we were quick. Had we not had the red flag, it may have been a different result, but that's how it is. So disappointing, but I don't regret decisions we made with Jenson. I think that was the right call. It could have paid off, it should have paid off, but it didn't."

Lost in the excitement was a brilliant performance by Webber. The Aussie wasted over 12s when he had a long pit stop in the immediate aftermath of the Vettel foul-up, and a great drive saw him eventually fight back to where he was originally, in fourth place. He made a point by setting fastest lap on the final lap.

Kamui Kobayashi ran a one-stop strategy for Sauber, and jumped up the order when the safety car gave him the perfect chance to pit. Initially, he ran behind Adrian Sutil, who used the same strategy, but the Sauber driver got by when he pushed the Force India out of the way.

A bitterly frustrated Hamilton ultimately finished sixth, after a wild race that saw him make a bad start and earn penalties after tangles with Massa and, most controversially, an impressive Pastor Maldonado. Had Lewis started from his rightful position – which surely wouldn't have been any lower than second – we might have had an even more dramatic battle at the front...

TOP LEFT Sauber's Kamui Kobayashi finished an excellent fifth, despite a clash with Adrian Sutil that earned the Japanese driver a reprimand

LEFT Sebastian Vettel passes the chequered flag again to take a remarkable fifth win from six races

SNAPSHOT FROM
MONACO

CLOCKWISE FROM RIGHT

The unmistakable landscape of Monte Carlo; Mark Webber takes the opportunity to check out details of the McLaren MP4-26; Sergio Perez's Sauber was in a sorry state after his crash in Q3; marshals on their way to work; the Monaco skyline reflected in the polished glass of the McLaren Brand Centre; the beautiful people flock to Monaco to see and be seen; Sebastian Vettel celebrates his win with a spectacular entrance to the Red Bull Racing pool; a water-powered jet pack demonstration provided entertainment off-track; Lewis Hamilton shows off his diamond-encrusted helmet to girlfriend Nicole Scherzinger and brother Nick; Vitaly Petrov fans unite

RACE RESULTS
MONACO
MONTE CARLO

RACE DATE May 29th
CIRCUIT LENGTH 2.075 miles
NO. OF LAPS 78
RACE DISTANCE 161.850 miles
WEATHER Sunny & dry, 24°C
TRACK TEMP 42°C
ATTENDANCE Not available
LAP RECORD Michael Schumacher, 1m14.439s, 100.373mph, 2004

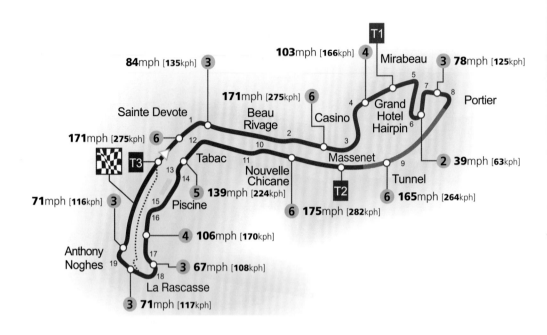

PRACTICE 1			
	Driver	Time	Laps
1	S Vettel	1m16.619s	25
2	F Alonso	1m16.732s	24
3	N Rosberg	1m17.139s	20
4	F Massa	1m17.316s	24
5	L Hamilton	1m17.350s	23
6	J Button	1m17.534s	24
7	P Maldonado	1m18.527s	30
8	A Sutil	1m18.578s	24
9	V Petrov	1m18.733s	16
10	M Schumacher	1m18.805s	14
11	N Heidfeld	1m18.928s	19
12	S Buemi	1m19.234s	24
13	R Barrichello	1m19.395s	24
14	D Ricciardo	1m19.463s	25
15	K Kobayashi	1m19.768s	25
16	S Perez	1m19.792s	26
17	H Kovalainen	1m20.083s	23
18	J Trulli	1m21.116s	27
19	P di Resta	1m21.548s	32
20	J d'Ambrosio	1m21.758s	31
21	T Glock	1m21.815s	17
22	V Liuzzi	1m22.840s	13
23	N Karthikeyan	1m23.885s	37
24	M Webber	No time	3

PRACTICE 2			
	Driver	Time	Laps
1	F Alonso	1m15.123s	42
2	L Hamilton	1m15.228s	33
3	N Rosberg	1m15.321s	44
4	J Button	1m15.448s	38
5	S Vettel	1m15.667s	46
6	F Massa	1m15.781s	45
7	M Schumacher	1m16.356s	33
8	M Webber	1m16.642s	42
9	A Sutil	1m17.101s	46
10	N Heidfeld	1m17.126s	38
11	V Petrov	1m17.337s	35
12	S Perez	1m17.541s	47
13	R Barrichello	1m17.570s	39
14	S Buemi	1m17.581s	32
15	P Maldonado	1m17.633s	49
16	K Kobayashi	1m17.706s	37
17	J Alguersuari	1m17.789s	43
18	H Kovalainen	1m18.266s	50
19	J Trulli	1m18.490s	39
20	P di Resta	1m19.053s	15
21	J d'Ambrosio	1m19.185s	40
22	T Glock	1m19.338s	35
23	N Karthikeyan	1m22.066s	33
24	V Liuzzi	No time	0

PRACTICE 3			
	Driver	Time	Laps
1	F Alonso	1m14.433s	18
2	J Button	1m14.996s	17
3	F Massa	1m15.024s	19
4	S Vettel	1m15.245s	19
5	M Schumacher	1m15.310s	21
6	L Hamilton	1m15.386s	14
7	M Webber	1m15.529s	19
8	J Alguersuari	1m16.617s	13
9	S Buemi	1m16.736s	15
10	S Perez	1m16.821s	19
11	P di Resta	1m16.990s	20
12	R Barrichello	1m17.196s	13
13	P Maldonado	1m17.333s	17
14	K Kobayashi	1m17.403s	18
15	V Petrov	1m17.779s	17
16	N Heidfeld	1m17.880s	17
17	A Sutil	1m18.069s	17
18	H Kovalainen	1m18.115s	20
19	T Glock	1m18.580s	21
20	J d'Ambrosio	1m18.808s	21
21	J Trulli	1m19.259s	19
22	V Liuzzi	1m20.115s	15
23	N Karthikeyan	1m20.278s	16
24	N Rosberg	No time	3

QUALIFYING 1		
	Driver	Time
1	L Hamilton	1m15.207s
2	J Button	1m15.397s
3	S Vettel	1m15.606s
4	P Maldonado	1m15.819s
5	N Rosberg	1m15.858s
6	S Perez	1m15.918s
7	F Alonso	1m16.051s
8	M Webber	1m16.087s
9	M Schumacher	1m16.092s
10	F Massa	1m16.309s
11	S Buemi	1m16.358s
12	V Petrov	1m16.378s
13	K Kobayashi	1m16.513s
14	A Sutil	1m16.600s
15	R Barrichello	1m16.807s
16	N Heidfeld	1m16.681s
17	P di Resta	1m16.813s
18	H Kovalainen	1m17.343s
19	J Trulli	1m17.381s
20	J Alguersuari	1m17.820s
21	T Glock	1m17.914s
22	J d'Ambrosio	1m18.736s
23	N Karthikeyan	No time
24	V Liuzzi	No time

QUALIFYING 2		
	Driver	Time
1	L Hamilton	1m14.275s
2	S Vettel	1m14.277s
3	J Button	1m14.545s
4	F Alonso	1m14.569s
5	F Massa	1m14.648s
6	N Rosberg	1m14.741s
7	M Webber	1m14.742s
8	M Schumacher	1m14.981s
9	S Perez	1m15.482s
10	P Maldonado	1m15.545s
11	V Petrov	1m15.815s
12	R Barrichello	1m15.826s
13	K Kobayashi	1m15.973s
14	P di Resta	1m16.118s
15	A Sutil	1m16.121s
16	N Heidfeld	1m16.214s
17	S Buemi	1m16.300s

Best sectors – Practice			Speed trap – Practice			Best sectors – Qualifying			Speed trap – Qualifying		
Sec 1	F Alonso	19.357s	1	A Sutil	176.096mph	Sec 1	S Vettel	19.162s	1	A Sutil	177.463mph
Sec 2	F Alonso	34.617s	2	P di Resta	176.034mph	Sec 2	S Vettel	34.367s	2	J Button	176.904mph
Sec 3	J Button	20.227s	3	V Petrov	175.723mph	Sec 3	S Vettel	20.027s	3	P di Resta	176.655mph

Sebastian Vettel
"I lost position to Jenson at the first stop. The safety car helped us, but it was hard to do 60 laps on the same tyres. I was pressed, but there was another safety car."

Jenson Button
"After the red flag for Vitaly, the teams were able to fit fresh tyres, which meant we couldn't do anything, as Seb, Fernando and I were on the same pace."

Fernando Alonso
"I looked after the tyres early on, before attacking Vettel. Then came the red flag. That meant it was over as, on new tyres, he was impossible to beat."

Michael Schumacher
"At the start, the anti-stall system kicked in. Then I had a clash with Lewis at Turn 1 that bent my wing, so I lost downforce. At the end, there was a fire in the airbox."

Nick Heidfeld
"I'm glad that Vitaly is OK. At the start, I almost got one of the Force Indias. When the safety car came out, I got a late call into the pits which definitely helped me."

Rubens Barrichello
"With six laps to go, I thought 10th was the best I could do. I ended up ninth, but not in the way I'd have liked, as it was at the expense of my team-mate."

Mark Webber
"I didn't go long enough on the first stint. When I arrived in the pits we didn't have tyres out, as there was a radio problem. When you wait here, you lose position."

Lewis Hamilton
"I made some strong moves on Michael, Felipe and Pastor, and got penalised for two of them. It's tough to overtake around here, and I was racing my heart out."

Felipe Massa
"After Lewis pushed me into Webber at Loews, the car was not right and I couldn't drive it. That put me on the dirt and then I ended up in the barrier."

Nico Rosberg
"I had a good start. After that, I thought that I'd be able to push, but unfortunately the rear tyres went off in the first stint, which really cost me performance."

Vitaly Petrov
"It was a big impact and I could not feel my legs. I didn't lose consciousness, but was in quite a lot of pain. It's a shame, as I had gained two places at the start."

Pastor Maldonado
"The result wasn't what we wanted, but the rest of the race was good until Hamilton tried an ambitious move at the first corner that ended my race."

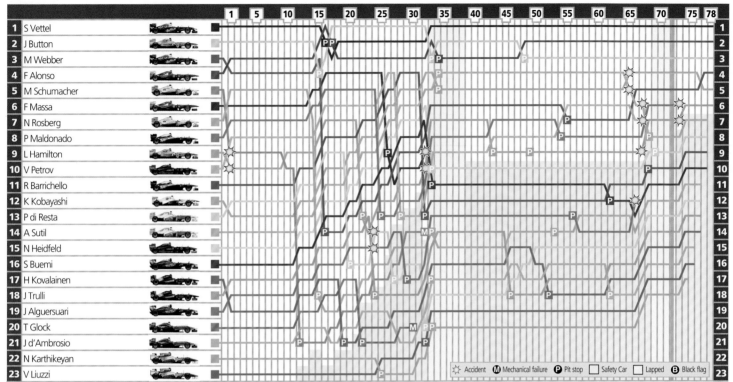

| | 1 | 5 | 10 | 15 | 20 | 25 | 30 | 35 | 40 | 45 | 50 | 55 | 60 | 65 | 70 | 75 | 78 |

	Driver
1	S Vettel
2	J Button
3	M Webber
4	F Alonso
5	M Schumacher
6	F Massa
7	N Rosberg
8	P Maldonado
9	L Hamilton
10	V Petrov
11	R Barrichello
12	K Kobayashi
13	P di Resta
14	A Sutil
15	N Heidfeld
16	S Buemi
17	H Kovalainen
18	J Trulli
19	J Alguersuari
20	T Glock
21	J d'Ambrosio
22	N Karthikeyan
23	V Liuzzi

☆ Accident · Ⓜ Mechanical failure · Ⓟ Pit stop · ☐ Safety Car · ☐ Lapped · Ⓑ Black flag

QUALIFYING 3

	Driver	Time
1	S Vettel	1m13.556s
2	J Button	1m13.997s
3	M Webber	1m14.019s
4	F Alonso	1m14.483s
5	M Schumacher	1m14.682s
6	F Massa	1m14.877s
7	N Rosberg	1m15.766s
8	P Maldonado	1m16.258s
9	L Hamilton	No time
10	S Perez	No time

GRID

	Driver	Time
1	S Vettel	1m13.556s
2	J Button	1m13.997s
3	M Webber	1m14.019s
4	F Alonso	1m14.483s
5	M Schumacher	1m14.682s
6	F Massa	1m14.877s
7	N Rosberg	1m15.766s
8	P Maldonado	1m16.258s
9	L Hamilton	No time
10	V Petrov	1m15.815s
11	R Barrichello	1m15.826s
12	K Kobayashi	1m15.973s
13	P di Resta	1m16.118s
14	A Sutil	1m16.121s
15	N Heidfeld	1m16.214s
16	S Buemi	1m16.300s
17	H Kovalainen	1m17.343s
18	J Trulli	1m17.381s
19	J Alguersuari	1m17.820s
20	T Glock	1m17.914s
21	J d'Ambrosio	1m18.736s
22	N Karthikeyan	No time
23	V Liuzzi	No time

RACE

	Driver	Car	Laps	Time	Avg. mph	Fastest	Stops
1	S Vettel	Red Bull-Renault RB7	78	2h09m38.373s	74.921	1m16.267s	1
2	F Alonso	Ferrari 150 Italia	78	2h09m39.511s	74.912	1m16.471s	2
3	J Button	McLaren-Mercedes MP4-26	78	2h09m40.751s	74.901	1m16.463s	3
4	M Webber	Red Bull-Renault RB7	78	2h10m01.474s	74.702	1m16.234s	2
5	K Kobayashi	Sauber-Ferrari C30	78	2h10m05.289s	74.665	1m18.308s	1
6	L Hamilton	McLaren-Mercedes MP4-26	78	2h10m25.583s*	74.471	1m17.847s	3
7	A Sutil	Force India-Mercedes VJM04	77	2h09m54.910s	73.806	1m18.724s	2
8	N Heidfeld	Renault R31	77	2h09m58.699s	73.770	1m17.857s	2
9	R Barrichello	Williams-Cosworth FW33	77	2h09m09.135s	73.672	1m18.584s	2
10	S Buemi	Toro Rosso-Ferrari STR6	77	2h10m09.637s	73.667	1m18.832s	2
11	N Rosberg	Mercedes MGP W02	76	2h09m54.060s	72.855	1m18.699s	3
12	P di Resta	Force India-Mercedes VJM04	76	2h09m55.850s	72.839	1m18.724s	3
13	J Trulli	Lotus-Renault T128	76	2h10m19.445s	72.619	1m21.277s	2
14	H Kovalainen	Lotus-Renault T128	76	2h10m19.884s	72.615	1m20.678s	2
15	J d'Ambrosio	Virgin-Cosworth MVR-02	75	2h10m18.135s	71.676	1m21.391s	2
16	V Liuzzi	HRT-Cosworth F111	75	2h10m21.400s	71.646	1m21.566s	1
17	N Karthikeyan	HRT-Cosworth F111	74	2h10m34.254s	70.574	1m22.731s	2
18	P Maldonado	Williams-Cosworth FW33	73	Accident	-	1m18.904s	2
R	V Petrov	Renault R31	67	Accident	-	1m20.058s	1
R	J Alguersuari	Toro Rosso-Ferrari STR6	66	Accident	-	1m18.608s	2
R	F Massa	Ferrari 150 Italia	32	Accident	-	1m20.202s	1
R	M Schumacher	Mercedes MGP W02	32	Airbox fire	-	1m19.801s	1
R	T Glock	Virgin-Cosworth MVR-02	30	Suspension	-	1m22.102s	1
NS	S Perez	Sauber-Ferrari C30	0	Driver injury	-	-	0

* 20-second penalty for colliding with Pastor Maldonado

CHAMPIONSHIP

	Driver	Pts
1	S Vettel	143
2	L Hamilton	85
3	M Webber	79
4	J Button	76
5	F Alonso	69
6	N Heidfeld	29
7	N Rosberg	26
8	F Massa	24
9	V Petrov	21
10	K Kobayashi	19
11	M Schumacher	14
12	A Sutil	8
13	S Buemi	7
14	R Barrichello	2
15	S Perez	2
16	P di Resta	2

	Constructor	Pts
1	Red Bull-Renault	222
2	McLaren-Mercedes	161
3	Ferrari	93
4	Renault	50
5	Mercedes	40
6	Sauber-Ferrari	21
7	Force India-Mercedes	10
8	Toro Rosso-Ferrari	7
9	Williams-Cosworth	2

Fastest lap
M Webber 1m16.234s
(98.006mph) on lap 78

Fastest speed trap
L Hamilton 179.576mph
Slowest speed trap
T Glock 170.007mph

Fastest pit stop
1 J Button 24.670s
2 P di Resta 24.970s
3 A Sutil 25.037s

Adrian Sutil
"When the first safety car came out, I pitted for options and knew I'd be on them for a long time. I tried to make them last, but I ran wide and picked up a puncture."

Kamui Kobayashi
"The team did a great job with strategy. It was no problem to do a long stint with the super-softs. But then I was stuck behind Sutil, and had to keep Webber back."

Sebastien Buemi
"I started 16th and finished 10th after a difficult grand prix, as by the end of it I have to admit I wasn't too sure where we were in terms of strategy and tyres."

Jarno Trulli
"That was a great team result. I kept up with the cars ahead, but the safety car hit our strategy hard, as the gap we had was wasted behind slower cars."

Narain Karthikeyan
"The car went well in the first stint. I was ahead of Tonio when I pitted, and then the safety car came out twice, which was unlucky and meant I lost a lap."

Timo Glock
"I was keeping up with the cars ahead, but unluckily the right-rear pushrod was damaged and collapsed in the chicane. Lucky it happened at a slow part."

Paul di Resta
"After my first stop, the team told me that I needed to pass Jaime, so I tried to pass him at the hairpin, but bent my wing, forcing me to make an early second stop."

Sergio Perez
Did not start due to accident in qualifying.

Jaime Alguersuari
"I was passing Heidfeld and I think Sutil had a problem with his rear tyre, so Hamilton braked hard in front of me and, although I braked as hard as I could, I couldn't stop."

Heikki Kovalainen
"Finishing 13th and 14th is a good result, but that was an average race for me. I lost a position at the start and that was pretty much the end of my race."

Vitantonio Liuzzi
"I had a problem from lap 1 with the power steering, so it was tough. Luckily, we made it to the end and 16th is a good result as it's good for motivating the team."

Jerome d'Ambrosio
"It went OK for 30 laps, but when Heidfeld passed I got pick-up from the marbles and couldn't clean the tyres, lost grip and the Lotuses were able to pass me."

FORMULA 1 GRAND PRIX
DU CANADA 2011
MONTREAL

JB BACK TO FRONT

After clashing with Lewis Hamilton and Fernando Alonso, pitting six times, including a stop-and-go penalty, and lying in last place on lap 37, Jenson Button drove an incredible race to take victory

Jenson Button scored a sensational victory in a dramatic rain-hit Canadian GP after leader Sebastian Vettel made a mistake on the very last lap of a thrilling contest.

Not for the first time in his career, Jenson made the right calls in a wet race and, more importantly, showed that he understood how to play the long game. In these races things can go awry very quickly, but, just as easily, fortune can swing back in your favour.

The Montréal numbers were extraordinary. Quite apart from his official winning average speed of 46mph – the clock was still running during a two-hour suspension – Jenson pushed the boundaries by making six visits to the pits, including a drive-through and two slow crawls back to replace punctured tyres after collisions.

Vettel's weekend had got off to a bad start when he crashed in FP1 on Friday. However, qualifying went routinely, and he safely secured pole. Meanwhile, team-mate Mark Webber missed the whole of FP3 with KERS issues, did not have the use of it in qualifying, and so was restricted to fourth place.

Ferrari was expected to be strong at a track that featured long straights, and where Pirelli was using the supersoft tyre, and Fernando Alonso and Felipe Massa did well to secure second and third places.

INSIDE LINE
JENSON BUTTON

**McLAREN
DRIVER**

"I really don't know what to say – last to first!

The incident with Lewis... I couldn't see anything when he was alongside me. I couldn't see anything in my mirrors. It was one of those things. Then it was really a fight. I got a drive-through penalty for speeding behind the safety car and I had to fight my way through about three times.

Eventually, on the last lap, I was chasing down Seb. He ran a little bit wide on to the wet and I was able to take the opportunity. Even if I hadn't won today I would still have enjoyed that race immensely.

It was one of those grands prix where you're nowhere, then you're somewhere, then you're nowhere and then you're somewhere. As we always say, the last lap is the important one to be leading and I led the right half of it!

It felt like I spent more time in the pits than on the track! The guys did a great job calling the strategy. At some points we definitely lucked out, especially when the red flag came out, but we called it very well going to slicks.

Fighting your way through is almost as good as winning: that feeling of getting one up on someone. A big thank-you to the whole team for staying calm in some very difficult circumstances, especially when I damaged the front left and the front wing. The car on the intermediates and the slicks felt fantastic. On the wet tyre it didn't really work.

I wouldn't have had a chance if we didn't have DRS here. If Sebastian hadn't made a mistake it would have been very tricky, but I was getting very close to making the move because of the DRS.

On the penultimate lap I got DRS but I wasn't really close enough to make a move, but I felt I was creeping closer and it could have been one of those moves on the last lap into the last corner.

It didn't get that far because Seb put a wheel on to the wet and ran wide, but I'll take that because I was pressuring him and he was trying to keep me out of the DRS zone. After Monaco, which again was a great race for me, to get the win here and have some luck, I think we deserved that."

McLaren had a disappointing qualifying. Hamilton could not better fifth place, complaining that his seventh gear ratio was too short, while Button was fifth. The team seemed to have brought a higher-downforce spec than some of its rivals, and that compromised straightline speed.

However, that was potentially a benefit in the wet and, as had been predicted, rain came on Sunday. The early laps were run under a safety car before the field was released. Vettel led away, while further back Hamilton clumsily tangled with Webber at Turn One, pitching the RBR driver into a spin. Button gained a spot from the Aussie and lost one to Schumacher, ending the first racing lap in seventh. On the next lap he gained another place when Lewis ran wide.

Hamilton was keen to make amends, and when his team-mate got the final chicane slightly wrong at the end of lap seven, Lewis made an ambitious move up the inside, close to the pit wall.

We'd seen them race wheel-to-wheel several times in the past without any dramas. This time, it didn't work out. Jenson insisted that he could only see a flash of orange in his mirrors, and thinking that it was his own rear wing, he moved across. The subsequent contact could have had catastrophic results, and yet somehow both men were able to continue in the right direction, although a bitterly frustrated Hamilton was told by his team to park later round the lap due to broken suspension.

Button, meanwhile, had a left-rear puncture, and had to crawl back to the pits for a replacement. In an attempt to salvage opportunity from disaster, McLaren put Jenson on to inters. He resumed in 12th place.

The safety car made the tyre choice a little less risky, in that there were four laps of slow running, which helped the track to dry further. Unfortunately, during the safety-car period, Jenson had exceeded the target speed, and that earned a drive-through. He couldn't take the penalty under the safety car, and came in at the first opportunity after the green. He rejoined 15th, but soon began to regain places.

There was a brief window when inters looked like an inspired choice, and Jenson's pace encouraged others to stop, including Alonso and both Mercedes drivers. But, even as those guys were pitting, the rain was coming down again.

Jenson rose as high as eighth on lap 18 – but his race was about to go badly wrong, and he wouldn't reach such dizzy heights again until lap 50. As the rain intensified, those on inters knew they were in serious trouble, and began to change back to wets. Jenson came in on lap 19, just as the conditions caused the safety car to be dispatched again. He dropped to 11th as he joined the safety-car queue, soon gaining another spot when Schumacher pitted for wets. After a few more fruitless laps, with the rain getting heavier, the red flag came out, and the field lined up on the grid behind leader Vettel.

The cars then sat there for two hours as the rain came and went, while Button took the opportunity to talk to Hamilton, and clear the air about their earlier incident.

When the FIA finally decreed that the track was dry enough, Button had a new set of wets for the resumption, while others stuck with a used set. After nine more laps behind the safety car, the field was finally released at the end of lap 34, and Vettel continued to look secure.

OPPOSITE With standing water on the track and heavy spray, the race started behind the safety car; when it pulled off after four laps, Sebastian Vettel sprinted into the lead pursued by the two Ferraris

BELOW On the run down to Turn 1 on the restart, Lewis Hamilton tried an over-optimistic move on Mark Webber, both cars spinning as Nico Rosberg, Jenson Button and Michael Schumacher passed

BOTTOM Lap 7, and the debris flies after the two McLarens make contact on the pit straight, Button inadvertently squeezing Hamilton into contact with the pit wall; Lewis retired with broken suspension

stranded on the kerbs the safety car emerged again, which limited the damage.

Jenson was now 21st, literally last. He also had to catch the back of the safety-car queue, something he didn't quite manage. When the green flag flew at the end of lap 40, he crossed the line still some 2.4s shy of Liuzzi's HRT, instead of being on his tail.

On the plus side, he'd run a couple of very fast laps catching up, so he was in the groove at the restart. He was soon weaving through the backmarkers and then the midfield, and was up to 10th by lap 49.

Now the window for slicks was beginning to open. Webber and Barrichello were the first of the cars ahead of Jenson to stop, coming in on lap 50. Encouraged by Webber's quick sector times, Button was duly called in, slipping briefly from eighth back to 10th. He only had used supersofts left, while of the frontrunners, only Schumacher had the advantage of a new set.

As others stopped, Jenson soon began to climb the order again, helped by the fact that, on slicks, he found an extra gear that no-one else had. Everyone else stopped within a couple of laps of Jenson, but they were too late, and he charged up to fifth, getting ahead of Barrichello, Rosberg, Petrov, Heidfeld and Massa (who had crashed) during the stop sequence. He then passed Kobayashi, leaving only Vettel, Schumacher and Webber still ahead.

With 15 laps to go, on lap 55, JB was 15s behind the leader – and on that lap he had taken an astonishing 4s out of Vettel, who was still finding his feet on slicks. The next lap JB sliced another 2s off Vettel's advantage, while also catching the Schumacher/Webber battle.

Then we had another safety-car interlude, triggered by a crash for Nick Heidfeld. Although he was already on schedule to catch Vettel, it made Button's life even easier, as all the gaps shrunk to nothing, although he had Jerome d'Ambrosio's lapped Virgin between himself and Webber.

After three laps under the safety car, the field was released at the end of lap 60, with exactly 10 to go. Button

ABOVE After the race was red-flagged on lap 25, the cars returned to the grid for a rain-soaked two-hour wait for the restart

BELOW With Vettel already ahead, Kamui Kobayashi battles with Felipe Massa for second place at the restart

OPPOSITE Michael Schumacher was unlucky not to finish on the podium after Webber passed him for third place with four laps to go

At the restart, several cars at the tail of the field went straight into the pits for inters, and Jenson came in at the end of the first racing lap. His team refitted the scrubbed intermediates that he had used earlier in the race. The stop dropped him down to 15th, but with others pouring into the pits, he soon bounced back to 11th. Alonso had pitted a lap later, and came out just in front. Jenson's tyres were up to temperature, and he was already dialled in, so he immediately took a run at the Ferrari – contact was made, and the Spaniard spun off.

Once again Button continued, albeit with a puncture, but he had another long crawl back to the pits, where he collected a set of fresh intermediates. With the Ferrari

TALKING POINT
HAMILTON UNREST

Post-Monaco, Lewis Hamilton was clearly unhappy and things got worse in Canada.

Monte Carlo and Montréal were down as 'must win' races for Lewis – respectively tracks at which the driver can have more input and which should have been well suited to the McLaren MP4-26.

In Monaco the decision to wait until the end of Q3 proved disastrous and then Hamilton had his race collisions with Felipe Massa and Pastor Maldonado. He was clearly at fault in both instances, but refused to accept blame, labelling his fellow competitors "frickin' ridiculous". Then came his well-documented Ali G remarks...

He carried on in similar vein in Canada. He spun Mark Webber out of the way at the first turn, for which he was fortunate to go unpenalised, then collided with team-mate Button trying to pull off a move that looked highly optimistic.

But it was not his on-track behaviour that got tongues wagging. Disappointed to qualify only fifth in a McLaren that was over-winged and geared too long, Hamilton then paid a visit to Red Bull Team Principal Christian Horner in somewhat bizarre circumstances.

No clandestine encounter, this. Hamilton phoned the Red Bull catering girl and asked if she could fix a meeting with Horner. Christian was sitting at a table next to a group of photographers when she arrived and said she had Lewis on the 'phone, wanting to meet up.

"Lewis who?" said Horner, who runs Lewis Williamson in GP3.

"Lewis Hamilton," she replied.

"OK, tell him to come on down."

Of course, in no time at all, photographers had told journalists and the story of Hamilton's meeting with Red Bull was all over the internet.

Simon Fuller's 19 Entertainment contingent, which now manages Hamilton, was back at McLaren's hospitality enclave and seemed blissfully unaware...

At McLaren's Saturday 'Meet the Team' press briefing, Hamilton's body language was telling. While Team Principal Martin Whitmarsh gave his opinion of the decision to run a big rear wing – which he didn't agree with, but which the engineers had opted for to look after rear tyres that actually proved more durable than expected – Button was supportive and amenable.

Hamilton, Monaco fresh in his memory, sat facing away from the pair, twiddled with his mobile phone and looked totally disinterested.

Hamilton's relationship with McLaren appeared to have reached a crossroads. In his mind, he's the best, but Vettel was winning all the races and looked set fair for a second consecutive title. Hamilton's title-winning 2008 season was starting to feel a long while ago.

If Whitmarsh felt that providing a rookie with a title-winning car and making him a world star warranted a degree of loyalty, it didn't look like he was getting it.

ABOVE Fernando Alonso was caught by Button on lap 35 and the two cars touched, leaving the Ferrari stranded and forcing a fifth appearance of the safety car – which allowed Button to pit to replace a punctured tyre without being lapped

BELOW An ecstatic Button heads towards *parc fermé* after pressuring Vettel into a mistake on the final lap to take an inspired victory ahead of the two Red Bulls

blasted past the Virgin, and for three laps sat on the tail of Webber's Red Bull, gaining a DRS boost as he did so.

At the end of lap 64, Webber got it wrong at the last corner, and JB sliced past. Soon glued to Schumacher's tail, he used DRS to shoot past at the end of lap 65.

"I think the car was obviously pretty good in the conditions, but I don't want to take anything from Jenson," said Martin Whitmarsh. "I think he found that time. In those conditions a driver has to believe what he's doing, and has to be confident. He did a fantastic job. I think if you're in that zone you get the tyres at the right temperature. It's a virtuous circle. He was going to overtake anyone that was in his way."

With five laps to go, Button was 3.1s behind leader Vettel. And so the gap came down, to 1.6s, 1,3s, 1.1s, despite Seb improving his pace dramatically. At the start of the last lap, the margin was just 0.9s.

We'll never know what Jenson could have done with DRS on the run to the final chicane on the last lap, but in the end, he didn't need it. Under the most extreme pressure, Vettel finally cracked, sliding wide at Turn Five, and ceding the lead.

It was an amazing turnaround. At one stage Jenson had made three pit stops – putting on intermediates and taking them off again, plus the drive-through – when many of those ahead hadn't stopped at all. In total, he spent 2m21s of his race in the pitlane.

He survived contact with Hamilton, Alonso and Pedro de la Rosa. One of his laps, returning to the pits with a puncture after the clash with the Ferrari, stretched out to 3m05s. Perhaps most astonishingly of all, from lap 37 to lap 40, he was 21st and last. And yet, somehow, he won the race…

"It felt like I spent more time in the pits than on the pit straight," said Button. "The guys did a great job of calling the strategy. At some points we definitely lucked out on the strategy, especially when the red flag came out, but we called it very well going to slicks. The car was working really well in these tricky conditions, so I enjoyed it very much coming through the field."

Behind Vettel, Webber claimed third, while Schumacher had the best race since his comeback to finish fourth. With a few laps to go he was, for a while, the fastest driver on the track, and ran as high as second before he lost momentum and was passed by Button and Webber.

Petrov claimed fifth for Renault, while Massa earned Ferrari its only points with sixth, after running in the top three for much of the race until he damaged his nose after sliding wide when lapping an HRT. The top 10 was completed by Kamui Kobayashi – who was lying second before the red flag – Jaime Alguersuari, Rubens Barrichello and Sébastien Buemi.

It was a truly remarkable race. But even in such lottery conditions, Vettel was still piling up the points…

SNAPSHOT FROM
CANADA

CLOCKWISE FROM RIGHT

The spray flies as the cars round the hairpin, running under the safety car after the restart; Lewis Hamilton congratulates Jenson Button on a superb win, as the media wait for a sound bite; a Lotus mechanic flies the Canadian flag; the safety car was deployed six times during the race; Sebastian Vettel crashed heavily during the first free practice session on Friday, recovering to take pole position on Saturday; the enthusiastic crowd was undeterred by the appalling weather; the track personnel did their best to clear the standing water; the weather on Friday was hot; a marshal picks up debris from the track during the race; the grid girls brightened up race day

RACE RESULTS
CANADA MONTREAL

RACE DATE June 12th
CIRCUIT LENGTH 2.710 miles
NO. OF LAPS 70
RACE DISTANCE 189.700 miles
WEATHER Wet the dry, 17°C
TRACK TEMP 20°C
ATTENDANCE 300,000
LAP RECORD Rubens Barrichello, 1m13.622s, 132.511mph, 2004

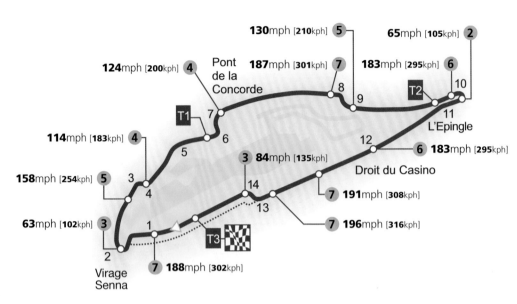

130mph [210kph] 5 — 65mph [105kph] 2
124mph [200kph] 4 — Pont de la Concorde — 187mph [301kph] 7 — 183mph [295kph] 6
8 — T2 — 10
T1 — 7 — 9 — 11 — L'Epingle
114mph [183kph] 4 — 6 — 12 — 6 183mph [295kph]
5 — 3 84mph [135kph] — Droit du Casino
158mph [254kph] 5 — 3 — 14 — 7 191mph [308kph]
4 — 13 — 7 196mph [316kph]
63mph [102kph] 3 — 1 — T3 —
2
7 188mph [302kph]
Virage Senna

PRACTICE 1

	Driver	Time	Laps
1	N Rosberg	1m15.591s	32
2	F Alonso	1m16.139s	27
3	M Schumacher	1m16.549s	30
4	F Massa	1m16.658s	26
5	J Button	1m16.676s	20
6	L Hamilton	1m16.842s	19
7	R Barrichello	1m16.990s	28
8	P di Resta	1m17.294s	26
9	N Heidfeld	1m17.445s	28
10	N Hulkenberg	1m17.549s	20
11	S Perez	1m17.662s	27
12	M Webber	1m17.820s	30
13	J Alguersuari	1m18.458s	31
14	V Petrov	1m18.506s	15
15	D Ricciardo	1m18.648s	35
16	S Vettel	1m18.852s	8
17	P Maldonado	1m18.932s	20
18	J Trulli	1m19.274s	29
19	H Kovalainen	1m19.422s	30
20	K Kobayashi	1m19.577s	26
21	J d'Ambrosio	1m19.838s	31
22	V Liuzzi	1m19.960s	23
23	T Glock	1m20.520s	21
24	N Karthikeyan	1m20.839s	27

PRACTICE 2

	Driver	Time	Laps
1	F Alonso	1m15.107s	34
2	S Vettel	1m15.476s	29
3	F Massa	1m15.601s	33
4	L Hamilton	1m15.977s	26
5	J Button	1m15.989s	25
6	P di Resta	1m16.089s	34
7	M Webber	1m16.102s	28
8	V Petrov	1m16.324s	32
9	N Heidfeld	1m16.422s	32
10	R Barrichello	1m16.687s	28
11	A Sutil	1m16.905s	16
12	P Maldonado	1m16.941s	39
13	S Buemi	1m17.051s	32
14	J Alguersuari	1m17.684s	34
15	K Kobayashi	1m17.757s	20
16	J Trulli	1m18.470s	33
17	H Kovalainen	1m18.482s	38
18	P de la Rosa	1m18.536s	14
19	N Rosberg	1m18.601s	38
20	M Schumacher	1m19.209s	28
21	T Glock	1m19.303s	25
22	V Liuzzi	1m20.284s	31
23	N Karthikeyan	1m20.311s	38
24	J d'Ambrosio	1m20.922s	26

PRACTICE 3

	Driver	Time	Laps
1	S Vettel	1m13.381s	21
2	F Alonso	1m13.701s	21
3	N Rosberg	1m13.919s	29
4	F Massa	1m13.956s	20
5	J Button	1m14.335s	18
6	L Hamilton	1m14.469s	16
7	M Schumacher	1m14.488s	23
8	V Petrov	1m14.917s	23
9	A Sutil	1m15.217s	18
10	P di Resta	1m15.243s	17
11	P Maldonado	1m15.312s	19
12	N Heidfeld	1m15.350s	22
13	S Buemi	1m16.138s	17
14	J Alguersuari	1m16.145s	19
15	K Kobayashi	1m16.236s	21
16	R Barrichello	1m16.438s	21
17	P de la Rosa	1m16.706s	22
18	H Kovalainen	1m17.093s	21
19	J Trulli	1m17.523s	24
20	V Liuzzi	1m18.910s	20
21	T Glock	1m19.073s	19
22	N Karthikeyan	1m19.213s	22
23	J d'Ambrosio	1m20.475s	19
24	M Webber	No time	0

QUALIFYING 1

	Driver	Time
1	F Alonso	1m13.822s
2	S Vettel	1m14.011s
3	F Massa	1m14.026s
4	L Hamilton	1m14.114s
5	J Button	1m14.374s
6	M Webber	1m14.375s
7	V Petrov	1m14.699s
8	P di Resta	1m14.874s
9	N Rosberg	1m14.920s
10	A Sutil	1m14.931s
11	M Schumacher	1m14.970s
12	N Heidfeld	1m15.096s
13	R Barrichello	1m15.331s
14	P Maldonado	1m15.585s
15	K Kobayashi	1m15.694s
16	S Buemi	1m15.901s
17	P de la Rosa	1m16.229s
18	J Alguersuari	1m16.294s
19	J Trulli	1m16.745s
20	H Kovalainen	1m16.786s
21	V Liuzzi	1m18.424s
22	T Glock	1m18.537s
23	N Karthikeyan	1m18.574s
24	J d'Ambrosio	1m19.414s

QUALIFYING 2

	Driver	Time
1	F Massa	1m13.431s
2	S Webber	1m13.486s
3	M Webber	1m13.654s
4	F Alonso	1m13.672s
5	L Hamilton	1m13.926s
6	N Rosberg	1m13.950s
7	J Button	1m13.955s
8	M Schumacher	1m14.242s
9	V Petrov	1m14.354s
10	N Heidfeld	1m14.467s
11	P di Resta	1m14.752s
12	P Maldonado	1m15.043s
13	K Kobayashi	1m15.285s
14	A Sutil	1m15.287s
15	S Buemi	1m15.334s
16	R Barrichello	1m15.361s
17	P de la Rosa	1m15.587s

Best sectors – Practice
Sec 1	S Vettel	20.296s
Sec 2	S Vettel	23.472s
Sec 3	S Vettel	29.412s

Speed trap – Practice
1	A Sutil	204.866mph
2	V Petrov	204.493mph
3	N Heidfeld	204.431mph

Best sectors – Qualifying
Sec 1	S Vettel	20.258s
Sec 2	S Vettel	23.195s
Sec 3	S Vettel	29.401s

Speed trap – Qualifying
1	J Alguersuari	201.448mph
2	S Buemi	201.075mph
3	A Sutil	200.081mph

Sebastian Vettel
"After the last safety car I didn't open the gap enough, then I saw Jenson coming and locked the rear. When you have it in your hands and give it away, it's not sweet."

Jenson Button
"That was my best win. Changing conditions are tricky, but I love it when you've got to search for grip on the track rather than knowing in advance where it is."

Fernando Alonso
"We fitted inters, then the rain came, along with the red flag, so those who hadn't changed could do it for nothing. Then there was my coming together with Button."

Michael Schumacher
"I'm half laughing, half crying. Having been second, I'd have loved to be on the podium again. Even though it didn't work out, I can be happy about the result."

Nick Heidfeld
"Kamui slowed suddenly in front of me and I hit him, which resulted in my front wing coming off and me going off the track when I was on course for fifth place."

Rubens Barrichello
"Starting 16th, I'm happy that I scored. It should have been more, but I lost a potential sixth when I went off line to avoid Kobayashi after the last safety car went in."

Mark Webber
"I had a few people to pass after the break. It wasn't hard until a dry line appeared and it was slippery off line. It was then hard to clear guys like Michael and Nick."

Lewis Hamilton
"I touched Mark after he braked early into the first turn. I got a run on Jenson and thought I was halfway alongside. As he hadn't seen me, he kept moving across."

Felipe Massa
"Karthikeyan was slow on the dry line but, as I was passing on the wet, he accelerated and I lost control, ending up in the wall. In the end, I climbed to sixth."

Nico Rosberg
"I made a mistake at the hairpin on lap 66. I was trying to pass Kobayashi and he slowed when I didn't expect it and I damaged my wing, which then came off."

Vitaly Petrov
"After the restart, I was fourth as I decided not to change tyres before the red flag. Finishing fifth after starting 10th is good, but I could have been on the podium."

Pastor Maldonado
"Kamui made a mistake at Turn 1, Rosberg braked in response and I collided with him. That broke my front wing so I had to make a stop. After that, I spun out."

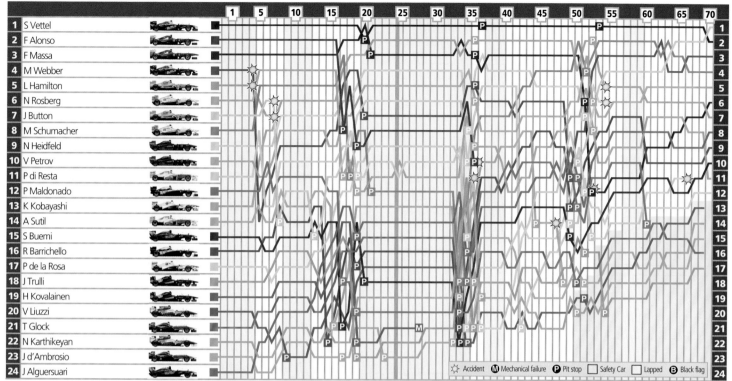

		1	5	10	15	20	25	30	35	40	45	50	55	60	65	70	
1	S Vettel																1
2	F Alonso																2
3	F Massa																3
4	M Webber																4
5	L Hamilton																5
6	N Rosberg																6
7	J Button																7
8	M Schumacher																8
9	N Heidfeld																9
10	V Petrov																10
11	P di Resta																11
12	P Maldonado																12
13	K Kobayashi																13
14	A Sutil																14
15	S Buemi																15
16	R Barrichello																16
17	P de la Rosa																17
18	J Trulli																18
19	H Kovalainen																19
20	V Liuzzi																20
21	T Glock																21
22	N Karthikeyan																22
23	J d'Ambrosio																23
24	J Alguersuari																24

☆ Accident   Ⓜ Mechanical failure   Ⓟ Pit stop   ☐ Safety Car   ☐ Lapped   Ⓑ Black flag

QUALIFYING 3

	Driver	Time
1	S Vettel	1m13.014s
2	F Alonso	1m13.199s
3	F Massa	1m13.217s
4	M Webber	1m13.429s
5	L Hamilton	1m13.565s
6	N Rosberg	1m13.814s
7	J Button	1m13.838s
8	M Schumacher	1m13.864s
9	N Heidfeld	1m14.062s
10	V Petrov	1m14.085s

GRID

	Driver	Time
1	S Vettel	1m13.014s
2	F Alonso	1m13.199s
3	F Massa	1m13.217s
4	M Webber	1m13.429s
5	L Hamilton	1m13.565s
6	N Rosberg	1m13.814s
7	J Button	1m13.838s
8	M Schumacher	1m13.864s
9	N Heidfeld	1m14.062s
10	V Petrov	1m14.085s
11	P di Resta	1m14.752s
12	P Maldonado	1m15.043s
13	K Kobayashi	1m15.285s
14	A Sutil	1m15.287s
15	S Buemi	1m15.334s
16	R Barrichello	1m15.361s
17	P de la Rosa	1m15.587s
18	J Alguersuari	1m16.294s
19	J Trulli	1m16.745s
20	H Kovalainen	1m16.786s
21	V Liuzzi	1m18.424s
22	T Glock	1m18.537s
23	N Karthikeyan	1m18.574s
24	J d'Ambrosio	1m19.414s

RACE

	Driver	Car	Laps	Time	Avg. mph	Fastest	Stops
1	J Button	McLaren-Mercedes MP4-26	70	4h04m39.537s	46.518	1m16.956s	6
2	S Vettel	Red Bull-Renault RB7	70	4h04m42.246s	46.510	1m17.217s	3
3	M Webber	Red Bull-Renault RB7	70	4h04m53.365s	46.474	1m19.572s	3
4	M Schumacher	Mercedes MGP W02	70	4h04m53.756s	46.473	1m19.138s	4
5	V Petrov	Renault R31	70	4h04m59.932s	46.454	1m19.054s	2
6	F Massa	Ferrari 150 Italia	70	4h05m12.762s	46.413	1m19.148s	4
7	K Kobayashi	Sauber-Ferrari C30	70	4h05m12.807s	46.413	1m20.213s	2
8	J Alguersuari	Toro Rosso-Ferrari STR6	70	4h05m15.501s	46.405	1m20.371s	3
9	R Barrichello	Williams-Cosworth FW33	70	4h05m24.654s	46.375	1m20.316s	4
10	S Buemi	Toro Rosso-Ferrari STR6	70	4h05m26.593s	46.369	1m19.371s	4
11	N Rosberg	Mercedes MGP W02	70	4h05m29.991s	46.359	1m20.371s	4
12	P de la Rosa	Sauber-Ferrari C30	70	4h05m43.144s	46.318	1m20.369s	2
13	V Liuzzi	HRT-Cosworth F111	69	4h05m53.138s	45.625	1m23.419s	3
14	J d'Ambrosio	Virgin-Cosworth MVR-02	69	4h06m01.652s	45.599	1m22.495s	5
15	T Glock	Virgin-Cosworth MVR-02	69	4h06m01.982s	45.597	1m24.590s	2
16	J Trulli	Lotus-Renault T128	69	4h06m02.312s	45.596	1m22.233s	4
17	N Karthikeyan	HRT-Cosworth F111	69	4h06m20.698s*	45.540	1m23.116s	2
18	P di Resta	Force India-Mercedes VJM04	67	Accident	-	1m19.395s	4
R	P Maldonado	Williams-Cosworth FW33	61	Accident	-	1m24.265s	5
R	N Heidfeld	Renault R31	55	Accident	-	1m25.135s	2
R	A Sutil	Force India-Mercedes VJM04	49	Suspension	-	1m30.171s	4
R	F Alonso	Ferrari 150 Italia	36	Accident	-	1m34.223s	3
R	H Kovalainen	Lotus-Renault T128	28	Driveshaft	-	1m38.460s	1
R	L Hamilton	McLaren-Mercedes MP4-26	7	Crash damage	-	1m37.761s	0

* 20s penalty for cutting a corner and gaining an advantage

CHAMPIONSHIP

	Driver	Pts
1	S Vettel	161
2	J Button	101
3	M Webber	94
4	L Hamilton	85
5	F Alonso	69
6	F Massa	32
7	V Petrov	31
8	N Heidfeld	29
9	M Schumacher	26
10	N Rosberg	26
11	K Kobayashi	25
12	A Sutil	8
13	S Buemi	8
14	J Alguersuari	4
15	R Barrichello	4
16	S Perez	2
17	P di Resta	2

	Constructor	Pts
1	Red Bull-Renault	255
2	McLaren-Mercedes	186
3	Ferrari	101
4	Renault	60
5	Mercedes	52
6	Sauber-Ferrari	27
7	Toro Rosso-Ferrari	12
8	Force India-Mercedes	10
9	Williams-Cosworth	4

Fastest lap
J Button 1m16.956s
(126.764mph) on lap 69

Fastest speed trap
M Webber 199.833mph
Slowest speed trap
J d'Ambrosio 184.609mph

Fastest pit stop
1 M Schumacher 22.832s
2 A Sutil 22.923s
3 N Rosberg 22.986s

Adrian Sutil
"Those ahead of me slowed a lot at the hairpin and I got caught out, damaging my front wing. I switched to dry tyres, but it was too early and I touched the wall."

Kamui Kobayashi
"I qualified 13th, so it isn't bad to finish seventh. On the other hand, I started second after the red-flag period and looking from there the result is disappointing."

Sebastien Buemi
"I'm disappointed as I think I could have done better, and I'm not sure if changing to slicks so early worked. Looking at the result, I'm happy for the team."

Jarno Trulli
"After my stop for dry tyres I had something moving around in the cockpit, so I came in for the team to investigate. They couldn't fix it, so I went back out again."

Narain Karthikeyan
"I'd have liked to have stayed longer on the last set of inters; I passed Tonio with them, so maybe one more lap would have got me a bit more track position."

Timo Glock
"When Narain came up, I tried to stay in front, but he made a move into the last turn and pushed me off. He cut the chicane and Jerome got by me then too."

Paul di Resta
"I lost my wing against Nick when he cut across me. That gave me a drive-through penalty. Then, after that, I pushed to pass Rubens and clipped the wall."

Pedro de la Rosa
"I came from 17th and resumed the race ninth behind the safety car. But, just before the restart, Jenson and I touched and I had to pit with a damaged front wing."

Jaime Alguersuari
"I'm very happy because to finish eighth having started last from the pitlane is a really good result. I'm also very pleased that I've scored my first points of the year."

Heikki Kovalainen
"My race came to an end with a driveshaft failure. When we restarted, I lost drive almost immediately and had to retire, which is very disappointing."

Vitantonio Liuzzi
"It was a crazy race. In these kinds of situations, you have to gamble. We made the right decisions and the team worked perfectly during pit stops."

Jerome d'Ambrosio
"There were lots of ups and downs. I stopped twice before the red flag, yet after the restart I found myself racing with Timo and thought, what's happening?"

2011 FORMULA 1
GRAND PRIX OF EUROPE
VALENCIA

VETTEL ON TOP AGAIN

After a forced error in Canada, Sebastian Vettel remained calm under pressure from Fernando Alonso and Mark Webber at Valencia, to preserve his tyres and take his sixth win from eight races

Sebastian Vettel took another big step in his campaign to retain the World Championship when he scored a finely judged victory at Valencia. The German made it look easy, but on a day when McLaren underperformed he had to see off an unexpectedly strong challenge from a resurgent Fernando Alonso and Ferrari.

Valencia has rarely produced much in the way of entertainment, and the trend continued with a race that lacked drama relative to previous grands prix in 2011.

There was at least some DRS-inspired passing, a lot of it when cars were on tyres at different stages of their life cycles, but nothing like the excitement we'd seen elsewhere. The consensus among drivers was that the first of the twin DRS zones wasn't long enough, and the second, preceded by a third-gear kink, was pretty much a waste of time.

The race wasn't totally devoid of spectacle, however, as for much of it Vettel enjoyed only a slender advantage, and behind him there was a great battle for second.

Valencia saw the FIA begin its planned two-stage clampdown on using engine mapping for aerodynamic gain by blowing exhaust gases into the diffuser. The first step saw teams banned from changing maps between qualifying and the race. That ensured drivers could no

INSIDE LINE
CHARLIE WHITING
FIA F1 RACE DIRECTOR

The hot topic as the paddock formed up in Valencia was how much a mid-season FIA ban on special qualifying engine maps and exhaust-blown diffusers – introduced in two stages at Valencia and Silverstone respectively – would change the competitive picture.

In Valencia, teams would have the same engine maps in qualifying and race. At Silverstone, there would be a limit on throttle openings with the driver off the throttle.

For aerodynamic purposes, many throttles were still 100% open with the driver off the pedal, increasing exhaust gas and hence diffuser effectiveness. At Silverstone, throttles would have to be a maximum 10% open at 12,000rpm and 20% open at 18,000rpm.

The mid-season changes brought to mind the mass damper issue of 2006. This, said the FIA's Charlie Whiting, was a good analogy.

"Mass damper use, when first introduced," he explained, "was fairly benign when it came to aerodynamics, but the more it got developed, the more extreme the designs were. There were four, five, six mass dampers on the car clearly being used for aerodynamic reasons. These things escalate to the point where something has to be done."

In an explanatory media session, Whiting was quizzed: "Everyone knows which team (Ferrari) made the pressure to stop the mass damper. Is it the same team stopping this system because they are not able to build a winning car?"

"No, I don't think so," Whiting said, "because everybody is doing this to some extent. Obviously some are doing it more extremely than others, but everyone is doing it."

The throttle-opening issue was difficult for commentators to explain. Just as everyone started to get a handle on it, understanding that the FIA had looked at '09 data to decide limitations, a curved ball was thrown in when it emerged that a throttle was not just a throttle.

"A lot depends on engine architecture," Whiting explained. "We have to be very careful not to disadvantage, for example, users of barrel throttles versus butterfly throttles, because they have a distinctly different way of working.

"If it's quite clear that in '09 one engine with a butterfly throttle only needed 15% opening, but the same engine with a barrel throttle needed 20%, then we could make a distinction. We don't want an across-the-board figure that will affect one team more than another."

The fact that the rule interpretation would be different, team to team, was, predictably enough, the cue for widespread paddock paranoia (see 'Talking Point').

longer run 'extreme' downforce-generating maps on Saturday that then couldn't be used over a race distance for reliability and fuel-consumption reasons.

The change may have cost Red Bull something of its advantage, but not enough to give the others a chance of stealing pole. Vettel ended up just under 0.2s clear of team-mate Mark Webber and some 0.4s ahead of RBR's closest rival, the McLaren of Lewis Hamilton.

Webber was the only top driver to make an improvement on the second and final runs in Q3, jumping up to second. Hamilton shared the second row with Alonso, the local hero putting in a strong performance and coming very close to usurping McLaren. Felipe Massa was fifth in the second Ferrari, while Montréal winner Jenson Button, who struggled with oversteer, was sixth.

The race turned into a three-stopper for almost everyone, with three stints on the soft Pirelli followed by a final one on the slower medium, which was making its debut at this race.

At the start, Vettel stayed safely ahead of Webber, while Alonso and Massa both jumped Hamilton and slotted into third and fourth. As so often, Vettel was able to control the pace from the front, staying just a few seconds clear of Webber, and preserving his tyres. While he successfully maintained a small gap, the identity of his pursuer changed three times.

"It was a really fascinating race, where it was really between our guys and Fernando," said Christian Horner. "The start for both went well. Fernando was able to stay within the DRS zone of Mark, and the three of them went away.

"You've got that first dilemma of where do you make your first stop? And the easiest thing in the world is not to be able to get it right with both of them. It's very easy to get it right with one, but to get it right with both is very, very difficult.

"Then, on the option tyres in the second stint, we were going OK, pulling away at the front and just

watching how the tyres wear, and so on. Through the next stop was fine, and again Sebastian going that little bit longer and just stopping when he needed to, the most important thing was to drop the guys into clear air at that stage."

Having stayed in touch during the second stint, Alonso managed to get past Webber in a well-judged move, one of the few in which any driver successfully used the DRS zones in Valencia. However, at the second round of stops, Webber came in earlier and did just enough on his one lap on fresher tyres to get back ahead.

At the third and final stops, the Aussie again came in before Alonso, after feeling that his tyres were past their best. However, his new medium tyres were no match for the old softs still fitted to the Ferrari.

A slight glitch on the pit entry cost Webber a few tenths, and he also had traffic. But the two laps on which Alonso stayed out on his softs were crucial, and ensured that the Spaniard came out ahead when he pitted. It was Webber's call to take the gamble and come in.

"Unfortunately he lost a little bit of time on the way into the pitlane and picked up some traffic," said Horner. "And the prime tyre didn't quite have the out-lap performance that we were hoping for. If anything it was

OPPOSITE After his qualifying lap in Q1 was ruined by traffic, Jaime Alguersuari started 18th, but drove an excellent race to finish as the first of the two-stoppers in eighth

TOP Michael Schumacher's magnetic attraction for Vitaly Petrov continued, the German this time hitting the Renault as he left the pits after his first stop, damaging the Mercedes' front wing and forcing him to stop again for a replacement

ABOVE Nico Rosberg qualified and finished seventh after a straightforward race, the Mercedes proving to be the fourth-fastest car at this stage of the season, behind the Red Bulls, McLarens and Ferraris

ABOVE Sergio Perez, seen here ahead of Nick Heidfeld and Kamui Kobayashi, opted for a less-than-ideal one-stopper, but coped well with his heavily worn second set of tyres to finish a lap down in 11th place

OPPOSITE TOP Local hero Fernando Alonso battled with Mark Webber for much of the race, eventually emerging ahead of the Australian after the final stops to take an excellent second place, splitting the Red Bulls

OPPOSITE Red Bull Racing's pit work was as slick as ever, and Mark Webber kept the pressure on team-mate Vettel in the early stages, but struggled to preserve his tyres later in the race, enabling Alonso to undercut him for second place at the final stop

as good as, but not a step better. That allowed Fernando to sneak ahead."

Intriguingly, Mark himself didn't blame the traffic, but said the prime simply wasn't fast enough at the start of its life. It's easy to suggest that Mark and RBR made a bad call, but Horner insisted that it was a nothing-to-lose situation because Webber, had he stayed out, would have been jumped by Alonso: "The options were finished anyway, but at that stage Alonso's were still going OK, so we needed to pit. We had nothing to lose, it was the only chance of beating Fernando."

With the pit stops behind him done, Vettel switched to the mediums for a short 10-lap run to the flag. With low fuel and tyres he could push as hard as he wanted, he could have some fun, opening up a gap on Alonso and scaring the pit wall with a fastest lap four laps from home.

"I think he knew at that point he could abuse the tyres," said Horner. "Suddenly you start to see the timing board go purple, and that's when I start to get nervous. That's when his engineer just reminded him! The key with these tyres is that the operating window is just so narrow that if you fall out of it then you see the tyres go away from you very, very quickly. He seems to have a fantastic ability to gauge where that performance is."

After his last-lap disappointment in Montréal, and the frustration of the engine-mapping clampdown that he presumably felt was targeted at him, Seb responded in style.

"Yesterday was the foundation, and today it was a long and tough race," said Vettel. "It was quite close, always between two, one-and-a-half, two-and-half, three seconds. Not too easy to really pull away and open a gap. It is a bit unknown. How long is the stint going to be? How many laps does it mean in the next stint and then at the end on the medium tyres?

"It helps having that little bit of a cushion, so we always came a lap later and others came earlier and came out closer, or they were closer behind me when I came out, so I had to build up a gap again, really trying to get a tenth or two every lap. All in all, it was a faultless race and I enjoyed it a lot. I didn't have a fight or anybody to race, but you race against yourself and the car and always against the guys behind, between one-and-a-half and three seconds, so I really enjoyed today."

Second place was a big boost for Ferrari, after a difficult start to the season for the Maranello team.

"I think that Fernando's race was really good," said team boss Stefano Domenicali. "It was a great race, pushing lap by lap, a lot of backmarkers in

TALKING POINT
PADDOCK PARANOIA

In truth, it seemed odd to embark on a round of wholesale regulation changes mid-season. Naturally, everyone wondered what the agenda was and who was driving it.

Purely technical, said the FIA. Engines and exhausts are to be used for combustion, not as aerodynamic devices. Things had gone too far.

But was that really all there was to it? Were we sure it wasn't political? Was it not a means of trying to slow down the Red Bulls to liven up the season and make sure that TV viewers didn't switch off in their droves?

Whenever something like this happens mid-season, for instance the sudden banning of the Renault mass dampers in 2006, there's widespread paranoia as everyone seeks to unravel what's really going on, where the objections have come from, and who stands to gain from any changes.

There was varying opinion about how much the Red Bulls would be affected by the diffuser changes at Silverstone. And many pointed out in advance that Silverstone may not be the best barometer for the rest of the season, given the performance level that Red Bull had demonstrated at the Northamptonshire track in the previous two visits.

On the subject of exhaust-blown diffusers, Red Bull Team Principal Christian Horner said: "For sure it's worth a few tenths of a second, but some teams have optimised it in different ways. Some have been blowing hot air, which is a bit more potent, and some have been blowing cold air. We've been blowing cold air, for example, so it's impossible to predict the effect it will have."

The assertion that Red Bull has not been hot-blowing (burning fuel in the exhaust off-throttle via spark advance) was met with scepticism by one of F1's more experienced technical men, who thought that Christian may have been insulting the media's intelligence. He pointed out that the Red Bull used the same engine as the Renault which, as he so eruditely put it, "sounded like a skeleton having a w*nk in a biscuit tin…"

Horner, however, was adamant, alleging that Red Bull had obviously tried hot-blowing, but could not do it to any great degree because they risked overheating their rear tyres.

One of the engine men explained that the subject of calibration was massively, massively complex. An intelligent man himself, he admitted that his calibration guys spoke a different language.

The complexity of the issue made people wonder why such a potential can of worms should be opened mid-season, despite Charlie Whiting's explanations (see 'Inside Line').

After predictable ructions in Friday practice at Silverstone, it was perhaps no surprise when, for the rest of the season, the governing body ordered, "As you were…"

the middle, so that was not really an easy job for anyone, unfortunately also for him too.

"I'm very pleased, because we saw that on race pace we were there. We beat one of the two Red Bulls on the track. The strategy applied was the right one to jump Mark on the track. So a positive outcome to the day."

Webber had a few worries about high gearbox temperatures and was told to take it easy. Having lost his second place in the stops, he was content to drop away from Alonso and safely secure a comfortable third.

McLaren was off the pace of those ahead all day, and Lewis Hamilton finished a lonely fourth, an incredible 46s down on the winner. He did at least get ahead of Massa at the first stops, and thereafter the Brit struggled to find pace while trying to keep his rear tyres alive.

"We just weren't quick enough, it's as simple as that," said a disappointed Hamilton. "The Ferraris were massively quicker than ourselves. I think we were quite lucky to stay ahead of Massa, really."

The Brazilian took more points for Ferrari with fifth place, while Button finished where he started, in a frustrated sixth, having been even further off the pace than Hamilton. He had lost out to Nico Rosberg at the start, but managed to get past the Mercedes driver on the sixth lap.

Meanwhile, Jaime Alguersuari went from 18th on the grid to eighth at the flag, on a day when most drivers finished one or two places from where they started. And he did that by running a two-stop strategy when all of those who finished ahead, and most of those who finished behind, ran three stops, shadowing each other in and out of the pits like a bunch of lemmings.

A few drivers and engineers were left scratching their heads and wondering how Toro Rosso did it. The bottom line – and not for the first time – was that Alguersuari was able to use brand-new tyres all the way through, because he didn't make it out of Q1. An ultra-long and consistently fast middle stint made all the difference.

Adrian Sutil gave Force India some useful points with ninth, having traded the place with Renault's Nick Heidfeld at the start. Aside from Alguersuari, the other big strategy gambler was Sergio Perez, the Mexican returning after missing two races, and using a bold one-stop to move up from 16th to 11th at the flag.

There were no penalties and no spins, and the only unscheduled pit stop occurred when Michael Schumacher crunched his front wing on Vitaly Petrov, and had to come in for a replacement. Remarkably, all 24 cars finished, which meant that Narain Karthikeyan became the first driver ever to finish 24th in a Grand Prix, the Indian having already set a record with 23rd in China...

ABOVE Vitantonio Liuzzi and Jerome d'Ambrosio battled early on, eventually finishing 23rd (three laps down) and 22nd (two laps down) respectively in a race that saw all 24 starters take the flag

LEFT "What happens if I pull this?" Vettel checks out the hardware on Alonso's Ferrari

SNAPSHOT FROM
EUROPE

CLOCKWISE FROM RIGHT

The Valencia podium occupies a unique setting in the paddock; a stunning view of the harbourside circuit; the sun sets over old-town Valencia; the McLaren mechanics leap into action ready for a pit stop, wearing the rubber gloves necessary when handling a car equipped with KERS; the unusually high track temperatures – reaching 47°C during the race – led to high tyre wear; Michael Schumacher arrives in the paddock on his scooter; a jubilant Red Bull Racing team celebrates Sebastian Vettel's win and Mark Webber's third place; Jarno Trulli prepares to qualify his Lotus; Heikki Kovalainen relaxes conspicuously in a subtle pair of sunglasses

RACE RESULTS
EUROPE
VALENCIA

Official Results © [2011]
Formula One Administration Limited,
6 Princes Gate, London, SW7 1QJ.
No reproduction without permission.
All copyright and database rights reserved.

RACE DATE June 26th
CIRCUIT LENGTH 3.367 miles
NO. OF LAPS 57
RACE DISTANCE 191.919 miles
WEATHER Sunny & dry, 28°C
TRACK TEMP 47°C
ATTENDANCE 163,061
LAP RECORD Timo Glock, 1m38.683s, 122.837mph, 2009

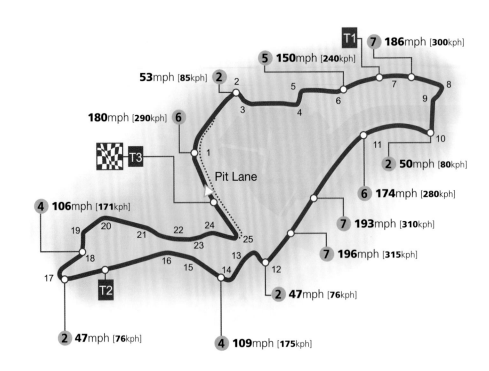

	PRACTICE 1				PRACTICE 2				PRACTICE 3				QUALIFYING 1			QUALIFYING 2	
	Driver	Time	Laps		Driver	Time	Laps		Driver	Time	Laps		Driver	Time		Driver	Time
1	M Webber	1m40.403s	22	1	F Alonso	1m37.968s	35	1	S Vettel	1m37.258s	15	1	F Massa	1m38.413s	1	S Vettel	1m37.305s
2	V Petrov	1m41.227s	20	2	L Hamilton	1m38.195s	26	2	F Alonso	1m37.678s	16	2	S Vettel	1m39.116s	2	L Hamilton	1m37.727s
3	F Alonso	1m41.239s	22	3	S Vettel	1m38.265s	31	3	F Massa	1m37.840s	17	3	M Schumacher	1m39.198s	3	J Button	1m37.749s
4	L Hamilton	1m41.510s	23	4	M Schumacher	1m38.315s	30	4	M Webber	1m38.068s	13	4	L Hamilton	1m39.244s	4	F Alonso	1m37.930s
5	N Heidfeld	1m41.580s	24	5	F Massa	1m38.443s	32	5	J Button	1m38.326s	13	5	N Rosberg	1m39.266s	5	M Webber	1m38.058s
6	F Massa	1m41.758s	23	6	J Button	1m38.483s	30	6	N Rosberg	1m38.580s	15	6	A Sutil	1m39.329s	6	M Schumacher	1m38.365s
7	J Button	1m41.926s	14	7	M Webber	1m38.531s	26	7	L Hamilton	1m38.741s	13	7	J Button	1m39.453s	7	N Rosberg	1m38.373s
8	A Sutil	1m41.955s	20	8	N Rosberg	1m38.981s	33	8	M Schumacher	1m38.799s	14	8	S Perez	1m39.494s	8	F Massa	1m38.566s
9	N Rosberg	1m42.043s	22	9	N Heidfeld	1m39.040s	35	9	V Petrov	1m38.822s	17	9	R Barrichello	1m39.602s	9	N Heidfeld	1m38.781s
10	J Alguersuari	1m42.216s	29	10	V Petrov	1m39.586s	27	10	N Heidfeld	1m39.113s	15	10	S Buemi	1m39.679s	10	A Sutil	1m39.034s
11	M Schumacher	1m42.270s	26	11	A Sutil	1m39.626s	31	11	A Sutil	1m39.411s	19	11	P Maldonado	1m39.690s	11	V Petrov	1m39.068s
12	D Ricciardo	1m42.412s	27	12	R Barrichello	1m40.020s	34	12	S Perez	1m39.778s	18	12	V Petrov	1m39.690s	12	P di Resta	1m39.422s
13	R Barrichello	1m42.704s	23	13	P Maldonado	1m40.301s	34	13	P di Resta	1m39.823s	18	13	F Alonso	1m39.725s	13	R Barrichello	1m39.489s
14	S Perez	1m42.738s	20	14	P di Resta	1m40.363s	7	14	K Kobayashi	1m39.848s	18	14	P di Resta	1m39.852s	14	K Kobayashi	1m39.525s
15	P Maldonado	1m42.841s	28	15	S Buemi	1m40.454s	32	15	S Buemi	1m39.888s	17	15	N Heidfeld	1m39.877s	15	P Maldonado	1m39.645s
16	S Vettel	1m42.941s	21	16	S Perez	1m40.531s	37	16	R Barrichello	1m39.987s	15	16	M Webber	1m39.956s	16	S Perez	1m39.657s
17	K Kobayashi	1m43.201s	18	17	K Kobayashi	1m42.083s	34	17	P Maldonado	1m40.004s	16	17	K Kobayashi	1m40.131s	17	S Buemi	1m39.711s
18	N Hulkenberg	1m43.769s	7	18	H Kovalainen	1m42.156s	39	18	J Alguersuari	1m40.239s	20	18	J Alguersuari	1m40.323s			
19	H Kovalainen	1m44.136s	17	19	J Trulli	1m42.239s	25	19	H Kovalainen	1m41.267s	15	19	H Kovalainen	1m41.664s			
20	J d'Ambrosio	1m45.026s	17	20	T Glock	1m42.273s	21	20	J Trulli	1m41.690s	18	20	J Trulli	1m42.234s			
21	T Glock	1m45.221s	19	21	J d'Ambrosio	1m42.809s	26	21	T Glock	1m42.557s	18	21	T Glock	1m42.553s			
22	V Liuzzi	1m45.494s	24	22	V Liuzzi	1m44.460s	29	22	V Liuzzi	1m43.243s	17	22	V Liuzzi	1m43.584s			
23	N Karthikeyan	1m46.926s	27	23	N Karthikeyan	1m46.906s	16	23	J d'Ambrosio	1m43.309s	18	23	J d'Ambrosio	1m43.735s			
24	K Chandhok	No time	2	24	J Alguersuari	No time	0	24	N Karthikeyan	1m44.630s	19	24	N Karthikeyan	1m44.363s			

Best sectors – Practice			Speed trap – Practice			Best sectors – Qualifying			Speed trap – Qualifying		
Sec 1	S Vettel	25.737s	1	P Maldonado	197.534mph	Sec 1	S Vettel	25.590s	1	N Rosberg	197.285mph
Sec 2	S Vettel	44.006s	2	N Rosberg	197.347mph	Sec 2	S Vettel	43.981s	2	R Barrichello	197.285mph
Sec 3	S Vettel	27.435s	3	M Schumacher	197.285mph	Sec 3	M Webber	27.320s	3	M Schumacher	196.726mph

Sebastian Vettel
"I'm not sure whether it seemed that much was happening, but I had pressure from behind, especially as the strategy was a bit different to Mark and Fernando."

Jenson Button
"The field bunched into Turn 2 and I was on the outside, where I lost out to Nico. I didn't have the straightline speed to pass easily, but I got him into Turn 2."

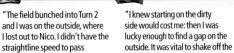

Fernando Alonso
"I knew starting on the dirty side would cost me: then I was lucky enough to find a gap on the outside. It was vital to shake off the McLarens, as they were slower."

Michael Schumacher
"I saw Petrov quite late, but I was aware that he was coming, and tried to brake as late as possible and corner with him. But I locked a wheel and slipped into him."

Nick Heidfeld
"I lost a place to Adrian at the start and finished where I'd been for most of the race (behind Sutil). I managed to pass him once, but he used DRS to get by."

Rubens Barrichello
"I didn't have the car beneath me, so I'm happy with what I delivered. The team has worked hard to bring upgrades, so I'm sorry that we didn't do better."

Mark Webber
"I should have finished second. It was a good race with Fernando, my best race of the year until the last stop. I probably pitted a bit early, but that was my call."

Lewis Hamilton
"I got a poor start and lost out to both Ferraris. After that, it was a long race – the team asked me to stay out for as long as I could, and I was pushing all the way."

Felipe Massa
"I passed Hamilton and Alonso, then attacked Webber, but he closed the door, so Alonso got back. I lost 4–5s in the pits, stopping me from fighting Hamilton."

Nico Rosberg
"I'm happy with seventh, as that's the most I could have done. It was great to overtake Jenson at the start, and we made the right choice to go for three stops."

Vitaly Petrov
"Schumacher seemed to exit the pits very quickly and didn't seem to be able to stop coming into the first corner. I saw him in my mirror, but there was still contact."

Pastor Maldonado
"I lost places off the line, then couldn't make the prime tyre work in the first stint, so had to pit early. The early stop forced us onto a three-stop strategy."

8·9 OFFICIAL FORMULA 1™ REVIEW

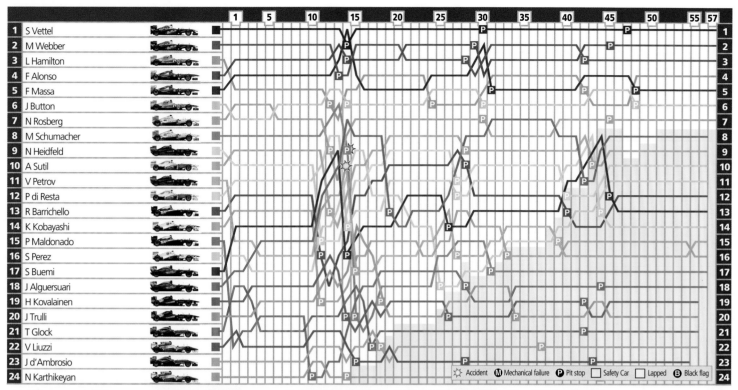

		1	5	10	15	20	25	30	35	40	45	50	55 57	
1	S Vettel													1
2	M Webber													2
3	L Hamilton													3
4	F Alonso													4
5	F Massa													5
6	J Button													6
7	N Rosberg													7
8	M Schumacher													8
9	N Heidfeld													9
10	A Sutil													10
11	V Petrov													11
12	P di Resta													12
13	R Barrichello													13
14	K Kobayashi													14
15	P Maldonado													15
16	S Perez													16
17	S Buemi													17
18	J Alguersuari													18
19	H Kovalainen													19
20	J Trulli													20
21	T Glock													21
22	V Liuzzi													22
23	J d'Ambrosio													23
24	N Karthikeyan													24

☆ Accident   Ⓜ Mechanical failure   Ⓟ Pit stop   ☐ Safety Car   ☐ Lapped   Ⓑ Black flag

QUALIFYING 3

	Driver	Time
1	S Vettel	1m36.975s
2	M Webber	1m37.163s
3	L Hamilton	1m37.380s
4	F Alonso	1m37.454s
5	F Massa	1m37.535s
6	J Button	1m37.645s
7	N Rosberg	1m38.231s
8	M Schumacher	1m38.420s
9	N Heidfeld	No time
10	A Sutil	No time

GRID

	Driver	Time
1	S Vettel	1m36.975s
2	M Webber	1m37.163s
3	L Hamilton	1m37.380s
4	F Alonso	1m37.454s
5	F Massa	1m37.535s
6	J Button	1m37.645s
7	N Rosberg	1m38.231s
8	M Schumacher	1m38.420s
9	N Heidfeld	No time
10	A Sutil	No time
11	V Petrov	1m39.068s
12	P di Resta	1m39.422s
13	R Barrichello	1m39.489s
14	K Kobayashi	1m39.525s
15	P Maldonado	1m39.645s
16	S Perez	1m39.657s
17	S Buemi	1m39.711s
18	J Alguersuari	1m40.323s
19	H Kovalainen	1m41.664s
20	J Trulli	1m42.234s
21	T Glock	1m42.553s
22	V Liuzzi	1m43.584s
23	J d'Ambrosio	1m43.735s
24	N Karthikeyan	1m44.363s

RACE

	Driver	Car	Laps	Time	Avg. mph	Fastest	Stops
1	S Vettel	Red Bull-Renault RB7	57	1h39m36.169s	115.617	1m41.852s	3
2	F Alonso	Ferrari 150 Italia	57	1h39m47.060s	115.407	1m42.308s	3
3	M Webber	Red Bull-Renault RB7	57	1h40m03.424s	115.093	1m42.534s	3
4	L Hamilton	McLaren-Mercedes MP4-26	57	1h40m22.359s	114.730	1m42.947s	3
5	F Massa	Ferrari 150 Italia	57	1h40m27.874s	114.625	1m42.705s	3
6	J Button	McLaren-Mercedes MP4-26	57	1h40m36.234s	114.467	1m42.340s	3
7	N Rosberg	Mercedes MGP W02	57	1h41m14.259s	113.750	1m43.649s	3
8	J Alguersuari	Toro Rosso-Ferrari STR6	56	1h39m43.385s	113.452	1m43.579s	2
9	A Sutil	Force India-Mercedes VJM04	56	1h39m43.880s	113.442	1m43.526s	3
10	N Heidfeld	Renault R31	56	1h39m52.277s	113.284	1m43.901s	3
11	S Perez	Sauber-Ferrari C30	56	1h39m59.029s	113.156	1m43.949s	1
12	R Barrichello	Williams-Cosworth FW33	56	1h40m04.146s	113.060	1m44.131s	3
13	S Buemi	Toro Rosso-Ferrari STR6	56	1h40m05.383s	113.037	1m44.103s	3
14	P di Resta	Force India-Mercedes VJM04	56	1h40m07.378s	112.999	1m43.851s	3
15	V Petrov	Renault R31	56	1h40m11.044s	112.930	1m43.151s	3
16	K Kobayashi	Sauber-Ferrari C30	56	1h40m12.498s	112.902	1m43.517s	2
17	M Schumacher	Mercedes MGP W02	56	1h40m27.320s	112.625	1m44.578s	3
18	P Maldonado	Williams-Cosworth FW33	56	1h40m45.308s	112.290	1m43.134s	3
19	H Kovalainen	Lotus-Renault T128	55	1h39m47.875s	111.343	1m45.055s	3
20	J Trulli	Lotus-Renault T128	55	1h40m25.816s	110.641	1m46.208s	2
21	T Glock	Virgin-Cosworth MVR-02	55	1h40m41.990s	110.345	1m46.628s	3
22	J d'Ambrosio	Virgin-Cosworth MVR-02	55	1h41m02.650s	109.969	1m47.164s	3
23	V Liuzzi	HRT-Cosworth F111	54	1h39m42.633s	109.414	1m47.418s	3
24	N Karthikeyan	HRT-Cosworth F111	54	1h41m18.345s	107.691	1m47.708s	3

CHAMPIONSHIP

	Driver	Pts
1	S Vettel	186
2	J Button	109
3	M Webber	109
4	L Hamilton	97
5	F Alonso	87
6	F Massa	42
7	N Rosberg	32
8	V Petrov	31
9	N Heidfeld	30
10	M Schumacher	26
11	K Kobayashi	25
12	A Sutil	10
13	J Alguersuari	8
14	S Buemi	8
15	R Barrichello	4
16	S Perez	2
17	P di Resta	2

	Constructor	Pts
1	Red Bull-Renault	295
2	McLaren-Mercedes	206
3	Ferrari	129
4	Renault	61
5	Mercedes	58
6	Sauber-Ferrari	27
7	Toro Rosso-Ferrari	16
8	Force India-Mercedes	12
9	Williams-Cosworth	4

Fastest lap
S Vettel 1m41.852s
(119.015mph) on lap 53

Fastest speed trap
K Kobayashi 197.596mph
Slowest speed trap
J d'Ambrosio 187.778mph

Fastest pit stop
1 F Alonso 20.136s
2 A Sutil 20.286s
3 M Webber 20.319s

Adrian Sutil
"I made a good start: getting ahead of Heidfeld and kept up with Schumacher in the first stint. However, after the final stop, I came out behind Alguersuari."

Kamui Kobayashi
"I struggled and never had the performance to fight. It was hard to manage the tyres. I tried to take care of them well, but they were gone pretty quickly."

Sébastien Buemi
"I had a good start, then ran at a strong pace. However, as soon as I had degradation from my tyres, my lap times slowed and I was no longer able to overtake."

Jarno Trulli
"We tried a couple of different strategies to cover all our options, and even though my second set of tyres was gone by the end, I really enjoyed myself out there."

Narain Karthikeyan
"The rear tyres were degrading and I had braking problems. I was trying to keep with Liuzzi and d'Ambrosio, but I locked the front and then had a lonely race."

Timo Glock
"I had a good opening lap and passed both the Lotuses and a Toro Rosso. But, once the DRS was enabled, I couldn't keep Heikki and Jarno behind me."

  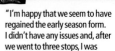 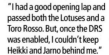

Paul di Resta
"There were a few laps when my tyres had gone off. I made up for that during the second stop, when I jumped Heidfeld and Barrichello, but lost out again."

Sergio Perez
"I had struggled with the harder tyres, but I also had a lack of grip with the softer ones and later in the race I lost time to blue flags. It wasn't an easy comeback."

Jaime Alguersuari
"I'm very happy, especially after starting 18th. I struggle to get the best out of the tyres in qualifying, but have a better understanding of how to use them in the race."

Heikki Kovalainen
"I'm happy that we seem to have regained the early season form. I didn't have any issues and, after we went to three stops, I was able to keep up a good pace."

Vitantonio Liuzzi
"It was a difficult race as I struggled with the rears, and that's why I was forced to do a three-stopper and, unluckily, was unable to cope with the Virgins."

Jerome d'Ambrosio
"I'm much happier with the race than with qualifying. Even though I lost time in the first stint when I was held up by Liuzzi, I had a good second stint."

2011 FORMULA 1 SANTANDER BRITISH GRAND PRIX
SILVERSTONE

FERNANDO RULES

Coinciding with a controversial change to the blown-diffuser rules, a raft of aero updates for Silverstone enabled Ferrari's Fernando Alonso to challenge the dominance of Red Bull Racing

Fernando Alonso scored a brilliant win for Ferrari in the British Grand Prix, after getting ahead of Sebastian Vettel when the German was delayed by a pitlane glitch. While he had some luck, Alonso's pace was such that he might well have beaten the Red Bull driver in a straight fight.

It was the first victory for the Maranello team in 2011, and with perfect timing it came on the 60th anniversary of its first ever World Championship win at Silverstone. Indeed during race morning Alonso enjoyed an emotional demonstration run in the ex-José Froilán González 375, owned by Bernie Ecclestone.

The big talking point of the weekend was the FIA's clampdown on exhaust blowing of diffusers, which dominated all paddock conversations. On Friday, the governing body relaxed the restrictions under pressure from Red Bull and Renault, but for qualifying they went back to the original plan, and the restrictions appeared to do Ferrari no harm.

Rain added some excitement to qualifying, but despite the chance of a random outcome (and the exhaust ruling in theory handicapping the blue cars) it was pretty much business as usual as the

INSIDE LINE
STEFANO DOMENICALI

FERRARI TEAM PRINCIPAL

"I'm not going to say I'm surprised that we won Silverstone. Surprise is a big word. For sure we were expecting to be competitive, but the win was a great result.

And it was good to win at Silverstone on the 60th anniversary of González. That history is something unique to this team. Correct me if I'm wrong but I think that in the last 18 years we've always been able to win something, and that means a lot.

We were expecting an improvement, for sure, but it was so big that we need to be cautious. We need to fully understand the data, but we saw that the performance of the car at Silverstone was really good in all conditions – wet, soft tyres, hard tyres.

Maybe it will be different at Nürburgring, but we don't have to be focused, as a lot of people are, on this saga of the hot and cold exhaust gas. We really need to look ahead and hope that our performance will be the basis for the next part of the season.

I don't know how much of this victory is owing to our step forward and how much to the blown-diffuser episode pulling back Red Bull. Anyone can say anything because nobody really knows. I hear so many things – that it makes a difference anything from three tenths to one second per lap.

I just want my people focused on car development. I've said to them, 'don't follow all the discussion, just focus on the job.'

I'm not going to talk about being back in the championship. But never say never. If in the next couple of races we get good results, then we will see.

I can confirm that we agreed to going back to the exhaust-blown diffusers. We need to draw a line under it. Even if I don't agree with the process taken, for the benefit of the sport we should have the gas. We need to look at the bigger picture even if, I have to say, I don't think all the people are behaving like we are.

If someone told me that this level of performance would apply to all the remaining circuits, I'd pay for it now!

Our Silverstone race pace was good, and even without the slow Red Bull pit stop, we could have won. We were strong."

Red Bulls hogged the front row – except that this time Mark Webber was ahead of Vettel.

Rain came and went through the course of qualifying, but in the end, when it mattered in the final session, everyone got in a dry lap. The rain then returned in the closing minutes of the session, so nobody was able to improve on a second timed lap, and we got a fairly standard grid. On the runs that counted, Webber beat Vettel by just 0.032s, enough to guarantee the Aussie his second pole of the year.

Ferrari had clearly gained more than McLaren from the regulation changes, and Alonso was less than a tenth behind Vettel, in a strong third place, despite a lucky escape when he went through the gravel in Q1. Felipe Massa started alongside him in fourth.

Jenson Button was fifth for McLaren, confused as to why he was 1.3s off Alonso. Meanwhile, after a disastrous first dry lap, Lewis Hamilton was unable to improve, and was stuck in 10th place.

A rain shower before the start left parts of the track soaked, and others – including the new pit straight – almost dry. Everyone started on intermediate tyres, and the early laps of the race proved very tricky as the drivers slithered around.

Despite the potential for some surprises, the race had a familiar look, as Vettel beat Webber off the line and shot straight into a lead that he extended by the lap.

The Ferraris seemed to be quick in all conditions, on a day when form varied wildly as the race developed. At the start, Alonso made an attempt to pass Webber into Turn 3, and having failed to make it past, dropped a couple of seconds back in the early laps – which at least kept him safely out of the spray. As the track dried and the first stops approached, he edged a little closer.

The move to slicks was triggered by Michael Schumacher, who was forced to come in on lap nine after a collision with Kamui Kobayashi. Nick Heidfeld came in a lap later, and by then Michael's sector times showed that the crossover point had been reached. Next time round, on lap 11, sixth-placed Button was the highest-placed driver to come in.

Vettel's lead was such that he could afford to stay out on lap 12, as RBR instead focused on Webber, who was under more immediate pressure. He came in, with Alonso and Hamilton following him down the pitlane. Ferrari had to briefly hold Fernando to let the McLaren go past, and in fact the Spaniard

OPPOSITE Lewis Hamilton charges into Club corner past Silverstone's new 'Wing' pit complex

ABOVE Michael Schumacher continued his wayward season, this time tangling with Kamui Kobayashi at Brooklands, losing his front wing and earning him a stop-go penalty

BELOW Promising Australian rookie Daniel Ricciardo replaced Narain Karthikeyan in the HRT

lost nearly 2.6s to Webber just in the stops, a huge amount given the margins involved.

Alonso was a little hesitant in those opening laps on slicks, and within three laps he was passed by a flying Hamilton, in a brilliant move at Copse that saw the Brit edge onto the wet line. Since they had pitted at the same time, it wasn't as if Lewis had any advantage from getting his tyres up to temperature – this was just a ballsy move by a man who had already taken a few risks as he battled his way up from 10th.

Was Alonso also taking his time, playing the long game, and protecting his tyres in those early dry laps? If so, it worked well. Within a few laps he was trading fastest laps with Lewis. And exactly 10 laps after Lewis passed him, Fernando repaid the favour, with a little DRS assistance, at Brooklands. Lewis ducked straight into the pits on lap 24, and from here on Fernando's focus was on the Red Bulls. He was 7.1s behind Vettel, and 3.0s behind Webber.

And everything would change over the next three laps. On lap 25 Alonso was 6.7s behind Seb, and on lap 26 the gap was 5.8s. Protecting those tyres at the beginning of the stint had paid dividends, and the pressure was now on Red Bull. Once again, Webber

was the most vulnerable to attack, so he got the first stop on lap 26. Alas, there was a minor wheel issue, and he lost around 1.5s.

On the next lap, Vettel dived into the pits, and Alonso followed him in, having by now cut the gap to 5.2s. Ferrari clearly felt it was better to have Fernando on the same tyre strategy as the leading Red Bull at this point, and hope that he could continue to close the gap on new tyres and perhaps, by extending their life, jump Vettel by going further to the final stops.

In the end he didn't need to, because it all went wrong for Red Bull when Seb's stop took almost 7.5s longer than Alonso's. The problem was an unprecedented rear-jack failure, rather than 'finger trouble', so in that sense the delay resulted from pure bad luck rather than a mistake generated by pressure from Ferrari.

Nevertheless, Alonso had to be close enough to take advantage, and it was his pass on Hamilton – and the fact that he brought the gap down to 5.2s – that put him in the right position.

Hamilton also got past Vettel, and in some ways that spoiled what could have been a great fight. Instead of seeing if Alonso could have closed that

OPPOSITE TOP Paul di Resta mastered tricky conditions in qualifying to take a stunning sixth place on the grid, but his race was compromised after being forced to queue behind team-mate Adrian Sutil – whose Force India had suffered a puncture – at his second stop

OPPOSITE BOTTOM Jenson Button was in contention for a podium place until he made his final stop on lap 39, when he was forced to retire after being mistakenly released before the front-right wheel nut had been fitted

BELOW Mark Webber put Sebastian Vettel under pressure for second place in the final laps, the two Red Bulls battling fiercely

TALKING POINT
A CRISIS AT McLAREN?

According to some of the British national newspapers post-Silverstone, McLaren was a team in crisis and Martin Whitmarsh was under pressure for his job.

One of the newspaper stories even claimed "growing discontent among engineering and design staff at McLaren about Whitmarsh's leadership."

If that was so, it was unusually well disguised for the F1 paddock. The only real evidence of any previous internal conflict was Montréal, where Whitmarsh said he would have gone in a different direction from the engineering staff on rear-wing level.

There have been operational mistakes, such as Hamilton's Monaco qualifying, but often ones that became errors only with the benefit of hindsight. Nobody, for instance, could have predicted that Sergio Perez would cause Monaco qualifying to be red-flagged.

Jenson Button's lost Silverstone wheel nut could have happened to anyone, as Ferrari would prove at Nürburgring.

If there was any dissent within the McLaren design and engineering ranks, it was more likely to surround the prioritising of Friday tasks rather than any serious underlying issue.

With no between-race testing, new components have to be track-tested in Friday practice. A race engineer and a driver will always want to concentrate on set-up, while design staff will have an eye on future races.

In the background, as FOTA Chairman, Whitmarsh had been spending a lot of time on political issues, not least the future engine regulations, which had become a bone of contention.

And, spending the time effectively. One engine man said: "In 24 hours he persuaded Ferrari to sign for a V6, which wasn't too difficult, but also got Renault, at main board level, to change its mind on a publicly declared direction.

"And he persuaded an independent manufacturer to sign up to a new engine, when Bernie was in everyone's ear about retaining V8s. It was all done and signed off in little more than a day, which was a phenomenal effort."

Much of the justification for the newspaper reports seemed to be that Whitmarsh had taken over from Ron Dennis as front man of the team in early 2009, since when McLaren had not won a title.

But, short of the absence of a double diffuser in early '09 (an affliction suffered by 75% of the grid) and the failure to organise a professional hit on Adrian Newey, what else has McLaren done so disastrously wrongly in the past couple of seasons?

After all, it's not as if they'd failed to score a point – they were second only to Red Bull in the constructors' championship.

Consider, too, that from 1998, the last time McLaren won the constructors' title, until the end of Ron Dennis's time in charge, they won only a single title when Hamilton snatched the drivers' crown on the last corner of the last lap at Interlagos in 2008.

ABOVE Felipe Massa and Hamilton had an intense battle towards the end of the race, for fourth place, running side-by-side through the final corner to the line, the McLaren losing a front-wing endplate and Massa having a heart-in-mouth moment as his Ferrari slid across the wet grass

BELOW Fernando Alonso's victory pointed towards a return to form for Ferrari, at a track where the Red Bulls were expected to be unbeatable

5.2s gap on Vettel and found a way by, we would have seen if Seb could have dealt with a 2.7s margin on Fernando.

Hamilton couldn't match the pace of the other two, and it would get worse when, as we later found out, he was forced to save fuel. It's easy to say that Lewis protected Alonso and allowed him to get away, but the fact is that getting past people is part of the game, and Vettel simply couldn't do it.

Lewis was quick enough where it mattered to make it hard, while Seb seemingly wasn't prepared to take any risks with the man who has perhaps the widest car in F1. It was impossible to judge Vettel's

potential performance on that set of tyres, as he spent the whole stint behind the McLaren. But Alonso also had more speed in his pocket.

"Without Hamilton keeping Sebastian behind, obviously the race was a little bit different, for sure," said Fernando. "We had to push more to open the gap. With Lewis there, the race was a little bit more comfortable for us and we could drop the revs a little bit and take a bit more care of the engine, the tyres, and things like that."

From that 2.7s on lap 28, the first lap out of the pits, the gap between Alonso and Vettel grew to 10.3s before Seb came in on lap 36. The stop finally allowed him to jump Lewis, who pitted a lap later.

Again, Alonso had protected his tyres and he was able to go three laps further, and while Vettel did make some inroads into the lead, with a later stop Ferrari ensured that Fernando's tyres would be in that much better shape come the closing laps, should he need to have a bit in reserve.

It wasn't necessary, because once Fernando got on to his fresh tyres, he simply pulled away. The evidence certainly suggests that he would have had a very good chance of beating Seb on pure speed, with or without the pit-stop glitch. It would have come down to a question of passing on track, or in the final stops. And, as Alonso made clear in Monaco, where he didn't get his chance to launch an attack on Vettel with his fresher tyres in the closing laps, the Red Bull man has a lot more to lose in any confrontation.

In fact, this time Vettel came under pressure from his own team-mate, and the German even tried to put some extra life into his tyres by cooling them in puddles. He was 10.3s behind Alonso when Lewis released him into clean air, and 19.9s behind on the penultimate lap, while fighting Webber, before Fernando finally slowed for his cruise to the line.

Not for the first time, Vettel faded in the final few laps, as the tyre situation played itself out, while Webber picked up speed in the latter stages of the race. The Aussie got close enough to launch an attack in the closing laps, despite requests from his engineer to maintain station. Team boss Christian Horner even personally got on the radio, and the positions remained unchanged.

Hamilton just managed to hang on to fourth place after surviving a last-corner attack from Massa that saw the two drivers make contact, although both continued unscathed.

Nico Rosberg took sixth for Mercedes, while Sauber's Sergio Perez had another good race to seventh. The final points went to Heidfeld, Schumacher (who had a stop-and-go penalty after hitting Kobayashi) and Jaime Alguersuari. Unluckiest man of the day was Paul di Resta, who qualified a superb sixth, but was a victim of a tyre mix-up in the Force India pits.

The most notable retirement was that of Button, who was battling with Webber for fourth when an error at a pit stop on lap 40 saw him leave without a front-right wheel nut. He stopped at the end of the pitlane and had to retire.

SNAPSHOT FROM
GREAT BRITAIN

CLOCKWISE FROM RIGHT The Silverstone 'Wing' dominates the new startline, as the pack heads into Abbey corner; Sebastian Vettel entertains the crowd at the post-race Grand Prix Party; former McLaren team-mates Fernando Alonso and Lewis Hamilton were all smiles; the crowd invades the track for the podium ceremony at the end of the race; McLaren's Martin Whitmarsh and Ferrari's Stefano Domenicali discuss the controversial changes to the blown-diffuser regulations; Vettel brought another helmet design to Silverstone, paying tribute to his mechanics; Alonso enjoyed demonstrating the 1951 British Grand Prix-winning Ferrari 375 of José Froilán González, 50 years after the Argentine driver's first grand prix victory for the Prancing Horse; will the real Felipe Massa please take a step forward; Prince Harry poses with McLaren's Jenson Button and Lewis Hamilton; the friendly face of British policing

RACE RESULTS
GREAT BRITAIN SILVERSTONE

RACE DATE July 10th
CIRCUIT LENGTH 3.659 miles
NO. OF LAPS 52
RACE DISTANCE 190.262 miles
WEATHER Sunny & dry, 20°C
TRACK TEMP 22°C
ATTENDANCE 315,000
LAP RECORD Fernando Alonso,
1m30.874s, 145.011mph, 2010

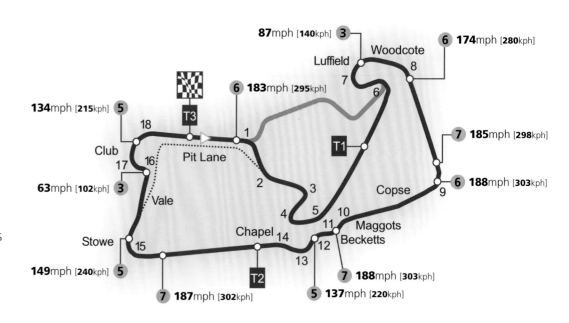

87mph [140kph] 3
Luffield 7
Woodcote 8
6 174mph [280kph]
6 183mph [295kph]
134mph [215kph] 5
T3
18
Club 1
17 16
Pit Lane
63mph [102kph] 3
Vale 2
T1
7 185mph [298kph]
6 188mph [303kph] 9
Copse
3
4 5 10
11 Maggots
Chapel 14 12 Becketts
Stowe 15 13
149mph [240kph] 5
T2
7 188mph [303kph]
7 187mph [302kph]
5 137mph [220kph]

PRACTICE 1			
	Driver	Time	Laps
1	M Webber	1m46.603s	19
2	M Schumacher	1m47.263s	20
3	R Barrichello	1m47.347s	23
4	S Perez	1m47.422s	22
5	F Massa	1m47.562s	13
6	N Rosberg	1m47.758s	23
7	F Alonso	1m48.161s	16
8	L Hamilton	1m48.549s	21
9	N Hulkenberg	1m48.598s	19
10	J Alguersuari	1m48.678s	22
11	P di Resta	1m48.730s	18
12	S Buemi	1m48.778s	18
13	S Vettel	1m48.794s	21
14	P Maldonado	1m48.809s	17
15	J Button	1m48.841s	23
16	N Heidfeld	1m48.941s	20
17	V Petrov	1m49.603s	15
18	K Kobayashi	1m50.133s	17
19	J Trulli	1m50.222s	14
20	K Chandhok	1m51.119s	17
21	T Glock	1m52.470s	17
22	V Liuzzi	1m53.143s	20
23	J d'Ambrosio	1m53.469s	26
24	D Ricciardo	1m54.334s	24

PRACTICE 2			
	Driver	Time	Laps
1	F Massa	1m49.967s	9
2	N Rosberg	1m50.744s	16
3	K Kobayashi	1m51.395s	16
4	L Hamilton	1m51.438s	6
5	J Button	1m51.518s	6
6	A Sutil	1m51.738s	18
7	P di Resta	1m51.781s	7
8	R Barrichello	1m51.992s	13
9	S Perez	1m52.169s	12
10	S Buemi	1m52.189s	21
11	V Petrov	1m52.198s	9
12	M Schumacher	1m52.325s	12
13	H Kovalainen	1m52.578s	16
14	M Webber	1m52.587s	6
15	F Alonso	1m52.869s	8
16	N Heidfeld	1m54.023s	8
17	J Alguersuari	1m54.274s	16
18	S Vettel	1m54.545s	4
19	J d'Ambrosio	1m54.714s	13
20	P Maldonado	1m55.155s	8
21	J Trulli	1m55.155s	12
22	T Glock	1m55.549s	10
23	D Ricciardo	1m55.828s	10
24	V Liuzzi	1m56.037s	6

PRACTICE 3			
	Driver	Time	Laps
1	S Vettel	1m31.401s	17
2	F Alonso	1m31.464s	20
3	M Webber	1m31.829s	12
4	F Massa	1m32.169s	20
5	P Maldonado	1m32.496s	20
6	J Button	1m32.956s	18
7	K Kobayashi	1m33.014s	20
8	N Rosberg	1m33.044s	23
9	S Perez	1m33.264s	21
10	P di Resta	1m33.423s	22
11	M Schumacher	1m33.551s	11
12	A Sutil	1m33.660s	22
13	L Hamilton	1m33.842s	16
14	R Barrichello	1m33.905s	21
15	V Petrov	1m34.042s	22
16	J Alguersuari	1m34.329s	20
17	S Buemi	1m34.799s	20
18	N Heidfeld	1m34.822s	21
19	H Kovalainen	1m35.225s	21
20	J Trulli	1m36.905s	21
21	T Glock	1m37.614s	18
22	J d'Ambrosio	1m38.068s	20
23	D Ricciardo	1m38.289s	19
24	V Liuzzi	1m38.568s	17

QUALIFYING 1		
	Driver	Time
1	M Webber	1m32.670s
2	P Maldonado	1m32.702s
3	F Massa	1m32.760s
4	S Vettel	1m32.977s
5	F Alonso	1m32.986s
6	R Barrichello	1m33.532s
7	L Hamilton	1m33.581s
8	S Perez	1m34.145s
9	M Schumacher	1m34.160s
10	N Rosberg	1m34.186s
11	J Button	1m34.230s
12	K Kobayashi	1m34.324s
13	V Petrov	1m34.428s
14	A Sutil	1m34.454s
15	P di Resta	1m34.472s
16	H Kovalainen	1m34.923s
17	N Heidfeld	1m35.132s
18	J Alguersuari	1m35.245s
19	S Buemi	1m35.749s
20	T Glock	1m36.203s
21	J Trulli	1m36.456s
22	J d'Ambrosio	1m37.154s
23	V Liuzzi	1m37.484s
24	D Ricciardo	1m38.059s

QUALIFYING 2		
	Driver	Time
1	F Massa	1m31.640s
2	M Webber	1m31.673s
3	F Alonso	1m31.727s
4	J Button	1m32.273s
5	N Rosberg	1m32.295s
6	S Vettel	1m32.379s
7	K Kobayashi	1m32.399s
8	L Hamilton	1m32.505s
9	P di Resta	1m32.569s
10	P Maldonado	1m32.588s
11	A Sutil	1m32.617s
12	S Perez	1m32.624s
13	M Schumacher	1m32.656s
14	V Petrov	1m32.734s
15	R Barrichello	1m33.119s
16	N Heidfeld	1m33.805s
17	H Kovalainen	1m34.821s

Best sectors – Practice			Speed trap – Practice			Best sectors – Qualifying			Speed trap – Qualifying		
Sec 1	S Vettel	28.949s	1	P Maldonado	194.489mph	Sec 1	M Webber	28.525s	1	N Rosberg	195.297mph
Sec 2	F Alonso	37.154s	2	M Schumacher	194.427mph	Sec 2	S Vettel	36.879s	2	M Schumacher	195.110mph
Sec 3	S Vettel	24.987s	3	N Rosberg	193.557mph	Sec 3	M Webber	24.824s	3	R Barrichello	194.986mph

Sebastian Vettel
"I was pulling away on inters, but we waited too long to go to dries. At the stop, we had to lift the car again. I got Lewis at the second stop, but Fernando was gone."

Jenson Button
"When Lewis, Seb and Mark pitted, I stayed out for a lap and I think I'd have come out alongside Mark. But, as I turned out, my right-front wheel came off."

Fernando Alonso
"I only realised I could win when I came out after the final stop. The problem at Vettel's stop helped, as did the fact that Hamilton had kept the Red Bulls behind him."

Michael Schumacher
"Using DRS for the first time, I arrived at the corner with overrun. Underestimating the effect, my braking wasn't good and this is how the collision happened."

Nick Heidfeld
"I was one of the first to change to slicks. Finding the balance between attacking, defending and not killing the tyres was great and brought four points."

Rubens Barrichello
"I didn't start well and fell back. Strangely, the car didn't feel good in the wet and it was a struggle to keep it on the track, so it was hard to keep up with those ahead."

Mark Webber
"I had to wait for slicks to come into play. On my in-lap, I had a moment at Becketts, so Fernando closed in. I felt strong at the start of each stint, less so later on."

Lewis Hamilton
"I stayed on Felipe's inside in the final corner. Luckily, we both got around the corner and I pipped him. The support when I crossed the line was as if I'd won."

Felipe Massa
"My floor was damaged after I hit something at Turn 6. Maybe we could have brought forward my second stop. I closed up to Hamilton, but just missed out."

Nico Rosberg
"I'm pleased. First of all because I had the potential to qualify in the top five, and secondly we had a good strategy. My start wasn't good, so sixth is a nice result."

Vitaly Petrov
"Traction was poor and others were able to go by like I wasn't there. They should move the DRS section position, as I was close to Adrian but just couldn't get past."

Pastor Maldonado
"It was difficult, especially with the rain before the start, as our set-up was geared towards a dry race. Towards the end, our performance became better."

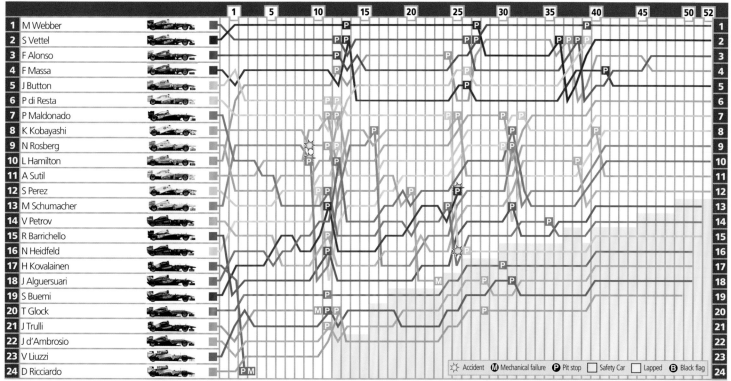

	Driver		
1	M Webber		
2	S Vettel		
3	F Alonso		
4	F Massa		
5	J Button		
6	P di Resta		
7	P Maldonado		
8	K Kobayashi		
9	N Rosberg		
10	L Hamilton		
11	A Sutil		
12	S Perez		
13	M Schumacher		
14	V Petrov		
15	R Barrichello		
16	N Heidfeld		
17	H Kovalainen		
18	J Alguersuari		
19	S Buemi		
20	T Glock		
21	J Trulli		
22	J d'Ambrosio		
23	V Liuzzi		
24	D Ricciardo		

Legend: ☼ Accident Ⓜ Mechanical failure Ⓟ Pit stop ☐ Safety Car ☐ Lapped Ⓑ Black flag

QUALIFYING 3

	Driver	Time
1	M Webber	1m30.399s
2	S Vettel	1m30.431s
3	F Alonso	1m30.516s
4	F Massa	1m31.124s
5	J Button	1m31.898s
6	P di Resta	1m31.929s
7	P Maldonado	1m31.933s
8	K Kobayashi	1m32.128s
9	N Rosberg	1m32.209s
10	L Hamilton	1m32.376s

GRID

	Driver	Time
1	M Webber	1m30.399s
2	S Vettel	1m30.431s
3	F Alonso	1m30.516s
4	F Massa	1m31.124s
5	J Button	1m31.898s
6	P di Resta	1m31.929s
7	P Maldonado	1m31.933s
8	K Kobayashi	1m32.128s
9	N Rosberg	1m32.209s
10	L Hamilton	1m32.376s
11	A Sutil	1m32.617s
12	S Perez	1m32.624s
13	M Schumacher	1m32.656s
14	V Petrov	1m32.734s
15	R Barrichello	1m33.119s
16	N Heidfeld	1m33.805s
17	H Kovalainen	1m34.821s
18	J Alguersuari	1m35.245s
19	S Buemi	1m35.749s
20	T Glock	1m36.203s
21	J Trulli	1m36.456s
22	J d'Ambrosio	1m37.154s
23	V Liuzzi	1m37.484s
24	D Ricciardo	1m38.059s

RACE

	Driver	Car	Laps	Time	Avg. mph	Fastest	Stops
1	F Alonso	Ferrari 150 Italia	52	1h28m41.196s	128.720	1m34.908s	3
2	S Vettel	Red Bull-Renault RB7	52	1h28m57.707s	128.322	1m35.565s	3
3	M Webber	Red Bull-Renault RB7	52	1h28m58.143s	128.311	1m35.665s	3
4	L Hamilton	McLaren-Mercedes MP4-26	52	1h29m10.182s	128.022	1m36.180s	3
5	F Massa	Ferrari 150 Italia	52	1h29m10.206s	128.021	1m35.474s	3
6	N Rosberg	Mercedes MGP W02	52	1h29m41.861s	127.269	1m37.073s	2
7	S Perez	Sauber-Ferrari C30	52	1h29m46.786s	127.152	1m36.656s	2
8	N Heidfeld	Renault R31	52	1h29m56.738s	126.918	1m37.117s	2
9	M Schumacher	Mercedes MGP W02	52	1h29m59.108s	126.862	1m37.034s	3
10	J Alguersuari	Toro Rosso-Ferrari STR6	52	1h30m00.304s	126.834	1m37.160s	2
11	A Sutil	Force India-Mercedes VJM04	52	1h30m00.908s	126.820	1m36.744s	3
12	V Petrov	Renault R31	52	1h30m01.877s	126.797	1m36.308s	2
13	R Barrichello	Williams-Cosworth FW33	51	1h28m42.272s	126.218	1m36.733s	2
14	P Maldonado	Williams-Cosworth FW33	51	1h28m43.098s	126.198	1m37.036s	3
15	P di Resta	Force India-Mercedes VJM04	51	1h29m33.432s	125.016	1m37.936s	3
16	T Glock	Virgin-Cosworth MVR02	50	1h29m28.458s	122.677	1m39.811s	2
17	J d'Ambrosio	Virgin-Cosworth MVR02	50	1h29m55.381s	122.065	1m40.560s	2
18	V Liuzzi	HRT-Cosworth F111	50	1h30m03.141s	121.890	1m40.524s	2
19	D Ricciardo	HRT-Cosworth F111	49	1h29m43.466s	119.887	1m40.910s	2
R	J Button	McLaren-Mercedes MP4-26	39	Loose wheel	-	1m36.982s	3
R	S Buemi	Toro Rosso-Ferrari STR6	25	Collision damage	-	1m40.224s	2
R	K Kobayashi	Sauber-Ferrari C30	23	Oil leak	-	1m40.703s	3
R	J Trulli	Lotus-Renault T128	10	Oil leak	-	1m55.491s	0
R	H Kovalainen	Lotus-Renault T128	2	Gearbox	-	2m10.404s	0

CHAMPIONSHIP

	Driver	Pts
1	S Vettel	204
2	M Webber	124
3	F Alonso	112
4	L Hamilton	109
5	J Button	109
6	F Massa	52
7	N Rosberg	40
8	N Heidfeld	34
9	V Petrov	31
10	M Schumacher	28
11	K Kobayashi	25
12	A Sutil	10
13	J Alguersuari	9
14	S Perez	8
15	S Buemi	8
16	R Barrichello	4
17	P di Resta	2

	Constructor	Pts
1	Red Bull-Renault	328
2	McLaren-Mercedes	218
3	Ferrari	164
4	Mercedes	68
5	Renault	65
6	Sauber-Ferrari	33
7	Toro Rosso-Ferrari	17
8	Force India-Mercedes	12
9	Williams-Cosworth	4

Fastest lap
F Alonso 1m34.908s
(138.848mph) on lap 41

Fastest speed trap
V Petrov 192.749mph
Slowest speed trap
H Kovalainen 109.827mph

Fastest pit stop
1 S Vettel 23.137s
2 F Massa 23.238s
3 J Button 23.292s

Adrian Sutil

"Things looked good in the first few laps and I think we made the right decision with the strategy to stop three times, but I didn't have the pace to hold on for points."

Kamui Kobayashi

"There isn't a lot for me to say about the accident with Michael. We weren't side by side, and he hit the rear of my car. After that, I had to drive with a damaged car."

Sébastien Buemi

"I'd like to see the footage with di Resta to see what happened. He tried to come up the inside where the surface was still wet. He touched my left rear, shredding it."

Jarno Trulli

"I was getting set to pass Timo, but had the call to stop to prevent any damage to the engine due to an oil leak, which was clearly not how we wanted the race to go."

Daniel Ricciardo

"Understanding the tyres, pit stops and strategy is something I've never done before. I was quite a bit off the other drivers, but as I learn I'll get closer."

Timo Glock

"The first few corners were a bit of a mess, but when everything settled I was in front of Jarno and could stay there. After they retired, I had a fairly easy time."

Paul di Resta

"I made the switch to dry tyres at the right moment. Then I got a call to pit again, but the team were expecting Adrian, so there was confusion that cost 25s."

Sergio Perez

"The conditions were difficult, but I managed to stay out of trouble. The strategy was good, but I just couldn't pass Nico, as he was too fast on the straights."

Jaime Alguersuari

"I was faster than Heidfeld and Schumacher around most of the lap, as in Valencia. But we couldn't make the most of this, as I then lost out down the straight."

Heikki Kovalainen

"What a shame! I had a really good start, but lost fourth gear and had to retire. The conditions out there were exactly what they should be for real drivers."

Vitantonio Liuzzi

"I had a good start with good pace and was able to fight our nearest rival, which is what we wanted to achieve, as we didn't have the pace to beat them."

Jerome d'Ambrosio

"It was very difficult when wet. I then had a good fight with Tonio in the second stint, passing him. But, after a couple of laps in the last stint I had no front-left grip."

FORMULA 1 GROSSER PREIS
SANTANDER VON DEUTSCHLAND 2011
NÜRBURGRING

VINTAGE HAMILTON

After a stunning qualifying performance, lining up second behind Mark Webber, Lewis Hamilton demonstrated his instinctive racecraft throughout the race and took a superb win

The Nürburgring proved once again that for all the excitement generated by the DRS and tyre degradation, in a 'normal' 2011 dry race there was no substitute for having pure qualifying speed, starting at the front, and controlling the race. Except this time, it wasn't Sebastian Vettel who proved that.

With Seb out of the picture for once, we had a great race at the front. As in Monaco, we saw three different cars running nose to tail, with nothing to choose between Lewis Hamilton, Mark Webber and Fernando Alonso. Unlike the Monaco race, the German GP ran to its natural conclusion, and Hamilton emerged as the winner. For the first time in 2011, Vettel failed to make the podium, settling instead for fourth.

Low temperatures added a little uncertainty to the proceedings in qualifying. Webber was in dominant form in the vital Q3 session, proving fastest on both his runs. It was his third pole of the year, and the second in a row after Silverstone.

Downbeat on Friday, Hamilton did a brilliant job, and ran what he described as his best qualifying lap of the year to take second. Vettel was clearly disappointed to be only third in front of his home fans, despite feeling that the car was better than it had been in Friday practice.

INSIDE LINE
LEWIS HAMILTON
McLAREN DRIVER

"Every win is special, but when we don't see results, I think all the emotion from the energy the team puts in slowly builds up. When you finally hit the sweet spot and get it, it's even better.

We never expected to come to Nürburgring and be so fast.

It was one of the best races I've ever done. Bit by bit, by learning more about how the car was behaving, and with my driving style, I learned to look after the tyres.

I was quickest in the first sector, quickest in the last sector, but struggling in the middle sector, so it was really down to improving my line in a lot of different places, particularly Turn 3.

At the apex of T3 I was sliding, but later on I was able to avoid it. At Turn 8, the fast chicane, I wasn't able to take it flat-out at the beginning. Webber could, and was catching me massively.

There are still areas we need to improve on, particularly on heavier fuel at the beginning, but this was a massive step forward and

I really hope that we can keep the momentum going.

The start was one of our best, a huge difference to what we had at places like Valencia. I got good temperature in my tyres, good temperature in my brakes and as we pulled away it felt just fantastic.

It was important to lead, otherwise we may have seen Mark pull away. Going into the chicane from lap to lap it was a little bit different under braking. Maybe it was just my car, but I would have a bit of rear-wheel locking, and slide.

I had a bit of a wide moment there, and Mark got past me, but fortunately I got him again into Turn 1. We had a good battle all the way to Turn 3. He was very fair and that's the kind of racing I love.

I thought we would be struggling behind both Red Bulls and Ferraris, but there was Mark, me and Fernando all within a tenth of each other, lap after lap. I was in a really good head space. The moves I did were some of the most precise I have pulled in a while. Being able to drive with your head all the time and get it right, just right, is massively satisfying."

Fernando Alonso had been tipped to be the closest challenger to RBR, but in the end he had to settle for fourth, and was somewhat surprised to see Hamilton get ahead. Felipe Massa backed him up in fifth place.

Nico Rosberg was the second-best local driver with a respectable sixth place for Mercedes, while Jenson Button struggled with set-up and even abandoned his final run. He was stranded back in seventh.

After heavy rain on Sunday morning, it was dry for the race, although there were a few spots of rain as the cars sat on the grid – and, crucially, it was still very cold. At the start, Webber appeared to bog down, and Hamilton was able to surge into the lead. Behind him, Alonso made an aggressive move on Vettel, and managed to take third place. On the second lap, however, Alonso ran wide, allowing Seb back into third place.

The Spaniard regained the spot with another great move into Turn One at the start of lap 8. Vettel's challenge for the podium faded when he had a spin, and he could never quite find the speed he needed to get back on terms with those ahead.

Meanwhile, Webber continued to chase Hamilton, and even managed to get past briefly at the end of lap 12 – only for Lewis to fight back and re-pass at

Turn One. That pinpointed the McLaren's superior straightline performance.

At the time, it seemed like a crucially important response from Lewis, but just a few laps later, Webber was in front anyway. A lap after he'd briefly taken the lead, RBR brought Mark in. Lewis drove a blistering couple of laps in response, but when he came in – with Alonso following him down the pitlane – he was passed by Webber. On his new tyres, Mark had simply been faster by more than enough to get himself in front.

So 17 laps into the race, a Red Bull was in front, albeit not the one we had usually seen there this year. However, this race had plenty more excitement in store.

By lap 25, Webber had opened up a handy lead of 1.4s, but at that stage, Lewis began to close the gap. The RBR simply didn't have the pace to generate a safe margin. By lap 29, the gap had come down to 0.8s, and a lap after that RBR brought the leader in.

Being ahead to start with, plus the new-tyre advantage over one lap, should have been enough to ensure that Mark stayed in front, but this time the undercut didn't work, because his out-lap simply wasn't fast enough – a reflection of the fact that it wasn't easy to switch the tyres on straight away.

LEFT Lewis Hamilton beats Mark Webber into the first corner to take the lead, with the rest of the field jostling for position behind

TOP Adrian Sutil made good use of a set of used option tyres to qualify eighth, driving his best race of the season thus far to finish sixth, beating both Mercedes cars

BELOW Vitantonio Liuzzi takes avoiding action in his HRT as Paul di Resta is pushed into a spin by Nick Heidfeld on the opening lap, the Force India driver rejoining at the back of the field before working his way back up to 13th place

The news that Turkey was likely to be off the provisional 2012 calendar caused some to voice concerns about the sport's future direction.

This wasn't because everyone loves Turkey, although Istanbul Park is widely reckoned to be the best of Hermann Tilke's circuits. It was simply that Turkey's unwillingness to pay a substantial hike in hosting fees is a recurring theme.

Although there are currently just five temporary venues on the calendar (Albert Park, Monte Carlo, Montréal, Valencia and Singapore), it seems that government funding is now all but a prerequisite for securing a slot on the Formula 1 calendar. And, increasingly, countries are electing to showcase a city, in the manner of Valencia and Singapore, rather than build a permanent venue such as the one in Austin, Texas.

Williams Technical Director Sam Michael said: "There's probably better racing on permanent tracks. So it's a shame that we're losing Turkey. One of the reasons you don't get good racing on non-permanent tracks is that the best ones for overtaking are the ones with natural undulations that have the ability to create different lines and sequences.

"Tracks that have a straight, a 90-degree corner and then a straight, have no sequence. It's point and squirt. Some street circuits do have sequences, like Tabac to the last corner at Monte Carlo. That's the most important thing."

Michael's opposite number at Red Bull, Adrian Newey, concurs: "The key thing is that we don't go too far down the temporary tracks route and that Formula 1 as an industry supports the permanent tracks.

"In Spain there's a danger that a permanent Barcelona could be lost to a temporary Valencia, and I think that would be a tragedy."

One of the problems is that in a country such as Turkey, which has not embraced Formula 1, attendance figures are low. Despite a claimed raceday crowd of 42,000 this year, many believe the real figure was more like half of that. In such instances, the official backing becomes the only reason to go there. Over time therefore, Formula 1 risks a situation where the racing becomes entirely secondary to dollar generation when, in reality, there needs to be a balance.

While nobody denies the spectacle that Singapore has added – the event has rapidly established itself as one of the classic events despite just three hostings so far – there is more scepticism over somewhere like Valencia.

"Give me Istanbul Park over Valencia any day," said one experienced team principal. "Istanbul's a great track, it's just a shame we can't pick it up and put it down somewhere else…"

Lewis came out of the pits, and was in front at Turn One, and while Mark had the advantage of his tyres by now being up to temperature, he couldn't quite find a way past through the first two or three corners. Lewis used every ounce of his racer's instinct to stay ahead.

"In these cold conditions it was quite a struggle to pull out in front of someone and stay in front of them," said Martin Whitmarsh. "From race to race you get situations where if you stop first and get on to fresh rubber, the level of degradation means that you're inherently quicker. Here, the degradation was less, and consequently it wasn't as clear-cut that when you jumped on to the new tyre, you were immediately quicker."

Lewis used his savvy again just a lap later. This time Alonso hadn't followed Hamilton into the pits, but chose instead to stay out a lap longer. And just as Lewis had come out ahead of Webber, so Fernando did the same to Lewis – but the McLaren's tyres were working just a tad better than Webber's had after one lap. And, of course, no way was Lewis going to let Alonso steal his lead.

Webber, it seemed, had shot his bolt, and in that third stint he fell away from the other two. Lewis, meanwhile, was awesome at the start of that stint. He opened up a margin of 1.7s in one lap, as Alonso struggled to get his tyres working, and then banged in a series of fastest laps. Just five laps after Fernando's stop, the gap was up to 3.1s. And then it began to fall.

From the outside, it looked as though Lewis might have taken too much out of his tyres too soon. This was going to be a long third stint and, crucially, it was open-ended in the sense that no-one really knew when the switch to primes would come, and thus for how long they would have to keep that set of options in good order.

Of course, slowing down Hamilton when he's in the mood to go quickly isn't an easy matter. In fact, Whitmarsh said Lewis did exactly what he was asked to do: "I think Lewis was well-judged and well-disciplined, and we were giving him quite a lot of data at that time,

because we wanted a 2.5–3s buffer, to give us the flexibility to manage that final stop."

The timing of that final stop was crucial. Everyone knew that the mediums would be used for only a very short final stint, and Pirelli had hinted earlier in the weekend that we might even get some last-minute changes, which is what happened with Vettel and Massa.

The key was to watch what happened to the first cars to switch to the prime. Some reasonably competitive drivers switched quite early – Maldonado lap 35, Buemi lap 36, Perez lap 41 – but they were two-stopping and committed to a long final stint. The first top-10 contender to change was Petrov, and while he was also two-stopping, the window for the top guys was fast approaching. Thus the Russian was the control sample.

Although Alonso had pulled back Hamilton's advantage to around 2s as the stops approached, that was still just enough to give Lewis maximum flexibility.

"We were watching Petrov, obviously," said Whitmarsh. "He was setting greens on the prime tyre. Our estimation at that time was that we had about a 1.8s degradation after about 20-ish laps on the option. The prime tyre was about 1.5s slower than the option, and a new prime should have been a little bit quicker.

OPPOSITE Sébastien Buemi squeezed Nick Heidfeld on to the grass on lap 9, causing the Renault to flip into the air as it hit a rut. The car thankfully landed on its wheels and slid to a halt in the gravel trap; a nonplussed Heidfeld gestured his disapproval to the Toro Rosso driver

TOP Mark Webber and Fernando Alonso kept the pressure on Hamilton during the early part of the race, before the first stops

ABOVE Daniel Ricciardo in the HRT battles with Karun Chandhok, who substituted for Jarno Trulli at Lotus; both drivers finished the race to take 19th and 20th places respectively

ABOVE Felipe Massa and Sebastian Vettel pitted together on the final lap, the German locking up to avoid hitting the back of the Ferrari. A wheel-nut problem delayed Massa, while a perfect stop for Red Bull allowed Vettel to exit the pits ahead to gain fourth place

BELOW Fernando Alonso hitched a lift back to *parc fermé* with Mark Webber after his Ferrari ran out of fuel on the slowing-down lap

"It was a difficult call. We all knew that we had to get on to that prime, and we all had to be comfortable that if you were on it for too long and it really was 1.5s slower, then it was going to be very difficult to get the job done."

Lewis came in on lap 51. The big question obviously was how quickly he could get up to speed on the medium, and he exceeded the team's expectations with a great out-lap.

"It was a critical time, and I think we got it right, personally," said Whitmarsh. "He was green on that tyre, and if he hadn't been... It was very easy in these sorts of conditions on that prime tyre not to fire it up, but he did. And as soon as he fired it up, from there

on, we had the job done, unless we made a mistake."

Surprisingly perhaps, Alonso stayed out for two more laps on the option, instead of coming straight in. When he did pit, he emerged still behind Lewis. Certainly McLaren felt that it would have been closer had he come in after one lap, although Hamilton would still have led.

"I was delighted!" said Whitmarsh of Ferrari's delayed response. "I think part of Ferrari's hesitation was, could you really switch the prime on? And I think they were probably a little bit more scared of it than we were. Actually, the only way they could have had a go at us was to have got on the prime before us, and as soon as they didn't, provided we could turn the prime on, they weren't going to beat us."

Clearly, in Germany it was all about tyre temperature, and specifically that critical first lap out of the pits.

"It's a combination of the team, the team giving the driver information, and setting the car up and getting it right," said Whitmarsh. "The teams deploy a lot of tactics and different equipment to try and manage the tyre into that sweet spot. We had determined a three-stop, and I think we made the stops at the right time, given where we were in the race."

Webber dropped away from the two leaders in third, taking a gamble by staying out longer on his primes. In fact, Massa and Vettel waited until the last possible opportunity – the start of the last lap – before pitting, and when the Ferrari crew had a glitch, Vettel jumped ahead.

Adrian Sutil did a great job to take sixth for Force India, beating the Mercedes pair of Nico Rosberg and Michael Schumacher. The final points went to Kamui Kobayashi and Vitaly Petrov.

Button would have ended up in a strong position if a hydraulic leak had not led to his retirement. He'd made a bad start, had been switched to a two-stop, and had to go through the pain of slipping back as his first stint dragged on. He knew that it would be worth it, but he never had the chance to reap the benefit as he retired for the second race in a row.

SNAPSHOT FROM GERMANY

CLOCKWISE FROM RIGHT

The surrounding forest echoes the spirit of the legendary *Nordschleife* circuit; Lewis Hamilton provides a focus for the photographers in *parc fermé*; Nico Rosberg poses for a fan; a flash of red as Fernando Alonso's Ferrari gets up close and personal to the snappers; Sebastian Vettel was hugely popular with the fans at his home race; Vitaly Petrov finds a new way to deal with 'helmet hair'; the grid girls had the legs in the paddock; smiley-face stickers in Sebastian Vettel's Red Bull Racing RB7 cockpit denote his 2011 race-win tally; Karun Chandhok made a one-off appearance standing in for Jarno Trulli at Lotus; former McLaren team-mates Mika Hakkinen and David Coulthard were reunited to demonstrate Silver Arrows race winners from the past

RACE RESULTS
GERMANY
NURBURGRING

Official Results © [2011]
Formula One Administration Limited,
6 Princes Gate, London, SW7 1QJ.
No reproduction without permission.
All copyright and database rights reserved.

RACE DATE July 24th
CIRCUIT LENGTH 3.196 miles
NO. OF LAPS 60
RACE DISTANCE 191.775 miles
WEATHER Overcast but dry, 14°C
TRACK TEMP 18°C
ATTENDANCE Not available
LAP RECORD Michael Schumacher, 1m29.468s, 128.721mph, 2004

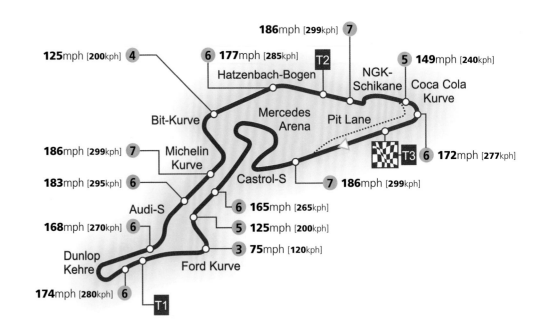

125mph [200kph] 4 — Bit-Kurve
186mph [299kph] 6 — 177mph [285kph] T2 Hatzenbach-Bogen
186mph [299kph] 7 — NGK-Schikane
5 149mph [240kph] — Coca Cola Kurve
186mph [299kph] 7 — Michelin Kurve
Mercedes Arena — Pit Lane
183mph [295kph] 6 — T3 — 6 172mph [277kph]
Audi-S — Castrol-S — 7 186mph [299kph]
168mph [270kph] 6 — 6 165mph [265kph]
— 5 125mph [200kph]
Dunlop Kehre — 3 75mph [120kph]
174mph [280kph] 6 — Ford Kurve
T1

PRACTICE 1

	Driver	Time	Laps
1	F Alonso	1m31.894s	30
2	M Webber	1m32.217s	24
3	S Vettel	1m32.268s	27
4	F Massa	1m32.681s	23
5	L Hamilton	1m32.996s	18
6	J Button	1m33.628s	22
7	N Rosberg	1m33.787s	33
8	A Sutil	1m33.832s	27
9	N Hulkenberg	1m33.858s	26
10	M Schumacher	1m33.863s	31
11	V Petrov	1m34.094s	22
12	J Alguersuari	1m35.115s	23
13	S Buemi	1m35.371s	20
14	R Barrichello	1m35.389s	24
15	N Heidfeld	1m35.444s	22
16	S Perez	1m36.371s	22
17	H Kovalainen	1m36.392s	29
18	P Maldonado	1m36.842s	29
19	K Kobayashi	1m36.882s	27
20	N Karthikeyan	1m38.504s	22
21	V Chandhok	1m38.765s	19
22	D Ricciardo	1m39.279s	24
23	T Glock	1m40.109s	23
24	J d'Ambrosio	1m40.428s	22

PRACTICE 2

	Driver	Time	Laps
1	M Webber	1m31.711s	34
2	F Alonso	1m31.879s	38
3	S Vettel	1m32.084s	28
4	F Massa	1m32.354s	36
5	M Schumacher	1m32.411s	31
6	N Rosberg	1m32.557s	32
7	L Hamilton	1m32.724s	28
8	N Heidfeld	1m33.098s	17
9	V Petrov	1m33.138s	22
10	A Sutil	1m33.211s	34
11	J Button	1m33.225s	17
12	P di Resta	1m33.299s	34
13	S Perez	1m34.113s	34
14	R Barrichello	1m34.344s	34
15	J Alguersuari	1m34.487s	37
16	K Kobayashi	1m34.491s	35
17	P Maldonado	1m34.996s	35
18	H Kovalainen	1m35.753s	42
19	T Glock	1m36.940s	32
20	K Chandhok	1m37.248s	33
21	J d'Ambrosio	1m37.313s	33
22	V Liuzzi	1m38.145s	31
23	D Ricciardo	1m40.737s	5
24	S Buemi	No time	3

PRACTICE 3

	Driver	Time	Laps
1	S Vettel	1m30.916s	15
2	M Webber	1m31.049s	16
3	F Alonso	1m31.138s	12
4	L Hamilton	1m31.578s	13
5	J Button	1m31.623s	14
6	N Rosberg	1m31.694s	19
7	F Massa	1m32.144s	13
8	A Sutil	1m32.391s	20
9	M Schumacher	1m32.523s	16
10	P Maldonado	1m32.751s	18
11	V Petrov	1m32.777s	18
12	P di Resta	1m32.813s	21
13	N Heidfeld	1m33.072s	18
14	R Barrichello	1m33.179s	17
15	S Perez	1m33.531s	20
16	K Kobayashi	1m33.671s	20
17	S Buemi	1m33.948s	21
18	J Alguersuari	1m34.125s	19
19	H Kovalainen	1m35.385s	13
20	T Glock	1m36.724s	21
21	V Liuzzi	1m36.804s	24
22	J d'Ambrosio	1m36.894s	23
23	K Chandhok	1m36.959s	18
24	D Ricciardo	1m37.554s	22

QUALIFYING 1

	Driver	Time
1	F Massa	1m31.826s
2	A Sutil	1m32.286s
3	N Heidfeld	1m32.505s
4	M Schumacher	1m32.603s
5	P di Resta	1m32.651s
6	N Rosberg	1m32.785s
7	F Alonso	1m32.916s
8	L Hamilton	1m32.934s
9	S Vettel	1m32.973s
10	M Webber	1m33.003s
11	P Maldonado	1m33.096s
12	V Petrov	1m33.187s
13	J Button	1m33.224s
14	S Perez	1m33.295s
15	S Buemi	1m33.635s
16	J Alguersuari	1m33.658s
17	R Barrichello	1m33.664s
18	K Kobayashi	1m33.786s
19	H Kovalainen	1m35.599s
20	T Glock	1m36.400s
21	K Chandhok	1m36.422s
22	J d'Ambrosio	1m36.641s
23	V Liuzzi	1m37.011s
24	D Ricciardo	1m37.036s

QUALIFYING 2

	Driver	Time
1	L Hamilton	1m30.998s
2	S Vettel	1m31.017s
3	F Alonso	1m31.150s
4	M Webber	1m31.311s
5	N Rosberg	1m31.343s
6	J Button	1m31.532s
7	F Massa	1m31.582s
8	A Sutil	1m31.809s
9	V Petrov	1m31.985s
10	M Schumacher	1m32.180s
11	N Heidfeld	1m32.215s
12	P di Resta	1m32.560s
13	P Maldonado	1m32.635s
14	R Barrichello	1m33.043s
15	S Perez	1m33.176s
16	S Buemi	1m33.546s
17	J Alguersuari	1m33.698s

Best sectors – Practice
Sec 1	S Vettel	30.100s
Sec 2	M Webber	37.433s
Sec 3	S Vettel	23.268s

Speed trap – Practice
1	N Rosberg	192.065mph
2	F Massa	191.755mph
3	M Schumacher	191.382mph

Best sectors – Qualifying
Sec 1	L Hamilton	29.713s
Sec 2	M Webber	36.883s
Sec 3	L Hamilton	23.164s

Speed trap – Qualifying
1	M Schumacher	192.873mph
2	N Rosberg	192.811mph
3	F Massa	192.500mph

 **Sebastian Vettel**

"It was a difficult race. I made a mistake, which dropped me to fifth place, and from there it was a tough recovery. I think fourth was the maximum I could achieve."

 **Jenson Button**

"I had a terrible first lap, so had to fight back from 10th. I got stuck behind Vitaly, but enjoyed fighting back. I'd passed Nico when my power steering got heavy."

 **Fernando Alonso**

"When I was behind Hamilton, I couldn't get close. Even though I came out ahead at the second stop, I had no grip and he passed me around the outside."

 **Michael Schumacher**

"It was a pretty exciting race with lots of action. My spin caught me out, but that spot is known to be tricky in the wet, even if the conditions weren't so wet today."

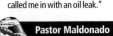 **Nick Heidfeld**

"Di Resta was on the outside at Turn 3. I locked my fronts and slid into him. Later, Buemi blocked the left. When I went to his right, he pushed me on to the grass."

Rubens Barrichello

"I was doing OK after making a good start and was looking fine for a two-stop strategy, but the team came on the radio and called me in with an oil leak."

Mark Webber

"I led the middle part, but could not get the tyre range around the stops to get the undercut on the second stop. I drove on the limit, but Lewis was able to cover us."

Lewis Hamilton

"To win is positive, but there's a long way to go, and it'll be about consistency as well as speed. The moves I made were some of the most precise I've ever pulled off."

 Felipe Massa

"I got away well, but Vettel closed the inside line and I tried the outside, as there was nowhere else to go if I wanted to make up places, but I lost one to Rosberg."

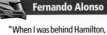 **Nico Rosberg**

"I moved up to fifth on lap 1, but the car wasn't working as well as in qualifying. I had a good battle with Massa, but it was impossible to keep him behind me."

 Vitaly Petrov

"I had some decent battles and it's another point gained, but we must analyse why we lost places and why we didn't pit earlier to fight with the group in front."

 Pastor Maldonado

"It was a tough race. I was quite competitive in the second stint on a new set of option tyres, but went on to the primes for the last stint and lost time and places."

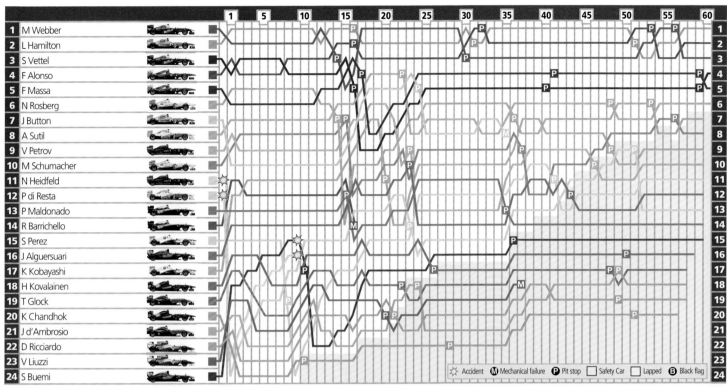

Lap by lap positions chart (laps 1–60), drivers 1–24:

1	M Webber
2	L Hamilton
3	S Vettel
4	F Alonso
5	F Massa
6	N Rosberg
7	J Button
8	A Sutil
9	V Petrov
10	M Schumacher
11	N Heidfeld
12	P di Resta
13	P Maldonado
14	R Barrichello
15	S Perez
16	J Alguersuari
17	K Kobayashi
18	H Kovalainen
19	T Glock
20	K Chandhok
21	J d'Ambrosio
22	D Ricciardo
23	V Liuzzi
24	S Buemi

Legend: ☆ Accident Ⓜ Mechanical failure Ⓟ Pit stop ☐ Safety Car ☐ Lapped Ⓑ Black flag

QUALIFYING 3

	Driver	Time
1	M Webber	1m30.079s
2	L Hamilton	1m30.134s
3	S Vettel	1m30.216s
4	F Alonso	1m30.442s
5	F Massa	1m30.910s
6	N Rosberg	1m31.263s
7	J Button	1m31.288s
8	A Sutil	1m32.010s
9	V Petrov	1m32.187s
10	M Schumacher	1m32.482s

GRID

	Driver	Time
1	M Webber	1m30.079s
2	L Hamilton	1m30.134s
3	S Vettel	1m30.216s
4	F Alonso	1m30.442s
5	F Massa	1m30.910s
6	N Rosberg	1m31.263s
7	J Button	1m31.288s
8	A Sutil	1m32.010s
9	V Petrov	1m32.187s
10	M Schumacher	1m32.482s
11	N Heidfeld	1m32.215s
12	P di Resta	1m32.560s
13	P Maldonado	1m32.635s
14	R Barrichello	1m33.043s
15	S Perez	1m33.176s
16	J Alguersuari	1m33.698s
17	K Kobayashi	1m33.786s
18	H Kovalainen	1m35.599s
19	T Glock	1m36.400s
20	K Chandhok	1m36.422s
21	J d'Ambrosio	1m36.641s
22	D Ricciardo	1m37.036s
23*	V Liuzzi	1m37.011s
24**	S Buemi	1m33.546s

* 5-place penalty for gearbox change.
** Excluded from qualifying for using illegal fuel.

RACE

	Driver	Car	Laps	Time	Avg. mph	Fastest	Stops
1	L Hamilton	McLaren-Mercedes MP4-26	60	1h37m30.334s	118.004	1m34.302s	3
2	F Alonso	Ferrari 150 Italia	60	1h37m34.314s	117.928	1m34.626s	3
3	M Webber	Red Bull-Renault RB7	60	1h37m40.122s	117.812	1m34.468s	3
4	S Vettel	Red Bull-Renault RB7	60	1h38m18.255s	117.050	1m34.587s	3
5	F Massa	Ferrari 150 Italia	60	1h38m22.586s	116.964	1m34.609s	3
6	A Sutil	Force India-Mercedes VJM04	60	1h38m56.542s	116.295	1m36.653s	2
7	N Rosberg	Mercedes MGP W02	59	1h37m36.053s	115.929	1m36.181s	3
8	M Schumacher	Mercedes MGP W02	59	1h37m45.987s	115.732	1m35.628s	3
9	K Kobayashi	Sauber-Ferrari C30	59	1h37m54.841s	115.558	1m36.659s	2
10	V Petrov	Renault R31	59	1h37m55.160s	115.552	1m36.186s	2
11	S Perez	Sauber-Ferrari C30	59	1h38m08.511s	115.290	1m37.033s	2
12	J Alguersuari	Toro Rosso-Ferrari STR6	59	1h38m14.571s	115.171	1m37.415s	2
13	P di Resta	Force India-Mercedes VJM04	59	1h38m15.040s	115.162	1m36.715s	2
14	P Maldonado	Williams-Cosworth FW33	59	1h38m21.319s	115.039	1m37.568s	2
15	S Buemi	Toro Rosso-Ferrari STR6	59	1h38m52.794s	114.429	1m37.863s	2
16	H Kovalainen	Lotus-Renault T128	58	1h38m10.881s	113.290	1m39.050s	2
17	T Glock	Virgin-Cosworth MVR02	57	1h37m51.795s	111.698	1m39.982s	2
18	J d'Ambrosio	Virgin-Cosworth MVR02	57	1h38m02.125s	111.502	1m39.787s	2
19	D Ricciardo	HRT-Cosworth F111	57	1h38m28.184s	111.010	1m40.489s	2
20	K Chandhok	Lotus-Renault T128	56	1h38m26.941s	109.086	1m40.435s	3
R	V Liuzzi	HRT-Cosworth F111	37	Electrical	-	1m40.683s	1
R	J Button	McLaren-Mercedes MP4-26	35	Hydraulics	-	1m36.258s	1
R	R Barrichello	Williams-Cosworth FW33	16	Oil leak	-	1m39.679s	0
R	N Heidfeld	Renault R31	9	Collision	-	1m39.452s	0

CHAMPIONSHIP

	Driver	Pts
1	S Vettel	216
2	M Webber	139
3	L Hamilton	134
4	F Alonso	130
5	J Button	109
6	F Massa	62
7	N Rosberg	46
8	N Heidfeld	34
9	V Petrov	32
10	M Schumacher	32
11	K Kobyashi	27
12	A Sutil	18
13	J Alguersuari	9
14	S Perez	8
15	S Buemi	8
16	R Barrichello	4
17	P di Resta	2

	Constructor	Pts
1	Red Bull-Renault	355
2	McLaren-Mercedes	243
3	Ferrari	192
4	Mercedes	78
5	Renqult	66
6	Sauber-Ferrari	35
7	Force India-Mercedes	20
8	Toro Rosso-Ferrari	17
9	Williams-Cosworth	4

Fastest lap
L Hamilton 1m34.302s
(122.115mph) on lap 59

Fastest speed trap
M Schumacher 192.687mph
Slowest speed trap
R Barrichello 179.141mph

Fastest pit stop
1 M Schumacher 19.930s
2 F Alonso 19.975s
3 F Alonso 20.035s

Adrian Sutil
"I had a great car all weekend and everything went perfectly. The tyres lasted well and we made the right calls, helping me to beat Nico in the final stint."

Kamui Kobayashi
"I was able to gain places in the first few corners, going from 17th to 12th. But then our pace wasn't good enough. The fact that I scored is down to good strategy."

Sébastien Buemi
"I had rain settings and the rain never came, so it wasn't the best set-up. I had quite a good start, but Heidfeld drove into me at the chicane and I got a puncture."

Karun Chandhok
"I need more time to get used to the tyres. When they start to go off there's very little give compared to 2010's rubber, but that's all part of the learning process."

Daniel Ricciardo
"I've made a good step from Silverstone, but there's still quite a long way to go. If I can keep this way then in a few races time the progress will be more obvious."

Timo Glock
"I struggled with the braking system from the middle of the race onwards, and I wasn't able to push late on in the race, so we'll have to look into the problem."

Paul di Resta
"I was racing with Michael into the first corner. Then I got hit from behind, which must have been Nick, and that spun me around and compromised my race."

Sergio Perez
"I made a mistake on lap 8, went off and was on the grass. This was why I had to pit early and change tyres. I recovered a bit from there, but not enough for points."

Jaime Alguersuari
"I did a good job in the race, given where I started on the grid. However, my pace wasn't as good as at Valencia or Silverstone and I struggled under braking."

Heikki Kovalainen
"It was lonely, as we're not quite with the guys ahead, yet well clear of those behind, so I wanted to make sure I could push as hard as possible over the full distance."

Vitantonio Liuzzi
"I passed a few cars on lap 1, then began to suffer brake-balance problems. After my stop, I recovered pace until an electronic issue forced me to retire."

Jerome d'Ambrosio
"I feel like I'm back on the right track and, although there are definitely more improvements I can make, particularly in qualifying, I'm going in the right direction."

FORMULA 1 ENI
MAGYAR NAGYDÍJ 2011
BUDAPEST

POLISHED BUTTON

With his instinctive ability to judge track grip in changing conditions and make the right tyre choices, Jenson Button drove superbly to take a deserved victory in his 200th grand prix

Jenson Button made it two wins in eight days for McLaren after a thrilling race in Hungary. As with the Canadian and British GPs, rain helped to trip up Red Bull Racing, although Sebastian Vettel still managed to finish second and extend his already huge lead over his title rivals.

There have been some pretty boring processions in Hungary over the 25 years of the event's history, but nobody could say that about the 2011 edition. Rain at the start, and again in the last third of the race, spiced up the action, but we would have had an intriguing contest even it had stayed dry all the way through.

Vettel had a below-par Friday, and RBR made a lot of changes to the car overnight, to the extent that the mechanics stayed late and broke the curfew – something they can do only four times a year before getting a penalty.

Lewis Hamilton was fastest after the first runs in Q3, but Vettel hit back right at the end to go some 0.16s faster. Hamilton's final hot lap couldn't improve on his first, so he had to settle for second. Like everyone in an even-numbered grid slot, the McLaren driver had to start from the less favourable dirty side of the grid.

McLaren's disappointment was lessened by the fact that Jenson Button was behind his team-mate in a solid third place. Meanwhile, for once Felipe Massa went faster than

INSIDE LINE
PADDY LOWE
McLAREN
TECHNICAL DIRECTOR

"Jenson didn't put a foot wrong. Like so often in those sort of mixed conditions, he just reads it so well.

We had a split strategy with Jenson and Lewis. It wasn't deliberately done that way, each car crew works independently in deciding. When it was still dry and Lewis went on to the option tyre and Jenson the prime; we thought the strategies would work out to be similar. Alonso stopped four laps before Lewis, and was going very fast on the options and there was uncertainty about how long the prime would last.

Also, Lewis seemed to be having a much tougher time wearing his left-front tyre than Jenson, so we thought that the more aggressive strategy, and extra stop, was better suited to him.

The interesting thing then was that the option tyre didn't seem to have the pace to make it work, because we started to see Jenson and Vettel doing personal-best lap times on the prime tyre. And so it became immediately evident that even without the rain, Lewis was on the wrong strategy.

That was a team call. A lap earlier, Lewis said it was OK for dry tyres, but then the conditions got quickly worse.

We'd seen quite a lot of people stop for the rain tyre, and the weather radar was indicating that it was going to get worse. In those situations you're normally better off getting on to the wet tyre earlier.

The complication was that watching Rosberg's times, the intermediate tyre seemed better in sector one, which was wetter, and the dry tyre looked better in sector two. You are trying to make these split-second decisions, and you haven't got the benefit of two or three laps to analyse it – you're looking at it sector by sector.

Why didn't Lewis win? First there was fitting the option tyres instead of the primes, although he might not have made the prime work anyway because of his front tyre wear. Then there was his spin, then his spin-turn in front of traffic. That looked pretty ambitious at the time, so I think that the penalty was fair enough.

If he hadn't done the spin-turn he'd have lost more places, because he'd have had to wait for Vettel and everyone else to come through. Then there was the drive-through penalty, then the wet-tyre decision. Considering everything, he did well to finish fourth!"

Paddy Lowe

Fernando Alonso, and the two Ferrari drivers lined up fourth and fifth. The Spaniard had looked a good bet for pole during the weekend, and was fastest in both Q1 and Q2, but didn't get it right when it mattered. After some KERS problems in qualifying, Mark Webber was relegated to sixth.

After an overcast couple of days, the rain finally came on Sunday morning. On-and-off showers meant the track was damp for the start, and everyone went to the grid on intermediates. From pole, Vettel got away safely in front, ahead of Hamilton and Button. Lewis was clearly in feisty mood, and after several attempts he made it through into the lead at Turn 2 on the fifth lap.

He continued to open up a gap on Vettel, until the window for dry tyres opened up around lap 10. Webber was the first to stop, from sixth place, and he immediately showed that the track was dry enough by doing a quick sector time on his out-lap.

The rest of the top guys followed over the next couple of laps, with Hamilton and Vettel staying out until lap 12. They emerged with Lewis still safely in front, while his team-mate also managed to get ahead of Vettel by stopping a lap earlier than the German.

Over the second stint, Hamilton continued to hold a handy lead over Button, while Vettel ran third and Webber fourth, and that pattern continued after the second round of stops.

The race became more interesting around this time, as it became clear that some teams expected to stop three times, while others were running a four-stop strategy. For the former, it was a question of putting the prime or soft on at the third stop, and doing a long stint on it.

Hamilton and Alonso chose to go for the supersoft and committed to four stops, while Vettel, Button and Webber went for the soft, and thus three stops.

Then, around lap 46, the rain returned. Still leading, and desperate to make the best of the situation he was in, Hamilton pushed a little too hard and spun. Button got

through, and at that point Lewis's hopes of winning were dead and buried, unless he could make the rain work for him. Then, later, he received a drive-through penalty for resuming a little too carelessly after the spin, into the path of Paul di Resta.

After a couple of laps, the rain eased off, and Alonso was able to make his final stop for primes on lap 47. This was a tricky one for Ferrari, as there was a threat of more rain coming soon, but the team had to bring him in.

So now Button, Vettel, Webber and Alonso were all on primes and able to go to the end. The one man who couldn't was Hamilton, and when the rain came back, heavier than before, it looked like he might luck in.

It was Nico Rosberg who kick-started a mini-rush for intermediates, coming in on lap 50. Just 46s later, Webber dashed in, and up and down the pitlane engineers urgently studied sector times and asked their drivers what state the track was in. These situations are always hugely complicated.

"It's a 50/50 thing at the end of the day," said Christian Horner. "Mark was on the radio saying, 'It's inters', and we couldn't disagree with him, because you're looking at the pitlane and it's wet, and cars are going off the track. You don't know whether that rain

OPPOSITE Winner of the 2010 Hungarian GP, Mark Webber had a difficult weekend, qualifying sixth and finishing the race an eventual fifth after being wrong-footed by a poor tyre choice at his first pit stop

BELOW Jarno Trulli returned to his Lotus, revitalised with a new power-steering system that suited his driving style, although he ran behind team-mate Kovalainen and retired with a water leak

BOTTOM Lewis Hamilton and Sebastian Vettel battled hard for the lead in the opening laps, Hamilton getting the better of the World Champion at the end of lap 4. Behind, Button leads Fernando Alonso and Nico Rosberg

a lot of people stop," said Technical Director Paddy Lowe. "The radar was indicating that this was just the beginning of the rain, and it was going to get worse. As with these things normally, you're better being earlier on to the wet tyre, than late, so that's the way we went.

"Then the complication was that one tyre was better in S1, which was more wet than S2 and S3. So you're trying to make these split-second decisions, and you don't have the benefit of two or three laps to analyse, you're analysing sector by sector, and making a quick call. Even if you had that data, it's immediately raining either more or less, so it's historical already."

Meanwhile, the rest continued to struggle round on dry tyres, losing chunks of time for a couple of laps when inters were the thing to have.

And then the rain stopped, and just as quickly inters were useless. In fact, Webber pitted to get back on to slicks just 2m09s after Hamilton had gone the other way!

"At the time, his [dry] tyres were shot and he had to come in," said Martin Whitmarsh of Hamilton's strategy. "Half the field fitted intermediates at that point, so we weren't actually alone in the thought process. If you can have a crystal ball, then you can always get it better."

Lewis in turn had to go back to slicks after just two laps on inters, and this extra stop sent him further down the order. It all became academic anyway, as his drive-through was announced.

Through all of this, Button and Vettel had carried on round at the front, staying clear of any pit activity. Their achievement should not be underestimated, not just in terms of keeping out of trouble, but also in dealing with tyres that lost temperature over those few cold and wet laps in the middle, and then had to be nursed to the end of the race.

Having earlier lapped in 1m24s, at the height of the rain Jenson ran a 1m41.2s lap and Vettel a 1m45.6s – but then they both ran wide at Turn 2 while ceding to the intermediate-shod Hamilton. That showed how easy it

ABOVE Nick Heidfeld's Renault got all fired up due to an exhaust problem on lap 23

BELOW Jerome d'Ambrosio struggled with his Virgin in changeable conditions, spinning down the pitlane and missing his pit box as he made his final stop

OPPOSITE Jenson Button and Lewis Hamilton fight it out, with Vettel following close behind

is going to stop or start, so it was right on the cusp, and obviously pretty much 50% of the field, Lewis included, followed the same route.

"Sebastian was asking the same questions, but we thought, 'OK, at this point we can't cover both options', so we split, and we left him, and he managed those conditions very well, because it's very easy to make a mistake, and it came right for him."

After Webber stopped, Petrov, Barrichello, Kovalainen, Sutil, Liuzzi and Maldonado all came into the pitlane within 90s of Rosberg stopping – and then McLaren brought Hamilton in.

"We needed to stop anyway, and we'd seen quite

TALKING POINT
SKY'S F1 TV DEAL

The news that Sky Sports and the BBC would share F1 coverage from 2012 until 2018, with Sky the only place to see all races live, stunned the paddock early on Friday morning.

Many of the BBC team, Martin Brundle among them, were clearly unimpressed, as much as anything because of the lack of information.

Parachuted in to report the news, they were somewhat dismayed to find that they were the news.

The over-riding reaction was negative. And it wasn't long before those who had been around the block were looking at the bigger picture.

Many believe that the teams should take control of their own commercial destiny when the current Concorde Agreement expires at the end of 2012.

As part of the existing agreement, however, the teams, FOTA or anyone acting on their behalf, are precluded from entering into negotiations with any existing circuits/promoters/broadcasters about a potential breakaway series until 1 January next year. Or from revealing any such details until 1 June 2012.

In the meantime, murmured one TV man, it is in the interests of Bernie and F1 commercial rights holder CVC to make any such possibility even more remote by doing as many long-term deals as possible bridging the existing Concorde.

What better way, in one of F1's major markets, than to sew up two broadcast giants such as the BBC and Sky Sports, until the end of 2018?

There was an understandable feeling of deflation among the BBC team. They produce excellent coverage that, in the opinion of Murray Walker, is the best in the world bar none. And from what we have in 2011, 2012 is a step backwards as far as the BBC is concerned. That much was inescapable.

But, when the BBC's Head of Sport, Barbara Slater, spoke of the need for pragmatism, flexibility and adaptability in a tough financial climate, it's because that was the reality.

Widespread BBC cuts are fact. Far better to have the BBC involved in F1 until 2018, albeit in a reduced capacity, than to have a thick red line scratched through the whole F1 budget, which could so easily have been the case.

There are significant numbers whose enthusiasm for Rupert Murdoch is luke-warm at best. And, surely only F1 and Mr Ecclestone would brazenly do a deal with Murdoch at that particular moment, with phone-hacking scandals, the 'News of the World' closure and parliamentary enquiries dominating the headlines.

The new combined deal means a revenue increase for F1. Which is good business. It becomes poor business, however, if audience numbers decline and more is lost in sponsorship – which depends on viewing figures – than is gained from the deal. Time will ultimately be the judge of that.

was to lose chunks of time if you made the wrong call.

"I think Sebastian was relying on our feedback," said Christian Horner. "We asked him to hang in there. He would possibly have been happy to hear 'Box for inters' at that stage. But then obviously the rain stopped within two minutes, and then the heat started coming back in the slicks, and quickly the slicks became the tyre to be on. It's the type of call that can go either way for you. That call could arguably have won Mark the race, if it had continued to rain. It didn't..."

In the end, staying out was the right choice, and Button and Vettel reaped the dividends, as indeed did Alonso, who salvaged third from his four-stopper,

when he could have ended up fourth or fifth in the normal run of events.

"It was an interesting race in that sense," said Paddy Lowe. "We saw half the field gamble one way in that second lot of rain, and half the field the other way. Unfortunately, Lewis got the wrong end of that gamble. Thankfully, we had a split strategy, you might say. It wasn't deliberately done that way; each team works independently in deciding what's best for them."

And, yet again, Vettel consolidated his championship lead with second. Horner was happy enough with that: "I think all things considered, on a day like today, when you've got a lot more ability for things to go wrong than right, to come away second having extended his lead in the driver's championship, after the conditions that we faced in that race, is a really positive result.

"I think the McLarens were quick at certain stages of the race, we were quick at other stages of the race, and it would have been fascinating had it been dry to the end after that last stop. We thought we were looking in good shape, we'd elected to take a different strategic route by going on the prime tyre, and then it rained.

"And for probably two or three laps, the slick was the wrong tyre to be on, and 50% of the grid came in for inters, and arguably for those two laps, it was the right thing to do. But then the rain stopped, and therefore an additional stop for Mark probably cost a podium today. I think he would have been third, because again he would have run to the end."

Hamilton fought back to claim fourth. The bottom line was that even without the move to intermediates he was not going to win, as he did not have the speed to make up for the extra stop that he would have made on his four-stop strategy.

Webber took fifth, while Massa survived an early spin and contact with the barriers to take sixth. Force India was again best of the rest, as di Resta took seventh ahead of Sébastien Buemi, Nico Rosberg and Jaime Alguersuari.

SNAPSHOT FROM
HUNGARY

CLOCKWISE FROM RIGHT The spray flies as the field jostles for position on lap 1; double vision as Nico Rosberg keeps an eye on things; grid girls prepare for work; Jenson Button's current and former bosses – Frank Williams, Ross Brawn and Martin Whitmarsh – got together with his father, John, to mark his 200th grand prix; John Button celebrates with a cigar; Michael Schumacher climbed the order early in the race, before a gearbox failure forced him to retire; the Renault team continued to send their good wishes to the injured Robert Kubica; a marshal brushes up on his Roman history; Mark Webber lost his front wing on Friday, resulting in a scooter with high-downforce set-up; the sun sets on another action-packed weekend

RACE RESULTS
HUNGARY
HUNGARORING

Official Results © [2011]
Formula One Administration Limited,
6 Princes Gate, London, SW7 1QJ.
No reproduction without permission.
All copyright and database rights reserved.

RACE DATE July 31st
CIRCUIT LENGTH 2.719 miles
NO. OF LAPS 70
RACE DISTANCE 190.340 miles
WEATHER Dry then rain then dry, 18°C
TRACK TEMP 17°C
ATTENDANCE 200,000
LAP RECORD Michael Schumacher,
1m19.071s, 123.828mph, 2004

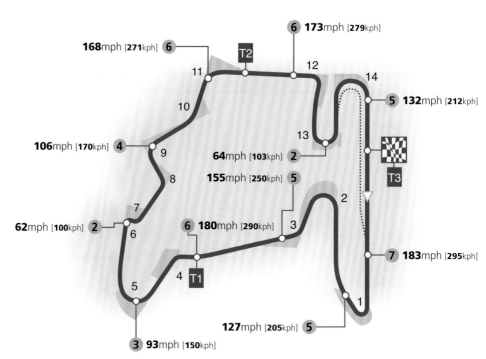

PRACTICE 1				PRACTICE 2				PRACTICE 3				QUALIFYING 1			QUALIFYING 2	
	Driver	Time	Laps		Driver	Time	Laps		Driver	Time	Laps		Driver	Time		Driver	Time
1	L Hamilton	1m23.350s	19	1	L Hamilton	1m21.018s	29	1	S Vettel	1m21.168s	17	1	F Alonso	1m21.578s	1	F Alonso	1m20.262s
2	S Vettel	1m23.564s	24	2	F Alonso	1m21.259s	40	2	F Alonso	1m21.469s	13	2	L Hamilton	1m21.636s	2	J Button	1m20.578s
3	F Alonso	1m23.642s	29	3	J Button	1m21.322s	34	3	J Button	1m21.639s	14	3	S Vettel	1m21.740s	3	M Webber	1m20.890s
4	M Webber	1m23.666s	12	4	M Webber	1m21.508s	35	4	M Webber	1m21.645s	18	4	J Button	1m22.038s	4	S Vettel	1m21.095s
5	J Button	1m23.772s	20	5	S Vettel	1m21.549s	31	5	F Massa	1m22.002s	14	5	F Massa	1m22.105s	5	F Massa	1m21.099s
6	F Massa	1m24.115s	25	6	F Massa	1m22.099s	40	6	N Rosberg	1m22.534s	22	6	M Webber	1m22.208s	6	L Hamilton	1m21.105s
7	N Rosberg	1m24.250s	22	7	N Rosberg	1m22.121s	36	7	L Hamilton	1m22.667s	14	7	A Sutil	1m22.237s	7	N Rosberg	1m21.243s
8	M Schumacher	1m24.369s	20	8	M Schumacher	1m22.440s	36	8	M Schumacher	1m23.037s	19	8	M Schumacher	1m22.876s	8	M Schumacher	1m21.852s
9	S Perez	1m24.620s	24	9	P di Resta	1m22.835s	40	9	V Petrov	1m23.175s	19	9	P di Resta	1m22.976s	9	A Sutil	1m22.000s
10	V Petrov	1m25.093s	22	10	A Sutil	1m22.981s	37	10	P di Resta	1m23.276s	18	10	N Rosberg	1m22.996s	10	S Perez	1m22.157s
11	K Kobayashi	1m25.113s	21	11	K Kobayashi	1m23.030s	34	11	N Heidfeld	1m23.281s	13	11	N Heidfeld	1m23.024s	11	P di Resta	1m22.256s
12	P di Resta	1m25.336s	22	12	S Perez	1m23.399s	37	12	S Perez	1m23.375s	18	12	S Perez	1m23.067s	12	V Petrov	1m22.284s
13	N Hulkenberg	1m25.357s	17	13	R Barrichello	1m23.679s	34	13	K Kobayashi	1m23.626s	25	13	V Petrov	1m23.070s	13	K Kobayashi	1m22.435s
14	R Barrichello	1m25.836s	24	14	N Heidfeld	1m23.861s	28	14	R Barrichello	1m23.663s	17	14	R Barrichello	1m23.075s	14	N Heidfeld	1m22.470s
15	B Senna	1m25.855s	25	15	P Maldonado	1m24.181s	39	15	P Maldonado	1m23.894s	17	15	K Kobayashi	1m23.278s	15	R Barrichello	1m22.684s
16	S Buemi	1m25.890s	28	16	J Alguersuari	1m24.182s	26	16	A Sutil	1m23.966s	18	16	J Alguersuari	1m23.285s	16	J Alguersuari	1m22.979s
17	J Alguersuari	1m26.099s	36	17	V Petrov	1m24.546s	21	17	J Alguersuari	1m23.998s	15	17	P Maldonado	1m23.847s	17	P Maldonado	No time
18	P Maldonado	1m26.124s	25	18	S Buemi	1m24.878s	35	18	S Buemi	1m25.061s	19	18	S Buemi	1m24.070s			
19	H Kovalainen	1m26.878s	26	19	J Trulli	1m24.994s	38	19	J Trulli	1m25.141s	20	19	H Kovalainen	1m24.362s			
20	K Chandhok	1m27.352s	21	20	H Kovalainen	1m25.447s	39	20	H Kovalainen	1m25.501s	20	20	J Trulli	1m24.534s			
21	T Glock	1m28.533s	30	21	T Glock	1m26.823s	33	21	J d'Ambrosio	1m26.955s	20	21	T Glock	1m26.294s			
22	J d'Ambrosio	1m28.903s	22	22	J d'Ambrosio	1m27.261s	28	22	D Ricciardo	1m26.991s	19	22	V Liuzzi	1m26.323s			
23	V Liuzzi	1m29.059s	24	23	D Ricciardo	1m27.730s	31	23	T Glock	1m27.174s	16	23	D Ricciardo	1m26.479s			
24	D Ricciardo	1m29.904s	26	24	V Liuzzi	1m28.255s	25	24	V Liuzzi	1m27.713s	20	24	J d'Ambrosio	1m26.510s			

Best sectors – Practice			Speed trap – Practice			Best sectors – Qualifying			Speed trap – Qualifying		
Sec 1	N Rosberg	28.713s	1	M Schumacher	186.411mph	Sec 1	F Massa	28.413s	1	M Schumacher	186.722mph
Sec 2	L Hamilton	29.017s	2	K Kobayashi	185.976mph	Sec 2	S Vettel	28.629s	2	N Rosberg	185.355mph
Sec 3	M Webber	22.834s	3	N Rosberg	185.106mph	Sec 3	L Hamilton	22.448s	3	F Alonso	185.168mph

 Sebastian Vettel

"I was struggling a bit in the first stint on the inters. Lewis was a bit faster, and then I went into Turn 2 too deep and I lost the lead, but still second is an important step."

 Jenson Button

"The car worked a treat in all conditions, we made all the right calls and I had a good battle with Lewis when we were running 1–2 and were driving on the limit."

 Fernando Alonso

"At Turn 1, I struggled for traction and Michael passed me. After that, I lost time behind the Mercedes, then Webber, so I changed to four stops."

 Michael Schumacher

"An unfortunate end to my race when I retired with a gearbox problem. We don't think that this had anything to do with the spin I had fighting with Felipe."

 Nick Heidfeld

"My second stop was longer than expected, the car overheated and I saw smoke coming from the rear. It worsened, then I noticed flames so I had to pull over."

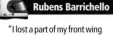 **Rubens Barrichello**

"I lost a part of my front wing early on. Then, when it began to rain, I saw a chance. But the rain only came for a lap or so, and so our stop for inters didn't work."

 **Mark Webber**

"I made the call to go for the slicks at the right time, but when the rain came I thought that it was going to be heavier, so I went for inters, but it didn't come."

 Lewis Hamilton

"I'm disappointed for spinning. I had to do a donut to get myself facing the right way, and that forced Paul on to the grass, which is why I got the drive-through."

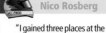 **Felipe Massa**

"I went off on lap 8. The back end hit the barriers and I was scared the car might be damaged, but was told to keep going. I lost so much time because of that."

Nico Rosberg

"I gained three places at the start. When the primes lost grip in increasingly damp conditions, we took the decision to put on inters, but I then had to switch to slicks."

 **Vitaly Petrov**

"When the rain returned near the end, I lost heat in my tyres. It looked like the wet conditions would continue, so I changed to inters, but it didn't last long."

Pastor Maldonado

"I made places, but it was hard to stay on-track on inters. I made a mistake coming into my first stop by not pushing the limiter button, so got a drive-through penalty."

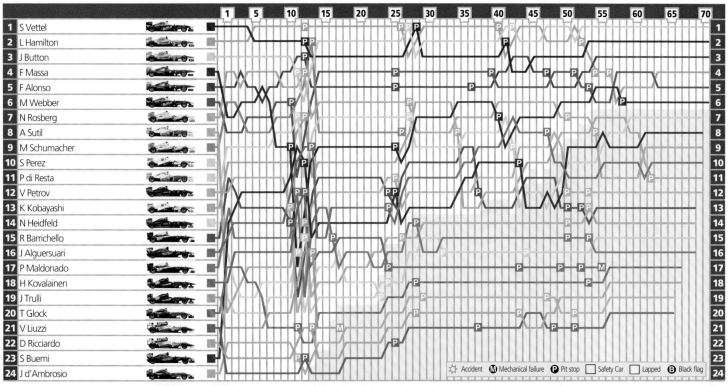

1	S Vettel	
2	L Hamilton	
3	J Button	
4	F Massa	
5	F Alonso	
6	M Webber	
7	N Rosberg	
8	A Sutil	
9	M Schumacher	
10	S Perez	
11	P di Resta	
12	V Petrov	
13	K Kobayashi	
14	N Heidfeld	
15	R Barrichello	
16	J Alguersuari	
17	P Maldonado	
18	H Kovalainen	
19	J Trulli	
20	T Glock	
21	V Liuzzi	
22	D Ricciardo	
23	S Buemi	
24	J d'Ambrosio	

☆ Accident Ⓜ Mechanical failure Ⓟ Pit stop ☐ Safety Car ☐ Lapped Ⓑ Black flag

QUALIFYING 3

	Driver	Time
1	S Vettel	1m19.815s
2	L Hamilton	1m19.978s
3	J Button	1m20.024s
4	F Massa	1m20.350s
5	F Alonso	1m20.365s
6	M Webber	1m20.474s
7	N Rosberg	1m21.098s
8	A Sutil	1m21.445s
9	M Schumacher	1m21.907s
10	S Perez	No time

GRID

	Driver	Time
1	S Vettel	1m19.815s
2	L Hamilton	1m19.978s
3	J Button	1m20.024s
4	F Massa	1m20.350s
5	F Alonso	1m20.365s
6	M Webber	1m20.474s
7	N Rosberg	1m21.098s
8	A Sutil	1m21.445s
9	M Schumacher	1m21.907s
10	S Perez	No time
11	P di Resta	1m22.256s
12	V Petrov	1m22.284s
13	K Kobayashi	1m22.435s
14	N Heidfeld	1m22.470s
15	R Barrichello	1m22.684s
16	J Alguersuari	1m22.979s
17	P Maldonado	No time
18	H Kovalainen	1m24.362s
19	J Trulli	1m24.534s
20	T Glock	1m26.294s
21	V Liuzzi	1m26.323s
22	D Ricciardo	1m26.479s
23*	S Buemi	1m24.070s
24	J d'Ambrosio	1m26.510s

* 5-place grid penalty for causing a collision in the German GP

RACE

	Driver	Car	Laps	Time	Avg. mph	Fastest	Stops
1	J Button	McLaren-Mercedes MP4-26	70	1h46m42.337s	107.134	1m23.937s	3
2	S Vettel	Red Bull-Renault RB7	70	1h46m45.925s	107.074	1m23.875s	3
3	F Alonso	Ferrari 150 Italia	70	1h47m02.156s	106.804	1m23.711s	4
4	L Hamilton	McLaren-Mercedes MP4-26	70	1h47m30.675s	106.331	1m23.661s	6
5	M Webber	Red Bull-Renault RB7	70	1h47m32.079s	106.308	1m23.718s	5
6	F Massa	Ferrari 150 Italia	70	1h48m05.513s	105.760	1m23.415s	4
7	P di Resta	Force India-Mercedes VJM04	69	1h47m33.222s	104.770	1m25.935s	3
8	S Buemi	Toro Rosso-Ferrari STR6	69	1h47m34.154s	104.756	1m25.977s	3
9	N Rosberg	Mercedes MGP W02	69	1h47m34.736s	104.746	1m24.857s	4
10	J Alguersuari	Toro Rosso-Ferrari STR6	69	1h47m41.807s	104.631	1m26.025s	3
11	K Kobayashi	Sauber-Ferrari C30	69	1h48m01.397s	104.315	1m24.664s	3
12	V Petrov	Renault R31	69	1h48m03.493s	104.281	1m24.664s	4
13	R Barrichello	Williams-Cosworth FW33	68	1h47m03.295s	103.733	1m25.018s	5
14	A Sutil	Force India-Mercedes VJM04	68	1h47m39.661s	103.149	1m25.579s	4
15	S Perez	Sauber-Ferrari C30	68	1h47m42.320s	103.106	1m24.999s	4
16	P Maldonado	Williams-Cosworth FW33	68	1h47m50.742s	102.972	1m25.724s	5
17	T Glock	Virgin-Cosworth MVR02	66	1h46m58.179s	100.762	1m28.022s	3
18	D Ricciardo	HRT-Cosworth F111	66	1h47m37.531s	100.148	1m28.876s	3
19	J d'Ambrosio	Virgin-Cosworth MVR02	65	1h46m59.876s	99.209	1m29.068s	4
20	V Liuzzi	HRT-Cosworth F111	65	1h47m19.517s	98.906	1m29.208s	5
R	H Kovalainen	Lotus-Renault T128	55	Water leak	-	1m27.149s	5
R	M Schumacher	Mercedes MGP W02	26	Electronics	-	1m29.781s	2
R	N Heidfeld	Renault R31	23	Engine fire	-	1m30.826s	2
R	J Trulli	Lotus-Renault T128	17	Water leak	-	1m35.252s	1

CHAMPIONSHIP

	Driver	Pts
1	S Vettel	234
2	M Webber	149
3	L Hamilton	146
4	F Alonso	145
5	J Button	134
6	F Massa	70
7	N Rosberg	48
8	N Heidfeld	34
9	V Petrov	32
10	M Schumacher	32
11	K Kobayashi	27
12	A Sutil	18
13	S Buemi	12
14	J Alguersuari	10
15	S Perez	8
16	P di Resta	8
17	R Barrichello	4

	Constructor	Pts
1	Red Bull-Renault	383
2	McLaren-Mercedes	280
3	Ferrari	215
4	Mercedes	80
5	Renault	66
6	Sauber-Ferrari	35
7	Force India-Mercedes	26
8	Toro Rosso-Ferrari	22
9	Williams-Cosworth	4

Fastest lap
F Massa 1m23.415s
(117.484mph) on lap 61

Fastest speed trap
S Perez 187.902mph
Slowest speed trap
J Trulli 173.859mph

Fastest pit stop
1 S Vettel 19.664s
2 F Alonso 19.936s
3 N Rosberg 19.939s

    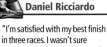

Adrian Sutil
"My chance of points ended on lap 1 when I locked up into the chicane. I was right behind Paul and to avoid an accident I had to go off and lost a lot of positions."

Kamui Kobayashi
"The team wanted me in for inters, but I didn't want to, as the track was improving. This is how I got up to seventh, but we waited too long for the next change."

Sébastien Buemi
"Starting from the back, I passed 10 cars on lap 1. Then, as it began to dry, I had too much understeer. When the rain returned, I was able to run at a good pace again."

Jarno Trulli
"I was really enjoying myself out there. I got past Timo pretty early on, and then had a good first stop, but it looks like a water leak brought my race to an early end."

Daniel Ricciardo
"I'm satisfied with my best finish in three races. I wasn't sure where I was on track, as a lot of cars made quite a few stops, so I didn't know how I was doing."

Timo Glock
"I got ahead of Heidfeld and others in faster cars, and was able to stay ahead until they got past after it started to dry and I just concentrated on my own race."

Paul di Resta
"I'm very happy with seventh. We went to supersofts for the middle two stints, then ended the race on the primes after losing track position at the last stop."

Sergio Perez
"I expected a lot more, but the race began to go wrong on lap 1, as I had no grip and dropped from 10th to 20th. The drive-through made matters worse."

Jaime Alguersuari
"I made one of my stops just as it began raining. With the tyres not up to temperature, I went off the track and lost another place after colliding with Kobayashi."

Heikki Kovalainen
"I was keeping pace with Maldonado, Sutil and Perez, and through the early stops I was able to push them. Later, I had to shut the engine off due to a water leak."

Vitantonio Liuzzi
"I got off to a good start, until someone hit me coming out of the chicane, causing me to spin. I lost a lot of time, and then the balance of the car wasn't ideal."

Jerome d'Ambrosio
"I chose to stop for inters when I should have stayed out on slicks. So I lost a lot of time with the pit stops and I also had a tough moment when I spun in the box."

2011 FORMULA 1 SHELL BELGIAN GRAND PRIX
SPA-FRANCORCHAMPS

RETURN TO VICTORY

Sebastian Vettel returned from the summer break to take his seventh victory of the season, ending a three-race losing streak as he led Mark Webber home in a Red Bull Racing 1–2

Sebastian Vettel and Red Bull bounced back in Belgium to score their first win since Valencia, after losing out in the three previous races.

But while the result might have a familiar look to it, Spa was far from a straightforward weekend for Red Bull Racing. The team went into the race with serious concerns about tyres, but by the end of the afternoon the blue cars had secured a 1–2 on a track that, thanks to its high-speed nature, was expected to favour the opposition.

As so often at Spa in the past, rain added a little extra edge to proceedings. Friday was very wet, and Q1 started on a damp track. It dried by the end, but there was another brief shower late in Q2. The big loser in the lottery was Jenson Button. Due to a communication error, he backed off to save his tyres as the fastest laps were being set, only to find he didn't have enough time for another flying lap. Having been fastest a few minutes earlier, he tumbled down to 13th.

The crucial third session started with a track that was drying rapidly, so everyone was able to go out on slicks. It was a question of pounding round and being out when the track was at its best. Pole changed hands rapidly, with Webber and Hamilton both topping the times, before Vettel went fastest right at the end.

Hamilton and Webber remained second and third, while Felipe Massa did a good job to take fourth, ahead of Nico Rosberg. Jamie Alguersuari was an excellent sixth for Toro Rosso, while Bruno Senna silenced the critics of Renault's decision to drop Nick Heidfeld by taking seventh. Fernando Alonso didn't get it right in Q3, and tumbled to eighth.

Before the race, concern emerged regarding front-tyre blistering seen in qualifying, especially at Red Bull. The team wanted dispensation to be allowed to start with fresh front tyres. However, it was deemed that they had created the problem by running extreme camber settings – outside Pirelli's recommended limit. After discussions with the FIA, all the top 10 drivers had to start on the tyres on which they qualified, as per usual.

Red Bull had also requested that it be allowed to reduce the camber for the start, so that the problem wouldn't recur during the race. The FIA's simple answer was that, as with any set-up change, the team was free to do it, but that would mean starting from the pitlane.

"There was a lot of debate about whether camber angles should be allowed to be reduced," said Adrian Newey after the race, "or whether the people who were in Q3 who'd suffered damage should be allowed to start on new fronts if they wished too.

"I don't know exactly what happened in the debates between Pirelli and the FIA, but in the end, it was decided that it was down to the teams, which for me was a very worrying and uncomfortable position to be in. Charlie [Whiting] of course is trying to keep it fair for everybody, but I just think where safety is concerned, it's tremendously difficult."

After two days of wet weather, Sunday was dry, as had been predicted. Rosberg was the star of the first lap, the Mercedes driver charging into the lead from fifth, ahead of Vettel, Massa, Hamilton and Alonso. Yet again Webber made a bad start, while there was chaos when Senna ran hard into Alguersuari at La Source, and several other drivers were caught up in the aftermath. Button's hopes of a quick climb from his 13th place were spoiled when he suffered front-wing damage, and had to make an early pit stop.

Inevitably, Rosberg's fun was short-lived, and he was soon passed by Vettel, while Alonso moved ahead of both Hamilton and Massa with some determined driving to take third.

RBR's tyre concerns saw Vettel stop as early as lap five for fresh tyres. Alonso then passed Rosberg for the lead before the Ferrari stopped, and then Hamilton led briefly

OPPOSITE Timo Glock misjudged his braking point at La Source on the first lap, causing chaos as he pushed Paul di Resta's Force India into Button's McLaren and the two Lotuses of Kovalainen and Trulli

BELOW Heikki Kovalainen's Lotus bears the brunt of the carnage, as Pastor Maldonado takes avoiding action to escape unscathed. The Williams driver went on to finish 10th, scoring his first-ever F1 point

OPPOSITE BELOW Michael Schumacher wore a special gold-painted helmet for the weekend, to celebrate the 20th anniversary of his F1 debut at Spa in 1991 in a Jordan

INSIDE LINE
ADRIAN NEWEY
RED BULL RACING CHIEF TECHNICAL OFFICER

"We were just a hair over Pirelli's four degrees maximum camber recommendation [the FIA reported 4.36]. If we'd known there was a safety concern we wouldn't have done it.

We'd had dialogue with Pirelli, they were in full knowledge that we were slightly over and didn't seem concerned about it.

I was emotional at the end of the race purely because of the worry about safety. It was a very tight call whether to change set-up and tyres and start from the pitlane, or not.

I don't think you can leave those things up to the drivers. I took the decision to make some changes – go to much higher tyre pressures to try and make it safer, and suffer the performance loss from that. Then do a very short first stint on those qualifying tyres.

Mark's were more damaged than Sebastian's, which is why we brought them in after three laps and five laps respectively.

Racing tyres have blistered since the sixties, but that wasn't the issue. The issue was the structural integrity and, because the blisters were so close to the inside shoulder where the tread meets the sidewall, Pirelli was telling us after qualifying that our tyres were very marginal.

At 5 o'clock on Saturday they couldn't say whether it would be after half a lap or five laps, but they were going to fail very soon. There was structural damage in the junction between the tyre wall and the tread. They felt that a failure was imminent on both cars.

You can take the performance aspect on the chin, it's the safety angle that was worrying.

Not using DRS helped, because damage is a function of speed and load, and with DRS it's a similar load at the front and it's only the rear that loses load and you are going a lot faster.

We did some internal calculations, combined with the results Pirelli gave us, as to how an increase in pressure would help the tyre life.

It wasn't a comfortable position to be in. It was one of the scariest races I've ever been involved in – heart in the mouth stuff.

First and foremost, our duty is to driver safety and you are trying to make the call as to what is going to make the car safe without excessively handicapping your performance. Frankly, at the end I was just very relieved."

TALKING POINT
A TIME FOR BRAVE MEN

At the end of the Belgian GP, a Red Bull 1–2, Adrian Newey sat quietly on his pit stool for a few extra moments, tears in his eyes. They were tears of relief.

Newey and Red Bull took a gamble at Spa and, happily, everything worked out fine (see 'Inside Line').

Having survived that worrying first stint, there was then more bravery from Mark Webber, of the type you don't see too often…

On Saturday, his 35th birthday, after a delay that had started plenty of speculation, Webber finally confirmed that he had put pen to paper to extend his Red Bull deal to the end of 2012.

You might have thought that with his new contract in the bag, Webber may not have seen the need to risk life and limb by going down the inside of Fernando Alonso's Ferrari into Eau Rouge.

"That was rather brave, wasn't it?" smiled Christian Horner, a sentiment echoed by Newey.

"I was still charged with frustration from the poor start when the anti-stall kicked in," admitted the Australian, who had qualified third, behind team-mate Vettel and Lewis Hamilton's McLaren.

"When Fernando came out from his first stop he was slightly ahead, but I had a bit of momentum down from the hairpin and we were obviously very, very close going down to Eau Rouge," Webber explained.

"I knew Fernando would have been using some KERS, so I did as well. I got a tow and thought that if I could get down the inside I would have the line.

"Both of us are very experienced, we don't give much too easily and it's even more rewarding when you can do it with someone like Fernando. He's a world-class driver and knows when enough is enough. My attitude might have been different with someone else.

"I was breathing in at the bottom of Eau Rouge. One of us had to lift and I had a slightly better line, so it was him…"

Webber wasn't the only one to breathe in when they saw what was shaping up. There have been a few similar examples of such moves over the years in various categories, but they are few and far between.

The one everyone does recall involved a couple of Porsche Group C cars, Jacky Ickx and Stefan Bellof, in 1985. On that occasion Bellof didn't quite get down the inside, the pair made contact and the up-and-coming young German died as a consequence.

In Webber's case, the shame of it was that Alonso swept by again practically unopposed on the following lap, with the aid of DRS. Webber's move deserved better!

before he too pitted. When it had all shaken out, Vettel was back in the lead. Hamilton had lost some ground around the pit stops, and in his hurry to make it up he clipped Kamui Kobayashi (who had yet to stop) at the end of the straight. The McLaren turned sharp left and crashed heavily, bringing out a safety car.

It seemed to be a simple misjudgement by the McLaren man, who was at a loss to explain what happened after seemingly being knocked out.

"I don't really remember much from hitting the wall, so it's potentially possible I was out for a couple of seconds, but I'm not really sure," he would later explain. "I don't remember the whole of hitting the wall and how I got to where I was. I remember going into the corner, or trying to go into the corner, and getting hooked, but after that, a bit blurry.

"I hit it quite hard. I was doing 200mph or whatever it was at the end of the straight. There wasn't much slowing down time between hitting him and into the wall, it was directly into the wall, so I hit it with a lot of force."

Hamilton had already been at the centre of controversy in qualifying, when he made contact with Pastor Maldonado and the Venezuelan appeared to retaliate, earning himself a grid penalty. Lewis received a reprimand for the incident.

When the safety car came out, leader Vettel pitted, and that proved to be a crucial move in ensuring that his strategy played out over the course of the race. He re-took the lead when Alonso made his second stop under green, and then led to the chequered flag, overcoming any worries about the tyres. When he crossed the line, the relief on the Red Bull pit wall was all too clear.

"I'm very proud," said Vettel. "Obviously you had to manage the tyres, going into the race wasn't easy, but then it turned out the pace was very good, and we went through some people, so it was a fun race, and I think it was one of the best we have had this year."

Newey's tearful reaction after the race gave some

indication of the emotions he had experienced over the previous 24 hours. As Chief Technical Officer he carries a major responsibility for the drivers, and we shouldn't forget that he knows what it's like to lose a driver in one of his cars.

However, the safety card can be played all too easily. The more cynical view was that RBR had messed up and was doing anything to avoid having to compromise its strategy, or face a pitlane start.

"If he was that worried, then he would have started in the pitlane," said Pirelli's Paul Hembery bluntly. "So he clearly couldn't have been that worried...

"The vast majority of the teams clearly knew where they were at, and made the adjustments themselves. There was more than one team that made that sacrifice. For the vast majority, as we saw in the race, it wasn't an issue at all, because they made the modifications to their set-up to avoid it.

"At the end of the day, imagine if we had given new tyres and the possibility to change camber to all the teams, and we got this result. I think you'd be asking some different questions about why I'd just handed Red Bull the championship! Myself and Charlie Whiting would probably have come in for a lot of questions in another direction.

OPPOSITE Bruno Senna returned to F1, replacing Nick Heidfeld at Renault, and qualifying a stunning seventh. A mistake on lap 1 saw him run into Jaime Alguersuari, forcing him to pit for a new nose and earning him a drive-through penalty

TOP Lewis Hamilton accepted the blame for clashing with Kamui Kobayashi on lap 13 on the approach to Les Combes, after passing the Japanese driver and moving back on to the racing line, not realising that the Sauber was still alongside

ABOVE After starting 13th, Jenson Button impressed with another superb drive through the field to take third place. Here, he passes Felipe Massa in a perfectly judged move at the chicane

ABOVE Mark Webber and Fernando Alonso had an epic battle, the Australian passing the Ferrari in a breathtaking seventh-gear, 180mph move around the outside at Eau Rouge, Alonso just giving him space

BELOW The Red Bull Racing duo congratulate each other on their first 1–2 of the 2011 season, Webber finishing 3.7s ahead of the charging Australian, who recovered from a disastrous start to take second

"So we knew we were in a no-win situation. But we tried to do what we felt was correct for the sport and for the majority of the teams. It was a tough decision, but with hindsight, we made the correct decision."

Like his team-mate, Webber had pitted very early, and went for medium tyres – which were less prone to blistering. His strategy also worked out well, as he moved up the order, passing Alonso for second in the closing stages as Ferrari again struggled on the harder compounds.

In fact, Mark passed Fernando in a breathtakingly close-fought move at Eau Rouge during an earlier pit-stop sequence. "It was a good battle," said Fernando. "With

Mark it's always quite good to battle, there's a lot of respect for everybody, and fair game, and no problems. So it was good. Eau Rouge, it's always very special to battle there…"

After his early stop for a new nose, Button had another strong race. He eventually charged up to third, and like Webber he was able to catch and displace Alonso, two laps from home.

"Turn One I think di Resta hit my rear wing or we made contact, so half the rear-wing endplate was gone," said Button. "Then, driving after Turn One to Eau Rouge, somebody's front wing blew off and went through my front wing and took the wing mirror off, which was a bit scary.

"Then I was really struggling for grip. The front wing was damaged and the guys said, 'We know it is, but keep going until we get to lap five'. We did. We came in and changed the front wing [actually on lap three], put option tyres on, and did the rest of the race on options.

"A fun race, lots of good overtaking, really enjoyed it out there today, but you're always going to wonder what could have been. But all in all, a good finish to get on the podium. It's good to finish here after Seb drove into me last year and we didn't finish."

Alonso held on to fourth. Meanwhile, Schumacher did a great job to take advantage of trouble for others, as he moved up from 24th to fifth. He enjoyed a good first lap as he avoided all the chaos, and put in perhaps the most convincing drive yet of his comeback.

Rosberg dropped to sixth by the flag, ceding his place to his team-mate when he had fuel-consumption concerns. Adrian Sutil made good progress from the start, and some consistent driving got him up to seventh by the flag.

Massa ran strongly in the opening laps, but he then fell off the pace. A puncture delayed the Brazilian, and ensured he crossed the line eighth, ahead of Vitaly Petrov and Maldonado, the latter scoring his first ever point.

SNAPSHOT FROM BELGIUM

CLOCKWISE FROM RIGHT A classic view of a classic circuit; Paul di Resta's Force India took a chunk out of Jenson Button's rear-wing endplate on the first lap; Michael Schumacher's fellow drivers gather to celebrate the 20th anniversary of his F1 debut; a Senna fan adopts a refreshing new helmet design; a pitlane marshal does her best to keep dry on Friday; Sebastian Vettel looks worried about the potentially risky tyre situation before the start; F1 enthusiast and guitar hero Eric Clapton made an appearance in the pitlane; the Shell grid girls were in touch with themselves outside the Ferrari hospitality area; Lotus Chief Technical Officer Mike Gascoyne shouts the odds on the grid; Sébastien Buemi was assaulted by Sergio Perez on lap 4, forcing him out with a broken rear wing

RACE RESULTS
BELGIUM
SPA-FRANCORCHAMPS

Official Results © [2011]
Formula One Administration Limited,
6 Princes Gate, London, SW7 1QJ.
No reproduction without permission.
All copyright and database rights reserved.

RACE DATE 28th August
CIRCUIT LENGTH 4.352 miles
NO. OF LAPS 44
RACE DISTANCE 191.488 miles
WEATHER Overcast but dry, 16°C
TRACK TEMP 26°C
ATTENDANCE Not available
LAP RECORD Sebastian Vettel,
1m47.263s, 146.065mph, 2009

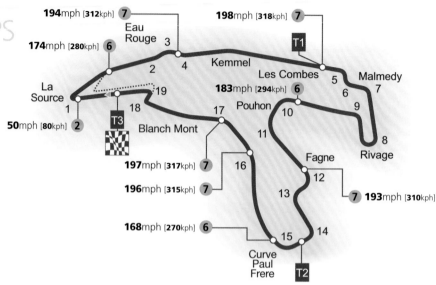

PRACTICE 1

	Driver	Time	Laps
1	M Schumacher	1m54.355s	13
2	N Rosberg	1m54.829s	15
3	J Button	2m02.740s	8
4	S Vettel	2m03.752s	10
5	L Hamilton	2m04.301s	7
6	A Sutil	2m04.663s	18
7	F Massa	2m04.728s	10
8	R Barrichello	2m05.391s	12
9	J Alguersuari	2m06.583s	16
10	K Kobayashi	2m06.886s	15
11	F Alonso	2m07.055s	12
12	S Perez	2m07.481s	15
13	J Trulli	2m08.233s	14
14	S Buemi	2m08.239s	14
15	P Maldonado	2m08.918s	10
16	M Webber	2m09.792s	8
17	T Glock	2m12.278s	13
18	V Liuzzi	2m12.389s	10
19	J d'Ambrosio	2m12.772s	13
20	P di Resta	2m13.058s	8
21	K Chandhok	2m13.090s	11
22	V Petrov	2m13.601s	10
23	B Senna	2m14.340s	7
24	D Ricciardo	2m14.933s	11

PRACTICE 2

	Driver	Time	Laps
1	M Webber	1m50.321s	22
2	F Alonso	1m50.461s	18
3	J Button	1m50.770s	9
4	L Hamilton	1m50.838s	9
5	F Massa	1m51.218s	14
6	N Rosberg	1m51.242s	22
7	S Perez	1m51.655s	20
8	N Hulkenberg	1m51.725s	17
9	P di Resta	1m51.751s	8
10	S Vettel	1m51.790s	13
11	M Schumacher	1m51.922s	22
12	P Maldonado	1m52.750s	20
13	K Kobayashi	1m52.780s	25
14	J Alguersuari	1m52.911s	24
15	S Buemi	1m53.009s	24
16	R Barrichello	1m53.156s	17
17	B Senna	1m53.835s	20
18	J Trulli	1m55.051s	20
19	T Glock	1m55.494s	22
20	P Kovalainen	1m56.202s	15
21	J d'Ambrosio	1m56.816s	20
22	V Liuzzi	1m57.450s	19
23	D Ricciardo	1m57.612s	24
24	V Petrov	2m02.234s	12

PRACTICE 3

	Driver	Time	Laps
1	M Webber	2m08.988s	7
2	L Hamilton	2m09.046s	8
3	J Alguersuari	2m09.931s	16
4	J Button	2m10.257s	7
5	S Vettel	2m10.402s	9
6	S Buemi	2m10.580s	15
7	N Rosberg	2m10.837s	12
8	A Sutil	2m11.437s	13
9	B Senna	2m11.664s	14
10	M Schumacher	2m11.667s	10
11	P di Resta	2m11.874s	13
12	H Kovalainen	2m13.036s	15
13	P Maldonado	2m13.074s	12
14	K Kobayashi	2m13.182s	12
15	V Petrov	2m13.290s	15
16	R Barrichello	2m13.778s	12
17	S Perez	2m14.334s	14
18	J Trulli	2m14.682s	11
19	J d'Ambrosio	2m17.159s	12
20	T Glock	2m18.039s	10
21	D Ricciardo	2m19.001s	12
22	V Liuzzi	2m19.597s	14
23	F Massa	2m22.454s	7
24	F Alonso	No time	5

QUALIFYING 1

	Driver	Time
1	J Button	2m01.813s
2	M Webber	2m02.827s
3	L Hamilton	2m03.008s
4	S Vettel	2m03.029s
5	F Alonso	2m04.450s
6	S Buemi	2m04.744s
7	B Senna	2m05.047s
8	N Rosberg	2m05.091s
9	V Petrov	2m05.292s
10	J Alguersuari	2m05.419s
11	P Maldonado	2m05.621s
12	R Barrichello	2m05.720s
13	F Massa	2m05.834s
14	A Sutil	2m06.000s
15	S Perez	2m06.284s
16	H Kovalainen	2m06.780s
17	K Kobayashi	2m07.194s
18	P di Resta	2m07.758s
19	J Trulli	2m08.773s
20	T Glock	2m09.566s
21	J d'Ambrosio	2m11.601s
22	V Liuzzi	2m11.616s
23	D Ricciardo	2m13.077s
24	M Schumacher	No time

QUALIFYING 2

	Driver	Time
1	F Alonso	2m02.768s
2	L Hamilton	2m02.823s
3	M Webber	2m03.302s
4	S Vettel	2m03.317s
5	V Petrov	2m03.466s
6	N Rosberg	2m03.723s
7	B Senna	2m04.452s
8	F Massa	2m04.507s
9	J Alguersuari	2m04.561s
10	S Perez	2m04.625s
11	S Buemi	2m04.692s
12	K Kobayashi	2m04.757s
13	J Button	2m05.150s
14	R Barrichello	2m07.349s
15	A Sutil	2m07.777s
16	P Maldonado	2m08.106s
17	H Kovalainen	2m08.354s

Best sectors – Practice
Sec 1 N Rosberg 31.891s
Sec 2 M Webber 48.181s
Sec 3 M Schumacher 29.337s

Speed trap – Practice
1 S Perez 185.665mph
2 S Vettel 185.603mph
3 M Schumacher 185.168mph

Best sectors – Qualifying
Sec 1 N Rosberg 31.582s
Sec 2 L Hamilton 47.708s
Sec 3 S Vettel 28.747s

Speed trap – Qualifying
1 S Perez 186.970mph
2 S Vettel 186.100mph
3 M Webber 185.665mph

Sebastian Vettel
"It wasn't easy with the tyres. We sacrificed a lot by stopping early. I came in again when the safety car came out, to see how they were. I'm happy with the win."

Jenson Button
"Somebody damaged my rear-wing endplate, then somebody's front wing went through mine and sliced my right-side mirror off. After that, I drove flat-out."

Fernando Alonso
"It would have been difficult to do better than fourth, given how much we suffered on the medium tyres: in these conditions, we were 1.5s slower than the best."

Michael Schumacher
"A wonderful ending to a great weekend. More than fifth would not have been possible, but making up 19 places was a good feeling with all my family here."

Bruno Senna
"I made a mistake in the first corner, which cost me the chance of causing a stir. However, once I'd paid the price with the drive-through, my pace was strong."

Rubens Barrichello
"I lost time fighting with Rosberg during the in-lap for my second pit stop, which was unfortunate as it lost me time and points which I think I could have scored."

Mark Webber
"The lights went out and I got anti-stall. We did a lot of damage to the tyres in qualifying and had to stop early to protect ourselves, which put us out of position."

Lewis Hamilton
"I'd got past one of the Ferraris, but then I was hit by Kamui. I don't really know what happened, but I hit the wall pretty hard and my race was over."

Felipe Massa
"I was in the fight for the top places, but then started to have tyre problems. With the mediums, things improved, but then it was too late. I also had a puncture."

Nico Rosberg
"It was a special feeling to lead in a Silver Arrow. It was great to see the traffic jam behind me, but it was hard to realise that we don't have the pace to stay at the top."

Vitaly Petrov
"We've made a big step forward. I was in top 10 contention, close to the Mercedes, so we need to keep working. I spun right at the end, as I'd lost my front brakes."

Pastor Maldonado
"I'm really happy to score. It's a big improvement. Our pace was very consistent and it was a hard race starting from the back, but I was pushing every single lap."

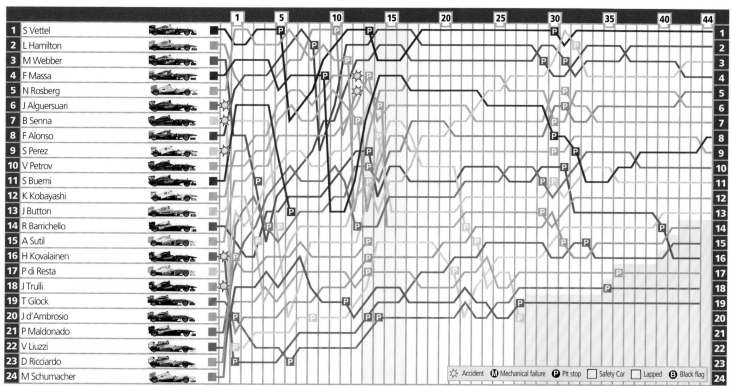

	Driver
1	S Vettel
2	L Hamilton
3	M Webber
4	F Massa
5	N Rosberg
6	J Alguersuari
7	B Senna
8	F Alonso
9	S Perez
10	V Petrov
11	S Buemi
12	K Kobayashi
13	J Button
14	R Barrichello
15	A Sutil
16	H Kovalainen
17	P di Resta
18	J Trulli
19	T Glock
20	J d'Ambrosio
21	P Maldonado
22	V Liuzzi
23	D Ricciardo
24	M Schumacher

☆ Accident Ⓜ Mechanical failure Ⓟ Pit stop ☐ Safety Car ☐ Lapped Ⓑ Black flag

QUALIFYING 3

	Driver	Time
1	S Vettel	1m48.298s
2	L Hamilton	1m48.730s
3	M Webber	1m49.376s
4	F Massa	1m50.256s
5	N Rosberg	1m50.552s
6	J Alguersuari	1m50.773s
7	B Senna	1m51.121s
8	F Alonso	1m51.251s
9	S Perez	1m51.374s
10	V Petrov	1m52.303s

GRID

	Driver	Time
1	S Vettel	1m48.298s
2	L Hamilton	1m48.730s
3	M Webber	1m49.376s
4	F Massa	1m50.256s
5	N Rosberg	1m50.552s
6	J Alguersuari	1m50.773s
7	B Senna	1m51.121s
8	F Alonso	1m51.251s
9	S Perez	1m51.374s
10	V Petrov	1m52.303s
11	S Buemi	2m04.692s
12	K Kobayashi	2m04.757s
13	J Button	2m05.150s
14	R Barrichello	2m07.349s
15	A Sutil	2m07.777s
16	H Kovalainen	2m08.354s
17	P di Resta	2m07.758s
18	J Trulli	2m08.773s
19	T Glock	2m09.566s
20	J d'Ambrosio	2m11.601s
21*	P Maldonado	2m08.106s
22	V Liuzzi	2m11.616s
23	D Ricciardo	2m13.077s
24	M Schumacher	No time

* 5-place penalty for causing a collision

RACE

	Driver	Car	Laps	Time	Avg. mph	Fastest	Stops
1	S Vettel	Red Bull-Renault RB7	44	1h26m44.893s	132.356	1m50.451s	3
2	M Webber	Red Bull-Renault RB7	44	1h26m48.634s	132.298	1m49.883s	2
3	J Button	McLaren-Mercedes MP4-26	44	1h26m54.562s	132.147	1m50.062s	3
4	F Alonso	Ferrari 150 Italia	44	1h26m57.915s	132.062	1m51.107s	2
5	M Schumacher	Mercedes MGP W02	44	1h27m32.357s	131.196	1m51.137s	3
6	N Rosberg	Mercedes MGP W02	44	1h27m33.567s	131.166	1m52.263s	2
7	A Sutil	Force India-Mercedes VJM04	44	1h27m44.606s	130.891	1m52.591s	2
8	F Massa	Ferrari 150 Italia	44	1h27m50.969s	130.733	1m51.564s	3
9	V Petrov	Renault R31	44	1h27ms56.810	130.588	1m52.432s	3
10	P Maldonado	Williams-Cosworth FW33	44	1h28m02.508s	130.447	1m53.362s	2
11	P di Resta	Force India-Mercedes VJM04	44	1h28m08.887s	130.290	1m53.223s	2
12	K Kobayashi	Sauber-Ferrari C30	44	1h28m16.869s	130.094	1m53.871s	2
13	B Senna	Renault R31	44	1h28m17.878s	130.069	1m53.585s	3
14	J Trulli	Lotus-Renault T128	43	1h26m55.773s	129.113	1m54.571s	2
15	H Kovalainen	Lotus-Renault T128	43	1h27m02.556s	128.945	1m54.051s	2
16	R Barrichello	Williams-Cosworth FW33	43	1h27m02.594s	128.944	1m50.424s	3
17	J d'Ambrosio	Virgin-Cosworth MVR02	43	1h27m52.627s	127.720	1m56.319s	2
18	T Glock	Virgin-Cosworth MVR02	43	1h27m54.328s	127.679	1m56.540s	4
19	V Liuzzi	HRT-Cosworth F111	43	1h28m33.305s	126.743	1m58.061s	3
R	S Perez	Sauber-Ferrari C30	27	Damage	-	1m57.244s	3
R	D Ricciardo	HRT-Cosworth F111	13	Vibration	-	1m59.831s	1
R	L Hamilton	McLaren-Mercedes MP4-26	12	Accident	-	1m55.647s	1
R	S Buemi	Toro Rosso-Ferrari STR6	6	Rear wing	-	1m56.790s	0
R	J Alguersuari	Toro Rosso-Ferrari STR6	1	Accident	-	-	0

CHAMPIONSHIP

	Driver	Pts
1	S Vettel	259
2	M Webber	167
3	F Alonso	157
4	J Button	149
5	L Hamilton	146
6	F Massa	74
7	N Rosberg	56
8	M Schumacher	42
9	V Petrov	34
10	N Heidfeld	34
11	K Kobayashi	27
12	A Sutil	24
13	S Buemi	12
14	J Alguersuari	10
15	P di Resta	8
16	S Perez	8
17	R Barrichello	4
18	P Maldonado	1

	Constructor	Pts
1	Red Bull-Renault	426
2	McLaren-Mercedes	295
3	Ferrari	231
4	Mercedes	88
5	Renault	68
6	Sauber-Ferrari	35
7	Force India-Mercedes	32
8	Toro Rosso-Ferrari	22
9	Williams-Cosworth	5

Fastest lap
M Webber 1m49.883s
(142.583mph) on lap 33

Fastest speed trap
M Webber 191.568mph
Slowest speed trap
D Ricciardo 174.170mph

Fastest pit stop
1 M Schumacher 20.153s
2 M Schumacher 20.226s
3 B Senna 20.756s

Adrian Sutil
"After starting 15th, I have to be happy with seventh. It was an exciting race. When the safety car came out, I pitted immediately, helping me make up two places."

Kamui Kobayashi
"My start was good, but I was slow on the straights. It was also hard to survive with the soft tyres. When I pitted on the second lap behind the safety car I lost places."

Sebastien Buemi
"I got a great start, moving from 11th to sixth. I was able to follow the pace of Alonso and Hamilton. Then Perez drove into the back of me, which destroyed my wing."

Jarno Trulli
"I had a great start, passing a few, but the accident in Turn 1 meant I suffered damage to the floor and I had to run the race like that, so to finish 14th is just fantastic."

Daniel Ricciardo
"I made a good start and gained from incidents ahead, but made the right choice which let me pick up a few spots. Then I had a problem with the rear of the car."

Timo Glock
"I made a mistake into Turn 1. I hit the brakes, locked the front tyres and had no chance to avoid the crash with Paul di Resta. I have to say sorry for that."

Paul di Resta
"There was an incident at La Source, and I thought I'd got by when I got hit by Timo. That put a hole in my floor and damaged my wing, giving me understeer."

Sergio Perez
"I was seventh when Buemi changed his line under braking. I couldn't avoid him. After my drive-through penalty, something felt wrong at the back of the car."

Jaime Alguersuari
"Going into La Source, I had Senna inside me and Alonso outside, then Senna missed his braking point and hit me, which pushed me into Alonso's path."

Heikki Kovalainen
"It all tightened up at the first corner and then someone else hit me. After I'd pitted and had a new nose it went pretty well from there."

Vitantonio Liuzzi
"I knew it would be tricky in the dry, but I made a good start and gained a few places. I was ahead of my rivals and, though our pace wasn't the best, kept on fighting."

Jerome d'Ambrosio
"I'm very pleased how things went in my first home grand prix. I focused on keeping it nice and clean, and in the end the team has another good two-car result."

FORMULA 1 GRAN PREMIO
SANTANDER D'ITALIA 2011
MONZA

SUPREME SEBASTIAN

Sebastian Vettel stamped his authority
on Monza with a stunning performance,
including a breathtaking move around the
outside of Fernando Alonso to take the lead

At Monza in 2008, Sebastian Vettel announced himself as a major talent with a shock wet-weather win for Scuderia Toro Rosso. Three years later, a second success in Italy all but secured a second World Championship for the German.

Monza was not supposed to be the ideal track for Red Bull, but after winning at Spa, a similarly high-speed venue, the team arrived with a perfect package. Despite a marked lack of overall top speed – a result of gearing and the aero set-up – the blue car was superb over a lap, and ultimately that proved to be the winning ticket.

DRS added a new element to the unique Monza aero package, and all the teams had to juggle overall downforce levels and seventh gear ratios, making sure that both parameters worked not only for lap time in qualifying, but also in race conditions, when DRS was available on the pit straight and into the Ascari chicane.

Vettel was beaten by Lewis Hamilton on the prime tyre in Q1, but he topped Q2 and was already fastest in Q3 before he put in an even quicker lap on his last run. His main rivals, Hamilton and Jenson Button, both aborted their last laps when they realised that they wouldn't improve. Nevertheless, the two McLaren drivers secured second and third places on the grid, with Lewis ahead.

"An unbelievable day. Fernando Alonso had an awesome start and looked like he was only ever going to be the leader out of the first chicane.

Sebastian was already pressuring him before the safety car. For anyone who doubted whether he could overtake, he demonstrated it very clearly with that very brave move on Fernando with two wheels on the grass!

He had tremendous pace. Obviously there had been a bit of debate about gear ratios, but we got it absolutely spot-on and it was a very well-executed race.

A lot of effort went into winning Monza. It's massively rewarding to win two races, Spa and Monza, which on paper should have been our weakest.

With our ratio choice we felt that the hit was potentially in qualifying, when you could use the DRS all the time, whereas for the race we were better placed. I think it was absolutely the right thing to do.

Both engineering sides of the table had the information and opportunity to go that route, but in the end went in different directions. From a team perspective it was impossible to say which one was right and which was wrong.

They both had pluses and minuses but Sebastian was adamant that he could make it work and he did just that.

Mark will bounce back. He was obviously going for it. With Felipe it was 50/50, a racing accident. He relied on Felipe being generous at the second part of the chicane and contact was made.

It was one of those things. It's our first DNF of the year. They are costly and he knows that.

I think we'd have handled the McLarens, even if they hadn't been delayed by Michael. You could see that the McLaren wasn't particularly quick, especially with the wing not activated.

Just watching Michael without his wing stalled still pulling away from a McLaren that was in the tow and had its wing open made it look like they maybe carried a bit too much downforce.

We have now equalled Tyrrell's 23 race wins in a seven-year period and that's a great team to be up there with. I think we've come a long way in a short space of time. Our philosophy is that you can always learn, so we'll keep pushing right up to Brazil.

Fernando Alonso took fourth place, to give Ferrari at least some hope of getting a podium. Mark Webber had something of a scrappy session and struggled with some KERS issues, the Aussie ending up in fifth place, ahead of Felipe Massa.

Having secured pole, Vettel had to break away at the start and ensure that he didn't come under threat from cars with superior straightline performance.

The plan nearly came unstuck when Sebastian was beaten into the first chicane by Fernando Alonso, to the delight of the *tifosi*. However, almost immediately there was a safety car, as backmarker Tonio Liuzzi lost control and spun across the grass into the middle of the pack. The errant HRT took out Vitaly Petrov and Nico Rosberg, and delayed several others. It was a great shame for Rosberg, who had saved tyres in qualifying and started on the prime with a strategy that could have paid off.

At the restart, Alonso was able to stay ahead for only one more lap before Vettel found a way by, the German showing that he can overtake through the tiniest of gaps by squeezing between the Ferrari and the grass. Once in the lead, Vettel began to pull away, helped by the fact that his main rivals – the two McLarens – had both made bad starts. In fact, at the end of the first lap Lewis Hamilton was fourth and Jenson Button only sixth.

"In the case of Jenson, I think the clutch didn't deliver enough torque," explains Whitmarsh. "And I think he instinctively dropped the paddle and had a bit of wheelspin. And on Lewis's car I think we probably had the opposite, and he had too much wheelspin.

"In truth, Lewis's wasn't a bad start, but there were some better ones around. It's all about position, and you've got to make a decision when you get down to the first chicane whether you come out with wings intact or not, and I think they both did a sensible job."

Hamilton was then passed by Michael Schumacher after the safety-car restart. Lewis admitted that he'd

allowed the German to get the jump on him, as Vettel and Alonso raced away in front: "Michael was on the outside of me, so I was looking at him in my mirrors, and then before I knew it, the guys had gone. I missed an opportunity to slipstream Sebastian – they caught me napping."

The Mercedes driver had much better straightline speed, and was soon vigorously defending his position, much to Hamilton's frustration.

Button lost a further place to Mark Webber, before the Aussie misjudged a move on fifth-placed Felipe Massa at the first chicane, and punted the Brazilian into a spin. Webber's front wing was broken, and as he headed to the pits, going into Parabolica, the wing folded under the car, sending him into the tyre wall. Incredibly, it was Red Bull's first retirement of 2011.

The loss of Webber and delay for Massa put Button up to fifth, and he began to catch the Schumacher/ Hamilton battle. Lewis was getting increasingly frustrated in his attempts to get by, as Michael used every trick in the book. The FIA even asked the team to tell him he was pushing the limits of what was acceptable, and the message was passed on by Ross Brawn.

OPPOSITE Tonio Liuzzi lost control at the start after Kamui Kobayashi braked hard in front of him, causing his HRT to slide across the grass into the middle of the pack and hit Vitaly Petrov and Nico Rosberg; the three wrecked cars partially blocked the track, triggering a safety car

TOP After starting 18th, Jaime Alguersuari jumped to 10th after the mayhem at the first chicane, and then drove an excellent race to finish a career-best seventh in Scuderia Toro Rosso's home grand prix

ABOVE Force India's Paul di Resta just missed out on making it through to Q3 and then fought hard to fend off a charging Bruno Senna to take eighth position in the race

TALKING POINT
MICHAEL'S DEFENCE

Monza sparked much debate about what exactly represents fair defensive driving. Did Michael Schumacher go too far?

Most controversy surrounded his crowding of Lewis Hamilton towards the grass on the inside of Curva Grande. But how many times has anyone got down the inside of a rival there? Even Hamilton's McLaren team-mate, Jenson Button, suggested that Lewis appeared to go for a gap that wasn't there.

It was also a move of questionable benefit, because Schumacher, in all probability, would have retained the all-important inside line for the Roggia chicane.

The move Vettel executed on Alonso was better – around the outside, giving him the inside for the following chicane. That, though, needed a bigger speed advantage than Hamilton had at that point. He would also have been putting himself at Schumacher's mercy on the outside of Curva Grande at close to 200mph…

Perhaps more controversial was Schumacher's defence into the first Lesmo. Quite a few times Hamilton got down the outside of the Mercedes into

the Roggia chicane and almost got a car's length advantage, so as to be able to turn in.

Repeatedly, though, Schumacher would go late on the brakes and claim the line from the middle of the road. Inevitably it compromised Michael's exit and, one lap in particular, Lewis got out much quicker and cleaner and headed down the inside into Lesmo 1.

It's a relatively short run and so, again, is difficult to pull off. Schumacher chopped right almost immediately, making the block much more blatant than the one at Curva Grande.

Having halted Lewis's momentum, he then flicked left again to take the ideal line through Lesmo.

Is that the permitted one move, or is it two? Having moved to defend, are you allowed to re-take the ideal line?

If you are, then it becomes very difficult for the attacking driver to make a move stick, and you could argue that what Schumacher did before Lesmo was not defensive driving but simple blocking.

Generally, the thinking is that F1 drivers are experienced and know what they're doing, so we shouldn't throw around penalties like confetti if we want to encourage racing.

At Monza, though, Ross Brawn's messages about one move and giving Hamilton 'racing room at Ascari' (a DRS zone) told you that the team had been warned.

Some have criticised the governing body for the warnings, pointing out that they are a luxury widely enjoyed.

Equally, Charlie Whiting knew he was looking at one of F1's most experienced drivers, with a speed advantage, instinctively placing his car to deny an opponent – an art as much as the incisive pass.

Charlie didn't want to spoil the show, but got the message across that he was watching. Fair enough?

However, just before the first round of stops, Button managed to pass both his own team-mate – wrongfooted by a Schumacher blocking move – and the Mercedes. He was really flying.

"The guys dealt with the frustration and difficulty of Schumacher incredibly well," said Whitmarsh. "It was frustrating enough to watch it from the pits; to have been watching it at close quarters must have been incredibly frustrating. In those situations it's very easy to lose a front wing.

"Not only did he make it difficult to get by, but you know lap by lap that the competition is getting away from you, so that's massively frustrating. All in all, both guys did a great job to keep their composure. A lot of people think that Lewis can be impetuous, but from being on the front row, and the frustration at the start, it was easy to make a mistake at that first corner and not yield."

Vettel continued to extend his lead over Alonso, and then, shortly after the second stops, the Spaniard struggled once again on the medium tyre, and Button was able to demote him to third.

Sebastian then controlled the gap over the McLaren, letting it come down from some 16s to 9.5s at the flag,

as he secured his eighth win of the season. After two difficult races with RBR, at Monza Vettel acknowledged that it was special to win again at the track where he took his debut victory.

"Friday already I had a very good feeling," he said. "Everyone is carrying quite a little wing around here to optimise the speed on the straight, and I think this year the balance was fantastic, so I really had a very good race car.

"The start wasn't that ideal. I don't know where Fernando came from, and it took me a while to understand it was three cars going side-by-side down to Turn One. After that, a great pass. Not that much room, but very enjoyable. Very hard, but fair, so it was great to be back in the lead, and from then onwards the car was fantastic.

"I was able to pull a big gap and benefit from that for the whole rest of the race. It is the best podium in the world. The only thing that could make it better is probably wearing a red suit, but all in all, great to be back on the podium here."

For the second race in a row, Button found the pace with which to catch and pass Alonso in the final stint, as once again the Ferrari underperformed on the

OPPOSITE Mark Webber tried to pass Felipe Massa for fifth at the first chicane on lap 4, but misjudged the move and broke his front wing as he pushed the Ferrari into a spin. Later in the lap, the Red Bull went off at Parabolica after the broken wing became stuck under the car

ABOVE Lewis Hamilton and Michael Schumacher battled furiously for 28 laps, the Mercedes driver blocking ruthlessly before Hamilton eventually made a successful pass to take fourth place

medium tyre. Lewis finally got clear of Michael, and also came very close to passing the Ferrari, but he didn't quite make it, and had to settle for fifth.

Button's recovery drive was awesome, and while it would have been a lot harder without the Webber/Massa collision conveniently clearing a path in front of him, it was another great drive by a guy whose reputation and standing within his team and in the paddock is as high as it has ever been.

"He had the worst start, but he kept his head down and kept pushing," said McLaren race engineer Phil Prew. "We've seen that time and again from Jenson; he doesn't allow setbacks to put him back. He had a good grid position and a bad start, but he still got his head down, and got on with the job.

"It was a fair race, they raced each other, as we've seen them do. Jenson getting ahead just before the first pit stop obviously gave him a bit of an advantage, and he took full advantage of it and pulled away and was able to have a reasonably good race."

However, the fact was that a shot at victory had slipped through McLaren's fingers once again, thanks to the bad starts both drivers made.

"Taking the positives out of this, we had the first and second fastest laps, so we had pace, and we came away with more points than any other team," said Whitmarsh. "Michael also helped them quite a bit today, not intentionally I'm sure, but it worked out..."

Hamilton, meanwhile, was clearly frustrated with Schumacher, although after the race he resolutely refused to criticise the former champ, fearing the media circus that would inevitably result.

"I got past eventually, and I was able to finish ahead," he said. "He was faster on the straight, even with my DRS. It was interesting being behind him, it was a real challenge to get past.

"It's not a great result to be honest. I started second, and I fell back two places. I'm definitely not happy, but that's motor racing. I'm happy that I finished and I got some points for the team, so that's a good step."

Meanwhile, Schumacher finished fifth for the second race in succession, the smile on his face revealing just how much he had enjoyed the tussle with Hamilton.

After his spin, Massa worked his way back to sixth, while the final points went to Jaime Alguersuari, Paul di Resta, Bruno Senna and Sébastien Buemi. It was the first ever score for Senna, who was quickly demonstrating that he is worthy of the Renault race seat.

TOP LEFT After a stunning start to take the lead from fourth place on the grid, local hero Fernando Alonso was passed by Sebastian Vettel and Jenson Button – seen here in pursuit – to take an eventual third place

LEFT Sebastian Vettel celebrates another well-deserved victory

SNAPSHOT FROM
ITALY

CLOCKWISE FROM RIGHT

The historic Monza Park circuit is a living monument to the history of F1; Fernando Alonso does a treble take during the Thursday press conference; Red Bull Racing reveal their secret exhaust system design; Ferrari's Stefano Domenicali tries to recruit a new driver; Paul di Resta fans unite to show their support; former Ferrari hero Michael Schumacher signs autographs for the appreciative tifosi; glamour on the grid; the fans and team members gather beneath the podium to show their appreciation; Mark Webber was one of five drivers to collaborate with artist Mark Dickens and Pirelli to create a unique piece of art using paint applied to F1 wet and intermediate tyre treads; Ducati MotoGP star Nicky Hayden chats to Bernie Ecclestone on the grid

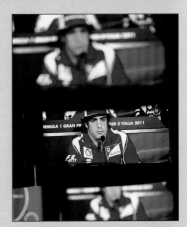

RACE RESULTS

ITALY MONZA

RACE DATE 11th September
CIRCUIT LENGTH 3.600 miles
NO. OF LAPS 53
RACE DISTANCE 190.800 miles
WEATHER Sunny and dry, 30°C
TRACK TEMP 42°C
ATTENDANCE 146,000
LAP RECORD Rubens Barrichello,
1m21.046s, 159.909mph, 2004

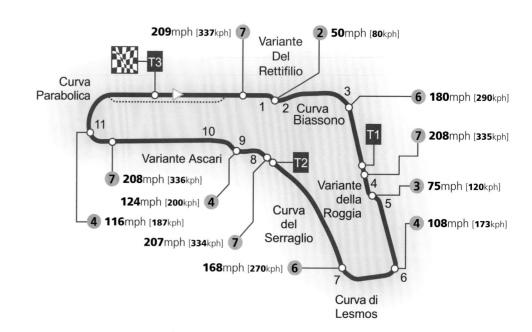

Curva Parabolica
209mph [337kph] 7
Variante Del Rettifilio
2 50mph [80kph]
6 180mph [290kph]
3 Curva Biassono
7 208mph [335kph]
Variante Ascari
7 208mph [336kph]
124mph [200kph] 4
4 116mph [187kph]
207mph [334kph] 7
Curva del Serraglio
3 75mph [120kph]
4 108mph [173kph]
168mph [270kph] 6
Curva di Lesmos
Variante della Roggia

PRACTICE 1

	Driver	Time	Laps
1	L Hamilton	1m23.865s	18
2	J Button	1m24.786s	19
3	S Vettel	1m25.231s	25
4	M Webber	1m25.459s	24
5	A Sutil	1m26.550s	23
6	V Petrov	1m26.625s	20
7	F Alonso	1m26.647s	20
8	F Massa	1m26.676s	24
9	S Perez	1m26.694s	28
10	J Alguersuari	1m26.696s	15
11	M Schumacher	1m26.699s	21
12	N Hulkenberg	1m26.826s	21
13	R Barrichello	1m26.836s	25
14	K Kobayashi	1m26.996s	29
15	P Maldonado	1m27.365s	25
16	B Senna	1m27.385s	23
17	S Buemi	1m27.433s	25
18	N Rosberg	1m27.492s	24
19	H Kovalainen	1m29.539s	10
20	K Chandhok	1m30.148s	19
21	D Ricciardo	1m30.609s	27
22	V Liuzzi	1m30.619s	24
23	T Glock	1m31.052s	12
24	J d'Ambrosio	1m31.899s	22

PRACTICE 2

	Driver	Time	Laps
1	S Vettel	1m24.010s	37
2	L Hamilton	1m24.046s	21
3	M Schumacher	1m24.347s	39
4	F Massa	1m24.366s	33
5	F Alonso	1m24.433s	31
6	M Webber	1m24.468s	32
7	J Button	1m24.508s	30
8	S Perez	1m25.097s	39
9	K Kobayashi	1m25.182s	37
10	B Senna	1m25.325s	38
11	V Petrov	1m25.450s	31
12	A Sutil	1m25.496s	39
13	P di Resta	1m25.683s	37
14	J Alguersuari	1m25.758s	29
15	R Barrichello	1m26.202s	36
16	P Maldonado	1m26.353s	40
17	S Buemi	1m28.347s	5
18	J Trulli	1m28.559s	32
19	H Kovalainen	1m28.605s	32
20	T Glock	1m28.804s	25
21	J Liuzzi	1m29.162s	34
22	N Rosberg	1m29.184s	29
23	J d'Ambrosio	1m29.622s	34
24	D Ricciardo	1m29.841s	7

PRACTICE 3

	Driver	Time	Laps
1	S Vettel	1m23.170s	18
2	M Webber	1m23.534s	19
3	F Massa	1m23.668s	14
4	L Hamilton	1m23.741s	17
5	J Button	1m23.787s	16
6	N Rosberg	1m23.875s	22
7	M Schumacher	1m24.114s	20
8	F Alonso	1m24.133s	14
9	A Sutil	1m24.543s	21
10	P di Resta	1m24.581s	22
11	B Senna	1m24.853s	20
12	V Petrov	1m25.889s	19
13	S Perez	1m24.948s	22
14	K Kobayashi	1m25.261s	21
15	R Barrichello	1m25.319s	19
16	J Alguersuari	1m25.426s	19
17	S Buemi	1m25.439s	22
18	P Maldonado	1m25.539s	19
19	J Trulli	1m27.328s	19
20	H Kovalainen	1m27.491s	21
21	J d'Ambrosio	1m28.186s	23
22	V Liuzzi	1m28.441s	22
23	T Glock	1m28.962s	17
24	D Ricciardo	1m30.316s	16

QUALIFYING 1

	Driver	Time
1	L Hamilton	1m23.976s
2	S Vettel	1m24.002s
3	J Button	1m24.013s
4	F Alonso	1m24.134s
5	M Webber	1m24.148s
6	V Petrov	1m24.486s
7	F Massa	1m24.523s
8	N Rosberg	1m24.550s
9	P di Resta	1m24.574s
10	A Sutil	1m24.595s
11	P Maldonado	1m24.798s
12	K Kobayashi	1m24.879s
13	B Senna	1m24.914s
14	R Barrichello	1m24.975s
15	M Schumacher	1m25.108s
16	S Perez	1m25.113s
17	S Buemi	1m25.164s
18	J Alguersuari	1m25.334s
19	J Trulli	1m26.647s
20	H Kovalainen	1m27.184s
21	T Glock	1m27.591s
22	J d'Ambrosio	1m27.609s
23	D Ricciardo	1m28.054s
24	V Liuzzi	1m28.231s

QUALIFYING 2

	Driver	Time
1	S Vettel	1m22.914s
2	J Button	1m23.031s
3	L Hamilton	1m23.172s
4	N Rosberg	1m23.335s
5	F Alonso	1m23.342s
6	M Webber	1m23.387s
7	M Schumacher	1m23.671s
8	F Massa	1m23.681s
9	V Petrov	1m23.741s
10	B Senna	1m24.157s
11	P di Resta	1m24.163s
12	A Sutil	1m24.209s
13	R Barrichello	1m24.648s
14	P Maldonado	1m24.726s
15	S Perez	1m24.845s
16	S Buemi	1m24.932s
17	K Kobayashi	1m25.065s

Best sectors – Practice

Sec 1	N Rosberg	27.001s
Sec 2	L Hamilton	28.037s
Sec 3	S Vettel	27.620s

Speed trap – Practice

1	V Petrov	215.678mph
2	B Senna	215.615mph
3	J Alguersuari	214.808mph

Best sectors – Qualifying

Sec 1	N Rosberg	26.880s
Sec 2	S Vettel	27.687s
Sec 3	S Vettel	27.319s

Speed trap – Qualifying

1	S Perez	216.982mph
2	B Senna	215.740mph
3	V Petrov	214.248mph

Sebastian Vettel
"The start wasn't good, Alonso was suddenly there and it took a while to see we were three wide into Turn 1. I kept second and, after the restart, I was able to get past."

Jenson Button
"I had a clutch problem at the start and fell to sixth. I was then delayed when Mark and Felipe tangled. I then got my head down and passed Lewis and Michael."

Fernando Alonso
"The start was magical, but I could do nothing about Vettel. It was better against the McLarens, as with the soft tyres I could defend, but not the mediums."

Michael Schumacher
"The fight against Lewis was fun. We're known for driving on the limit, and I had to make my car as wide as a truck, but in the end, as expected, he was still faster."

Bruno Senna
"Everybody cut the chicane, forcing me to the outside and to lose several positions. If the race had been a lap longer, I may have been able to pass di Resta."

Rubens Barrichello
"I had a brilliant start, but then I saw an HRT come past. He did not hit me, but I was then in the middle of the action. I didn't hit anyone, but Rosberg hit my nose."

Mark Webber
"I was trying to get inside Felipe at Turn 2, but I touched the kerb and clipped him. Driving back to the pits, the wing went under the car, so I couldn't turn or brake."

Lewis Hamilton
"At the restart, I was looking at Michael in my mirrors. Then, all of a sudden, the guys ahead had gone, so I missed an opportunity to slipstream Sebastian."

Felipe Massa
"I'm disappointed with sixth, as I could have fought for the podium. However, the incident caused by Webber cost me too much time and I fell to 10th."

Nico Rosberg
"I had a difficult start on my prime tyres, but managed to gain a place at the first corner. Then Liuzzi flew like a torpedo over the grass and put me out of the race."

Vitaly Petrov
"As I was heading into the first chicane, Liuzzi's HRT came from nowhere and hit me, bringing my race to an end. There's nothing I could have done to avoid this."

Pastor Maldonado
"I had a great start and made up a lot of places while avoiding the accident. In the second stint, I began to lose time and it was hard to maintain that rhythm."

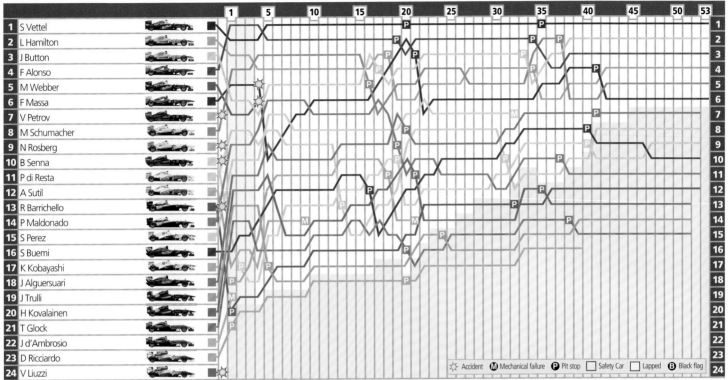

	Driver
1	S Vettel
2	L Hamilton
3	J Button
4	F Alonso
5	M Webber
6	F Massa
7	V Petrov
8	M Schumacher
9	N Rosberg
10	B Senna
11	P di Resta
12	A Sutil
13	R Barrichello
14	P Maldonado
15	S Perez
16	S Buemi
17	K Kobayashi
18	J Alguersuari
19	J Trulli
20	H Kovalainen
21	T Glock
22	J d'Ambrosio
23	D Ricciardo
24	V Liuzzi

☆ Accident Ⓜ Mechanical failure Ⓟ Pit stop ☐ Safety Car ☐ Lapped Ⓑ Black flag

QUALIFYING 3

	Driver	Time
1	S Vettel	1m22.275s
2	L Hamilton	1m22.725s
3	J Button	1m22.777s
4	F Alonso	1m22.841s
5	M Webber	1m22.972s
6	F Massa	1m23.188s
7	V Petrov	1m23.530s
8	M Schumacher	1m23.777s
9	N Rosberg	1m24.477s
10	B Senna	No time

GRID

	Driver	Time
1	S Vettel	1m22.275s
2	L Hamilton	1m22.725s
3	J Button	1m22.777s
4	F Alonso	1m22.841s
5	M Webber	1m22.972s
6	F Massa	1m23.188s
7	V Petrov	1m23.530s
8	M Schumacher	1m23.777s
9	N Rosberg	1m24.477s
10	B Senna	No time
11	P di Resta	1m24.163s
12	A Sutil	1m24.209s
13	R Barrichello	1m24.648s
14	P Maldonado	1m24.726s
15	S Perez	1m24.845s
16	S Buemi	1m24.932s
17	K Kobayashi	1m25.065s
18	J Alguersuari	1m25.334s
19	J Trulli	1m26.647s
20	H Kovalainen	1m27.184s
21	T Glock	1m27.591s
22	J d'Ambrosio	1m27.609s
23	D Ricciardo	1m28.054s
24	V Liuzzi	1m28.231s

RACE

	Driver	Car	Laps	Time	Avg. mph	Fastest	Stops
1	S Vettel	Red Bull-Renault RB7	53	1h20m46.172s	141.578	1m26.557s	2
2	J Button	McLaren-Mercedes MP4-26	53	1h20m55.762s	141.298	1m26.207s	2
3	F Alonso	Ferrari 150 Italia	53	1h21m03.081s	141.086	1m27.191s	2
4	L Hamilton	McLaren-Mercedfes MP4-24	53	1h21m03.589s	141.071	1m26.187s	2
5	M Schumacher	Mercedes MGP W02	53	1h21m18.849s	140.630	1m27.402s	2
6	F Massa	Ferrari 150 Italia	53	1h21m29.165s	140.333	1m26.924s	2
7	J Alguersuari	Toro Rosso-Ferrari STR6	52	1h20m54.891s	138.654	1m28.357s	2
8	P di Resta	Force India-Mercedes VJM04	52	1h20m58.821s	138.542	1m28.054s	2
9	B Senna	Renault R31	52	1h20m59.687s	138.518	1m26.895s	3
10	S Buemi	Toro Rosso-Ferrari STR6	52	1h21m10.095s	138.209	1m28.202s	2
11	P Maldonado	Williams-Cosworth FW33	52	1h21m22.769s	137.863	1m28.934s	2
12	R Barrichello	Williams-Cosworth FW33	52	1h21m38.443s	137.422	1m28.377s	2
13	H Kovalainen	Lotus-Renault T128	51	1h20m47.072s	136.204	1m29.639s	2
14	J Trulli	Lotus-Renault T128	51	1h21m18.239s	135.334	1m29.825s	2
15	T Glock	Virgin-Cosworth MVR02	51	1h21m36.845s	134.820	1m30.783s	2
NC	D Ricciardo	HRT-Cosworth F111	39	1h22m09.502s	102.382	1m32.013s	2
R	S Perez	Sauber-Ferrari C30	32	Gearbox	-	1m29.403s	0
R	K Kobayashi	Sauber-Ferrari C30	21	Gearbox	-	1m30.000s	2
R	A Sutil	Force India-Mercedes VJM04	9	Hydraulics	-	1m31.455s	0
R	M Webber	Red Bull-Renault RB7	4	Accident	-	1m30.994s	0
R	J d'Ambrosio	Virgin-Cosworth MVR02	1	Gearbox	-	-	0
R	V Petrov	Renault R31	0	Accident	-	-	0
R	N Rosberg	Mercedes MGP W02	0	Accident	-	-	0
R	V Liuzzi	HRT-Cosworth F111	0	Accident	-	-	0

CHAMPIONSHIP

	Driver	Pts
1	S Vettel	284
2	F Alonso	172
3	J Button	167
4	M Webber	167
5	L Hamilton	158
6	F Massa	82
7	N Rosberg	56
8	M Schumacher	52
9	V Petrov	34
10	N Heidfeld	34
11	K Kobayashi	27
12	A Sutil	24
13	J Alguersuari	16
14	S Buemi	13
15	P di Resta	12
16	S Perez	8
17	R Barrichello	4
18	B Senna	2
19	P Maldonado	1

	Constructor	Pts
1	Red Bull-Renault	451
2	Mclaren-Mercedes	325
3	Ferrari	254
4	Mercedes	108
5	Renault	70
6	Force India-Mercedes	36
7	Sauber-Ferrari	35
8	Toro Rosso-Ferrari	29
9	Williams-Cosworth	5

Fastest lap
L Hamilton 1m26.187s
(150.371mph) on lap 52

Fastest speed trap
B Senna 215.615mph
Slowest speed trap
J d'Ambrosio 132.911mph

Fastest pit stop
1	S Vettel	21.378s
2	J Button	21.660s
3	F Massa	21.821s

Adrian Sutil
"The biggest problem at Turn 1 was Liuzzi hitting the field. I was on the inside and had to go into the gravel to avoid it. A few laps later the power steering went."

Kamui Kobayashi
"I started on the harder tyres and the plan was to stay out for a long time. But in the accident in Turn 1, not only did my front wing come loose, but I damaged a tyre."

Sébastien Buemi
"I made a very good start, but when Liuzzi triggered the crash, the back of my car took a knock. If that hadn't happened, maybe I could've finished ninth or eighth."

Jarno Trulli
"Massa got into trouble into Turn 1, so I had to go off to avoid him. Then, while going into the second corner, Massa hit me, forcing me into the car next to me."

Daniel Ricciardo
"The car went into anti-stall, jammed in third, then the engine switched off. The mechanics got it going, but engine temperature rose and they called me back in."

Timo Glock
"The race was OK, even though the car was a bit difficult to drive, which is disappointing after qualifying. Over the weekend, though, we've seen a step forward."

Paul di Resta
"My start wasn't great. Going into Turn 1 I could see a Williams approaching, so I moved to the outside, but there was no option but to bump across the chicane."

Sergio Perez
"My strategy was to do a long stint on the harder tyres, then a short stint on the softs. I'd been seventh, but first I couldn't use third, then I couldn't shift gear."

Jaime Alguersuari
"It seems that whenever I have a poor grid position, I score points! I'm a bit surprised at the way the car performance came good in the race, as I didn't expect it."

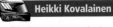
Heikki Kovalainen
"I had a great start, passing Jarno and then seeing the HRT coming into Turn 1 in hardcore style, so I avoided that and was then up into a good position early on."

Vitantonio Liuzzi
"I got past both Virgins, Lotuses and Daniel, but then I went for another overtaking move and got closed out. That put me on to the grass and I lost control."

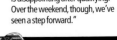
Jerome d'Ambrosio
"During the formation lap, I realised that I had no second gear. I started the race, but the car was undriveable, so I had to come back into the garage and retire."

2011 FORMULA 1 SINGTEL SINGAPORE GRAND PRIX
SINGAPORE

SINGAPORE FLYER

Another pole and another commanding lights-to-flag victory for Sebastian Vettel saw him leave Singapore needing a single further point to take the 2011 Drivers' World Championship

F ollowing his successes in Belgium and Italy, Sebastian Vettel scored another dominant win in the Singapore Grand Prix, and yet fate decreed that the German failed to secure his second title by the tiniest of margins.

The only driver who could now mathematically beat him was Jenson Button, who finished second. The McLaren man was now 124 points behind, with 125 on offer if he won all five remaining races. The chances of that happening, and Vettel failing to add to his post-Singapore score, were best described as slim...

Red Bull had a big corporate presence in Singapore – the company has its roots in Thailand – and Button postponed their party, the visiting VIPs missing out on celebrating the World Championship. But winning what has quickly become one of the highest-profile events on the calendar was a pretty good consolation prize.

Vettel may have made it look easy, but his victory was earned the hard way. It was the result of a typically polished performance from the irrepressible German, and another faultless weekend from the team that works so tirelessly to customise its car for each and every circuit.

It may have appeared routine, but Seb and the team still had to get everything right though Friday and Saturday. And while pole for car No1 was no great surprise,

managing Q3 was no easy task for anybody, as the sheer length of the lap made for a very short break between the first and second runs. There was no margin for error.

In the end, Red Bull showed a clear edge over the opposition, as Mark Webber took second place and locked out the front row for the team. Button took third, after Lewis Hamilton was bumped down to fourth when he was unable to make his second run in Q3. McLaren made a mistake when fuelling the car, and, given the short turnaround time, there was no time to rectify it. Hamilton also had a puncture in Q2, so he lost a set of supersoft tyres for the race. The Ferraris of Fernando Alonso and Felipe Massa lined up fifth and sixth.

At the start, Vettel blasted into the lead, leaving the opposition trailing. He was helped by the fact that Hamilton was squeezed by Webber, and lost a lot of momentum. Button jumped up to second place, and led the pursuit.

What stunned Vettel's rivals, and the whole pitlane, was his storming pace over the first 10 laps. His margin over Jenson went 2.5s, 3.5s, 4.4s, 5.5s, 7.0s, 8.2s, 9.1s, 9.9s, 10.9s, 11.6s, at which point the gap pretty much stabilised. It was astonishing progress that showed there wasn't going to be any kind of battle for the lead.

"They were amazing opening laps," said Adrian

Newey. "He felt comfortable in the car all weekend, and somewhere like this, he felt confident. He felt confidence in the car and therefore confidence in himself to chuck it around a bit...

"You want to get enough of a gap to not be undercut, but there's probably no point in opening it further."

Despite his pace, Vettel still had some life in his supersoft tyres, in stark contrast to Ferrari, where both drivers found themselves in trouble after just seven or eight laps, and had to pit. Seb stretched his first set out to 14 laps, and Button followed him in, so Vettel retained the lead, extending his advantage by a second here and there through the second stint. Indeed, it was up to 18.4s at

the point when Michael Schumacher crashed into Sergio Perez, and the safety car emerged.

The interruption was hardly unexpected given the event's history of at least one safety car per year. However, it was Red Bull's good fortune that once the pit stops had shaken out and the queue had formed up, Vettel had the lapped cars of Jarno Trulli, Tonio Liuzzi and Kamui Kobayashi between himself and Button as a cushion.

"It was frustrating to lose the gap," admitted Newey. "But he had the pace in the opening stint, so no reason to think that he couldn't open it back out again. After the restart, Button was stuck in traffic, and Seb was able to make the most of that."

OPPOSITE TOP Sebastian Vettel leads the field on his way to pulling out a lead of 2.5s on the first lap, while Nico Rosberg takes a short-cut

OPPOSITE BOTTOM Daniel Ricciardo damaged his HRT's nose after contact with Timo Glock's Virgin on the opening lap

ABOVE Jarno Trulli ran as high as 11th before his first pit stop, but he later retired with gearbox problems

INSIDE LINE
SEBASTIAN VETTEL
RED BULL RACING DRIVER

"The car was fantastic all the way through. When we had to push, we could pull away quite easily. The safety car didn't fit our plans, as we had a big gap, but I had a very good restart.

I was a bit lucky that there were back-markers between Jenson and

I. I got back into the rhythm straight away and opened the gap again.

On the last lap I faced five cars, a large group, but there was plenty of room. It wasn't that big a margin when I crossed the line, but I was in control.

I love the challenge of Singapore. It's a long race and it's hard to put the sectors together, not only in qualifying, but also the race. There's a lot of humidity and you sweat a lot.

Last year it was a tough fight to the end with Fernando, shadowing him. I felt I could have gone a little bit quicker and so it was great to come back this time and get the job done.

I used DRS only when I had to pass lapped cars. We were in a luxury position today. In the speed

was phenomenal. The car I had, every time I had to push there was so much more lap time in it. At stages we were more than a second quicker than the cars behind.

We didn't need to make the final pit stop, but when the others pitted, we decided to cover them in case there was another safety car. We could have been vulnerable on a used or scrubbed set of tyres at the end.

I wasn't thinking about the championship. It wasn't important for me to know where the other people were. I was given the gap to Jenson, who was second, and then the race order at the end, so crossing the line I didn't know whether it was enough. With just the one point needed I can work it out for myself from here!

My biggest worry was probably when Kovalainen and I went into the pits together. Lotus have a system with lights, I think, so I watched their lollipop and saw them going off when I was just approaching. I was aware of the situation.

I think initially Heikki didn't see me – it's a difficult angle. If I hadn't lifted I'd have lost the front wing, but it was more a misunderstanding, not really Heikki's fault."

as has become standard practice, he pitted in response to Button coming in, to head off any danger of a second safety car closing up the field and giving Jenson a chance to jump him with fresher rubber.

"Strategy-wise we were just covering what the others did," said Christian Horner. "We could have run to the end on the prime – we stopped to cover Jenson and the other cars on the eventuality of a safety car. We could have run options at the first stop for the second stint, but it was a situation where we were able to respond and look at what others were doing. We decided not to go a different route, to effectively mirror the strategy of the cars behind."

After his last stop, and with 11 laps to go, Seb was 9.5s clear of Jenson. And then the gap began to come down. Was there a problem with fuel consumption or something else? McLaren urged Button to push, and the margin continued to shrink, while traffic made life difficult for both men. In fact, Seb had it all under control.

"We were just managing the car," Newey insisted. "It's a tough race round here, there's no point in taking more out of it than we needed to. There were a few things we were worried about, so we were prepared to sacrifice a bit of pace to manage it."

"There was a lot of traffic, and they were all fighting for positions," said Horner. "He picked his timing to move through that traffic, which was the right thing to do, but at no point was he under any real pressure."

It didn't look that way from the outside, especially when the gap came down to 3.7s with three laps to go, and Jenson appeared to be on a mission.

"As they went through traffic, it concertinaed down to that," said Horner. "But the reality was the net loss was never more than five or six seconds. It was something Seb managed. I think he's driven some fantastic races this year, but that one is certainly well up there."

"That was a function of traffic," Newey confirmed. "Seb had to get through the traffic, and then obviously Button had the same."

ABOVE The front wing of Lewis Hamilton's McLaren flies through the air after contact with the right-rear tyre of Felipe Massa's Ferrari

BELOW A safety car led to battles throughout the field, Paul di Resta here lapping Jerome d'Ambrosio on his way to a superb sixth place

OPPOSITE Jenson Button closed to within 1.7s of Vettel on the final lap, his pursuit hampered by traffic

A clear track would have given Button some kind of shot, and created extra stress for Vettel, but Jenson had no chance. Just crossing the line for the restart he was already 4.0s behind the leader, so slow were the backmarkers.

Button soon dealt with the two Italians, but Kobayashi proved intransigent, and sat in front of the McLaren for over a lap. After just one lap of green running, Button was an amazing 8.9s behind Vettel. Quite rightly, the Sauber driver earned himself a drive-through penalty.

Even with a clear track Button couldn't hold the gap, and over the next few laps it edged out to around 12–13s, the number with which Seb appeared to be comfortable.

Vettel could have gone to the end on those tyres. But,

TALKING POINT
HAMILTON'S WOES

Lewis Hamilton's difficult 2011 season continued in Singapore, when he attracted another drive-through penalty after a coming-together with Felipe Massa.

Hamilton had 20s added to his race time in Malaysia after weaving in front of Fernando Alonso, received two drive-through penalties in Monaco for incidents with Massa and Pastor Maldonado, was fortunate to go unpenalised in Canada after spinning Mark Webber and colliding with team-mate Jenson Button.

In Hungary he had a drive-through for resuming in front of Paul di Resta's Force India after a spin, and at Marina Bay he was penalised when an attempt to pass Felipe Massa in the DRS zone resulted in a damaged front wing for the McLaren and a punctured right-rear tyre for the Ferrari.

Ironically, Hamilton was attacked in the media for further evidence of an 'over-aggressive' approach when, in fact, during the Singapore incident he was backing out of his attempt to pass Massa when it became obvious he wasn't going to make the move stick.

Hamilton was attempting to come back through the field after starting fourth and trying to pass Mark Webber's front-row Red Bull into Turn 1. Webber blocked him, forcing him to back off, and the McLaren lost a number of places at Turn 1, completing the opening lap in eighth place.

Hamilton initially looked like he would fly past Massa in the DRS zone, but the Ferrari driver used his KERS to defend, and was ahead as they reached the Turn 7 braking area.

Hamilton, on the outside line at the very corner he ended his 2010 Singapore GP in a collision with Webber, tried to tuck in too early and clipped the Ferrari. Massa was obliged to make an unscheduled stop to replace a punctured tyre.

After the race, as Hamilton was conducting TV interviews in the media pen, an obviously disgruntled Massa patted him on the shoulder, and said, sarcastically, "Good job, bro..."

"Don't touch me, man. Don't touch me," Hamilton responded.

The pair had almost come together in qualifying, when Hamilton wanted to clear the Ferrari before starting a hot lap.

"He cannot use his mind – even in qualifying," Massa said. "He has done it to me so many times this year. Again, he could have caused a big accident. He's paying for it and he doesn't understand that. It's important the FIA study this and penalise him every time."

It was just the latest incident in what was developing into an ever more frustrating year for the 2008 World Champion. He left Singapore fifth in the World Championship, 17 points adrift of McLaren team-mate Button, now the only man with a mathematical chance of stopping Vettel from taking the title.

ABOVE Fernando Alonso heads into his pit box for his first tyre stop, which allowed him to jump Mark Webber for fourth place. The Australian would re-pass the off-the-pace Ferrari as the safety car pulled in, consigning Alonso to fourth place, 55s adrift of winner Vettel

BELOW Pastor Maldonado just missed out on points, finishing in 11th place, two places ahead of team-mate Rubens Barrichello

Indeed any excitement was dulled when Button came across the scrapping Williams drivers. But Seb did cut it pretty fine on the last lap, dropping seven seconds off the pace to give himself just 1.7s as he cruised past the flag.

"After the safety car, I thought I might have a go, but I sat behind Kobayashi for a lap," said Button. "I think I lost about three or four seconds. I finally got past, but again the pace wasn't quick enough. I was told to look after the tyres. I also was always a little bit careful with fuel around here, so the last stint I was able to drive as fast as I could.

"It was putting 10 to 12 qualifying laps together. I could not have gone any quicker. That was it – that was all I could get out of the car. I took a lot of risks, enjoyed it. I

said coming here that I wanted to win the race, so we had to have a go. But I had to settle for second."

Webber, meanwhile, paid the price for another bad start, losing out to both Button and Alonso. He eventually recovered third, but he was 29s behind, and a fastest lap that was 1.6s off that of his team-mate spoke volumes.

"Mark had a good day," Horner insisted. "His start from the dirty side of the grid – it looked like that whole line lost out into Turn One, but thereafter his recovery and his performance were good. He seemed to enjoy passing Fernando, he did that twice today! It was a good drive from him at a circuit that probably isn't among his favourites."

Having lost his battle with Webber, Alonso dropped back to finish a distant fourth, after a disappointing day for the former winner. Meanwhile, once again Hamilton had an eventful race. While in recovery mode after his bad start, he damaged his front wing trying to pass Massa. The Brazilian picked up a puncture, while Lewis had to pit for a new nose, and then lost more time with a drive-through penalty for causing a collision. Good strategy and some hard driving gave him the chance to make up places, and he managed to work his way back to fifth.

Paul di Resta did a brilliant job to take sixth for Force India, after taking a strategy gamble and starting on the harder tyre. He ran as high as third before his first stop, and managed to beat the Mercedes of Nico Rosberg fair and square. Adrian Sutil made it a great race for Force India by taking eighth.

The puncture dropped Massa way down the field, but he worked his way back to ninth. Meanwhile, Perez survived the early thump from Schumacher to take 10th, and the final point, for Sauber.

Following the race, Massa made his displeasure known to Hamilton when the latter was conducting TV interviews, and there was a little incident between the two that once again drew attention to the Brit's recent run of disastrous races. His season wasn't getting any better, and now the whole world was wondering whether he had lost the plot...

SNAPSHOT FROM
SINGAPORE

CLOCKWISE FROM RIGHT

The packed grandstands provided a superb view of the floodlit action; Rubens Barrichello attempts to stay cool before the start; Sebastian Vettel celebrates another victory by getting intimate with his TV audience; the sparks fly from Fernando Alonso's Ferrari during qualifying; identity parade – the grid girls go head-to-head with the top five drivers on the grid, and in the World Championship; Nico Rosberg checks his lightly tinted visor; circuit workers make repairs to the trackside kerbing after problems in Friday practice; the post-race fireworks light up the night sky; the Renault team watch their man, Vitaly Petrov, during Q1 on Saturday evening; Bernie Ecclestone in animated discussion with FIA President Jean Todt

RACE RESULTS
SINGAPORE MARINA BAY

RACE DATE September 25th
CIRCUIT LENGTH 3.148 miles
NO. OF LAPS 61
RACE DISTANCE 192.028 miles
WEATHER Humid but dry, 32°C
TRACK TEMP 35°C
ATTENDANCE 330,000
LAP RECORD Kimi Räikkönen, 1m45.599s, 107.358mph, 2008

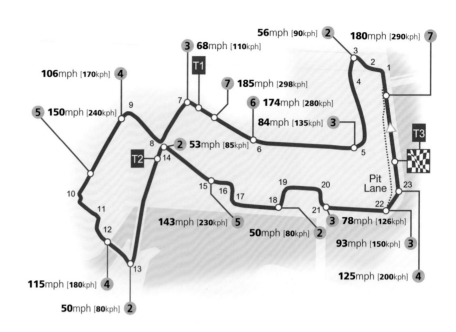

PRACTICE 1				PRACTICE 2				PRACTICE 3				QUALIFYING 1			QUALIFYING 2	
	Driver	Time	Laps		Driver	Time	Laps		Driver	Time	Laps		Driver	Time		Driver	Time
1	L Hamilton	1m48.599s	10	1	S Vettel	1m46.374s	33	1	M Webber	1m46.081s	15	1	S Vettel	1m46.397s	1	S Vettel	1m44.931s
2	S Vettel	1m49.005s	15	2	F Alonso	1m46.575s	28	2	J Button	1m46.108s	17	2	J Button	1m46.956s	2	J Button	1m45.472s
3	M Webber	1m50.066s	16	3	L Hamilton	1m47.115s	22	3	S Vettel	1m46.345s	14	3	L Hamilton	1m47.014s	3	M Webber	1m45.651s
4	F Alonso	1m50.596s	11	4	F Massa	1m47.120s	23	4	F Alonso	1m46.396s	14	4	F Alonso	1m47.054s	4	F Alonso	1m45.779s
5	J Button	1m50.952s	12	5	M Webber	1m47.265s	28	5	L Hamilton	1m46.936s	20	5	M Webber	1m47.332s	5	F Massa	1m45.955s
6	F Massa	1m52.043s	14	6	M Schumacher	1m48.418s	27	6	N Rosberg	1m47.831s	14	6	N Rosberg	1m47.688s	6	M Schumacher	1m46.043s
7	A Sutil	1m52.251s	13	7	A Sutil	1m48.866s	32	7	M Schumacher	1m47.837s	12	7	S Perez	1m47.717s	7	N Rosberg	1m46.405s
8	M Schumacher	1m52.416s	12	8	S Perez	1m49.578s	27	8	F Massa	1m48.711s	12	8	F Massa	1m47.945s	8	L Hamilton	1m46.829s
9	P di Resta	1m52.435s	13	9	K Kobayashi	1m49.730s	29	9	K Kobayashi	1m49.057s	15	9	A Sutil	1m47.952s	9	A Sutil	1m47.093s
10	N Rosberg	1m52.815s	13	10	J Button	1m49.751s	10	10	A Sutil	1m49.304s	16	10	P di Resta	1m48.022s	10	P di Resta	1m47.486s
11	R Barrichello	1m52.991s	17	11	J Alguersuari	1m49.792s	14	11	S Perez	1m49.583s	17	11	K Kobayashi	1m48.054s	11	S Perez	1m47.616s
12	J Alguersuari	1m53.050s	17	12	B Senna	1m50.241s	31	12	S Buemi	1m49.679s	18	12	R Barrichello	1m48.061s	12	R Barrichello	1m48.082s
13	P Maldonado	1m53.399s	18	13	P di Resta	1m50.345s	8	13	P di Resta	1m49.816s	18	13	S Buemi	1m48.753s	13	P Maldonado	1m48.270s
14	S Perez	1m53.703s	19	14	V Petrov	1m50.399s	29	14	P Maldonado	1m49.851s	17	14	M Schumacher	1m48.819s	14	S Buemi	1m48.634s
15	K Kobayashi	1m53.749s	12	15	N Rosberg	1m50.790s	28	15	R Barrichello	1m50.189s	15	15	B Senna	1m48.861s	15	B Senna	1m48.662s
16	B Senna	1m53.765s	17	16	R Barrichello	1m50.897s	24	16	V Petrov	1m50.229s	15	16	J Alguersuari	1m49.588s	16	J Alguersuari	1m49.862s
17	S Buemi	1m53.785s	16	17	P Maldonado	1m50.937s	30	17	B Senna	1m50.523s	14	17	P Maldonado	1m49.710s	17	K Kobayashi	Notime
18	V Petrov	1m54.736s	8	18	H Kovalainen	1m51.950s	26	18	J Alguersuari	1m50.547s	17	18	V Petrov	1m49.835s			
19	J Trulli	1m54.821s	9	19	S Buemi	1m52.257s	15	19	H Kovalainen	1m52.510s	17	19	H Kovalainen	1m50.948s			
20	H Kovalainen	1m56.198s	8	20	J Trulli	1m52.489s	25	20	J d'Ambrosio	1m52.697s	19	20	J Trulli	1m51.012s			
21	J d'Ambrosio	1m57.798s	13	21	T Glock	1m53.579s	25	21	D Ricciardo	1m53.728s	15	21	T Glock	1m52.154s			
22	T Glock	1m58.792s	6	22	J d'Ambrosio	1m54.649s	25	22	J Trulli	1m53.823s	18	22	J d'Ambrosio	1m52.363s			
23	D Ricciardo	1m59.169s	17	23	D Ricciardo	1m54.754s	29	23	T Glock	1m53.829s	16	23	D Ricciardo	1m52.404s			
24	N Kartikheyan	1m59.214s	18	24	V Liuzzi	1m55.198s	26	24	V Liuzzi	1m55.203s	17	24	V Liuzzi	1m52.810s			

Best sectors – Practice			Speed trap – Practice			Best sectors – Qualifying			Speed trap – Qualifying		
Sec 1	S Vettel	28.326s	1	A Sutil	181.813mph	Sec 1	M Webber	27.935s	1	A Sutil	182.124mph
Sec 2	J Button	41.075s	2	F Massa	180.446mph	Sec 2	J Button	40.688s	2	N Rosberg	181.999mph
Sec 3	S Vettel	36.183s	3	M Schumacher	180.197mph	Sec 3	S Vettel	35.560s	3	F Massa	181.626mph

 Sebastian Vettel

"The car was fantastic. The safety car didn't fit to our plan, but I had a very good restart and was lucky that there were backmarkers between me and Jenson."

 Jenson Button

"I was being told all race to look after the car and the tyres; the only time I was able to push was in the last 12 laps, when I chased Seb on the supersoft tyre."

 Fernando Alonso

"It was impossible to finish on the podium. We weren't fast enough and, even if we were third at points, I knew that sooner or later I would be overtaken."

Michael Schumacher

"It was an unfortunate end to my race. It was a misunderstanding between Perez and me. He was about to go inside and lifted, and I wasn't expecting him to do that."

 **Bruno Senna**

"I had high tyre degradation. When we put the soft tyres on, they didn't have the same bite. Then my wheels locked into the hairpin and I hit the wall."

 Rubens Barrichello

"We said that the tyres would have a hard time. With the safety car deployed when it was, the only option was to stay out to have a chance of scoring."

 Mark Webber

"I'm having to come back through the field too often. I can't make the starts I made last year and it's risky to try to regain positions when the DRS isn't working."

 Lewis Hamilton

"I had fun picking off cars after my penalty, but it was frustrating to again be down the field when I felt we had a car that could have challenged up at the front."

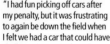 **Felipe Massa**

"There's no point in hiding my anger. The damage after contact with Hamilton penalised me, as I lost so much time early on when the traffic was still heavy."

Nico Rosberg

"The optimum would have been sixth place, but it just didn't quite work out for us, as I was struggling with the rear end and our car just didn't suit this track."

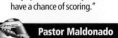 **Vitaly Petrov**

"I had KERS problems, which made it hard to pass. Then the tyres started to behave poorly; when cars started lapping me, I had to slow and the pressure fell."

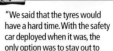 **Pastor Maldonado**

"The car had a lot of oversteer, particularly in the first stint. We tried everything to get rid of it to save the rear tyres, but the wear rate forced us to pit early."

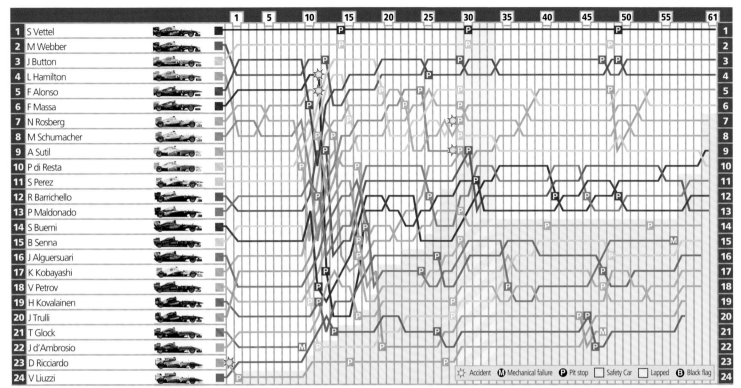

	Driver		
1	S Vettel		
2	M Webber		
3	J Button		
4	L Hamilton		
5	F Alonso		
6	F Massa		
7	N Rosberg		
8	M Schumacher		
9	A Sutil		
10	P di Resta		
11	S Perez		
12	R Barrichello		
13	P Maldonado		
14	S Buemi		
15	B Senna		
16	J Alguersuari		
17	K Kobayashi		
18	V Petrov		
19	H Kovalainen		
20	J Trulli		
21	T Glock		
22	J d'Ambrosio		
23	D Ricciardo		
24	V Liuzzi		

☆ Accident Ⓜ Mechanical failure Ⓟ Pit stop ☐ Safety Car ☐ Lapped Ⓑ Black flag

QUALIFYING 3

	Driver	Time
1	S Vettel	1m44.381s
2	M Webber	1m44.732s
3	J Button	1m44.804s
4	L Hamilton	1m44.809s
5	F Alonso	1m44.874s
6	F Massa	1m45.800s
7	N Rosberg	1m46.013s
8	M Schumacher	No time
9	A Sutil	No time
10	P di Resta	No time

GRID

	Driver	Time
1	S Vettel	1m44.381s
2	M Webber	1m44.732s
3	J Button	1m44.804s
4	L Hamilton	1m44.809s
5	F Alonso	1m44.874s
6	F Massa	1m45.800s
7	N Rosberg	1m46.013s
8	M Schumacher	No time
9	A Sutil	No time
10	P di Resta	No time
11	S Perez	1m47.616s
12	R Barrichello	1m48.082s
13	P Maldonado	1m48.270s
14	S Buemi	1m48.634s
15	B Senna	1m48.662s
16	J Alguersuari	1m49.862s
17	K Kobayashi	No time
18	V Petrov	1m49.835s
19	H Kovalainen	1m50.948s
20	J Trulli	1m51.012s
21	T Glock	1m52.154s
22	J d'Ambrosio	1m52.363s
23	D Ricciardo	1m52.404s
24*	V Liuzzi	1m52.810s

* 5-place penalty for causing a collision

RACE

	Driver	Car	Laps	Time	Avg. mph	Fastest	Stops
1	S Vettel	Red Bull-Renault RB7	61	1h59m06.757s	96.816	1m48.688s	3
2	J Button	McLaren-Mercedes MP4-26	61	1h59m08.494s	96.792	1m48.454s	3
3	M Webber	Red Bull-Renault RB7	61	1h59m36.036s	96.420	1m50.088s	3
4	F Alonso	Ferrari 150 Italia	61	2h00m02.206s	96.070	1m50.891s	3
5	L Hamilton	McLaren-Mercedes MP4-26	61	2h00m14.523s	95.906	1m50.832s	5
6	P di Resta	Force India-Mercedes VJM04	61	2h00m57.824s	95.334	1m54.239s	2
7	N Rosberg	Mercedes MGP W02	60	1h59m07.583s	95.217	1m54.383s	3
8	A Sutil	Force India-Mercedes VJM04	60	1h59m07.965s	95.211	1m54.564s	2
9	F Massa	Ferrari 150 Italia	60	1h59m08.346s	95.206	1m52.550s	4
10	S Perez	Sauber-Ferrari C30	60	1h59m10.653s	95.176	1m54.615s	2
11	P Maldonado	Williams-Cosworth FW33	60	1h59m19.332s	95.060	1m53.198s	3
12	S Buemi	Toro Rosso-Ferrari STR6	60	1h59m19.941s	95.052	1m52.197s	3
13	R Barrichello	Williams-Cosworth FW33	60	1h59m35.807s	94.842	1m55.235s	2
14	K Kobayashi	Sauber-Ferrari C30	59	1h59m40.313s	93.202	1m51.239s	4
15	B Senna	Renault R31	59	1h59m58.610s	92.965	1m53.774s	4
16	H Kovalainen	Lotus-Renault T128	59	2h00m20.977s	92.677	1m54.063s	3
17	V Petrov	Renault R31	59	2h00m36.150s	92.483	1m54.204s	3
18	J d'Ambrosio	Virgin-Cosworth MVR02	59	2h01m08.205s	92.075	1m58.730s	2
19	D Ricciardo	HRT-Cosworth F111	57	1h59m46.220s	89.968	1m59.064s	3
20	V Liuzzi	HRT-Cosworth F111	57	2h00m50.864s	89.165	1m58.283s	4
21	J Alguersuari	Toro Rosso-Ferrari STR6	56	Accident	-	1m53.676s	3
R	J Trulli	Lotus-Renault T128	47	Gearbox	-	1m57.126s	3
R	M Schumacher	Mercedes MGP W02	28	Accident	-	1m53.906s	2
R	T Glock	Virgin-Cosworth MVR02	9	Accident	-	2m00.412s	0

CHAMPIONSHIP

	Driver	Pts
1	S Vettel	309
2	J Button	185
3	F Alonso	184
4	M Webber	182
5	L Hamilton	168
6	F Massa	84
7	N Rosberg	62
8	M Schumacher	52
9	V Petrov	34
10	N Heidfeld	34
11	A Sutil	28
12	K Kobayashi	27
13	P di Resta	20
14	J Alguersuari	16
15	S Buemi	13
16	S Perez	9
17	R Barrichello	4
18	B Senna	2
19	P Maldonado	1

	Constructor	Pts
1	Red Bull-Renault	491
2	McLaren-Mercedes	353
3	Ferrari	268
4	Mercedes	114
5	Renault	70
6	Force India-Mercedes	48
7	Sauber-Ferrari	36
8	Toro Rosso-Ferrari	29
9	Williams-Cosworth	5

Fastest lap
J Button 1m48.454s
(104.672mph) on lap 54

Fastest speed trap
B Senna 182.248mph
Slowest speed trap
T Glock 169.013mph

Fastest pit stop
1 N Rosberg 29.417s
2 M Schumacher 29.473s
3 N Rosberg 29.549s

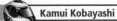

Adrian Sutil
"We've been aiming to get both cars in the points for a while. It was a normal race for me, though I lost track position under the safety car as Rosberg got ahead."

Kamui Kobayashi
"Our pace was OK, but due to traffic and a strategy error when the safety car was out, it didn't work out. I was surprised when I got the drive-through penalty."

Sebastien Buemi
"We didn't have enough downforce, reflected in the fact we had very good top speed down the straights, but weren't fast enough through the corners."

Jarno Trulli
"I got ahead of the Renaults and a Toro Rosso and was able to keep ahead. Mid-race, Jaime hit my left rear and I had to pit. Later I had a gearbox problem."

Daniel Ricciardo
"I got my nose clipped on lap 1. It was bunched into Turn 8 and I didn't have a clear line, so wanted to keep that line for the next corner and had a touch."

Timo Glock
"I had a good start, but lost my position with Jerome. Ricciardo drove into my rear right, and after that I had bad degradation then lost the rear and hit the wall."

Paul di Resta
"My first Singapore GP was fun. I don't think the safety car helped, as I still had a lot of life left in the supersoft tyres mid-race, but it didn't really hurt me either."

Sergio Perez
"I was on a two-stop strategy, starting on the supersofts and changing after 15 laps to the softs. For my second stop I had to pit earlier, as I had a puncture."

Jaime Alguersuari
"I wasn't expecting much from the race. I had a lot of oversteer after the first few laps. With a couple of laps to go I hit the barriers and that was my race over."

Heikki Kovalainen
"The strategy worked out well for us and the boys worked brilliantly to get me out quickly each time, helping me make sure I could stay ahead of Petrov at each stop."

Vitantonio Liuzzi
"I was forced to change to my last set of tyres early, as the rear was going. Immediately I felt I had less grip, locked the front in Turn 14 and broke my wing."

Jerome d'Ambrosio
"I had a good start, pushed hard on the first two laps, then tried to save the tyres, as we were following a two-stop strategy, so the last stint was long and not easy."

2011 FORMULA 1
JAPANESE GRAND PRIX
SUZUKA

JB WON, SEB TWO

Jenson Button drove a superb race to win, ahead of Fernando Alonso and a jubilant Sebastian Vettel, whose third place confirmed him as back-to-back World Champion

Sebastian Vettel finally put the 2011 World Championship title beyond any mathematical doubt in Japan, and he did it at a track where so many titles have been won in the past.

But on this day Vettel had to cede a little of the limelight to Jenson Button. The Brit has scored some great wins during his McLaren career, but he was in danger of being typecast as someone who truly thrives only when rain provides an opportunity to claim a victory through clever strategy. In Suzuka everything finally fell into place, and he achieved a brilliantly judged victory on one of the most challenging tracks on the calendar, displaying the perfect combination of speed and savvy.

The previous day, Vettel had given RBR yet another pole, but this time the German cut it fine, beating Button by the tiny margin of 0.009s.

Lewis Hamilton was fastest on the first runs in Q3, and had every chance of holding on to pole after the second. However, he failed to get round before the chequered flag in order to start his crucial last lap. Backing off to find a gap behind his team-mate, he found himself shuffled out when Mark Webber and Michael Schumacher – both of whom were equally

Things very nearly came unstuck for Jenson at the start. Having got away well, he found himself squeezed towards the grass on the right by Vettel, and in backing off he also allowed his team-mate through. All that hard work done in practice and qualifying to outpace Lewis meant nothing.

"I think he had a fairly aggressive manoeuvre pulled on him at the start," said Martin Whitmarsh. "He had to lift out of KERS and throttle and steer to avoid, otherwise without his actions there would have been a big shunt there, and if he needed any more motivation, I'm sure that gave him a bit more!"

Jenson had to bide his time behind Hamilton in the early laps, which became a bit frustrating when Lewis began to lose performance, with what the team believed at the time to be a slow puncture. When Hamilton really began to struggle, Jenson finally hustled his way past. He then had Vettel in his sights, albeit 5.4s up the road.

Although the handling issue prompted Hamilton's early first stop on lap 8, that decision also helped to encourage Red Bull to bring Seb in a lap later. Jenson came in a lap after that, and in the pitlane alone he gained almost 1.2s on the German, so the gap shrank a little.

In fact, McLaren's pitlane times would be consistently quicker all day. As Webber pointed out, Suzuka, like Silverstone, is a track where having the last pit box is a disadvantage – the Red Bull drivers could not get up to 100kph by the time they got to the line that allowed them to release the limiter, and that cost vital tenths.

Over the second stints, the gap from Vettel to Button came down to 2.5s, and then shrank further to 1.6s by lap 18. Sebastian was suddenly under distinct pressure.

Seb stopped for a second time on lap 19, and Jenson again came in a lap later, this time gaining

ABOVE As the field streams away, Sebastian Vettel mounts a robust defence of his pole position, forcing Jenson Button on to the grass

BELOW The magnetic attraction between Lewis Hamilton and Felipe Massa continued at Suzuka, the two drivers clashing once again

OPPOSITE Local hero Kamui Kobayashi qualified an excellent seventh, but faded to 13th in the race

keen to start a new lap and beat the flag – hustled their way past.

Hamilton's problems left Vettel free to set a last-lap time that put him on top, and Button just failed to dislodge him with his final effort. Vettel was helped by the fact that a new front wing arrived just before the session. The team had arrived with only two of the latest-spec wings, and Vettel had to revert to an old one after crashing in practice.

Behind Button and Hamilton, Felipe Massa took a good fourth place, ahead of Fernando Alonso. Webber had a scrappy session, and was at a loss to explain why he ended up only sixth.

INSIDE LINE
JENSON BUTTON
McLAREN DRIVER

"This circuit is very special to all of us. We love this place, so to get a victory here really does mean a lot. I need to say a big thanks to the team for the improvements we have had over the last few races.

It's good to see three different cars so close. It shows how competitive F1 is at the moment. The fans in Japan are so supportive, and we've all tried to plant a good memory in their minds after a tough year for Japan.

My start was very good, maybe too good, and I ended up on the grass! I said on the radio that I thought Sebastian would get a penalty for that – I'm not going to lie. From my point of view I had half my car up the inside. I thought he was coming across more than I expected and didn't give me any room.

Maybe when I watch it back on TV I will have a different opinion. The stewards said it was fair, so that's it. Sometimes, when you get a good start and the guy in front doesn't, these things happen. If we all get off the line at the same speed, it's not normally an issue. We'll put it behind us. But I might not lift off next time…

I was looking after the tyres during the race and also conserving some fuel at times, so the last five laps weren't the most enjoyable, under pressure from Fernando, but we got it home.

The car was really great around Suzuka all weekend. The Red Bulls are always so strong on these fast circuits, especially with the changes of direction, so for us to win here really does mean a lot, as we've been fighting these characteristics for two years now.

It was a very interesting race, because the tyre wear was massive, and it wasn't just down to being quick over one lap. You really had to think the race through and I enjoyed it out there.

Suzuka's always a special place to race. It's a fast, flowing track that's also unforgiving, so one little mistake and it's game over. To win here is among my most special victories. I don't think I've ever won a race on such a high-speed circuit – even if Monza last year was close! – so it means a lot to me."

0.9s just in the pitlane. Helped also by a mega in-lap, Button came out in front of Vettel, an eventuality that even McLaren had not foreseen.

"I think we were all very pleasantly surprised to see Jenson come out ahead at that stop," said McLaren Technical Director Paddy Lowe. "A nice surprise! I can only assume we had a very good stop that time, and Vettel didn't. I think when we saw Vettel stop earlier than Jenson, the thinking wasn't particularly, 'Oh dear he's going to get the jump', but more 'great we've got more laps on the tyre than him, and that's going to help us out'."

A clash between Massa and Hamilton at the chicane left debris on the track, and a safety car was deployed between laps 24 and 27, making the second half of the race potentially more interesting.

The intervention didn't really affect the lead battle, since all the top runners had made their second stops, and it gave everyone an equal chance to give their tyres a little break. But what it did do was close up the rest of the field so that as soon as the third-stop sequence began, there was a much greater chance that the top guys would come out in traffic.

The crucial thing was now that third stop, and the

transition to the medium tyre. Vettel set the ball rolling when he came in on lap 33, earlier than McLaren had expected. And sure enough, thanks to the safety car having bunched the field up, he came out in traffic.

McLaren was happy enough with Jenson's pace on a clear track with older softs relative to Vettel on his new mediums, and Button was duly kept out for another three laps. Again, he had a much faster pitlane time, gaining 0.7s on Vettel, but he didn't even need it, as by now he had such an advantage. He easily came out of the pits still in front. Indeed, Vettel also lost second place to Alonso during the pit-stop sequence.

It's easy to suggest that RBR made a tactical misjudgement with the early stop, but the tyre situation had forced Vettel's hand, and he had to pit when he did.

"Seb put himself back into some traffic," said Whitmarsh. "The tyres fell away fairly quickly, so when they went, I'm sure they didn't have a choice. That was the key moment of the race really, conserving tyres, opening up a sufficient gap."

After his final stop, Jenson had to run 17 laps to the flag on the medium tyre. But his main rival now

was Alonso, who was clearly making his tyres last well – and his later stop meant that his were a lap younger.

Jenson spent the rest of the race brilliantly managing the gap to the Ferrari, while also paying urgent heed to fuel consumption, as the team began to have concerns about getting to the flag and having enough left for the FIA fuel sample.

"He looked after his tyres, and he was looking after them in each stint," said Whitmarsh. "And this race was about what you could do to make those tyres last. Overall, great control, but he still had the pace at the end, and still did the fastest lap of the race. I think we were just taking it easy at the end, he controlled himself, let them get close enough, but didn't let them in the DRS zone, and just did a good job."

The fuel situation was tight, however, and that's why Jenson pulled over just after the finish line, just as Alonso had stopped on the slowing-down lap in Germany earlier in the season. You can't do that in qualifying, but the FIA turns a blind eye in races, as long as it doesn't become routine. The argument from the teams is that they can't be accurate enough to run fuel that low as a matter of course, so we would never see 20 cars stopping after the flag. Jenson

TALKING POINT
VETTEL'S DOUBLE

Sebastian Vettel's title-winning season made him the youngest back-to-back World Champion in the sport's history, at just 24.

Vettel is the ninth man to achieve the feat, joining Alberto Ascari, Juan Manuel Fangio, Jack Brabham, Alain Prost, Ayrton Senna, Michael Schumacher,

Mika Häkkinen and Fernando Alonso.

His speed has been obvious ever since he memorably won his first grand prix for Toro Rosso, in mixed conditions at Monza in 2008. Toro Rosso's technical chief, Giorgio Ascanelli, remembers the first time he realised he had something special on his hands.

"It was Valencia that year. I decided to run many laps in the Friday morning practice and we topped the timing sheet for the first time. In the afternoon he had tyres that were already worn, he had full tanks, and I was looking at the times thinking, 'Where did this come from?'

"In the evening I said to him, 'you were the fastest guy on the circuit.'

"He said, 'Yes, this morning.'

"I said: 'No, this afternoon on full tanks.'

"He said: 'How do you mean?'

"I said: 'You've done one lap which completely stands out from anything else.' I got the traces, showed him and told him to go away and think about it. He did. And he never missed a beat after that!

"In the last part of '08, Sebastian knew he was going to Red Bull. His first comment was, 'Webber… That'll be OK. He makes some mistakes that I don't understand.'

"I said to him: 'Wait…'

"The second race of '09, he grabbed my arm in the paddock and said, 'Oops… he's fast!'

"I said: 'Told you…' and laughed. He took about a year and a half to take the size of it and then…

"He's grown. Enormously. He's on a learning curve that's atomic, and if you look at how few mistakes he has made this year, it's amazing.

"Last year I had to stay at home for Korea, but I called him after the race and said, 'Bad that you blew the engine. You've got to push now and forget the rest.' He said 'Well, I'm doing it all the time.' And he is.

"When I hear about drivers producing an extraordinary lap, I'm asking myself the question: what makes it extraordinary? Only because they don't do it all the time! When Vettel does it all the time it's no longer extraordinary, and that's what he's doing.

"I really think the guy has an edge on everybody now. He's happy, confident. He reminds me of Casey Stoner on the Ducati – couldn't put a foot wrong. He's fit, he's strong, he doesn't make mistakes, he enjoys it, he likes the team. Perfect. Life is sweet!"

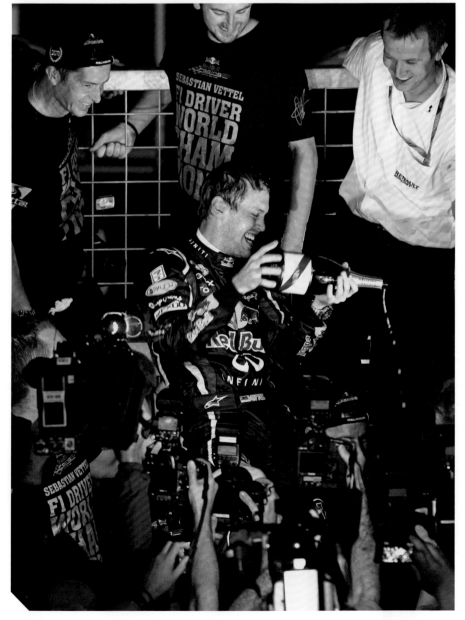

couldn't have driven back to *parc fermé* and provided a sample – it was that tight.

"We were not taking any chances!" conceded Whitmarsh. "One thing you can guarantee is that if you stop, you're going to have at least a litre of fuel taken out, and we knew we were OK. We were able to get twice as much as we needed out of the car to do that.

"I think Jenson was just driving with great confidence and great smoothness to score a fantastic win. He was the guy who did the fastest lap, which he did two weeks ago as well, so he had the pace. And he just knew how to control it. He used his experience and he used his intellect to preserve tyres and be truly competitive."

Vettel was right behind Alonso in third, and happy to be on the podium to celebrate his second championship. Alonso conceded that it wasn't easy to stay ahead.

"With Sebastian, it was difficult to keep him behind, as at that part of the race he was quicker than us," he said. "I tried to defend the position in braking for the last corners and into the first corner as well, where the DRS was active. After we had done this job we saw we were catching Jenson a little bit, so we tried in the last couple of laps but, as we saw later on, Jenson was taking care about tyres, about his car, so it was impossible to fight for victory this time."

Webber made it a good day for Red Bull with fourth place, while Hamilton was a distant fifth after he fell off the pace in the second half of the race. In fact he finished 24 seconds behind his team-mate, and this in a race where a safety car had allowed him to regain time lost in the first half of the race.

"We knew after three or four laps that we had quite a big pressure differential across the rear axle [McLaren speak for puncture!]," said Whitmarsh. "At that point we knew that it wasn't helping him, but we also knew that if he stopped, he was destined to four-stop.

"So we tried to hang on as long as we could. But that harmed him a little bit, probably ultimately cost him a couple of places, but the alternative would have been a four-stop, which would have been very difficult. He was struggling a bit more on the tyres and a bit more for balance than Jenson."

Behind Hamilton, Massa took sixth, ahead of Schumacher. Clever two-stop strategies helped to earn eighth for Sergio Perez, and ninth for Vitaly Petrov. Meanwhile Nico Rosberg rose from a disastrous 23rd on the grid to take a welcome point for 10th.

ABOVE LEFT After taking the flag, Jenson Button parked his car at the end of the pitlane due to concerns about running out of fuel on the slowing-down lap. His girlfriend, Jessica Michibata, shows her appreciation as he jogs down the pitlane towards the podium.

LEFT The back-to-back World Champion celebrates with his team

SNAPSHOT FROM
JAPAN

CLOCKWISE FROM RIGHT Sebastian Vettel passes the Suzuka ferris wheel on his way to a second succcessive World Championship; the 2011 grid's five World Champions sign paintings of their Championship-winning cars for a charity auction; a range of 'official' puppets was on sale to raise money for the Japanese tsunami victims, Bernie Ecclestone and Kamui Kobayashi proving popular; several drivers wore special helmets in memory of the tsunami victims; John Button, Jenson Button's girlfriend, Jessica Michibata, and her sister Angelica watch the podium celebrations; Sebastian Vettel had a light 'off' on Friday morning, nudging the barriers; enthusiastic local Red Bull fans; veteran Japanese driver Satoru Nakajima demonstrated his 1990 Lotus 102; a message from the marshals

RACE RESULTS

JAPAN
SUZUKA

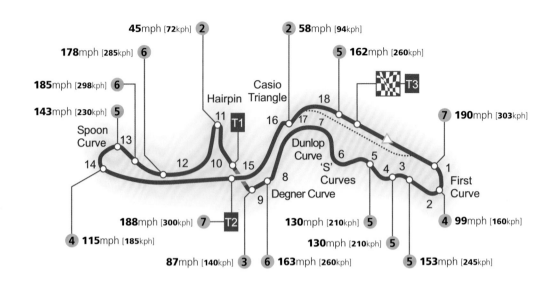

RACE DATE October 9th
CIRCUIT LENGTH 3.608 miles
NO. OF LAPS 53
RACE DISTANCE 191.224 miles
WEATHER Sunny & dry, 24°C
TRACK TEMP 31°C
ATTENDANCE 199,000
LAP RECORD Kimi Räikkönen,
1m31.540s, 141.904mph, 2005

PRACTICE 1

	Driver	Time	Laps
1	J Button	1m33.634s	20
2	L Hamilton	1m33.725s	18
3	S Vettel	1m34.090s	22
4	F Alonso	1m34.372s	24
5	M Webber	1m34.426s	25
6	J Alguersuari	1m34.937s	23
7	F Massa	1m35.585s	27
8	S Buemi	1m35.590s	25
9	M Schumacher	1m36.033s	22
10	V Petrov	1m36.370s	18
11	B Senna	1m36.487s	18
12	N Hulkenberg	1m36.700s	21
13	K Kobayashi	1m36.948s	24
14	P di Resta	1m36.949s	22
15	S Perez	1m37.103s	29
16	N Rosberg	1m38.197s	18
17	R Barrichello	1m38.331s	11
18	P Maldonado	1m38.446s	8
19	J Trulli	1m39.168s	10
20	K Chandhok	1m39.946s	22
21	T Glock	1m40.872s	13
22	J d'Ambrosio	1m41.019s	24
23	D Ricciardo	1m41.106s	25
24	N Karthikeyan	1m41.775s	25

PRACTICE 2

	Driver	Time	Laps
1	J Button	1m31.901s	32
2	F Alonso	1m32.075s	33
3	S Vettel	1m32.095s	35
4	M Webber	1m32.147s	28
5	F Massa	1m32.448s	34
6	M Schumacher	1m32.710s	26
7	N Rosberg	1m32.982s	27
8	L Hamilton	1m33.245s	26
9	V Petrov	1m33.446s	36
10	S Buemi	1m33.681s	33
11	J Alguersuari	1m33.705s	25
12	A Sutil	1m33.790s	36
13	S Perez	1m34.393s	35
14	B Senna	1m34.557s	27
15	P di Resta	1m34.601s	33
16	K Kobayashi	1m36.038s	33
17	H Kovalainen	1m36.225s	35
18	R Barrichello	1m37.123s	14
19	T Glock	1m37.440s	30
20	J d'Ambrosio	1m38.093s	30
21	P Maldonado	1m38.387s	16
22	D Ricciardo	1m38.763s	36
23	J Trulli	1m39.800s	24
24	V Liuzzi	1m42.480s	4

PRACTICE 3

	Driver	Time	Laps
1	J Button	1m31.255s	13
2	L Hamilton	1m31.762s	16
3	S Vettel	1m32.122s	18
4	F Alonso	1m32.279s	16
5	M Webber	1m32.401s	14
6	F Massa	1m32.429s	16
7	M Schumacher	1m32.725s	19
8	N Rosberg	1m32.878s	17
9	V Petrov	1m33.058s	15
10	A Sutil	1m33.424s	14
11	S Buemi	1m33.469s	18
12	J Alguersuari	1m33.545s	18
13	K Kobayashi	1m33.818s	17
14	S Perez	1m33.836s	21
15	P di Resta	1m33.990s	16
16	P Maldonado	1m34.321s	21
17	B Senna	1m35.389s	5
18	R Barrichello	1m35.651s	18
19	J Trulli	1m36.327s	16
20	H Kovalainen	1m36.912s	14
21	J d'Ambrosio	1m37.938s	17
22	T Glock	1m38.011s	16
23	D Ricciardo	1m38.355s	19
24	V Liuzzi	1m41.097s	8

QUALIFYING 1

	Driver	Time
1	K Kobayashi	1m32.626s
2	A Sutil	1m32.761s
3	F Alonso	1m32.817s
4	L Hamilton	1m32.843s
5	V Petrov	1m32.877s
6	J Button	1m32.947s
7	S Vettel	1m33.051s
8	S Buemi	1m33.064s
9	M Webber	1m33.135s
10	F Massa	1m33.235s
11	B Senna	1m33.359s
12	P di Resta	1m33.499s
13	M Schumacher	1m33.748s
14	P Maldonado	1m33.781s
15	R Barrichello	1m33.921s
16	S Perez	1m34.704s
17	J Alguersuari	1m35.111s
18	H Kovalainen	1m35.454s
19	J Trulli	1m35.514s
20	J d'Ambrosio	1m36.439s
21	T Glock	1m36.507s
22	D Ricciardo	1m37.846s
23	N Rosberg	No time
24	V Liuzzi	No time

QUALIFYING 2

	Driver	Time
1	L Hamilton	1m31.139s
2	S Vettel	1m31.424s
3	J Button	1m31.434s
4	M Webber	1m31.576s
5	F Alonso	1m31.612s
6	F Massa	1m31.909s
7	M Schumacher	1m32.116s
8	V Petrov	1m32.245s
9	B Senna	1m32.297s
10	K Kobayashi	1m32.380s
11	A Sutil	1m32.463s
12	P di Resta	1m32.746s
13	R Barrichello	1m33.079s
14	P Maldonado	1m33.224s
15	S Buemi	1m33.227s
16	J Alguersuari	1m33.427s
17	S Perez	No time

Best sectors – Practice
Sec 1	J Button	32.427s
Sec 2	J Button	41.116s
Sec 3	S Vettel	17.676s

Speed trap – Practice
1	M Webber	192.500mph
2	J Alguersuari	192.438mph
3	S Vettel	192.438mph

Best sectors – Qualifying
Sec 1	M Webber	32.111s
Sec 2	J Button	40.695s
Sec 3	F Alonso	17.468s

Speed trap – Qualifying
1	F Alonso	193.246mph
2	F Massa	191.320mph
3	B Senna	191.133mph

Sebastian Vettel
"We set ourselves the target to win the championship this year and so, to win it by Japan, with four more races to go, is hard and confusing to put into words."

Jenson Button
"Seb came across at me at the start, so I got on the grass and had to back off, losing a place. Fighting back was so satisfying, second only to a home victory."

Fernando Alonso
"I did my best and came close to winning. We know we're behind the Red Bulls and McLarens in qualifying, but in the race, with variables, we can exploit chances."

Michael Schumacher
"I'm very happy with what we achieved, as we maximised our potential. The team did a great job in finding performance and transforming it into the race."

Bruno Senna
"Vitaly squeezed me in the second corner, which made it hard for me to recover. For the rest of the race, I encountered lots of traffic and my tyres were degrading a lot."

Rubens Barrichello
"Everything seemed to be going our way, then the safety car was deployed. That was bad timing, as it closed the pack up and left us on the wrong tyre at the end."

Mark Webber
"I had contact with Michael, but he got away with it, while it bent my front wing at a crucial part of the race, just as I was trying to come back through the pack."

Lewis Hamilton
"I wasn't able to compete today, so I'll look at the data. I don't know what happened with Felipe – the car's mirrors vibrate at high speed, so I couldn't see him."

Felipe Massa
"The footage of the contact with Hamilton speaks for itself: he was struggling with his tyres and I had almost come alongside him and he moved over and hit me."

Nico Rosberg
"I had fun with a few nice passing moves. This is one of the toughest tracks for overtaking, so starting from the back of the grid meant that I had a pretty tough job."

Vitaly Petrov
"I started on the medium tyre, and it was hard to tell how the strategy was working, and it was a challenge for the first two stints against those on softer tyres."

Pastor Maldonado
"We started on the prime tyres and this hurt our pace in the first stint. We went onto the options at the second stop and that improved our pace considerably."

	Driver			1	5	10	15	20	25	30	35	40	45	50	53	
1	S Vettel															1
2	J Button															2
3	L Hamilton															3
4	F Massa															4
5	F Alonso															5
6	M Webber															6
7	K Kobayashi															7
8	M Schumacher															8
9	B Senna															9
10	V Petrov															10
11	A Sutil															11
12	P di Resta															12
13	R Barrichello															13
14	P Maldonado															14
15	S Buemi															15
16	J Alguersuari															16
17	S Perez															17
18	H Kovalainen															18
19	J Trulli															19
20	J d'Ambrosio															20
21	T Glock															21
22	D Ricciardo															22
23	N Rosberg															23
24	V Liuzzi															24

☼ Accident Ⓜ Mechanical failure Ⓟ Pit stop ☐ Safety Car ☐ Lapped Ⓑ Black flag

QUALIFYING 3

	Driver	Time
1	S Vettel	1m30.466s
2	J Button	1m30.475s
3	L Hamilton	1m30.617s
4	F Massa	1m30.804s
5	F Alonso	1m30.886s
6	M Webber	1m31.156s
7	K Kobayashi	No time
8	M Schumacher	No time
9	B Senna	No time
10	V Petrov	No time

GRID

	Driver	Time
1	S Vettel	1m30.466s
2	J Button	1m30.475s
3	L Hamilton	1m30.617s
4	F Massa	1m30.804s
5	F Alonso	1m30.886s
6	M Webber	1m31.156s
7	K Kobayashi	No time
8	M Schumacher	No time
9	B Senna	No time
10	V Petrov	No time
11	A Sutil	1m32.463s
12	P di Resta	1m32.746s
13	R Barrichello	1m33.079s
14	P Maldonado	1m33.224s
15	S Buemi	1m33.227s
16	J Alguersuari	1m33.427s
17	S Perez	No time
18	H Kovalainen	1m35.454s
19	J Trulli	1m35.514s
20	J d'Ambrosio	1m36.439s
21	T Glock	1m36.507s
22	D Ricciardo	1m37.846s
23	N Rosberg	No time
24	V Liuzzi	No time

RACE

	Driver	Car	Laps	Time	Avg. mph	Fastest	Stops
1	J Button	McLaren-Mercedes MP4-26	53	1h30m53.427s	126.121	1m36.568s	3
2	F Alonso	Ferrari 150 Italia	53	1h30m54.587s	126.094	1m36.882s	3
3	S Vettel	Red Bull-Renault RB7	53	1h30m55.433s	126.074	1m36.926s	3
4	M Webber	Red Bull-Renault RB7	53	1h31m01.498s	125.934	1m36.828s	3
5	L Hamilton	McLaren-Mercedes MP4-26	53	1h31m17.695s	125.562	1m37.645s	3
6	M Schumacher	Mercedes MGP W02	53	1h31m20.547s	125.497	1m37.916s	3
7	F Massa	Ferrari 150 Italia	53	1h31m21.667s	125.471	1m37.800s	3
8	S Perez	Sauber-Ferrari C30	53	1h31m32.804s	125.217	1m36.569s	2
9	V Petrov	Renault R31	53	1h31m36.034s	125.143	1m37.053s	2
10	N Rosberg	Mercedes MGP W02	53	1h31m37.749s	125.104	1m36.614s	3
11	A Sutil	Force India-Mercedes VJM04	53	1h31m47.874s	124.874	1m38.133s	3
12	P di Resta	Force India-Mercedes VJM04	53	1h31m55.753s	124.695	1m37.970s	3
13	K Kobayashi	Sauber-Ferrari C30	53	1h31m57.132s	124.664	1m39.724s	2
14	P Maldonado	Williams-Cosworth FW33	53	1h31m57.621s	124.654	1m37.645s	3
15	J Alguersuari	Toro Rosso-Ferrari STR6	53	1h32m00.050s	124.598	1m37.411s	2
16	B Senna	Renault R31	53	1h32m06.055s	124.463	1m38.407s	2
17	R Barrichello	Williams-Cosworth FW33	53	1h32m07.618s	124.540	1m39.080s	3
18	H Kovalainen	Lotus-Renault T128	53	1h32m21.251s	124.122	1m39.297s	3
19	J Trulli	Lotus-Renault T128	53	1h32m29.567s	123.936	1m39.561s	3
20	T Glock	Virgin-Cosworth MVR02	51	1h31m41.117s	120.305	1m41.704s	3
21	J d'Ambrosio	Virgin-Cosworth MVR02	51	1h31m42.392s	120.277	1m41.794s	3
22	D Ricciardo	HRT-Cosworth F111	51	1h31m44.888s	120.222	1m41.437s	3
23	V Liuzzi	HRT-Cosworth F111	50	1h30m59.218s	118.849	1m42.409s	3
R	S Buemi	Toro Rosso-Ferrari STR6	11	Lost wheel	-	1m42.107s	1

CHAMPIONSHIP

	Driver	Pts
1	S Vettel	324
2	J Button	210
3	F Alonso	202
4	M Webber	194
5	L Hamilton	178
6	F Massa	90
7	N Rosberg	63
8	M Schumacher	60
9	V Petrov	36
10	N Heidfeld	34
11	A Sutil	28
12	K Kobayashi	27
13	P di Resta	20
14	J Alguersuari	16
15	S Perez	13
16	S Buemi	13
17	R Barrichello	4
18	B Senna	2
19	P Maldonado	1

	Constructor	Pts
1	Red Bull-Renault	518
2	McLaren-Mercedes	388
3	Ferrari	292
4	Mercedes	123
5	Renault	72
6	Force India-Mercedes	48
7	Sauber-Ferrari	40
8	Toro Rosso-Ferrari	29
9	Williams-Cosworth	5

Fastest lap
J Button 1m36.568s
(134.515mph) on lap 52

Fastest speed trap
P Maldonado 189.953mph
Slowest speed trap
V Liuzzi 177.588mph

Fastest pit stop
1 N Rosberg 20.575s
2 N Rosberg 20.665s
3 M Schumacher 20.667s

Adrian Sutil

"My start was excellent, though I lifted as Kobayashi had a poor start. But what hurt my race was making my second stop the lap before the safety car came out."

Kamui Kobayashi

"The car went into anti-stall and I lost five places. Then the safety car came out at a bad moment for my strategy, as I then had to go to the end on the mediums."

Sebastien Buemi

"I had a great start, later running 10th before my first stop. I felt vibration at Turn 1, then saw the right front wheel wasn't on properly and it came off at Turn 4."

Jarno Trulli

"After a few laps, it felt like I had a gearbox problem, but then the safety car came out and I was able to close on Heikki and we both had a good run to the end."

Daniel Ricciardo

"We've got to be happy about being only a few tenths behind the Virgins. At one stage I was in front, but the safety car came out at a time that didn't suit us."

Timo Glock

"I passed Jerome at the start, then went for an early stop, but my right rear didn't go on well. We switched to three stops with the safety car and I got by Jerome."

Paul di Resta

"I made an awesome start, gaining four places, but the safety car spoilt our strategy, as it helped those making two stops, so they caught us in the final laps."

Sergio Perez

"I'm very happy to have scored after technical problems in qualifying. I had to start 17th, but the strategy worked out very well, but it was hard as I had flu."

Jaime Alguersuari

"I had the same strategy as Perez, but he seemed to be 1s faster. I was hitting the limiter, so couldn't find the speed to pass and was losing downforce behind others."

Heikki Kovalainen

"I got up to 14th at the start. The car worked well on the soft tyres, then the safety car came out and bunched everyone up. From there, it was a race to the flag."

Vitantonio Liuzzi

"I paid the price for doing hardly any laps before the race. I went out with a blind set-up and suffered huge degradation with the rear tyres, especially the rear left."

Jerome d'Ambrosio

"I had a good start and first part of the race, but I'm not sure if we went for the best strategy option, as I lost my position to Timo in the pits, which is a shame."

**2011 FORMULA 1
KOREAN GRAND PRIX**
YEONGAM

RED BULL'S RETAINER

Sebastian Vettel's tenth win of the season, together with a third-place finish for Mark Webber, ensured that Red Bull Racing retained the constructors' world title in Korea

Many times in 2011 we had seen Sebastian Vettel secure pole position, make a good start, build up a lead, and control the race from the front. However, in Korea a superb pole effort from Lewis Hamilton gave us the enticing prospect of a different kind of race, one in which Seb would have to do the chasing.

Vettel didn't have to chase for long. He snuck past Hamilton on the first lap, and thereafter recreated the familiar scenario from past races, staying safely ahead, his win helping to clinching the constructors' title for his team. It was the opposite of the normal situation, in that this time McLaren had the quicker qualifying package, and Red Bull had the faster car on Sunday.

Fortunately, Hamilton and Mark Webber kept us entertained with a fabulous battle for second – one that was eventually joined by Jenson Button and Fernando Alonso. The 2011 championships may have been sewn up, but there was still potential for entertainment.

Korea was always going to be interesting given Pirelli's decision to bring its soft and supersoft tyres. After the soggy 2010 weekend, the teams still had relatively little dry-weather knowledge of the venue, and the learning process was not helped when Friday was washed out.

"Lewis Hamilton should be proud of what he did here in Korea. He will never be satisfied unless he's winning races easily, but I think it was a great, great drive.

He should leave Korea feeling that it was a thorough, professional, brilliant piece of race driving – to be in a position to defend like that throughout the race, with a car that wasn't performing like it should have done.

Lewis, fairly early on, lost about 10 points of downforce, which was caused by congealed tyre rubber blocking a slot gap in the front wing.

That's why, although we want to win races, in the circumstances it was a brilliant piece of race driving. It's easy to win races when you're in front and you've got the best car, but real style and real class come when you've clearly got a car that's not performing as it should do.

When you haven't got DRS and you've got a quicker car behind you with a determined driver like Webber, then to be able to hold on and hold on like that, was a truly brilliant drive.

When Lewis looks at all the data, I think he will be really satisfied with the weekend's work. Satisfied with his job, satisfied with what he did – but not satisfied with being second and not first.

He may have talked about redeeming himself, but he didn't have to redeem himself with me. I don't think he has to redeem himself with anyone, and I can't speak more highly of the job he did in those circumstances. I think he should be delighted with it.

Equally, Jenson produced another brilliant, measured drive. On Jenson's car, too, we discovered after the race that he was also hurting from damage to his car – caused by a rock hitting the front wing.

The resulting understeer doubtless impaired Jenson's ability to close down Mark Webber in the track's final sector, and therefore meant he was unable to mount a sustained attack in the DRS zone.

Nevertheless, today showed that we have a very good car. While we acknowledge the achievement of Red Bull Racing in securing the constructors' championship, we have scored 65 points in the last two races. There are three races remaining in 2011 – and I know I speak for the whole team when I say that we will want to win all three."

It was clear even in Friday's rain that McLaren were more comfortable than RBR. Accepting that this time the team might have to give up on pole, RBR focused much more on race running in the single, dry FP3 session than did McLaren. And that led to RBR's unusual decision to use supersofts all the way through qualifying, and save three brand-new sets of softs per driver for the race.

It was a fascinating scenario, in that it signalled RBR's provisional plan for Sunday, with a choice of three stops and an option–prime–prime–prime strategy.

Meanwhile, Hamilton bounced back from his recent slump to take pole. Lewis was fastest in Q1, Q2 and on the first run in Q3, and he went even faster on his second and final run in Q3. It was the first pole for both the driver and his team since Canada the previous year and, remarkably, also the first time that Red Bull had been knocked off the top spot in 2011.

Vettel had to settle for second, and for a while it looked as though Seb might be behind both McLarens. However, Jenson Button's challenge faded in Q3 as he had to settle for third. Webber abandoned his final run, but had earlier set a time that was good enough for fourth, while for the second race in a row Felipe Massa beat Ferrari team-mate Fernando Alonso as the pair secured fifth and sixth.

Going into Sunday, McLaren had the boost of knowing that both Red Bulls would be starting from the dirty side of the track. So it was that the silver cars duly made good initial getaways, but later round the lap things went wrong.

Vettel made a great pass on Hamilton at Turn 4, in what was arguably his best move of the season. It was certainly an important one, on a par with his pass of Alonso in Italy after the safety car. On both occasions he knew he had to recover his usual place at the front as soon as possible.

Further back, Jenson was bundled down to eighth by the end of the first lap.

"We had good launches, but I think our first lap could have been better," said Whitmarsh with some understatement. "Jenson got bumped by Massa and, probably in his desire to get back, locked up, and that let a few more through. We were eighth at the end of the first lap, and that took a little bit to come back from..."

Vettel didn't disappear into the distance, as had often been the case in 2011, but after a few laps he began edging away from Hamilton. It was soon apparent that the McLarens didn't have the expected race pace.

"An unbelievable start from the dirty side," said Christian Horner. "A great move from Seb, he made it stick and then got his head down and got on with it. After the Friday and Saturday morning performance, we really didn't expect that. We expected the McLarens to be a lot, lot stronger."

In fact, understeer problems soon proved to be a massive handicap for both McLaren drivers – in Hamilton's case tyre debris had lodged itself in the front wing.

"We had it on both cars," said Whitmarsh. "Particularly on Lewis's, we lost front downforce. We couldn't really dial it out of the car all race, so that was ruining the tyres. As a consequence of that we weren't quite quick enough to get the job done this afternoon."

OPPOSITE TOP Sebastian Vettel passed pole-position man Lewis Hamilton on lap 1, with a decisive move down the inside between turns 3 and 4 – a move that determined the outcome of the race. Here, the field snakes past the pit boards on lap 2

OPPOSITE BOTTOM Jaime Alguersuari qualified strongly and drove a fine race to take seventh from Nico Rosberg on the final lap

TOP Vitaly Petrov misjudged his braking while battling with Fernando Alonso, and hit Michael Schumacher, resulting in the retirement of both the Mercedes and the Renault

ABOVE Heikki Kovalainen had a sound race for Lotus, finishing 14th, ahead of both Saubers

ABOVE Bruno Senna takes in the industrial views on his way to a disappointing 13th place for Renault

BELOW Jenson Button kept a watching brief on the 30-lap battle for second between Mark Webber and Lewis Hamilton

OPPOSITE Felipe Massa led team-mate Fernando Alonso for much of the race, until the Spaniard emerged ahead following the final pit stops

Lewis knew early on that he wouldn't be able to stay on terms with Vettel, although through the first stint he stayed safely clear of Webber, who'd enjoyed a better-than-usual first lap.

At the first stops, the focus for McLaren was more on Jenson. He lost a drag race out of the pits with Nico Rosberg, passed him when the Merc ran wide, and then lost out on DRS on the following straight!

He soon got back past again and, by pitting earlier, he also jumped both the Ferraris. Almost immediately after the first stops – mere seconds in the case of Vettel, who had waited until everyone else was done before coming in – the safety car came out after

a spectacular collision between a clumsy Vitaly Petrov and Michael Schumacher.

On-track for laps 17–20, the safety car closed up the gaps and ensured that we had a much more interesting race when it went green. Crucially, Vettel soon got out of Hamilton's DRS range, so by the time it was enabled after the restart, Lewis could do nothing about the German. Instead, he had his mirrors full of Webber.

What made the contest interesting was that Mark had followed RBR's pre-race plan and gone on to the soft, whereas Vettel went for more supersofts. The team literally didn't know which would be the perfect solution.

"We were still undecided at that point which was the better tyre," said Horner. "So we decided to split the cars. The tyres looked pretty evenly matched in fairness, so, give it to Pirelli, they got the choice right."

McLaren, meanwhile, stayed with the supersoft. Hamilton remained pretty close to Vettel through that middle stint, despite the distraction of the close attentions of Webber. A 'don't talk to me when I'm braking' radio message was indicative of how hard he was working...

The second stops were to be crucial, given that – thanks to the safety car giving everyone a breather – they were also to be the last.

Hamilton was the first to pit and, to the surprise of many, he was followed in by Webber. The stop was Mark's big chance to pass, so he could come in either before or after Lewis – doing it on the same lap was relying on a foul-up in the McLaren pits. There wasn't one, so Webber just followed him out. Mark himself made his disappointment pretty clear after the race.

"In the end, I think the second or the last pit stop was really what snookered us, I suppose," said Webber. "I was informing the team that my tyres were still good, but we still pitted. Yeah, that was

TALKING POINT
RED BULL'S DOUBLE

The Red Bull Racing 1–3 in Korea sealed back-to-back constructors' championships for Christian Horner's squad.

With his team having been somewhat sniffily referred to as "just a drinks manufacturer" in the past, it was time for Horner to reflect on a second crown with three races remaining.

"That race certainly made up for Korea last year, which was the most depressing race of our season!" he said.

"It was a great race between Mark and Lewis. Lewis was firm but fair, and Mark couldn't get off Turn 1 well enough to make use of the DRS and get us a 1–2. The DRS didn't seem to be particularly powerful, and McLaren looked to be good on torque on the way out of Turn 1.

"The priority now is to get Mark into second place in the championship. With the titles decided, the remaining races will be like three FA Cup Finals – they should be really exciting races and, I think, tight between us, McLaren and Ferrari.

"Winning the title feels very special. When you do it for the first time there's all the emotion of achieving it, but going into a year as champions means pressure to retain it.

"The team has improved in all areas, and we are a stronger unit than 12 months ago. Looking at the level of consistency, operationally and strategically the team has worked in total harmony, and that has allowed us to achieve the results that we have.

"I'm very proud to lead the team, and it's also special for Dietrich Mateschitz, who had the vision to buy Jaguar and should feel proud of what his team has achieved.

"What sets the team apart is the ambition and desire, and how it works as unit. Yes, they play their music loud, but they work longer and tougher hours against tight deadlines. It's that spirit that facilitated what we have achieved this year.

"We'd be foolish to underestimate the likes of Ferrari and McLaren and their pedigrees, and the likes of Mercedes-Benz. We're not foolish or arrogant enough to think that this performance is normal. It's abnormal and takes a superhuman effort to achieve.

"For us to win it once, they could probably tolerate, to do it twice probably upsets them a little and we've got continuity in all areas. But we've got less than four months to design and build a new car, which is why Adrian Newey elected not to attend in Korea.

"The remaining races are the only track time other than the young-driver tests between now and the birth of RB8, so we will be pushing right up until the chequered flag in Brazil. We want to do the hat-trick!"

ABOVE After narrowly losing out to his team-mate, Pastor Maldonado, in the battle to reach Q2, Rubens Barrichello leaves the pits on his way to a 12th-place finish for Williams as the final unlapped runner

BELOW Sebastian Vettel celebrates with his team after taking his 10th win of the season, and the 20th of his career, to seal back-to-back victories in the Constructors' World Championship for Red Bull Racing

a bit disappointing to do the same thing as Lewis, because we should have done something different..."

Horner explained it thus: "We looked at going for the undercut, because we could see Mark's performance on his out-lap on the previous set of tyres was very strong. Unfortunately, McLaren picked exactly the same lap as us, so it was a race in the pitlane."

The problem was that the team was also focusing on Vettel up ahead. Had they kept Mark out for that extra lap, Seb would have had to stay out for two laps longer than Lewis, and Hamilton was still close enough to be a threat. By bringing in Mark at the same time, Vettel could come in just a lap later, and the team could be confident that he would retain his lead.

Without enough time to change his troublesome front wing at the stop, Lewis was left to defend his second place with a car that was clearly giving him problems. He did it in great style.

Crucially, as the race played out, third-placed Webber couldn't get a perfect run on Lewis into the DRS zone. "Mark was quicker, but he couldn't get off Turn 1 and 2," said Horner. "We tried everything, but he just couldn't make the move stick."

All of this was of no concern to Vettel, who opened up a 12s advantage while the four cars behind closed up on each other, Alonso having joined the party after clearing Massa and finding some performance in the final stint. At the end of an intriguing contest, just 3.6s covered Hamilton, Webber, Button and Alonso.

It was ironic that after qualifying second so often, Hamilton converted his first pole into second place. Given his robust defence of his position, could he have hung on in front had he completed the first lap ahead of Vettel?

"It would have been tough, but no reason why he couldn't," said Whitmarsh. "There are lots of ifs and buts! In fairness, I think Sebastian did a great job, as he's done all year. We weren't quite quick enough to beat him today."

"I thought it was going to be a very, very hard race with the McLarens today," said Horner. "Our preparation yesterday morning was crucial. We put quite a bit of focus into the race, perhaps sacrificing something in qualifying, and it paid dividends. The other teams chose to focus on their qualifying preparation."

Behind the top five, Massa fell away from Alonso to finish sixth. Jaime Alguersuari worked his way up to seventh in great style, the Toro Rosso showing good pace and the Spaniard benefiting from a 'free' pit stop under the safety car. Rosberg took eighth, while the final points went to Sébastien Buemi and Paul di Resta.

SNAPSHOT FROM
KOREA

CLOCKWISE FROM RIGHT Pastor
Maldonado heads through the final
series of corners towards Yeongam
circuit's distinctive startline bridge; Lewis
Hamilton's McLaren cocooned overnight
in *parc fermé* conditions; Sebastian
Vettel sends the spray flying during wet
Friday-morning practice; a few words
of reassurance from Martin Whitmarsh
for Lewis Hamilton before the start; the
spoils of victory for Red Bull Racing;
Michael Schumacher's Mercedes looks
worse for wear after Vitaly Petrov's
assault; the well-drilled marshals spring
into action to clear debris from the track;
Felipe Massa looks rather despondent
about his prospects, even after out-
qualifying his team-mate; a huge floral
sculpture at the entrance to the circuit; a
peaceful welcome to Korea

RACE RESULTS
KOREA
YEONGAM

Official Results © [2011]
Formula One Administration Limited,
6 Princes Gate, London, SW7 1QJ.
No reproduction without permission.
All copyright and database rights reserved.

RACE DATE October 16th
CIRCUIT LENGTH 3.492 miles
NO. OF LAPS 55
RACE DISTANCE 192.060 miles
WEATHER Overcast, 22°C
TRACK TEMP 28°C
ATTENDANCE 160,236
LAP RECORD Sebastian Vettel,
1m39.605s, 126.101mph, 2011

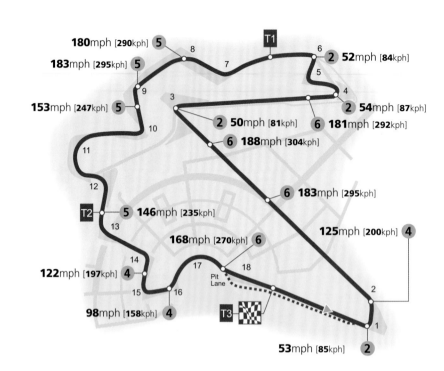

180mph [290kph] 5
183mph [295kph] 5
153mph [247kph] 5
2 52mph [84kph]
2 54mph [87kph]
2 50mph [81kph]
6 181mph [292kph]
6 188mph [304kph]
6 183mph [295kph]
5 146mph [235kph]
168mph [270kph] 6
125mph [200kph] 4
122mph [197kph] 4
98mph [158kph] 4
53mph [85kph] 2

#	PRACTICE 1 Driver	Time	Laps
1	M Schumacher	2m02.784s	10
2	S Vettel	2m02.840s	8
3	P di Resta	2m02.912s	12
4	A Sutil	2m03.141s	12
5	S Buemi	2m03.182s	9
6	K Kobayashi	2m03.292s	13
7	L Hamilton	2m03.391s	6
8	N Rosberg	2m04.311s	12
9	S Perez	2m04.797s	8
10	M Webber	2m05.183s	5
11	K Chandok	2m06.350s	11
12	P Maldonado	2m06.852s	11
13	J-E Vergne	2m07.541s	9
14	R Barrichello	2m08.218s	5
15	N Karthikeyan	2m08.832s	14
16	D Ricciardo	2m09.232s	14
17	J d'Ambrosio	2m12.658s	7
18	T Glock	2m14.508s	4
19	F Alonso	No time	5
20	F Massa	No time	1
21	B Senna	No time	1
22	V Petrov	No time	1
23	H Kovalainen	No time	1
24	J Button	No time	1

#	PRACTICE 2 Driver	Time	Laps
1	L Hamilton	1m50.828s	26
2	J Button	1m50.932s	19
3	S Vettel	1m52.646s	30
4	F Alonso	1m52.774s	25
5	M Webber	1m53.049s	27
6	J Alguersuari	1m53.402s	25
7	F Massa	1m53.707s	24
8	N Rosberg	1m53.914s	18
9	S Buemi	1m53.948s	27
10	P di Resta	1m53.957s	32
11	V Petrov	1m54.200s	26
12	A Sutil	1m54.392s	26
13	R Barrichello	1m54.831s	30
14	M Schumacher	1m54.965s	21
15	B Senna	1m55.187s	28
16	S Perez	1m55.203s	24
17	K Kobayashi	1m55.544s	23
18	P Maldonado	1m56.067s	22
19	H Kovalainen	1m56.669s	20
20	J Trulli	1m57.173s	19
21	T Glock	1m58.269s	25
22	J d'Ambrosio	1m59.458s	26
23	D Ricciardo	1m59.958s	19
24	V Liuzzi	2m00.165s	20

#	PRACTICE 3 Driver	Time	Laps
1	J Button	1m36.910s	18
2	L Hamilton	1m37.199s	18
3	M Webber	1m37.723s	23
4	F Alonso	1m38.029s	21
5	F Massa	1m38.434s	18
6	M Schumacher	1m39.559s	23
7	V Petrov	1m39.612s	20
8	A Sutil	1m39.660s	22
9	S Vettel	1m39.695s	22
10	N Rosberg	1m39.743s	25
11	P di Resta	1m39.847s	22
12	J Alguersuari	1m39.851s	20
13	S Buemi	1m39.964s	21
14	K Kobayashi	1m40.005s	17
15	S Perez	1m40.030s	18
16	B Senna	1m40.451s	19
17	P Maldonado	1m40.529s	20
18	R Barrichello	1m40.711s	22
19	H Kovalainen	1m41.909s	18
20	J Trulli	1m41.945s	13
21	T Glock	1m43.275s	19
22	J d'Ambrosio	1m44.377s	16
23	V Liuzzi	1m44.421s	22
24	D Ricciardo	1m45.143s	11

#	QUALIFYING 1 Driver	Time
1	L Hamilton	1m37.525s
2	J Button	1m37.929s
3	V Petrov	1m38.378s
4	F Alonso	1m38.393s
5	N Rosberg	1m38.426s
6	M Schumacher	1m38.502s
7	P di Resta	1m38.549s
8	F Massa	1m38.670s
9	A Sutil	1m38.789s
10	M Webber	1m39.071s
11	S Vettel	1m39.093s
12	S Perez	1m39.097s
13	B Senna	1m39.316s
14	S Buemi	1m39.352s
15	J Alguersuari	1m39.392s
16	K Kobayashi	1m39.464s
17	P Maldonado	1m39.436s
18	R Barrichello	1m39.538s
19	H Kovalainen	1m40.522s
20	J Trulli	1m41.101s
21	T Glock	1m42.091s
22	J d'Ambrosio	1m43.483s
23	V Liuzzi	1m43.758s
24	D Ricciardo	No time

#	QUALIFYING 2 Driver	Time
1	L Hamilton	1m36.526s
2	S Vettel	1m37.285s
3	M Webber	1m37.292s
4	J Button	1m37.302s
5	F Massa	1m37.313s
6	F Alonso	1m37.352s
7	N Rosberg	1m37.892s
8	V Petrov	1m38.186s
9	A Sutil	1m38.219s
10	P di Resta	1m38.254s
11	J Alguersuari	1m38.315s
12	M Schumacher	1m38.354s
13	S Buemi	1m38.508s
14	K Kobayashi	1m38.775s
15	B Senna	1m38.791s
16	P Maldonado	1m39.189s
17	S Perez	1m39.443s

Best sectors – Practice			Speed trap – Practice			Best sectors – Qualifying			Speed trap – Qualifying		
Sec 1	L Hamilton	34.322s	1	J Alguersuari	199.211mph	Sec 1	J Button	34.168s	1	J Alguersuari	199.025mph
Sec 2	J Button	42.312s	2	S Buemi	199.087mph	Sec 2	L Hamilton	41.834s	2	S Buemi	198.838mph
Sec 3	L Hamilton	20.101s	3	M Schumacher	196.291mph	Sec 3	L Hamilton	19.730s	3	M Schumacher	196.601mph

 Sebastian Vettel

"I knew passing Lewis near the start would be difficult and I nearly went off under braking, but he was very fair and it was vital for us to get track position."

 Jenson Button

"I braked into Turn 3 on lap 1, but Felipe went inside and I got stuck outside. I fell to sixth, but I don't think that poor first lap would have changed my end result."

 **Fernando Alonso**

"As usual, Red Bull and McLaren were stronger in qualifying, but on Sunday we were all much closer. All in all, an interesting race with plenty of action."

 Michael Schumacher

"Another unfortunate end to a race that could have been encouraging. It's a pity, as the car was again very good in race trim and I'd already gained positions."

 **Bruno Senna**

"I got a bad start, and from then on it was always going to be an uphill battle. Being stuck behind a number of other cars again restricted my ability to score."

 **Rubens Barrichello**

"Once again the safety car didn't go my way, and that cost me places. That said, I still enjoyed the race and I had fun overtaking. It's just a pity we didn't score."

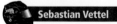 **Mark Webber**

"It's not easy to pass a driver of Lewis's calibre. I tried some moves and it was a good battle, as our cars had weaknesses and strengths in different areas."

 Lewis Hamilton

"There was so much pressure from Mark behind and it would have been easy to make a mistake, lock up or go wide. It feels good to be back."

Felipe Massa

"I made up some places on lap 1. Then, at the first stop, I rejoined behind Rosberg and Button, as the team had to keep me on my spot as Michael was coming in."

Nico Rosberg

"I flat-spotted my front tyres in the middle stint, so had to pit early, which made my last stint on primes long and I just wasn't able to defend against Jaime."

Vitaly Petrov

"I tried to defend my position from Fernando, but was in the braking zone on the dirty side of the track, which meant I locked my wheels and hit Michael."

Pastor Maldonado

"My pace was OK, but I made a mistake coming into the pits which cost me a drive-through. My race ended when the team spotted an engine problem."

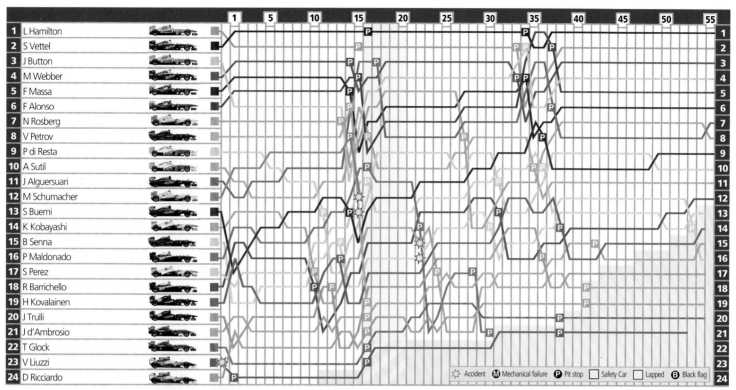

1	L Hamilton	
2	S Vettel	
3	J Button	
4	M Webber	
5	F Massa	
6	F Alonso	
7	N Rosberg	
8	V Petrov	
9	P di Resta	
10	A Sutil	
11	J Alguersuari	
12	M Schumacher	
13	S Buemi	
14	K Kobayashi	
15	B Senna	
16	P Maldonado	
17	S Perez	
18	R Barrichello	
19	H Kovalainen	
20	J Trulli	
21	J d'Ambrosio	
22	T Glock	
23	V Liuzzi	
24	D Ricciardo	

☆ Accident Ⓜ Mechanical failure Ⓟ Pit stop ▢ Safety Car ▢ Lapped Ⓑ Black flag

QUALIFYING 3

	Driver	Time
1	L Hamilton	1m35.820s
2	S Vettel	1m36.042s
3	J Button	1m36.126s
4	M Webber	1m36.468s
5	F Massa	1m36.831s
6	F Alonso	1m36.980s
7	N Rosberg	1m37.754s
8	V Petrov	1m38.124s
9	P di Resta	No time
10	A Sutil	No time

GRID

	Driver	Time
1	L Hamilton	1m35.820s
2	S Vettel	1m36.042s
3	J Button	1m36.126s
4	M Webber	1m36.468s
5	F Massa	1m36.831s
6	F Alonso	1m36.980s
7	N Rosberg	1m37.754s
8	V Petrov	1m38.124s
9	P di Resta	No time
10	A Sutil	No time
11	J Alguersuari	1m38.315s
12	M Schumacher	1m38.354s
13	S Buemi	1m38.508s
14	K Kobayashi	1m38.775s
15	B Senna	1m38.791s
16	P Maldonado	1m39.189s
17	S Perez	1m39.443s
18	R Barrichello	1m39.538s
19	H Kovalainen	1m40.522s
20	J Trulli	1m41.101s
21	T Glock	1m42.091s
22	J d'Ambrosio	1m43.483s
23	V Liuzzi	1m43.758s
24	D Ricciardo	No time

RACE

	Driver	Car	Laps	Time	Avg. mph	Fastest	Stops
1	S Vettel	Red Bull-Renault RB7	55	1h38m01.994s	117.372	1m39.605s	2
2	L Hamilton	McLaren-Mercedes MP4-26	55	1h38m14.013s	117.133	1m40.459s	2
3	M Webber	Red Bull-Renault RB7	55	1h38m14.471s	117.124	1m40.294s	2
4	J Button	McLaren-Mercedes MP4-26	55	1h38m16.688s	117.080	1m40.709s	2
5	F Alonso	Ferrari 150 Italia	55	1h38m17.683s	117.060	1m40.547s	2
6	F Massa	Ferrari 150 Italia	55	1h38m27.127s	116.873	1m40.541s	2
7	J Alguersuari	Toro Rosso-Ferrari STR6	55	1h38m51.532s	116.392	1m40.940s	2
8	N Rosberg	Mercedes MGP W02	55	1h38m56.047s	116.310	1m41.770s	2
9	S Buemi	Toro Rosso-Ferrari STR6	55	1h39m04.756s	116.133	1m40.537s	2
10	P di Resta	Force India-Mercedes VJM04	55	1h39m10.596s	116.019	1m42.102s	2
11	A Sutil	Force India-Mercedes VJM04	55	1h39m13.223s	115.968	1m42.014s	2
12	R Barrichello	Williams-Cosworth FW33	55	1h39m35.062s	115.544	1m42.371s	2
13	B Senna	Renault R31	54	1h38m08.447s	115.111	1m42.549s	2
14	H Kovalainen	Lotus-Renault T128	54	1h38m10.371s	115.073	1m42.456s	2
15	K Kobayashi	Sauber-Ferrari C30	54	1h38m23.507s	114.817	1m42.080s	3
16	S Perez	Sauber-Ferrari C30	54	1h38m23.897s	114.809	1m42.425s	3
17	J Trulli	Lotus-Renault T128	54	1h38m45.660s	114.387	1m43.009s	2
18	T Glock	Virgin-Cosworth MVR02	54	1h39m25.059s	113.632	1m44.536s	2
19	D Ricciardo	HRT-Cosworth F111	54	1h39m33.977s	113.462	1m44.870s	2
20	J d'Ambrosio	Virgin-Cosworth MVR02	54	1h39m36.409s	113.416	1m44.746s	2
21	V Liuzzi	HRT-Cosworth F111	52	1h38m34.293s	110.360	1m46.173s	3
R	P Maldonado	Williams-Cosworth FW33	30	Engine	-	1m44.689s	3
R	V Petrov	Renault R31	16	Accident damage	-	1m45.469s	1
R	M Schumacher	Mercedes MGP W02	15	Accident	-	1m45.327s	2

CHAMPIONSHIP

	Driver	Pts
1	S Vettel	349
2	J Button	222
3	F Alonso	212
4	M Webber	209
5	L Hamilton	196
6	F Massa	98
7	N Rosberg	67
8	M Schumacher	60
9	V Petrov	36
10	N Heidfeld	34
11	A Sutil	28
12	K Kobayashi	27
13	J Alguersuari	22
14	P di Resta	21
15	S Buemi	15
16	S Perez	13
17	R Barrichello	4
18	B Senna	2
19	P Maldonado	1

	Constructor	Pts
1	Red Bull-Renault	558
2	McLaren-Mercedes	418
3	Ferrari	310
4	Mercedes	127
5	Renault	72
6	Force India	49
7	Sauber	40
8	Toro Rosso-Ferrari	37
9	Williams-Cosworth	5

Fastest lap
S Vettel 1m39.605s
(126.101mph) on lap 55

Fastest speed trap
S Buemi 199.211mph
Slowest speed trap
V Liuzzi 189.207mph

Fastest pit stop
1 S Vettel 19.985s
2 N Rosberg 20.091s
3 S Vettel 20.170s

Adrian Sutil

"Our strategy was good, and I made my stop when the safety car came out, but our main rival was Toro Rosso and we didn't have the pace to beat them."

Kamui Kobayashi

"I changed to supersoft tyres after 10 laps, but when the safety car came out we lost the fresh-tyre advantage. I also had some damage to my rear wing."

Sébastien Buemi

"Someone hit me at the first corner, which cost me four places. After that, I had to work hard to pass the two Williams, the Saubers and Force Indias."

Jarno Trulli

"The start wasn't good, as I lost places into Turn 1, but made them back up again on the first set of tyres, and when we changed to the primes my times were great."

Daniel Ricciardo

"I had strong pace all race and had a good fight with the Virgins, so that's two races in a row in which we have been much more competitive with them."

Timo Glock

"I had a good car all race, very consistent to push. The problems that we thought we had were less of an issue. The Pirellis were very good and very consistent."

Paul di Resta

"Sadly, we didn't have the performance to match Toro Rosso. It looked like I might be able to hold off Buemi, but we came up six or seven laps short with the tyres."

Sergio Perez

"My start was good, but I got stuck behind some others and the places gained were lost. Early on with the soft tyres it was good, but I struggled with the supers."

Jaime Alguersuari

"Our two-stop strategy was the right one and it worked perfectly. The car had fantastic straight-line speed which is how I managed to overtake Nico on the final lap."

Heikki Kovalainen

"This is another big step forward for us, finishing 14th ahead of both Saubers and within touching distance of Senna on the final lap is our strongest race ever."

Vitantonio Liuzzi

"There must have been contact into Turn 3, as there was carbon flying. I hit something and then had problems locking the front, causing my contact in Turn 4."

Jerome d'Ambrosio

"It wasn't a great race. Compared to yesterday, though, and bearing in mind that we couldn't do big changes on the car because of the rules, today went pretty well."

2011 FORMULA 1 AIRTEL GRAND PRIX OF INDIA
BUDDH INTERNATIONAL CIRCUIT

SUPREME SEBASTIAN

The inaugural Indian Grand Prix saw another sublime performance from a dominant Sebastian Vettel as he took pole position, led every lap of the race and also set fastest lap

S ebastian Vettel may have taken pole, fastest lap and led every lap of the Indian GP, but his victory wasn't as easy as he made it look. In fact, the race was an intriguing one in terms of strategy, and there was plenty going on at the sharp end of the field. As so often in 2011, Vettel and his Red Bull team got their sums right at this brand-new venue.

Designed – like so many other circuits – by Hermann Tilke, the Buddh International Circuit attracted rave reviews from the drivers and teams, thanks to its challenging nature and dramatic gradients. There were some logistical issues – everything had an unfinished feel to it and there were problems with sewage and power cuts – but for the most part, F1 folk were won over by the enthusiasm of the locals, and wowed by the novel experience of being in such an extraordinary country.

And India certainly seemed to embrace F1. Although there were a few spaces in the grandstands come Sunday afternoon, there was still a large and enthusiastic crowd for this groundbreaking event.

The venue might have been new, but the outcome of qualifying was very familiar. Vettel was

INSIDE LINE
CHRISTIAN HORNER
**RED BULL RACING
TEAM PRINCIPAL**

Despite the fact that we turned KERS off and the engine down, Sebastian was still setting purple sectors! That was one of his best drives of the year. He was faultless.

He always wants to have the perfect weekend. We told him off about setting the fastest lap at the end of races. He said it wouldn't happen again after the last race and two weeks later here we are…

But he's a sensible boy and I think he builds in a margin. He just wanted to show what he was capable of. Short of putting a cow on the circuit there was nothing we could do to stop him!

It was fitting that Adrian Newey was up on the podium, too. He's had a remarkable year, and it's probably the most successful part of his career so far. We've broken the pole record this year, and now Sebastian has led more laps in a season than any other driver.

That record belonged to Nigel Mansell – also in an Adrian Newey car in '92. Adrian hasn't changed much, but Nigel has! Adrian's family were here too, which was nice.

We pitted Mark Webber when we did because he'd signalled to us that he wanted to come in. The dilemma was that because his tyres were effectively finished, he was going to be overtaken – or else Alonso would come in and get the undercut.

The only real chance of staying ahead was to pit him for the hard tyres, but unfortunately the out-lap performance wasn't strong enough. And, although Mark got a run on Fernando while the Ferrari was warming up its tyres, he couldn't make it stick, so just missed out on a podium.

He tried hard to pass Jenson early on, and we were concerned he was giving the tyres a hard time, then he found a reasonable rhythm. But when Fernando closed in, he was exposed either way.

I think the Indian Grand Prix was a brilliant event. There was strong reaction from the Indian public, and the fans felt excited and privileged to have a race.

Hats off to JayPee for building the track, to Bernie for putting it on, and Vijay Mallya as well, who had a hand in it. I think next year it will be even bigger. It's a really interesting place to come to. Driving to the circuit makes you feel like you're in a grand prix!

0.3s faster than nearest challenger Lewis Hamilton, although the McLaren driver was demoted to fifth after a yellow-flag speeding offence in Friday practice. Mark Webber thus moved up to second, ahead of Fernando Alonso, Jenson Button and Hamilton. Felipe Massa, who suffered a spectacular suspension failure after striking a kerb in qualifying, started sixth.

As for Sunday, the strategy challenge was the performance difference between the soft and hard Pirellis, the latter in use for the first time since Silverstone. The key was making the switch to the harder tyre at the right time, and not leaving yourself exposed to being overtaken because it was slow to warm up. The bottom line was that, if possible, you had to make the switch to the hard later than the guy you were racing.

Vettel made his customary good getaway, and, as has become his habit, began opening up an advantage on the first lap. Button got ahead of both Alonso and Webber to claim second place, while Hamilton had a bad start and lost a spot to Massa as he dropped to sixth. Meanwhile, there was some contact in the pack on the busy first lap, at both Turn 1 and Turn 3, and several drivers down the field had to make early pit visits.

Button had to work hard to fend off Webber in the early laps. Meanwhile, true to form, Vettel gradually edged away from his main pursuers and then waited for those behind him to pit, before coming in himself.

Most of the other key players came in on laps 16 and 17, Button stayed out until lap 18, and then Vettel came in a lap after that. It meant his tyres were a lap fresher than Button's for the rest of the middle stint, and it also helped to ensure that he could eventually make that crucial switch to the hards that much later.

"What we were very keen to do was establish a gap and then to ensure that we were always on slightly fresher tyres," said Christian Horner. "We would concede the undercut to McLaren by them pitting first, and of course they would eat into that gap on the out-lap. But our tyres were always that one lap fresher. We felt we'd got enough in hand to manage that."

Webber was the first of the quick guys to make that crucial change to hards, coming in on lap 37. It didn't seem to help him much – ultimately he lost a spot to Alonso – and that encouraged both Button and Vettel to stay out even longer. Jenson finally

OPPOSITE A dominant Sebastian Vettel leads away at the start of the first-ever Indian GP to build a gap ahead of the battling pack

ABOVE Kamui Kobayashi was hit at the first corner, resulting in his retirement due to a fractured oil line

BELOW Jenson Button fought hard with Mark Webber for second place early in the race, before taking the fight to Vettel in the closing laps

came in on lap 46, and Seb followed a lap later, giving himself a 13-lap run to the flag on hards.

He did actually lose a couple of seconds to Jenson during the stop sequence, but he was still 2.8s ahead after he pitted, and that was more than enough to allow him to pace himself to the flag.

He allowed himself one little luxury as he tried to complete a statistically perfect weekend. After Webber set fastest lap in his pursuit of Alonso, Seb suddenly found some pace and went quicker on the penultimate lap, and then faster still on the very last lap. Hearts skipped a beat on the RBR pit wall.

"At the end of the day, we have complete trust in him. I'm sure there was still a margin in there. He likes that little statistic to complete a perfect weekend," said Horner.

It was another brilliant drive to second from Button, and the only frustration for McLaren was that he had endured such a below-par qualifying. Had Jenson started a little higher – perhaps on the front row alongside Vettel – he might have had a better shot at a win.

"Once again it's the thing of, 'if only we could start from pole, and make it stick'," admitted

McLaren Technical Director Paddy Lowe. "Lewis had the pole in Korea, and didn't manage to make it stick on the first lap. I think we could control the race and we could win races, but again we weren't there. If Jenson had got P2, maybe the win would have been there for him. Unfortunately Sebastian had the pace to control it."

It wasn't just about a good start – in the early laps Jenson had to work hard to hang on to the second place he'd gained.

"For me, what was particularly impressive was how he defended from Webber once the DRS came through," said Lowe. "There were three or four laps there when Webber had the DRS, and I thought Jenson was a goner. He took some brilliant lines through Turn 4 to just defend the position legitimately. It was very, very close.

"It was a fantastic drive, really well controlled, as we're seeing more and more from Jenson. I think if he'd had a better day on Saturday he could have won the race."

Webber was in the unwelcome position of starting a promising second and then later in the race finding himself in fourth, trying to recover third

LEFT A busy scene on the undulating back straight early in the race, as Bruno Senna battles with Jaime Alguersuari at the head of the second half of the field

OPPOSITE BOTTOM After yet another tangle with Lewis Hamilton, Felipe Massa was forced to pit for a new nose, and later received a controversial drive-through penalty for his part in the clash, eventually retiring with suspension failure

BELOW Narain Karthikeyan made a return to HRT for his home race, finishing ahead of team-mate Daniel Ricciardo in 17th place

TALKING POINT
MASSA'S PENALTY

David Coulthard was among those who came down firmly on the side of Felipe Massa over the collision with Lewis Hamilton, their sixth this year, that saw the Ferrari driver given a drive-through penalty.

"For me it was a racing incident," Coulthard said. "At worst I felt Lewis was more to blame. I simply can't

understand how Felipe could have been deemed the guilty party.

"As drivers, we are always taught that the car behind is responsible so, to my mind, the stewards misinterpreted what happened. It was almost as if they felt that with Lewis receiving so many decisions against him this year, they were trying to redress the balance."

The fact is that Hamilton almost got alongside Massa early in the run to Turn 5 on lap 24, by deploying KERS. That then ran out, and he no longer had the additional momentum that would have brought him fully alongside.

KERS and DRS are complicating the analysis of such incidents, because drivers can make larger gains on rivals than was possible in the past merely by getting a better exit from the previous corner.

But, it is the position of the two cars at the turn-in point that is significant. Hamilton was on the dirty side of the track, as evidenced by the dust the McLaren was kicking up, while Massa headed right to take the normal racing line.

The stewards interpreted that as Massa giving Hamilton room and then closing the door, but the Brazilian said not.

"That was the normal line, the grippy part, and I braked later than him," Massa said. "When I turned he hit me in the back, not the side or wheel-to-wheel, in which case I wouldn't have closed the door."

The key point is that about the driver behind being responsible. The reasoning behind such etiquette is simple enough. On the run along a straight to a corner, drivers can

jockey for position, check their mirrors, attack, defend, feint, whatever, but when they reach the turn-in point and commit, they are looking ahead.

A full field of peripheral vision is 180 degrees. Not many have it. For most it's somewhere between 140 degrees and 180 degrees. If you're looking ahead, therefore, and someone isn't right alongside you or even slightly ahead, you aren't going to see them. You might know they're there, of course, but in the widely understood laws of motor racing, if someone is behind you, you aren't obliged to accommodate them.

Most agreed, however, that the situation between Hamilton and Massa is becoming highly charged, to the extent that they needed to have a quiet chat and get it sorted.

ABOVE Michael Schumacher had a strong race, making an excellent start and looking after his tyres to finish in fifth place, ahead of his Mercedes team-mate Nico Rosberg

BELOW Fernando Alonso and Jenson Button give Sebastian Vettel a champagne shower on the podium after one of his most emphatic performances of the season: he took pole, led every lap on his way to victory, and set fastest lap

you're exposed whether you stay out, or try and pit ahead of him. You're almost in a vicious circle by that stage."

When he came in on lap 37, Mark was about 1.5s ahead of Alonso. But after Fernando stayed out for two crucial laps on his old, soft tyres, the Ferrari emerged from its stop safely in front.

"Mark had signalled to us that he wanted to pit that lap," said Horner. "And the dilemma that you find yourself in is that because his tyres were effectively finished, he's either possibly going to be overtaken, maybe go off because the tyres are in such bad shape, or Fernando comes in and gets the undercut on the other tyres.

"The only real chance we had of staying ahead – despite the fact that we knew the out-lap performance of the hard tyre wasn't great – was to pit, and so we pitted for the hard. Unfortunately, the out-lap performance just wasn't strong enough. Despite getting a run on him whilst Fernando was struggling to get his tyres up to speed, he just couldn't make the move stick."

The big surprise was that Alonso was able to hold on at all in the final stint, given the form Ferrari had previously shown on the hard and medium tyre. At several earlier races, the Spaniard had drifted down the order after proving a sitting duck for quicker cars. This was another great race from Alonso, the man who always delivers the goods – and arguably had been flattering the Ferrari all year.

"Fernando did a really great performance, after a difficult start when he lost a position in the first corner," said team boss Stefano Domenicali. "In that respect, the only chance we could have had to overtake Mark was to do something different in terms of strategy, so I think on that, the team reacted very well.

"We said to Fernando we needed to push one or two laps depending on how the tyres were behaving, and I think we did the right choice, and I'm very happy for that. At the end he was able to match the pace and control Mark, who was very aggressive behind, so I think he did a very good race."

Massa and Hamilton had been battling for fifth place, but on lap 23 they collided in spectacular fashion, when Lewis made a move down the inside. This time the stewards decreed that the Ferrari driver was at fault, and Massa duly received a drive-through penalty, although he didn't accept blame. It was the sixth time this year that the pair had made contact on the track. Had Hamilton started from his rightful second place, we might have seen a different kind of race.

Later, Massa retired due to another front suspension breakage after clipping a kerb, while Hamilton eventually slipped to seventh as he lost out to both Mercedes drivers. Nico Rosberg had been in front initially, but Michael Schumacher put in a great drive from 11th on the grid to climb to fifth with an ultra-late switch to hards. Behind Rosberg and Hamilton, the top 10 was completed by Jaime Alguersuari, Adrian Sutil and Sergio Perez.

from Alonso. The Aussie ultimately lost out because he was struggling more than most with soft-tyre degradation, and that forced him to declare his hand and make that early stop for hards.

Mark had already got himself into tyre trouble in the first stint, using them a little too aggressively in his pursuit of Button.

"That's what we were concerned about, that early on he was giving the tyres a hard time," said Horner. "But then he seemed to find a rhythm that was reasonable. Then, in the second stint, the tyres went away from him, and obviously Fernando closed in, and had more in hand at that point. And then

SNAPSHOT FROM
INDIA

CLOCKWISE FROM RIGHT

Buddh International Circuit is the latest design from German architect Hermann Tilke; any off-track excursions resulted in clouds of dust; Jarno Trulli was one of several drivers to adopt a special helmet design as a tribute to Marco Simoncelli and Dan Wheldon; a Ferrari team member takes a break from the action; Rowan Atkinson was a guest of McLaren; the enthusiastic marshals were recruited and trained locally; the circuit logo adorns the main startline building; drivers, team members and officials stand in silence before the start in remembrance of IndyCar driver Dan Wheldon and MotoGP rider Marco Simoncelli who sadly lost their lives on consecutive weekends prior to the Indian GP; Jenson Button tries out a tuk-tuk

RACE RESULTS
INDIA
BUDDH INTERNATIONAL

RACE DATE October 30th
CIRCUIT LENGTH 3.185 miles
NO. OF LAPS 60
RACE DISTANCE 191.100 miles
WEATHER Sunny, 31°C
TRACK TEMP 38°C
ATTENDANCE 230,000
LAP RECORD Sebastian Vettel,
1m27.249s, 131.397mph, 2011

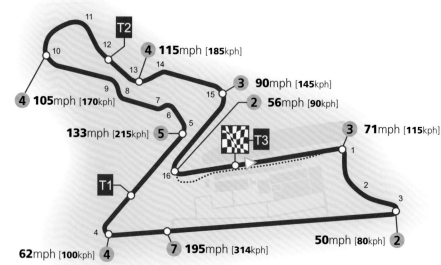

PRACTICE 1			
	Driver	Time	Laps
1	L Hamilton	1m26.836s	22
2	S Vettel	1m27.416s	23
3	M Webber	1m27.428s	27
4	J Button	1m28.394s	23
5	M Schumacher	1m28.531s	23
6	N Rosberg	1m28.542s	29
7	F Massa	1m28.644s	22
8	A Sutil	1m28.705s	23
9	S Buemi	1m29.219s	24
10	K Kobayashi	1m29.355s	29
11	P di Resta	1m29.700s	24
12	V Petrov	1m29.705s	22
13	B Senna	1m29.799s	20
14	S Perez	1m30.132s	25
15	R Barrichello	1m30.367s	21
16	J Alguersuari	1m30.556s	19
17	P Maldonado	1m30.669s	22
18	J Trulli	1m30.818s	22
19	K Chandhok	1m32.487s	24
20	T Glock	1m32.771s	24
21	D Ricciardo	1m33.928s	27
22	N Karthikeyan	1m34.113s	30
23	J d'Ambrosio	1m35.796s	19
24	F Alonso	1m35.899s	4

PRACTICE 2			
	Driver	Time	Laps
1	F Massa	1m25.706s	33
2	S Vettel	1m25.794s	34
3	F Alonso	1m25.930s	34
4	L Hamilton	1m26.454s	26
5	M Webber	1m26.500s	30
6	J Button	1m26.714s	28
7	A Sutil	1m27.316s	34
8	B Senna	1m27.498s	36
9	P di Resta	1m27.853s	35
10	S Buemi	1m27.868s	35
11	V Petrov	1m27.890s	37
12	K Kobayashi	1m28.050s	34
13	S Perez	1m28.289s	36
14	J Alguersuari	1m28.552s	31
15	R Barrichello	1m28.691s	29
16	P Maldonado	1m28.708s	24
17	J Trulli	1m29.332s	39
18	H Kovalainen	1m30.241s	41
19	N Rosberg	1m31.098s	38
20	T Glock	1m31.469s	32
21	M Schumacher	1m31.804s	25
22	J d'Ambrosio	1m32.593s	12
23	D Ricciardo	1m32.768s	33
24	N Karthikeyan	1m32.824s	33

PRACTICE 3			
	Driver	Time	Laps
1	S Vettel	1m24.824s	18
2	J Button	1m25.191s	15
3	M Webber	1m25.203s	19
4	L Hamilton	1m25.288s	16
5	F Alonso	1m25.784s	17
6	F Massa	1m26.058s	16
7	P di Resta	1m26.785s	19
8	N Rosberg	1m26.873s	22
9	A Sutil	1m26.958s	19
10	S Buemi	1m27.146s	20
11	M Schumacher	1m27.217s	21
12	B Senna	1m27.235s	20
13	K Kobayashi	1m27.262s	19
14	V Petrov	1m27.280s	18
15	J Alguersuari	1m27.387s	20
16	S Perez	1m27.749s	21
17	P Maldonado	1m27.793s	17
18	R Barrichello	1m27.875s	20
19	J Trulli	1m29.355s	21
20	H Kovalainen	1m29.750s	19
21	T Glock	1m30.683s	23
22	N Karthikeyan	1m30.900s	25
23	J d'Ambrosio	1m32.851s	19
24	D Ricciardo	1m33.246s	16

QUALIFYING 1		
	Driver	Time
1	V Petrov	1m26.189s
2	S Vettel	1m26.218s
3	J Button	1m26.225s
4	A Sutil	1m26.271s
5	N Rosberg	1m26.364s
6	M Webber	1m26.473s
7	J Alguersuari	1m26.557s
8	L Hamilton	1m26.563s
9	S Buemi	1m26.608s
10	B Senna	1m26.766s
11	F Alonso	1m26.774s
12	M Schumacher	1m26.790s
13	P Maldonado	1m26.829s
14	P di Resta	1m26.864s
15	F Massa	1m27.012s
16	S Perez	1m27.249s
17	R Barrichello	1m27.479s
18	K Kobayashi	1m27.876s
19	H Kovalainen	1m28.565s
20	J Trulli	1m28.752s
21	D Ricciardo	1m30.216s
22	N Karthikeyan	1m30.238s
23	J d'Ambrosio	1m30.866s
24	T Glock	1m34.046s

QUALIFYING 2		
	Driver	Time
1	S Vettel	1m24.657s
2	L Hamilton	1m25.091s
3	F Alonso	1m25.158s
4	M Webber	1m25.282s
5	J Button	1m25.299s
6	F Massa	1m25.522s
7	N Rosberg	1m25.555s
8	A Sutil	1m26.140s
9	S Buemi	1m26.161s
10	J Alguersuari	1m26.319s
11	V Petrov	1m26.319s
12	M Schumacher	1m26.337s
13	P di Resta	1m26.503s
14	P Maldonado	1m26.537s
15	B Senna	1m26.651s
16	R Barrichello	1m27.247s
17	S Perez	1m27.562s

Best sectors – Practice			Speed trap – Practice		
Sec 1	S Vettel	41.282s	1	J Alguersuari	201.200mph
Sec 2	M Webber	22.584s	2	S Perez	201.075mph
Sec 3	S Vettel	20.805s	3	S Buemi	200.827mph

Best sectors – Qualifying			Speed trap – Qualifying		
Sec 1	L Hamilton	41.009s	1	J Alguersuari	201.448mph
Sec 2	S Vettel	22.226s	2	S Buemi	201.200mph
Sec 3	S Vettel	20.675s	3	S Perez	200.951mph

 Sebastian Vettel

"I had a fight with Jenson, who was always around 4s away, but he kept closing in around the pit stops. I was pushing hard into the box, but we lost a little bit there."

Jenson Button

"I made up places on lap 1 and settled down to keep Mark behind me. I think we 'broke' his rears, which let me open a gap. Then I set about Seb."

Fernando Alonso

"I didn't get away well, and Button was able to pass me. Then when Webber slowed, I closed up and, staying out a few laps longer, was able to get ahead."

Michael Schumacher

"At the start, it worked to my strategy as I didn't want to use KERS in the first two turns, and saved it for the straight, where I knew I could make up places."

Bruno Senna

"I got a very strong start and jumped four places, so was very happy with that. But, unluckily I suffered a KERS problem, so I had to finish the race without it."

Rubens Barrichello

"I lost my nose going into Turn 1 at the start, so I had to pit, and that ruined my race. After that, we had to change our strategy to a one-stop to avoid losing more time."

Mark Webber

"We lost the podium mid-race. It's pretty much the story of this year; I just don't have the pace at the end of the stints, so I run out of tyres and then lose strategy."

Lewis Hamilton

"The contact with Felipe was just one of those things. During the race, it felt like there was a vibration through the right-handers, like the floor was scraping."

Felipe Massa

"I'm unhappy that I wasn't able to finish a race in which I showed I had the pace for the podium. As for the clash with Hamilton, I don't share the stewards' opinion."

Nico Rosberg

"I'm pleased to have gained a place on my grid position, but I lost time in my second pit stop which meant that I wasn't able stay ahead of Michael."

Vitaly Petrov

"My start was good, especially as I started with the hard tyres. I made an early stop, but made a mistake with the clutch that lost me time, as I couldn't pull away."

Pastor Maldonado

"I had a problem with the gearbox, but we don't know the exact cause. My pace was good before that, and the tyres were working well. It was just bad luck."

1	S Vettel
2	M Webber
3	F Alonso
4	J Button
5	L Hamilton
6	F Massa
7	N Rosberg
8	A Sutil
9	S Buemi
10	J Alguersuari
11	M Schumacher
12	P di Resta
13	P Maldonado
14	B Senna
15	R Barrichello
16	V Petrov
17	K Kobayashi
18	H Kovalainen
19	J Trulli
20	S Perez
21	J d'Ambrosio
22	T Glock
23	D Ricciardo
24	N Karthikeyan

Legend: ☼ Accident · Ⓜ Mechanical failure · Ⓟ Pit stop · ☐ Safety Car · ☐ Lapped · Ⓑ Black flag

QUALIFYING 3

	Driver	Time
1	S Vettel	1m24.178s
2	L Hamilton	1m24.474s
3	M Webber	1m24.508s
4	F Alonso	1m24.519s
5	J Button	1m24.950s
6	F Massa	1m25.122s
7	N Rosberg	1m25.451s
8	A Sutil	No time
9	S Buemi	No time
10	J Alguersuari	No time

GRID

	Driver	Time
1	S Vettel	1m24.178s
2	M Webber	1m24.508s
3	F Alonso	1m24.519s
4	J Button	1m24.950s
5*	L Hamilton	1m24.474s
6	F Massa	1m25.122s
7	N Rosberg	1m25.451s
8	A Sutil	No time
9	S Buemi	No time
10	J Alguersuari	No time
11	M Schumacher	1m26.337s
12	P di Resta	1m26.503s
13	P Maldonado	1m26.537s
14	B Senna	1m26.651s
15	R Barrichello	1m27.247s
16**	V Petrov	1m26.319s
17	K Kobayashi	1m27.876s
18	H Kovalainen	1m28.565s
19	J Trulli	1m28.752s
20*	S Perez	1m27.562s
21	J d'Ambrosio	1m30.866s
22	T Glock	1m34.046s
23^	D Ricciardo	1m30.216s
24%	N Karthikeyan	1m20.238s

* 3-place penalty for ignoring yellow flags, ** 5-place penalty for causing an avoidable accident, ^ 5-place penalty for changing gearbox, % 5-place penalty for impeding

RACE

	Driver	Car	Laps	Time	Avg. mph	Fastest	Stops
1	S Vettel	Red Bull-Renault RB7	60	1h30m35.002s	126.457	1m27.249s	2
2	J Button	McLaren-Mercedes MP4-26	60	1h30m43.435s	126.261	1m27.967s	2
3	F Alonso	Ferrari 150 Italia	60	1h30m59.303s	125.894	1m27.953s	2
4	M Webber	Red Bull-Renault RB7	60	1h31m00.531s	125.866	1m27.520s	2
5	M Schumacher	Mercedes MGP W02	60	1h31m40.423s	124.953	1m28.549s	2
6	N Rosberg	Mercedes MGP W02	60	1h31m41.853s	124.920	1m28.600s	2
7	L Hamilton	McLaren-Mercedes MP4-26	60	1h31m59.185s	124.528	1m28.721s	3
8	J Alguersuari	Toro Rosso-Ferrari STR6	59	1h30m54.422s	123.905	1m29.239s	2
9	A Sutil	Force India-Mercedes VJM04	59	1h31m10.160s	123.548	1m29.269s	2
10	S Perez	Sauber-Ferrari C30	59	1h31m12.750s	123.490	1m29.345s	2
11	V Petrov	Renault R31	59	1h31m13.627s	123.470	1m29.289s	2
12	B Senna	Renault R31	59	1h31m25.298s	123.207	1m29.310s	2
13	P di Resta	Force India-Mercedes VJM04	59	1h31m29.243s	123.119	1m28.679s	3
14	H Kovalainen	Lotus-Renault T128	58	1h30m41.595s	122.090	1m30.294s	2
15	R Barrichello	Williams-Cosworth FW33	58	1h30m56.557s	121.756	1m28.635s	2
16	J d'Ambrosio	Virgin-Cosworth MVR02	57	1h30m51.481s	119.766	1m31.990s	2
17	N Karthikeyan	HRT-Cosworth F111	57	1h30m52.067s	119.753	1m31.988s	2
18	D Ricciardo	HRT-Cosworth F111	57	1h31m23.903s	119.058	1m31.674s	3
19	J Trulli	Lotus-Renault T128	55	1h30m58.940s	115.411	1m31.691s	3
R	F Massa	Ferrari 150 Italia	32	Suspension	-	1m30.243s	3
R	S Buemi	Toro Rosso-Ferrari STR6	24	Engine	-	1m30.956s	1
R	P Maldonado	Williams-Cosworth FW33	12	Gearbox	-	1m33.573s	0
R	T Glock	Virgin-Cosworth MVR02	2	Crash damage	-	2m09.008s	1
R	K Kobayashi	Sauber-Ferrari C30	0	Crash damage	-	-	0

CHAMPIONSHIP

	Driver	Pts
1	S Vettel	374
2	J Button	240
3	F Alonso	227
4	M Webber	221
5	L Hamilton	202
6	F Massa	98
7	N Rosberg	75
8	M Schumacher	70
9	V Petrov	36
10	N Heidfeld	34
11	A Sutil	30
12	K Kobayashi	27
13	J Alguersuari	26
14	P di Resta	21
15	S Buemi	15
16	S Perez	14
17	R Barrichello	4
18	B Senna	2
19	P Maldonado	1

	Constructor	Pts
1	Red Bull-Renault	595
2	McLaren-Mercedes	442
3	Ferrari	325
4	Mercedes	145
5	Renault	72
6	Force India-Mercedes	51
7	Sauber-Ferrari	41
8	Toro Roso-Ferrari	41
9	Williams-Cosworth	5

Fastest lap
S Vettel 1m27.249s
(131.397mph) on lap 60

Fastest speed trap
S Perez 201.137mph
Slowest speed trap
T Glock 176.842mph

Fastest pit stop
1 M Schumacher 20.893s
2 P di Resta 20.984s
3 J Button 21.092s

Adrian Sutil
"In the early laps, I struggled with the rear and couldn't hold off the Toro Rossos. But in the later stints the car balance improved and I was able to keep Perez back."

Kamui Kobayashi
"Sadly, my race is a very short story. After the start I was hit from behind and immediately saw smoke and fire coming from my car, so had to stop and switch off."

Sebastien Buemi
"I was having a very good race. When the car stopped, I'd just passed Hamilton, I was lying eighth and I think I could have finished in the top eight."

Jarno Trulli
"One of the HRTs hit me as we came out of Turn 3, and that was the end of my race, as I had a puncture and had to do almost a full lap to get back to the pits."

Narain Karthikeyan
"To finish 17th in my home race is the best I could have wished for with the car we have, and beating my team-mate and a Lotus makes it all the more satisfying."

Timo Glock
"I came into Turn 1 on the outside and saw bits flying. I braked early and, when I turned, Kamui drove straight into me. My front wing and one side were damaged."

Paul di Resta
"I started on the hard tyre, and it was always the plan to pit early with the hope of a safety-car period as a gamble to get rid of the hard tyre early on."

Sergio Perez
"I'm very happy to have scored a point. At least I can now pay back something after I made a mistake on Friday, for which I received the three-place grid penalty."

Jaime Alguersuari
"We had a pace as quick as in Korea. I managed to pass Senna, then Sutil. I was also ahead of the Saubers, and this result reflects where we should be in the order."

Heikki Kovalainen
"I had a really strong race and even ran 10th. After the first stop I was able to keep pace with Senna, but when I went on to the hards it was harder to keep up."

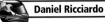
Daniel Ricciardo
"I passed a few people, then Narain, but in the second stint the front felt odd after a few laps. It might have been a puncture, but I had to make an extra pit stop."

Jerome d'Ambrosio
"It was strange in terms of the tyres. On the one hand this was good, as we could do long stints without degradation, but it wasn't optimum for the start."

2011 FORMULA 1 ETIHAD AIRWAYS ABU DHABI GRAND PRIX
YAS MARINA CIRCUIT

LEWIS RETURNS

Sebastian Vettel's first retirement of the season, after leading from pole position, took nothing away from Lewis Hamilton's return to form to take a dominant victory

Inevitably, the headline story in Abu Dhabi was the first-lap retirement of Sebastian Vettel, after the German suffered an unexplained puncture as he headed out of Turn One. It was the first time since Korea the previous year that Seb failed to see the chequered flag.

However, his absence did not detract from the brilliant performance of winner Lewis Hamilton, who still had to get the job done. Lewis drove a faultless race as Fernando Alonso stayed close enough to keep him honest.

In the light of his recent troubles, it was a great day for Hamilton, and it spoke volumes that this was the first time since his win in Germany that he had finished ahead of his grid position.

Vettel was certainly due some bad luck. Of course, both he and RBR had done a magnificent job all year, especially in qualifying, but the stats had been skewed by the fact that nothing had gone wrong for him. Sadly, his retirement robbed us of a potentially thrilling battle with Hamilton. Had Lewis beaten the Red Bull on the track, victory would surely have been that much sweeter.

"I think it would have been a close one," said Martin Whitmarsh. "We had a strong race car, and I think it would have been a thrilling race with Sebastian. I'd like to have felt that we could have beaten him in a straight fight."

ABOVE Sebastian Vettel limps back to the pits with damage to the right-rear corner of his car after a sudden tyre failure on the first lap

OPPOSITE TOP Nico Rosberg battled hard with team-mate Michael Schumacher early in the race

OPPOSITE BOTTOM Fernando Alonso once again maximised the performance of his Ferrari and was the only man to challenge Hamilton

"The whole team was frustrated, because we were in a great position to win the race today," said Christian Horner. "Sebastian did a superb job yesterday, one of the best laps of his career to nail that position, and he'd done everything right. He'd made the start, he made it comfortably into the lead in the first corner, and it was cruel luck to be forced to retire in the way he did. So of course he's disappointed."

In qualifying, Vettel was made to work hard by McLaren. Hamilton topped FP2, FP3, Q1 and Q2, and he was also quickest after the first runs in Q3. He was fastest again on his second run, but Vettel dug deep, and from somewhere he found the extra time on his last lap.

Jenson Button lost out to Hamilton by less than a hundredth of a second as he took third place, while Mark Webber was frustrated to be down in fourth. Alonso qualified fifth for the ninth time in 18 races, but was confident that he had a shot at a podium.

Initially, Vettel got everything right, shooting into the lead at Turn One and emerging with a handy advantage over Hamilton. But, at the second left-hander, his right rear suffered an instant deflation, and he spun wildly off the track. He crawled back to the pits, but the initial spin – with the collapsed tyre pushing unusual forces through the right-rear corner – had done enough damage to force his retirement.

INSIDE LINE
LEWIS HAMILTON
McLAREN DRIVER

"Fantastic. It was my Mum's birthday and great to be able to win while she was here at the race.

I feel fantastic. I think it was one of my best races. I said that to myself as I slowed down. Just being able to hold off one of the best drivers in the world throughout the race is something that is very, very tough to do.

I was just looking after the tyres and managing the gap. Obviously the team did a fantastic job at the pit stops but I'm ecstatic. I'm really happy to be back on the top step of the podium. I can get on my flight tonight and smile!

It's early days but hopefully this is the start of something very good. We've got another great race ahead of us in Brazil and I've just got to focus on that and keep up the momentum.

When I saw Sebastian go off I didn't know which way he would go and I was just trying not to collect him as he came across the track.

It's rare for me this year to be able to maintain a gap and control the race but today I had the pace to do that. I was able to respond when Fernando went quicker, whenever he closed the gap. It seemed like he would start off a stint a bit slower than me and then get faster towards the end, so his tyres would last a bit longer.

I think some of the backmarkers just didn't see us when they were being lapped because they were in their own race. I lost seconds behind certain people and Rubens overtook me with the DRS; there was nothing I could do about that. I came up alongside him thinking, "I'm in the lead, we're not racing..." But he came and congratulated me after the race, so that's fine.

I was really surprised to see as much support out there for me in the crowd. It may not have been too exciting for everyone just watching me go around, but I'm very pleased with that performance in terms of not making any mistakes.

I don't feel that I made a single one in the race and with the pressure I've been under and the doubts surrounding me, I just feel massively proud to have put that kind of performance together and to have come out on top.

We were quick and I think it would have been close if Sebastian had not gone off."

Hamilton was grateful to accept this gift, and in fact Lewis was able to match what Vettel has been doing all year. By the end of a superb first lap, he was already 2.5s clear of his nearest pursuer, ensuring that he would be safely out of DRS range once it became available.

And the man leading the chase was not Button, but Alonso, who managed to pass Webber and then Jenson with aggressive first-lap moves. Fernando in turn did well to maintain the 2.5s gap for the duration of the first stint, while, behind him, Button found himself struggling to fend off Webber as he battled with faulty KERS.

"From early on in the first stint he had KERS failure," said Whitmarsh. "We couldn't get it running, and then after about 20 minutes we got it running again. We got it back, but frankly it wouldn't stay working, so we had to continually re-set it, which was a real challenge.

"He had a variable car, and it's very, very difficult for a driver to get into any rhythm when you're in those situations. So it wasn't ideal for him, but just to cope with that, all the various switching he has to do, and the rhythm, and the brake balance being changed all the time. And in all that time he was subjected to a lot of pressure, and was racing hard. It was massively impressive."

At the front the margin remained the same, until on

lap 15 Alonso suddenly gained half a second. A lap after that, McLaren brought Lewis in. Fernando followed him down the pitlane – there was no point in staying out given that Lewis would have fresh soft tyres – so everything depended on the second stops.

In fact, a better out-lap gave Lewis an extra second on his rival immediately after the first stops, and over the course of the stint his advantage grew as high as 5.6s, before slipping back to around 4s, as traffic played a role.

"I think it was a time-trial race, like an individual race," said Alonso. "I was doing like qualifying laps every lap, trying to close the gap, but one-tenth up, one-tenth down for the whole stint."

Nevertheless, despite being the first to pit, Lewis maintained a comfortable margin.

"We wanted to open a four-second gap and hold it," said Whitmarsh. "That's what Lewis planned to do if he got into that position, so he was just running that. Traffic was quite bad to be honest, that was a bit frightening."

Then, on lap 39, Hamilton's lead dropped to 3.1s. It was time to get rid of the soft tyres, and thus he came in on the next lap. Ferrari's only chance was to extend Fernando's stint on the softs and hope that he could gain some ground while Lewis was on the mediums.

Many times we'd seen Ferrari struggling on the prime in the final stint – although strangely it didn't happen in India, where Fernando held off Webber – so that was another reason to keep the Spaniard out.

"We knew that maybe we could overtake the McLaren at the second stop," Alonso acknowledged. "Because when we saw Lewis pitting, we had the tyres in more-or-less good condition to push for another two or three laps. So we did some good timed laps, so the team was informing me that we should be OK maybe to exit in front of him, or maybe on the limit, very close."

"Lewis pushed then," said Whitmarsh. "We felt pretty comfortable on the prime, it wasn't quite as quick a tyre, but we felt we could switch it on, and Lewis was able to go and do decent, quick times. In fact within a lap he was quicker than Fernando, but Fernando was obviously pushing as well. It's one of those situations where from halfway round the first lap it was our race to lose and we had to make sure we got it right…"

The tiny chance that Alonso had of challenging Lewis ended when, on his in-lap, he came across Daniel Ricciardo, who was minding his own business and also heading for the pits.

"Definitely, with the traffic on the pit entry, maybe we lost the opportunity to be close at the exit of the pits," said Fernando. "But I don't think that we lost the victory there. It was extremely difficult to beat the McLaren today."

It still wasn't over, as Lewis had to stay out of trouble in traffic and bring the car home, but he had more speed than Fernando on the primes, and was able to eke out a safe cushion.

"I have to say, today with the backmarkers it was not easy for everyone, and Lewis had the same issue with some backmarkers," said Stefano Domenicali. "But for sure it was really unfortunate about the last two corners, behind the last car that was coming in on the same lap."

For Alonso, this was another superb performance, as

BELOW Action in the pitlane at the first stops, as leader Lewis Hamilton heads out on to the track while a chasing Fernando Alonso leaves his pit box, and Jenson Button runs down the pitlane towards his crew

BOTTOM Felipe Massa passed Mark Webber after the Red Bull driver was delayed at his first pit stop. A spin during the last stint dropped Massa back behind the Australian to finish fifth

OPPOSITE Ths sun sets over Yas Marina Circuit as Jenson Button, hampered by KERS problems, takes his McLaren to a third-place finish

TALKING POINT
SEB'S FIRST RETIREMENT

"It's just a good job it happened this year as opposed to last!"

That was Christian Horner's verdict after the Abu Dhabi Grand Prix as he contemplated Sebastian Vettel's first retirement of 2011, courtesy of an instant right-rear tyre deflation on the first lap.

"It was cruel for Sebastian's challenge to end the way it did after such a superlative qualifying lap, one of his very best," Horner reckoned.

There was nothing riding on Abu Dhabi this time but there was still no hiding Vettel's disappointment at the loss of his 100 per cent scoring record in 2011.

Sebastian, though, did not head for an early shower. Instead, he inspected the damaged rear end of his car with chief mechanic Kenny Handkammer and then headed straight for the pit wall.

"He's like a sponge for information," said Horner. "I think he saw an opportunity not only to help his team-mate but also to experience what the pit wall was like and to see how we make decisions."

Once the race was done, Vettel switched his attention from the Red Bull technicians to their counterparts at Pirelli.

"We've just been out there with Seb having a walk around to see if there's any debris on the circuit," explained Pirelli's motorsport boss Paul Hembery early Sunday evening. "To be honest, we can't find anything. We're chatting to Red Bull now and working together to try to understand what happened and give Seb some answers.

"We'll work late tonight and if we haven't got the equipment here to analyse it properly, we'll send our bag of bits to Milan to try to get him some explanation," Hembery added.

Vettel was not angry but he likes answers, especially with suggestions that the failure may have been linked to blowing hot exhaust gas in the vicinity of the tyre.

It seemed unlikely given that Red Bull has exploited the technique to such good effect all season. By the middle of the following week, following their investigations, Pirelli were none the wiser.

But Vettel's sense of humour was still very much intact. He said he was honoured to have received a letter from Nigel Mansell congratulating him on beating Nigel's record for the number of race laps led in a season and wishing him the best with his bid for a record 15 poles. He had, he said, first met Mansell as a child – in Madame Tussauds!

Asked whether he thought they'd do a Vettel waxwork, he replied:

"I shouldn't think so. They've got one German in there already, and I gather he's not very popular." He meant Adolf, not Michael…

he continued to outperform the car. He was gifted a place by Vettel, but the rest he did himself, as he passed Webber and Button on the first lap to put himself in a position to challenge Lewis.

It has been a long time since we've seen Jenson left trailing behind his team-mate, but the KERS issue meant his hands were tied.

"The problem is, it is not just when you accelerate, it is when you brake," he explained. "When you have KERS you have a lot of engine braking from the KERS, and when you don't have it you don't have any braking performance. Every time I arrived at a corner, I didn't know what I was going to get, either engine braking or not, so it was pretty tricky."

As in India, Jenson enjoyed an entertaining fight with Webber, one that was again conducted without the sort of dramas that inevitably surround any Hamilton/Massa confrontation.

Button's job was made easier when Webber was the victim of a rare Red Bull glitch in the first pit stop. It not only cost the Aussie priceless time to Jenson, but stranded him behind Massa as well.

"We had a nut come out of the socket on the right rear, which unfortunately cost him about two or three seconds," Horner explained. "Otherwise I think we would have been able to jump Jenson. But that then dropped him behind both Jenson and Felipe."

When Mark stayed on the soft tyre at his second stop – giving him some speed, but guaranteeing that he would have to come in again – it came as a surprise. With stalemate at the front, Webber's tyre choice did at least add a little variety to the last part of the race, as he began to run very quickly. It was always going to be hard to gain enough to make up for an extra stop, which he made at the start of the last lap. He did at least jump Massa, if not Button.

"That was a situation where because of the issue at the first stop, we were behind Jenson and Felipe," said Horner. "And if we had adopted the same strategy as them, then we were likely to finish behind them. So at that point you say we've got nothing to lose. Unfortunately, Jenson was a bit too quick on the prime. We got to about 12s, we needed 20s. It just wasn't enough today, but it was worth the roll of the dice."

Staying ahead of Webber would have given Massa a boost, but instead he had a very public spin as he struggled for grip on the prime in the final stint. The race turned into a real struggle for him, in part because Ferrari reverted to the old wing for qualifying and the race.

Behind the Brazilian, Nico Rosberg took sixth place, with the remaining points going to Michael Schumacher, Adrian Sutil, Paul di Resta (who stopped only once) and Kamui Kobayashi.

With Vettel keen to make amends for his Abu Dhabi disappointment, and Hamilton and Button on three 2011 wins each for McLaren, the scene was set for a potentially thrilling season finale in Brazil.

LEFT TOP Rubens Barrichello charged through to finish 12th after starting on the final row of the grid due to an engine failure

LEFT BOTTOM Lewis Hamilton celebrates victory with his mother

SNAPSHOT FROM
ABU DHABI

CLOCKWISE FROM RIGHT

A twilight view of the unmistakable Yas Marina hotel; buttons galore on Bruno Senna's steering wheel; Sam Michael spent his first weekend in the McLaren garage as incoming Sporting Director; a stiff, hairy upper lip for Jenson Button as he grows a moustache in aid of a prostate cancer charity; Etihad Airways stewardesses performed the grid-girl duties; McLaren's guests included golfer Rory McIlroy with his girlfriend, Danish tennis player Caroline Wozniacki; Lewis Hamilton celebrates with the McLaren team and his mother, Carmen; Sir Paul McCartney attended the race and performed a concert in the evening; Vitaly Petrov and Bruno Senna pose with Brazilian soccer legend Ronaldo; Mercedes men in silver prepare for action

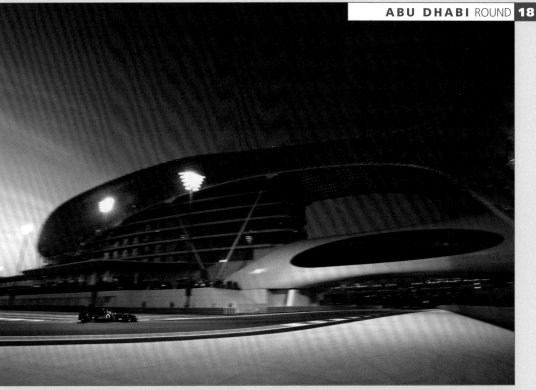

RACE RESULTS
ABU DHABI
YAS MARINA

RACE DATE November 13th
CIRCUIT LENGTH 3.450 miles
NO. OF LAPS 55
RACE DISTANCE 189.7385 miles
WEATHER Bright and dry, 28°C
TRACK TEMP 35°C
ATTENDANCE Not available
LAP RECORD Sebastian Vettel, 1m40.279s, 123.890mph, 2009

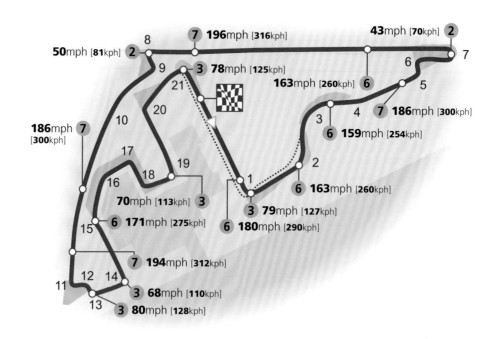

PRACTICE 1

	Driver	Time	Laps
1	J Button	1m40.263s	21
2	M Webber	1m40.389s	26
3	L Hamilton	1m40.403s	27
4	S Vettel	1m40.755s	27
5	F Alonso	1m40.801s	25
6	F Massa	1m41.260s	17
7	A Sutil	1m41.340s	23
8	N Rosberg	1m42.130s	26
9	P di Resta	1m42.151s	28
10	J Alguersuari	1m42.377s	26
11	J-E Vergne	1m42.633s	26
12	R Grosjean	1m42.685s	29
13	R Petrov	1m43.118s	13
14	P Maldonado	1m43.255s	29
15	M Schumacher	1m43.389s	24
16	S Perez	1m44.412s	28
17	K Kobayashi	1m44.484s	18
18	H Kovalainen	1m44.565s	27
19	J Trulli	1m44.898s	25
20	V Liuzzi	1m46.385s	28
21	D Ricciardo	1m46.532s	27
22	T Glock	1m48.024s	20
23	R Wickens	1m48.551s	23
24	R Barrichello	No time	3

PRACTICE 2

	Driver	Time	Laps
1	L Hamilton	1m39.586s	31
2	J Button	1m39.785s	30
3	F Alonso	1m39.971s	20
4	F Massa	1m39.980s	24
5	M Webber	1m40.104s	35
6	S Vettel	1m40.132s	26
7	M Schumacher	1m40.553s	34
8	A Sutil	1m40.951s	34
9	P di Resta	1m41.021s	37
10	K Kobayashi	1m41.490s	34
11	S Perez	1m41.565s	34
12	S Buemi	1m41.680s	33
13	V Petrov	1m41.947s	31
14	J Alguersuari	1m41.983s	34
15	B Senna	1m42.369s	36
16	R Barrichello	1m42.798s	35
17	P Maldonado	1m42.910s	34
18	H Kovalainen	1m43.562s	36
19	J Trulli	1m44.050s	38
20	N Rosberg	1m44.265s	41
21	T Glock	1m45.486s	34
22	J d'Ambrosio	1m46.142s	32
23	V Liuzzi	1m46.249s	21
24	D Ricciardo	1m46.328s	34

PRACTICE 3

	Driver	Time	Laps
1	L Hamilton	1m38.976s	17
2	S Vettel	1m39.403s	18
3	M Webber	1m39.427s	18
4	J Button	1m39.429s	16
5	F Alonso	1m39.661s	16
6	N Rosberg	1m40.135s	19
7	F Massa	1m40.183s	18
8	A Sutil	1m40.429s	21
9	P di Resta	1m40.511s	19
10	M Schumacher	1m40.938s	18
11	B Senna	1m41.509s	21
12	K Kobayashi	1m41.527s	21
13	S Perez	1m41.566s	20
14	V Petrov	1m41.594s	18
15	S Buemi	1m41.622s	18
16	J Alguersuari	1m41.855s	18
17	P Maldonado	1m42.025s	19
18	H Kovalainen	1m43.409s	22
19	R Barrichello	1m43.861s	5
20	T Glock	1m45.262s	23
21	V Liuzzi	1m45.302s	20
22	J d'Ambrosio	1m45.509s	22
23	D Ricciardo	1m45.732s	20
24	J Trulli	No time	1

QUALIFYING 1

	Driver	Time
1	L Hamilton	1m39.782s
2	M Webber	1m40.167s
3	J Button	1m40.227s
4	S Vettel	1m40.478s
5	A Sutil	1m40.595s
6	V Petrov	1m40.955s
7	P di Resta	1m41.064s
8	N Rosberg	1m41.120s
9	S Perez	1m41.311s
10	F Alonso	1m41.380s
11	J Alguersuari	1m41.386s
12	B Senna	1m41.391s
13	F Massa	1m41.592s
14	K Kobayashi	1m41.613s
15	S Buemi	1m41.737s
16	P Maldonado	1m42.258s
17	M Schumacher	1m42.605s
18	H Kovalainen	1m42.979s
19	J Trulli	1m43.884s
20	T Glock	1m44.515s
21	D Ricciardo	1m44.641s
22	J d'Ambrosio	1m44.699s
23	V Liuzzi	1m45.159s
24	R Barrichello	No time

QUALIFYING 2

	Driver	Time
1	L Hamilton	1m38.434s
2	S Vettel	1m38.516s
3	M Webber	1m38.821s
4	F Alonso	1m39.058s
5	J Button	1m39.097s
6	N Rosberg	1m39.420s
7	F Massa	1m39.623s
8	A Sutil	1m40.205s
9	P di Resta	1m40.414s
10	M Schumacher	1m40.554s
11	S Perez	1m40.874s
12	V Petrov	1m40.919s
13	S Buemi	1m41.009s
14	B Senna	1m41.079s
15	J Alguersuari	1m41.162s
16	K Kobayashi	1m41.240s
17	P Maldonado	1m41.760s

Best sectors – Practice

Sec 1	M Webber	17.267s
Sec 2	M Schumacher	40.771s
Sec 3	L Hamilton	39.268s

Speed trap – Practice

1	J Alguersuari	200.951mph
2	J-E Vergne	200.951mph
3	S Buemi	200.951mph

Best sectors – Qualifying

Sec 1	S Vettel	17.408s
Sec 2	S Vettel	41.857s
Sec 3	L Hamilton	38.886s

Speed trap – Qualifying

1	S Perez	200.951mph
2	K Kobayashi	200.578mph
3	J Alguersuari	198.963mph

Sebastian Vettel
"Turning into Turn 2, I could feel something odd on the rear right. I had to catch the car, and the second time I couldn't do it, as I'd lost too much air, and spun off."

Jenson Button
"It was difficult, as I had a KERS issue, and it stopped working after 15 laps and that doesn't just affect your power out of corners, it affects engine braking too."

Fernando Alonso
"My podium trophy collection is complete! I have 73 top-three finishes and I've stood on the podium of all the F1 circuits used over the past 10 years."

Michael Schumacher
"Considering that I wasn't able to find the perfect balance, I got the maximum out of our situation, but I lost some parts of the car that cost us balance."

Bruno Senna
"There's not a crumb of comfort to take from that. We suffered a KERS failure, a drive-through penalty and a car that wasn't on the money at this track."

Rubens Barrichello
"It was a well-considered race. I started from the back, but fought all the way through and almost ended up fighting for points. We did well to finish where we did."

Mark Webber
"On the second stop, we fitted the option tyre. In the first DRS zone it was easy to pass, but in the second you couldn't, so if I passed Jenson there, he'd get me back."

Lewis Hamilton
"This result is fantastic and I felt I maximised everything. For most of the race, I was focusing on managing the gap to Fernando. Victory is good for the soul."

Felipe Massa
"Things were OK while I was on the softs, but with the mediums I struggled to keep on track. That's why I spun, losing any hope of staying ahead of Webber."

Nico Rosberg
"At the start, I tried to pass Felipe, but there was no space. Michael passed me and we had fun before I took the place back. After that, I could handle my tyres."

Vitaly Petrov
"It was frustrating, as my DRS wasn't working. We thought we could have a good fight with those in front, but were helpless, so decided to change strategy."

Pastor Maldonado
"Our pace was a bit slow, but improved when we switched to the soft tyre. Sadly, my drive-through penalty cost us a lot of time and a better result."

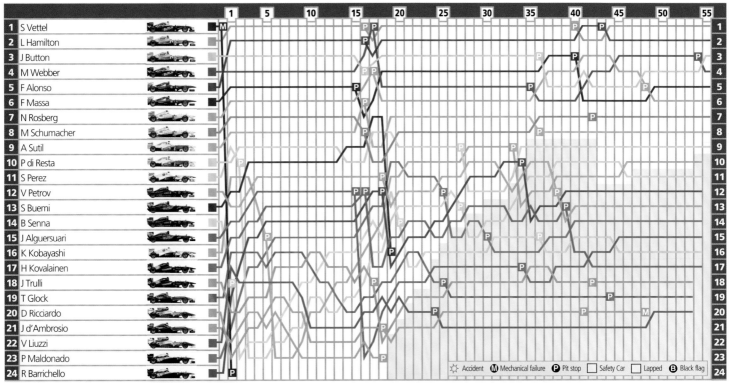

		1	5	10	15	20	25	30	35	40	45	50	55	
1	S Vettel													1
2	L Hamilton													2
3	J Button													3
4	M Webber													4
5	F Alonso													5
6	F Massa													6
7	N Rosberg													7
8	M Schumacher													8
9	A Sutil													9
10	P di Resta													10
11	S Perez													11
12	V Petrov													12
13	S Buemi													13
14	B Senna													14
15	J Alguersuari													15
16	K Kobayashi													16
17	H Kovalainen													17
18	J Trulli													18
19	T Glock													19
20	D Ricciardo													20
21	J d'Ambrosio													21
22	V Liuzzi													22
23	P Maldonado													23
24	R Barrichello													24

Accident ☆ | Mechanical failure Ⓜ | Pit stop Ⓟ | Safety Car □ | Lapped □ | Black flag Ⓑ

QUALIFYING 3

	Driver	Time
1	S Vettel	1m38.481s
2	L Hamilton	1m38.622s
3	J Button	1m38.631s
4	M Webber	1m38.858s
5	F Alonso	1m39.058s
6	F Massa	1m39.695s
7	N Rosberg	1m39.773s
8	M Schumacher	1m40.662s
9	A Sutil	1m40.768s
10	P di Resta	No time

GRID

	Driver	Time
1	S Vettel	1m38.481s
2	L Hamilton	1m38.622s
3	J Button	1m38.631s
4	M Webber	1m38.858s
5	F Alonso	1m39.058s
6	F Massa	1m39.695s
7	N Rosberg	1m39.773s
8	M Schumacher	1m40.662s
9	A Sutil	1m40.768s
10	P di Resta	No time
11	S Perez	1m40.874s
12	V Petrov	1m40.919s
13	S Buemi	1m41.009s
14	B Senna	1m41.079s
15	J Alguersuari	1m41.162s
16	K Kobayashi	1m41.240s
17	H Kovalainen	1m42.979s
18	J Trulli	1m43.884s
19	T Glock	1m44.515s
20	D Ricciardo	1m44.641s
21	J d'Ambrosio	1m44.699s
22	V Liuzzi	1m45.159s
23	R Barrichello	No time
24*	P Maldonado	1m41.760s

*10-place penalty for using 9th engine

RACE

	Driver	Car	Laps	Time	Avg. mph	Fastest	Stops
1	L Hamilton	McLaren-Mercedes MP4-26	55	1h37m11.886s	117.125	1m43.461s	2
2	F Alonso	Ferrari 150 Italia	55	1h37m20.343s	116.955	1m43.914s	2
3	J Button	McLaren-Mercedes MP4-26	55	1h37m37.767s	116.607	1m43.154s	2
4	M Webber	Red Bull-Renault RB7	55	1h37m47.670s	116.410	1m42.612s	3
5	F Massa	Ferrari 150 Italia	55	1h38m02.464s	116.117	1m44.288s	2
6	N Rosberg	Mercedes MGP W02	55	1h38m04.203s	116.083	1m43.993s	2
7	M Schumacher	Mercedes MGP W02	55	1h38m27.850s	115.618	1m44.916s	2
8	A Sutil	Force India-Mercedes VJM04	55	1h38m29.008s	115.596	1m44.709s	2
9	P di Resta	Force India-Mercedes VJM04	55	1h38m52.973s	115.129	1m44.120s	1
10	K Kobayashi	Sauber-Ferrari C30	54	1h37m13.417s	114.964	1m43.521s	2
11	S Perez	Sauber-Ferrari C30	54	1h37m26.738s	114.702	1m44.566s	2
12	R Barrichello	Williams-Cosworth FW33	54	1h37m27.448s	114.688	1m44.438s	2
13	V Petrov	Renault R31	54	1h37m31.300s	114.612	1m43.673s	2
14	P Maldonado	Williams-Cosworth FW33	54	1h38m24.633s*	113.577	1m44.628s	2
15	J Alguersuari	Toro Rosso-Ferrari STR6	54	1h38m25.938s**	113.552	1m44.093s	2
16	B Senna	Renault R31	54	1h38m34.408s	113.389	1m46.150s	3
17	H Kovalainen	Lotus-Renault T128	54	1h38m37.753s	113.325	1m46.610s	2
18	J Trulli	Lotus-Renault T128	53	1h37m53.904s	112.057	1m47.444s	2
19	T Glock	Virgin-Cosworth MVR02	53	1h38m23.176s	111.500	1m48.085s	2
20	V Liuzzi	HRT-Cosworth F111	53	1h38m55.177s	110.900	1m49.242s	1
R	D Ricciardo	HRT-Cosworth F111	48	Alternator	-	1m48.274s	2
R	S Buemi	Toro Rosso-Ferrari STR6	19	Hydraulics	-	1m47.094s	0
R	J d'Ambrosio	Virgin-Cosworth MVR02	18	Brakes	-	1m51.196s	0
R	S Vettel	Red Bull-Renault RB7	1	Puncture	-	-	0

* 30s penalty for ignoring blue flags   ** 20s penalty for ignoring blue flags

CHAMPIONSHIP

	Driver	Pts
1	S Vettel	374
2	J Button	255
3	F Alonso	245
4	M Webber	233
5	L Hamilton	227
6	F Massa	108
7	N Rosberg	83
8	M Schumacher	76
9	V Petrov	36
10	N Heidfeld	34
11	A Sutil	34
12	K Kobayashi	28
13	J Alguersuari	26
14	P di Resta	23
15	S Buemi	15
16	S Perez	14
17	R Barrichello	4
18	B Senna	2
19	P Maldonado	1

	Constructor	Pts
1	Red Bull-Renault	607
2	McLaren-Mercedes	482
3	Ferrari	353
4	Mercedes GP	159
5	Renault	72
6	Force India-Mercedes	57
7	Sauber Ferrari	42
8	Toro Ross-Ferrari	41
9	Williams-Cosworth	5

Fastest lap
M Webber 1m42.612s
(121.076mph) on lap 51

Fastest speed trap
S Perez 200.516mph
Slowest speed trap
H Kovalainen 189.456mph

Fastest pit stop
1 L Hamilton 19.350s
2 M Webber 19.525s
3 M Schumacher 19.660s

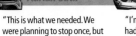

Adrian Sutil
"This is what we needed. We were planning to stop once, but decided to run a two-stopper strategy, as the soft tyre didn't last as long as we reckoned."

Kamui Kobayashi
"I'm happy to have scored. I had a good start and made up five places on lap 1. Actually, the performance of the tyres after the start was better than expected."

Sebastien Buemi
"I had to retire because of a loss of fluid from the hydraulic system, which I first felt through the lack of power steering. After that, I couldn't change gear."

Jarno Trulli
"I lost a few places at the start with clutch slip, but I soon got past the cars we needed to fight, then focused on making sure I got the car to the end of the race."

Daniel Ricciardo
"I could keep up with Glock in the second stint. I was then caught in traffic and, three laps from the end, my car stopped. It was a shame to end like that."

Timo Glock
"I had a strong start and was in front of a few quicker guys, even though they caught me up. I just drove my race and my engineer kept me updated about the gap."

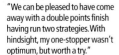

Paul di Resta
"We can be pleased to have come away with a double points finish having run two strategies. With hindsight, my one-stopper wasn't optimum, but worth a try."

Sergio Perez
"There was a queue into Turn 7 and I couldn't miss Sutil. It was not clear how much damage I had, but I was told my front wing was broken and I had to pit."

Jaime Alguersuari
"We'd opted for an aerodynamic strategy for ease of passing, but my tyres degraded. Then there was a mistake in the pit stop from which I couldn't recover."

Heikki Kovalainen
"Another pretty good start, and from there the race was straightforward. I didn't have any issues all race, the stops were good and the strategy worked as planned."

Vitantonio Liuzzi
"My car suffered from balance problems. The team worked all night to fix it, but unfortunately there was understeer on left turns and oversteer on right turns."

Jerome d'Ambrosio
"I had a good start and was fighting against the HRTs, but I had a brake problem and that was my race over. But we will work hard and continue to be motivated."

FORMULA 1 GRANDE PRÊMIO PETROBRAS DO BRASIL 2011
SÃO PAULO

MARK A WINNER

Red Bull's Mark Webber finished on a high by finally winning a race in 2011, while team-mate Sebastian Vettel, slowed by gearbox gremlins, followed him home

All week a downpour was forecast for Sunday in Brazil, but in the end it didn't materialise. Instead of the element of chance provided by rain, we had a pretty straightforward race, with Red Bull at the front, and McLaren and Ferrari giving chase.

The difference this time, however, was that Sebastian Vettel didn't cross the line first, as Mark Webber ended his frustrating 2011 season by scoring his maiden win of the year – but only after his team-mate was slowed by gearbox gremlins. With a drive that Vettel likened to that of Ayrton Senna's at the same venue in 1991, the new World Champion managed the situation brilliantly, and defied the odds to bring the car safely home in second place.

The threat of rain for Sunday meant that teams went into qualifying with one eye on a wet set-up. Indeed, rain was also in the air as the first session began, which led to an extra sense of urgency, but in the end it stayed dry throughout. Intriguingly, the Red Bulls were lacking a bit of straightline speed, the team having added downforce for a potentially wet race.

Vettel was fastest in Q2, and on the first runs in Q3, when he set a lap of 1m12.2s. As it turned out, that would have been good enough for pole, but he

went even faster on his second run with a 1m11.9s. It was his 15th pole of the season, breaking a record established by Nigel Mansell in 1992.

Jenson Button held second place for a few seconds, but was pushed down to third by Mark Webber, who was frustrated not to beat his team-mate.

"I tried to help old Nigel out today, but it didn't work out," he joked...

Button shared the second row with team-mate Lewis Hamilton, who was almost 0.2s slower. Fernando Alonso took his customary fifth place for Ferrari, while Nico Rosberg was sixth for Mercedes, ahead of Felipe Massa. Adrian Sutil did a good job to take eighth for Force India, while Bruno Senna pleased his home fans with ninth for Renault. Michael Schumacher completed the top 10.

Sunday morning saw a little nostalgia, as Nelson Piquet took to the track in Bernie Ecclestone's Brabham BT49 to celebrate the 30th anniversary of his first World Championship. He had not sat in an F1 car since his last season with Benetton in 1991.

As the start drew near, it became obvious that the expected rain was not going to come, and we were going to have a dry race. For once, everyone got

through the first lap at Interlagos unscathed. Vettel and Webber stayed safely in front, while further back Alonso jumped ahead of Hamilton to claim fourth.

Vettel soon opened up his customary gap, to ensure that he was safely out of Webber's DRS range once it became available on the third lap. He gradually began to edge away, opening the gap to 3.8s by lap 10.

However, by then the Red Bull Racing team had already become aware of a gearbox problem, as the oil level was starting to drop. Initially, Seb was told to short-shift in second and third, and the team continued to tell him to take care of the gearbox as the race progressed, with ever-increasing urgency.

Vettel did his best to adjust his driving to compensate, and inevitably his lead began to shrink, a tenth here, a tenth there. He was still 2.8s ahead before he pitted on lap 17, with Webber coming in a lap later. After the stops, he further moderated his pace, and fell back into the clutches of Webber. He offered no resistance when the Aussie got on to his tail, and the lead swapped at the first corner at the start of lap 30.

"I got through the first pit stop and obviously gained a little bit on Mark," said Vettel, "because I came in a lap earlier. But then at some stage I realised that it was still pretty early in the race, our main

OPPOSITE TOP Sebastian Vettel shows his delight, patting his trusty RB7 after taking his record-breaking 15th pole position of the season

OPPOSITE BELOW A trouble-free start saw the Red Bulls lead away, with Button third and Alonso fourth

ABOVE Jarno Trulli finished 18th, ahead of the Virgins and HRTs to cement Team Lotus's 10th position in the Constructors' Championship

INSIDE LINE
MARK WEBBER
RED BULL RACING DRIVER

"In motorsport you take wins as they come. It was actually brewing into a reasonable little battle between Seb and me.

The pace wasn't too bad at the end of my stints and I'm not exactly sure when he started to have a few issues. I thought that he was either

in tyre trouble way earlier than he should be, or had no KERS or something. One thing Seb doesn't do is forget how to drive from one lap to the next!

When I started to take a pretty big chunk out of him per lap, Ciaron [Pilbeam] informed me that he had a gearbox problem and I could smell it when I got close. There was also a little bit of fluid.

It was mixed feelings; there was the chance to win but I know how hard the guys worked on Seb's gearbox on Saturday night and in the end something let them down. With that far to go I thought he obviously wouldn't finish, but the car still got home.

With 10 laps to go, I started to think 'OK, it's nice to finish the year with a win, nice to finish with the

car feeling good underneath you, nice to have my second victory here in Brazil.' It's been a pretty good year but not like 2010 obviously, so for all the guys on my car, I was happy.

The last three laps were all fastest race laps. I kept pinching the front a little into turn eight and in the last laps I got it a little bit better and kept pushing hard. That's what it's about – pushing yourself, backing yourself and having a crack. I was only racing myself at that point so it was a nice little feeling.

I think I can have a stronger 2012 season. Clearly I started off poorly for lots of different reasons. You've got to look at all the different areas to get to the

highest level, and when the bar's high it's obviously not just Seb.

I didn't come here thinking about just him. We've got some class operators in other teams: JB, Lewis, Fernando. These boys are on the case, so that's what makes it rewarding.

I want to dedicate this win to a close friend of myself and my family, Bob Woods, who's a very ill man at the moment, so this win is for him."

BELOW Felipe Massa celebrated his 10th year as an F1 driver by finishing fifth at his home race, adopting a special gold helmet livery for the occasion

BOTTOM Bruno Senna gesticulates as the debris flies during his 10th-lap clash with Michael Schumacher, the Renault suffering damage to a right front-wing endplate which punctured the left-rear tyre on the Mercedes

OPPOSITE Rubens Barrichello races past the shanty-town backdrop of the Interlagos circuit on his way to 14th place and an uncertain future

priority was to finish the race, and Mark would be catching up, and the most important thing would be to help the team to win the race.

"I tried to be very clear on the radio that I couldn't keep first position with the pace that we were going, or whatever they asked me to do that was required to manage the gearbox. And then I told them, 'Tell Mark that I would let him through', to give him the chance to keep pushing. 'Don't lose any time getting past me', because at that stage I didn't know whether I would see the chequered flag or not."

Webber may have been handed the lead, but he still had to run 41 laps and stay out of trouble. The team had a little scare when Button made an early change to the prime tyre – potentially allowing him to get to the end without another pit stop – but it proved to be a false alarm, and when Button came in for an extra set of primes, RBR could relax. Mark finished the race with three consecutive fastest laps, crossing the line some 16.9s ahead of Vettel.

Vettel kept up an incredible pace while keeping the gearbox alive, and by the flag virtually all of its oil was gone. At one stage he told his engineer, "I feel like Senna in '91," referring to Ayrton's heroic drive to

victory with a crippled McLaren with serious gearbox problems. "Good for you, you should feel proud," was the reply.

Button ran third in the early laps, but he struggled for pace and was pushed hard by Alonso. The Ferrari driver then got ahead of Button with a superb pass around the outside on lap 10. Jenson changed his strategy by switching to the harder tyre for his third stint, having felt more comfortable on them in practice.

It paid off, as ultimately he was able to reel in Alonso during his fourth and final stint. Once again, the Ferrari struggled on the prime tyre, and Button was able to close on the Spaniard and pass him with DRS on lap 61. After that, he pulled away, and indeed brought the gap to Vettel down as he hoped to take advantage of the German's gearbox problems. The margin shrank below 10s, but right at the end Jenson himself slowed, and was told to pull over after the flag, as saving fuel became an issue.

"I couldn't look after the tyre and I really struggled with degradation, especially at the rear end, which was a little bit of a shock," said Button of his first stint. "The problem in the first stint was Fernando, he pushed me very hard, and when someone's doing that, you have to drive a little bit harder, so I was pushing the tyres pretty hard.

"I pitted early, because I couldn't look after the tyres, put a second set on, exactly the same thing happened, and then we went to the prime tyre where the pace was much better. The car felt more consistent, and the good thing was that we could get a good feeling on that tyre for the last stint, when I stuck on some new primes and I was able to hunt down Fernando."

Alonso took fourth, and wasn't disappointed also to be demoted by Webber from third to fourth place in the World Championship – it meant he avoided

TALKING POINT
PREMATURE GOODBYES?

It was at this race three years ago that many in the paddock felt a little uneasy around Rubens Barrichello.

David Coulthard, we knew, was having his last grand prix. He'd announced it and there were celebratory cakes and people stopping by to exchange anecdotes and wish him well.

Everyone suspected that it might also be Barrichello's last race too, with the word on the street suggesting he wouldn't be retained by Honda. Bruno Senna was the man hotly tipped to take the seat alongside Jenson Button. Rubens himself, however, was keeping the faith. He didn't intend hanging up his helmet just yet.

Nobody knew then that Honda would withdraw, that Ross Brawn would take over, sign Rubens for his safe hands and sure feedback, and that Rubinho would go on to win twice the following year in a Mercedes-powered Brawn! It's an unpredictable business, is F1…

Rubens was back in the same boat again this time around. The rumour mill had been suggesting that his seat at Williams could go to any number of drivers – Kimi Räikkönen, Adrian Sutil or Valtteri Bottas, the Williams test driver and GP3 champion who impressed in the Abu Dhabi young-driver tests.

The Räikkönen idea was now being discounted and, at Force India, the recent performances of Adrian Sutil made it look as if the world would be an unjust place if he were to lose his seat next year. But that's the way it seemed. You couldn't imagine Nico Hulkenberg sitting on the pit wall all year without the promise of a race seat in 2012 but, by the same token, Paul di Resta had done more than enough to retain his place.

Sutil is also a Mercedes-Benz man, so might there also be some three-pointed-star money to keep Sutil in the game somewhere? Then there was the talk of Pastor Maldonado's money from PDVSA, the Venezuelan state-owned petroleum company, coming under threat, so maybe Williams would need cash from another source. All in all, it didn't look too good for Rubens.

But was F1's most experienced man looking downcast? Not a bit of it. As far as Barrichello was concerned, he has as much passion for the sport as the day he arrived and he looked confident that he would be on the grid for his 20th – yes, 20th! – season of F1 in 2012.

"If you haven't got the motivation any more, that's one thing," he said, "but that's not a problem for me. This is where I belong, it's what I love and I think I could even change my name to Rubens F1 Barrichello!"

You had to admire the spirit, and hope that it wasn't misplaced…

the trip to Delhi for the FIA Prizegiving, compulsory for the top three! Behind him, Felipe Massa took fifth place, ending the year without a podium finish to his name. His race was compromised by the loss of a set of soft tyres from qualifying due to a puncture, which forced him to make just two stops and run a less-than-optimal option/option/prime strategy.

At one stage, the local hero found himself battling with his nemesis Hamilton, but the Brit was handicapped by gearbox problems. Lewis lost seventh gear, but still kept up a good pace, before the 'box failed completely, and he coasted to a halt.

Adrian Sutil drove a strong race to sixth place for Force India, passing Nico Rosberg along the way, and moving himself up to ninth in the World Championship. His team also secured a solid sixth in the constructors' table, beating Sauber and Toro Rosso and earning some vital extra cash.

Rosberg took seventh, ahead of Paul di Resta (another to be troubled by gearbox problems), Kamui Kobayashi and Vitaly Petrov. After qualifying a superb 12th, Rubens Barrichello had a disastrous start, and fought back to finish 14th. He was at least ahead of Michael Schumacher, who was a lowly 15th after a clash with Bruno Senna left him with a rear puncture. The Renault driver was handed a drive-through penalty for his troubles.

At the tail end of the field, Heikki Kovalainen and Jarno Trulli finished 16th and 18th respectively to confirm 10th place in the Constructors' Championship for Team Lotus, with Jerome d'Ambrosio and Daniel Ricciardo the final finishers in 19th and 20th places.

The three other retirees joining Lewis Hamilton were Pastor Maldonado, who spun his oversteering Williams out of the race on lap 26, Timo Glock, who stopped his three-wheeling Virgin at the pit exit after losing a wheel following his first stop, and Vitantonio Liuzzi, whose HRT developed alternator problems, forcing him to retire 10 laps from the finish.

So a very long season – one that finished later in the year than ever before – came to its conclusion. There was a pleasant ambience in the paddock afterwards as rival teams bosses congratulated each other, and Hamilton and Massa even found time to kiss and make up after their stormy season. With Christmas decorations already on view in São Paulo, everyone agreed it was time for a break...

TOP Paul di Resta came home eighth, taking him to 13th place, and top rookie, in the Drivers' World Championship

LEFT Third-placed Jenson Button helps Mark Webber celebrate his victory on the podium

SNAPSHOT FROM
BRAZIL

CLOCKWISE FROM RIGHT

The sun sets over the São Paulo skyline; singers Macy Gray and Jessie J were guests of the Lotus Renault team; Team Lotus personnel assemble for an end-of-term photograph; Felipe Massa's family and colleagues attended as he was presented with a cake to celebrate his 10th year in F1; a Pirelli tyre engineer checks his wares between practice sessions; Vitantonio Liuzzi poses for a photograph with a fan; Felipe Massa kept the fans entertained with a series of doughnuts at the end of the race before returning to *parc fermé*; Lewis Hamilton was one of several drivers to use a special helmet livery for the weekend, taking cues from the iconic design of Brazilian hero Ayrton Senna; a helmeted Mercedes team member ready for pit-crew duty

RACE
RESULTS
BRAZIL
INTERLAGOS

Official Results © [2011]
Formula One Administration Limited,
6 Princes Gate, London, SW7 1QJ.
No reproduction without permission.
All copyright and database rights reserved.

RACE DATE November 27th
CIRCUIT LENGTH 2.677 miles
NO. OF LAPS 71
RACE DISTANCE 190.067 miles
WEATHER Bright & dry, 26°C
TRACK TEMP 47°C
ATTENDANCE 143,921
LAP RECORD Juan Pablo Montoya,
1m11.473s, 134.837mph, 2004

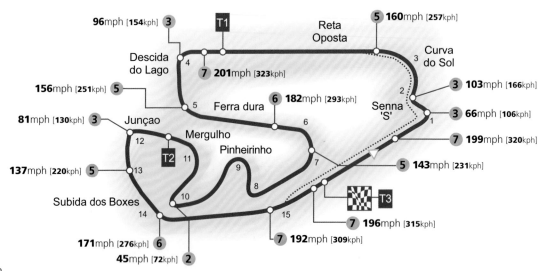

PRACTICE 1

	Driver	Time	Laps
1	M Webber	1m13.811s	26
2	J Button	1m13.825s	25
3	L Hamilton	1m13.961s	20
4	S Vettel	1m14.025s	28
5	F Massa	1m14.507s	34
6	F Alonso	1m14.541s	26
7	M Schumacher	1m15.162s	28
8	N Hulkenberg	1m15.178s	28
9	P di Resta	1m15.241s	31
10	N Rosberg	1m15.321s	29
11	J Alguersuari	1m15.468s	29
12	R Grosjean	1m15.547s	18
13	R Barrichello	1m15.663s	27
14	B Senna	1m15.732s	32
15	K Kobayashi	1m15.747s	31
16	P Maldonado	1m15.836s	27
17	S Perez	1m15.979s	35
18	J-E Vergne	1m16.052s	33
19	H Kovalainen	1m16.514s	33
20	L Razia	1m17.595s	31
21	T Glock	1m18.140s	29
22	J d'Ambrosio	1m18.653s	29
23	D Ricciardo	1m18.952s	33
24	J Charouz	1m19.577s	37

PRACTICE 2

	Driver	Time	Laps
1	L Hamilton	1m13.392s	35
2	S Vettel	1m13.559s	41
3	M Webber	1m13.587s	41
4	F Alonso	1m13.598s	35
5	M Schumacher	1m13.723s	38
6	F Massa	1m13.750s	39
7	J Button	1m13.787s	36
8	N Rosberg	1m13.872s	42
9	A Sutil	1m14.144s	41
10	P di Resta	1m14.807s	48
11	V Petrov	1m14.856s	38
12	B Senna	1m14.931s	37
13	S Perez	1m14.970s	32
14	K Kobayashi	1m15.019s	45
15	S Buemi	1m15.264s	44
16	J Alguersuari	1m15.388s	41
17	P Maldonado	1m15.679s	43
18	R Barrichello	1m15.903s	40
19	J Trulli	1m16.298s	36
20	H Kovalainen	1m16.338s	48
21	J d'Ambrosio	1m18.031s	39
22	T Glock	1m18.051s	45
23	D Ricciardo	1m18.367s	42
24	V Liuzzi	1m18.476s	42

PRACTICE 3

	Driver	Time	Laps
1	S Vettel	1m12.460s	21
2	J Button	1m12.547s	19
3	M Webber	1m12.597s	21
4	L Hamilton	1m12.622s	15
5	F Alonso	1m12.765s	17
6	A Sutil	1m13.113s	22
7	N Rosberg	1m13.286s	21
8	M Schumacher	1m13.393s	19
9	P di Resta	1m13.419s	19
10	F Massa	1m13.583s	18
11	V Petrov	1m13.838s	20
12	R Barrichello	1m14.283s	19
13	J Alguersuari	1m14.286s	20
14	K Kobayashi	1m14.311s	24
15	P Maldonado	1m14.454s	22
16	S Perez	1m14.547s	24
17	B Senna	1m14.551s	15
18	J Trulli	1m15.843s	24
19	H Kovalainen	1m16.026s	22
20	J d'Ambrosio	1m16.616s	26
21	V Liuzzi	1m17.143s	23
22	D Ricciardo	1m17.296s	23
23	T Glock	1m17.984s	23
24	S Buemi	No time	3

QUALIFYING 1

	Driver	Time
1	J Button	1m13.281s
2	L Hamilton	1m13.361s
3	M Webber	1m13.467s
4	A Sutil	1m13.480s
5	S Vettel	1m13.664s
6	M Schumacher	1m13.694s
7	P di Resta	1m13.733s
8	V Petrov	1m13.859s
9	F Alonso	1m13.969s
10	N Rosberg	1m14.083s
11	R Barrichello	1m14.117s
12	J Alguersuari	1m14.225s
13	F Massa	1m14.269s
14	S Perez	1m14.430s
15	B Senna	1m14.453s
16	S Buemi	1m14.500s
17	K Kobayashi	1m14.571s
18	P Maldonado	1m14.625s
19	H Kovalainen	1m15.068s
20	J Trulli	1m15.358s
21	V Liuzzi	1m16.631s
22	D Ricciardo	1m16.890s
23	J d'Ambrosio	1m17.019s
24	T Glock	1m17.060s

QUALIFYING 2

	Driver	Time
1	S Vettel	1m12.446s
2	N Rosberg	1m12.569s
3	M Webber	1m12.658s
4	L Hamilton	1m12.811s
5	J Button	1m12.820s
6	F Alonso	1m12.870s
7	A Sutil	1m13.261s
8	F Massa	1m13.291s
9	B Senna	1m13.300s
10	M Schumacher	1m13.571s
11	P di Resta	1m13.584s
12	R Barrichello	1m13.801s
13	J Alguersuari	1m13.804s
14	S Buemi	1m13.919s
15	V Petrov	1m14.053s
16	K Kobayashi	1m14.129s
17	S Perez	1m14.182s

Best sectors – Practice

Sec 1	M Webber	18.385s
Sec 2	S Vettel	36.851s
Sec 3	M Schumacher	17.018s

Speed trap – Practice

1	J Alguersuari	199.273mph
2	J-E Vergne	199.087mph
3	S Buemi	197.844mph

Best sectors – Qualifying

Sec 1	S Vettel	18.239s
Sec 2	S Vettel	36.468s
Sec 3	N Rosberg	17.043s

Speed trap – Qualifying

1	J Alguersuari	196.477mph
2	S Perez	195.359mph
3	K Kobayashi	195.110mph

Sebastian Vettel
"I got the message that I had a problem, which was a shame as I had a great start. After that, it was obvious that I had to shift early and save the gearbox."

Jenson Button
"I couldn't really get the soft tyre working – we had degradation on each set – and that prompted the decision to run two sets of prime tyres in my final two stints."

Fernando Alonso
"I got a very good start, putting a move on Button, but then, on the medium tyres, we no longer had the speed to fend him off. I also had a problem with the DRS."

Michael Schumacher
"It was a shame with the incident with Bruno, which was caused perhaps by a lack of experience. Otherwise I could have had a nice race with some solid points."

Bruno Senna
"It's been a difficult day, and I'm disappointed, as the incident with Michael and the gearbox problem both prevented me from having a better race."

Rubens Barrichello
"We were running a long first gear. I started at the foot of the hill, and as it was dry, I slipped back. It was fun, but we don't have a car to finish in the points."

Mark Webber
"It's always nice to win. The battle with Seb wasn't a strong one in the end as he had a problem, but even so, my pace was strong and I felt very good in the car"

Lewis Hamilton
"I lost a position to Fernando at the start. After that, I had decent pace and was able to stay close to Fernando and Jenson until I suffered a gearbox problem."

Felipe Massa
"Yesterday's puncture robbed me of a set of softs for the race, and the race summed up my year: fairly good on the soft, then struggling on the harder compound."

Nico Rosberg
"This wasn't an ideal last race and, though I scored, I expected to finish higher. I had problems with my tyres overheating, so I had to manage my tyres."

Vitaly Petrov
"It's good to finish with a point. I lost out behind the Toro Rossos, as it was hard to pass them. I lost a lot of time, otherwise I think I could have beaten Kobayashi."

Pastor Maldonado
"I had a good start until I lost position fighting. My retirement came after I overtook Senna on lap 26. The car had too much oversteer and I lost control."

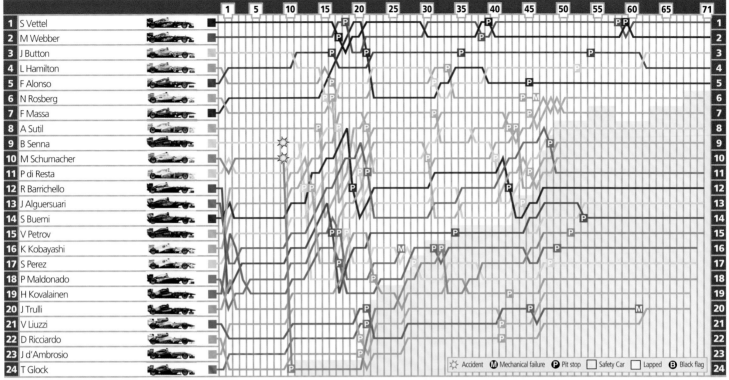

Legend: ☆ Accident Ⓜ Mechanical failure Ⓟ Pit stop ☐ Safety Car ☐ Lapped Ⓑ Black flag

QUALIFYING 3

	Driver	Time
1	S Vettel	1m11.918s
2	M Webber	1m12.099s
3	J Button	1m12.283s
4	L Hamilton	1m12.480s
5	F Alonso	1m12.591s
6	N Rosberg	1m13.050s
7	F Massa	1m13.068s
8	A Sutil	1m13.298s
9	B Senna	1m13.761s
10	M Schumacher	No time

GRID

	Driver	Time
1	S Vettel	1m11.918s
2	M Webber	1m12.099s
3	J Button	1m12.283s
4	L Hamilton	1m12.480s
5	F Alonso	1m12.591s
6	N Rosberg	1m13.050s
7	F Massa	1m13.068s
8	A Sutil	1m13.298s
9	B Senna	1m13.761s
10	M Schumacher	No time
11	P di Resta	1m13.584s
12	R Barrichello	1m13.801s
13	J Alguersuari	1m13.804s
14	S Buemi	1m13.919s
15	V Petrov	1m14.053s
16	K Kobayashi	1m14.129s
17	S Perez	1m14.182s
18	P Maldonado	1m14.625s
19	H Kovalainen	1m15.068s
20	J Trulli	1m15.358s
21	V Liuzzi	1m16.631s
22	D Ricciardo	1m16.890s
23	J d'Ambrosio	1m17.019s
24	T Glock	1m17.060s

RACE

	Driver	Car	Laps	Time	Avg. mph	Fastest	Stops
1	M Webber	Red Bull-Renault RB7	71	1h32m17.464s	123.576	1m15.324s	3
2	S Vettel	Red Bull-Renault RB7	71	1h32m34.447s	123.198	1m16.076s	3
3	J Button	McLaren-Mercedes MP4-26	71	1h32m45.102s	122.962	1m15.580s	3
4	M Webber	Ferrari 150 Italia	71	1h32m52.512s	122.798	1m16.181s	3
5	F Massa	Ferrari 150 Italia	71	1h33m24.197s	122.104	1m17.271s	2
6	A Sutil	Force India-Mercedes VJM04	70	1h32m24.235s	121.686	1m17.161s	3
7	N Rosberg	Mercedes MGP W02	70	1h32m33.036s	121.493	1m17.207s	2
8	P di Resta	Force India-Mercedes VJM04	70	1h32m42.985s	121.245	1m17.452s	2
9	K Kobayashi	Sauber-Ferrari C30	70	1h32m47.575s	121.176	1m17.644s	2
10	V Petrov	Renault R31	70	1h32m50.293s	121.117	1m17.011s	3
11	J Alguersuari	Toro Rosso-Ferrari STR6	70	1h32m53.541s	121.047	1m17.162s	2
12	S Buemi	Toro Rosso-Ferrari STR6	70	1h33m04.884s	120.801	1m17.428s	2
13	S Perez	Sauber-Ferrari C30	70	1h33m15.629s	120.569	1m17.780s	2
14	R Barrichello	Williams-Cosworth FW33	70	1h33m19.956s	120.476	1m16.684s	3
15	M Schumacher	Mercedes MGP W02	70	1h33m24.115s	120.386	1m16.681s	3
16	H Kovalainen	Lotus-Renault T128	69	1h32m56.493s	119.254	1m18.023s	3
17	B Senna	Renault R31	69	1h33m26.183s	118.622	1m18.274s	4
18	J Trulli	Lotus-Renault T128	69	1h33m34.391s	118.449	1m18.596s	2
19	J d'Ambrosio	Virgin-Cosworth MVR02	68	1h33m06.717s	117.310	1m19.902s	2
20	D Ricciardo	HRT-Cosworth F111	68	1h33m27.563s	116.874	1m19.649s	2
R	V Liuzzi	HRT-Cosworth F111	61	Alternator	-	1m20.648s	2
R	L Hamilton	McLaren-Mercedes MP4-26	46	Gearbox	-	1m17.209s	3
R	P Maldonado	Williams-Cosworth FW33	26	Spun off	-	1m19.706s	1
R	T Glock	Virgin-Cosworth MVR02	21	Lost wheel	-	1m21.773s	1

CHAMPIONSHIP

	Driver	Pts
1	S Vettel	392
2	J Button	270
3	M Webber	258
4	F Alonso	257
5	L Hamilton	227
6	F Massa	118
7	N Rosberg	89
8	M Schumacher	76
9	A Sutil	42
10	V Petrov	37
11	N Heidfeld	34
12	K Kobayashi	30
13	P di Resta	27
14	J Alguersuari	26
15	S Buemi	15
16	S Perez	14
17	R Barrichello	4
18	B Senna	2
19	P Maldonado	1

	Constructor	Pts
1	Red Bull-Renault	650
2	McLaren-Mercedes	497
3	Ferrari	375
4	Mercedes	165
5	Renault	73
6	Force India-Mercedes	69
7	Sauber-Ferrari	44
8	Toro Rosso-Ferrari	41
9	Williams-Cosworth	5

Fastest lap
M Webber 1m15.324s
(127.966mph) on lap 71

Fastest speed trap
J Button 188.959mph
Slowest speed trap
F Massa 181.316mph

Fastest pit stop
1 L Hamilton 20.396s
2 S Vettel 20.652s
3 N Rosberg 20.658s

Adrian Sutil
"My result completes a weekend where everything went to plan. We also made the right calls with the strategy, as we knew there was a chance to beat Mercedes."

Kamui Kobayashi
"We worked a lot on the race pace, and I'm happy I was able to score in the final two races of the season. It was vital for us to finish ahead of Scuderia Toro Rosso."

Sebastien Buemi
"I got a good start, passing Jaime and Rubens, but I suffered tyre degradation, partly because we didn't have the best set-up for the conditions. I did the best I could."

Jarno Trulli
"I didn't have a great start, but was ahead of the cars we needed to beat, and it was just about getting the car home so we could seal our championship position."

Daniel Ricciardo
"The race was a bit up and down, as the pace was mixed. It took a few laps for the primes to start working, but once they did the times were better than ever."

Timo Glock
"It was a disappointing way to end the season. It's a shame to have had to retire after losing the left-rear tyre after my first pit stop, but these things happen."

Paul di Resta
"Eighth is a great result after a tough race. There was a concern with the gearbox about halfway through, so the team told me to just try and bring the car home."

Sergio Perez
"My start was fine, but we had opted for wet conditions and so the rear tyres overheated. The car was quite difficult to drive and I'm sorry for the spin."

Jaime Alguersuari
"I had low grip in the first stint on the softer tyre, and I struggled to follow Buemi and Perez. Fortunately, the second stint on the harder tyre was better."

Heikki Kovalainen
"The car felt great, and we managed to make the most of our qualifying performance. I had another great start, and from there I got into a good rhythm."

Vitantonio Liuzzi
"Everything went well in qualifying, and during the race we had a good pace and competed well with the Virgins, so it's a shame that I suffered alternator failure."

Jerome d'Ambrosio
"This was a great way to end the year. We did a good job in qualifying, and this was one of my best races. I'm happy this happened in Brazil, as I love this track."

DRIVER RESULTS

	Driver	Nationality	Car	ROUND 1 March 27 AUSTRALIAN GP	ROUND 2 April 10 MALAYSIAN GP	ROUND 3 April 17 CHINESE GP	ROUND 4 May 18 TURKISH GP	ROUND 5 May 12 SPANISH GP	ROUND 6 May 29 MONACO GP
1	Sebastian Vettel	German	Red Bull-Renault RB7	1P	1P	2P	1P	1	1P
2	Jenson Button	British	McLaren-Mercedes MP4-26	6	2	4	6	3	3
3	Mark Webber	Australian	Red Bull-Renault RB7	5	4F	3F	2F	4P	4F
4	Fernando Alonso	Spanish	Ferrari 150 Italia	4	6	7	3	5	2
5	Lewis Hamilton	British	McLaren-Mercedes MP4-26	2	8	1	4	2F	6
6	Felipe Massa	Brazilian	Ferrari 150 Italia	7F	5	6	11	R	R
7	Nico Rosberg	German	Mercedes MGP W02	R	12	5	5	7	11
8	Michael Schumacher	German	Mercedez MGP W02	R	9	8	12	6	R
9	Adrian Sutil	German	Force India-Mercedes VJM04	9	11	15	13	13	7
10	Vitaly Petrov	Russian	Renault R31	3	17	9	8	11	R
11	Nick Heidfeld	German	Renault R31	12	3	12	7	8	8
12	Kamui Kobayashi	Japanese	Sauber-Ferrari C30	D8	7	10	10	10	5
13	Paul di Resta	British	Force India-Mercedes VJM04	10	10	11	R	12	12
14	Jaime Alguersuari	Spanish	Toro Rosso-Ferrari STR6	11	14	R	16	16	R
15	Sébastien Buemi	Swiss	Toro Rosso-Ferrari STR6	8	13	14	9	14	10
16	Sergio Perez	Mexican	Sauber-Ferrari C30	D7	R	17	14	9	NS
17	Rubens Barrichello	Brazilian	Williams-Cosworth FW33	R	R	13	15	17	9
18	Bruno Senna	Brazilian	Renault R31						
19	Pastor Maldonado	Venezuelan	Williams-Cosworth FW33	R	R	18	17	15	18
20	Pedro de la Rosa	Spanish	Sauber-Ferrari C30						
21	Jarno Trulli	Italian	Lotus-Renault T128	13	R	19	18	18	13
22	Heikki Kovalainen	Finnish	Lotus-Renault T128	R	15	16	19	R	14
23	Vitantonio Liuzzi	Italian	HRT-Cosworth F111	NQ	R	22	22	R	16
24	Jerome d'Ambrosio	Belgian	Virgin-Cosworth MVR-02	14	R	20	20	20	15
25	Timo Glock	German	Virgin-Cosworth MVR-02	NC	16	21	NS	19	R
26	Narain Karthikeyan	Indian	HRT-Cosworth F111	NQ	R	23	21	21	17
27	Daniel Ricciardo	Australian	HRT-Cosworth F111						
28	Karun Chandhok	Indian	Lotus-Renault T128						

RACE SCORING

1st	25	POINTS
2nd	18	POINTS
3rd	15	POINTS
4th	12	POINTS
5th	10	POINTS
6th	8	POINTS
7th	6	POINTS
8th	4	POINTS
9th	2	POINTS
10th	1	POINT

DATA KEY

D	DISQUALIFIED
F	FASTEST LAP
NC	NON-CLASSIFIED
NS	NON-STARTER
NQ	NON-QUALIFIER
P	POLE POSITION
R	RETIRED
W	WITHDRAWN

QUALIFYING HEAD-TO-HEAD

Red Bull-Renault
Vettel–Webber **16–3**

McLaren-Mercedes
Hamilton–Button **13–6**

Ferrari
Alonso–Massa **15–4**

Mercedes
Rosberg–Schumacher **16–3**

Renault
Petrov–Heidfeld **8–3**
Senna–Petrov **5–3**

Williams-Cosworth
Barrichello–Maldonado **10–9**

Force India-Mercedes
Sutil–di Resta **10–9**

Sauber-Ferrari
Perez–Kobayashi **10–7**
Kobayashi–de la Rosa **1–0**

Toro Rosso-Ferrari
Buemi–Alguersuari **13–6**

Lotus-Renault
Kovalainen–Trulli **16–2**
Kovalainen–Chandhok **1–0**

HRT-Cosworth
Liuzzi–Karthikeyan **7–1**
Liuzzi–Ricciardo **5–5**
Ricciardo–Karthikeyan **1–0**

Virgin-Cosworth
Glock–d'Ambrosio **14–5**

Race results for both drivers; ie, first and second listed as 1/2 with team's best result listed first.

CONSTRUCTOR RESULTS

1	Red Bull-Renault
2	McLaren-Mercedes
3	Ferrari
4	Mercedes
5	Renault
6	Force India-Mercedes
7	Sauber-Ferrari
8	Toro Rosso-Ferrari
9	Williams-Cosworth
10	Lotus-Renault
11	HRT-Cosworth
12	Virgin-Cosworth

ROUND 7 June 12 CANADIAN GP	ROUND 8 June 26 EUROPEAN GP	ROUND 9 July 10 BRITISH GP	ROUND 10 July 24 GERMAN GP	ROUND 11 July 31 HUNGARIAN GP	ROUND 12 August 28 BELGIAN GP	ROUND 13 September 11 ITALIAN GP	ROUND 14 September 25 SINGAPORE GP	ROUND 15 October 9 JAPANESE GP	ROUND 16 October 16 KOREAN GP	ROUND 17 October 30 INDIAN GP	ROUND 18 November 13 ABU DHABI GP	ROUND 19 November 27 BRAZILIAN GP	
2P	1PF	2	4	2P	1P	1P	1P	3P	1F	1PF	RP	2P	392
1F	6	R	R	1	3	2	2F	1F	4	2	3	3	270
3	3	3P	3P	5	2F	R	3	4	3	4	4F	1F	258
R	2	1F	2	3	4	3	4	2	5	3	2	4	257
R	4	4	1F	4	R	4F	5	5	2P	7	1	R	227
6	5	5	5	6F	8	6	9	7	6	R	5	5	118
11	7	6	7	9	6	R	7	10	8	6	6	7	89
4	17	9	8	R	5	5	R	6	R	5	7	15	76
R	9	11	6	14	7	R	8	11	11	9	8	6	42
5	15	12	10	12	9	R	17	9	R	11	13	10	37
R	10	8	R	R									34
7	16	R	9	11	12	R	14	13	15	R	10	9	30
18	14	15	13	7	11	8	6	12	10	13	9	8	27
8	8	10	12	10	R	7	21	15	7	8	15	11	26
10	13	R	15	8	R	10	12	R	9	R	R	12	15
	11	7	11	15	R	R	10	8	16	10	11	13	14
9	12	13	R	13	16	12	13	17	12	15	12	14	4
					13	9	15	16	13	12	16	17	2
R	18	14	14	16	10	11	11	14	R	R	14	R	1
12													
16	20	R		R	14	14	R	19	17	19	18	18	
R	19	R	16	R	15	13	16	18	14	14	17	16	
13	23	18	R	20	19	R	20	23	21		20	R	
14	22	17	18	19	17	R	18	21	20	16	R	19	
15	21	16	17	17	18	15	R	20	18	R	19	R	
17	24										17		
		19	19	18	R	NC	19	22	19	18	R	20	
			20										

ROUND 1 March 27 AUSTRALIAN GP	ROUND 2 April 10 MALAYSIAN GP	ROUND 3 April 17 CHINESE GP	ROUND 4 May 8 TURKISH GP	ROUND 5 May 22 SPANISH GP	ROUND 6 May 29 MONACO GP	ROUND 7 June 12 CANADIAN GP	ROUND 8 June 26 EUROPEAN GP	ROUND 9 July 10 BRITISH GP	ROUND 10 July 24 GERMAN GP	ROUND 11 July 31 HUNGARIAN GP	ROUND 12 August 28 BELGIAN GP	ROUND 13 September 11 ITALIAN GP	ROUND 14 September 25 SINGAPORE GP	ROUND 15 October 9 JAPANESE GP	ROUND 16 October 16 KOREAN GP	ROUND 17 October 30 INDIAN GP	ROUND 18 November 13 ABU DHABI GP	ROUND 19 November 27 BRAZILIAN GP	TOTAL POINTS
1/5	1/4	2/3	1/2	1/4	1/4	2/3	1/3	2/3	3/4	2/5	1/2	1/R	1/3	3/4	1/3	1/4	4/R	1/2	650
2/6	2/8	1/4	4/6	2/3	3/6	1/R	4/6	4/R	1/R	1/4	3/R	2/4	2/5	1/5	2/4	2/7	1/3	3/R	497
4/7	5/6	6/7	3/11	5/R	2/R	6/R	2/5	1/5	2/5	3/6	4/8	3/6	4/9	2/7	5/6	3/R	2/5	4/5	375
R/R	9/12	5/8	5/12	6/7	11/R	4/11	7/17	6/9	7/8	9/R	5/6	5/R	7/R	6/10	8/R	5/6	6/7	7/15	165
3/12	3/17	9/12	7/8	8/11	8/R	5/R	10/15	8/12	10/R	12/R	9/13	9/R	15/17	9/16	13/R	11/12	13/16	10/17	73
9/10	10/11	11/15	13/R	12/13	7/12	18/R	9/14	11/15	6/13	7/14	7/11	8/R	6/8	11/12	10/11	9/13	8/9	6/8	69
D/D	7/R	10/17	10/14	9/10	5/NS	7/12	11/16	7/R	9/11	11/15	12/R	R/R	10/14	8/13	15/16	10/R	10/11	9/13	44
8/11	13/14	14/R	9/16	14/16	10/R	8/10	8/13	10/R	12/15	8/10	R/R	7/10	12/21	15/R	7/9	8/R	15/R	11/12	41
R/R	R/R	13/18	15/17	15/17	9/18	9/R	12/18	13/14	14/R	13/16	10/16	11/12	11/13	14/17	12/R	15/R	12/14	14/R	5
13/R	15/R	16/19	18/19	18/R	13/14	16/R	19/20	R/R	16/20	R/R	14/15	13/14	16/R	18/19	14/17	14/19	17/18	16/18	
NQ/NQ	R/R	22/23	21/22	21/R	16/17	13/17	23/24	18/19	19/R	18/20	19/R	NC/R	19/20	22/23	19/21	17/18	20/R	20/R	
14/NC	16/R	20/21	20/NS	19/20	15/R	14/15	21/22	16/17	17/18	17/19	17/18	15/R	18/R	20/21	18/20	16/R	19/R	19/R